THE USES OF
DISCRETION

edited by
KEITH HAWKINS

CLARENDON PRESS · OXFORD

*This book has been printed digitally and produced in a standard design
in order to ensure its continuing availability*

OXFORD
UNIVERSITY PRESS

Great Clarendon Street, Oxford OX2 6DP

Oxford University Press is a department of the University of Oxford.
It furthers the University's objective of excellence in research, scholarship,
and education by publishing worldwide in

Oxford New York

Athens Auckland Bangkok Bogotá Buenos Aires Cape Town
Chennai Dar es Salaam Delhi Florence Hong Kong Istanbul Karachi
Kolkata Kuala Lumpur Madrid Melbourne Mexico City Mumbai Nairobi
Paris São Paulo Shanghai Singapore Taipei Tokyo Toronto Warsaw

with associated companies in Berlin Ibadan

Oxford is a registered trade mark of Oxford University Press
in the UK and in certain other countries

Published in the United States
by Oxford University Press Inc., New York

ISBN 0–19–825950–6

Preface

DISCRETION, though an elusive phenomenon, has long been a matter of scholarly interest for both lawyers and social scientists. Among lawyers, discretion has primarily attracted particular attention from those who work in jurisprudence and administrative law. They have been concerned with decision-making procedures and questions about the scope for the play of individual judgment afforded within a structure of rules; they have been concerned also with the nature of discretionary power, with the ways in which official authority is used, and with questions of legitimacy. Another area of interest has been the means by which discretion may be limited or guided in desirable directions. Most lawyers think, characteristically, in terms of legal forms of constraint by rules, procedures, or forms of accountability.

Discretion is of interest to social scientists because they want to advance understanding of the ways in which people reach decisions, and how various social, economic, and political constraints act upon the exercise of choice. Many social scientists tend not, however, to think in terms of discretion at all but are interested instead in decision-making behaviour more generally, and the processes by which individuals and organizations arrive at decisions about a course of action to follow. In keeping with this approach, social scientists view law as merely one set of restraints upon, or guidance for, individual action among a varied array of social forces. And, while social scientists recognize constraint upon human choice that comes from rules or standards, they are aware also that other kinds of constraints upon choice operate, including those which officials and organizations impose upon themselves. The social scientist's conception of the desirable means by which to guide or control discretion accordingly emphasizes matters such as the role of decision objectives, the incentives or disincentives to forms of behaviour, questions of socialization or training, or the importance of organizational routines.

Significant contributions to the literature of discretion and decision-making continue to appear. It is now, however, more than ten years since the publication of the excellent collection of essays on *Discretion and Welfare* edited by Michael Adler and Stewart Asquith (1981*a*), and more than five since Denis Galligan's important book *Discretionary Powers* (1986) appeared. Given the continuing interest in the subject, it seemed time to revisit and reappraise some of the key issues currently attracting scholarly attention. The topic is huge, however, and different disciplines have their own interests and priorities. No monograph can make claims to comprehensiveness. The purpose of this collection is to use the contributions and ideas of both the law and the social sciences to explore some of the central issues involved in the use of discretion by legal actors—those individuals who work in the legal system, or in legal bureaucracies, making decisions in the exercise of an authority conferred on them by law. In doing so I thought it desirable to invite contributions from authors who had not published in the book by Adler and Asquith.

My intention has been to focus on generic matters connected with the use of discretion and the forces that shape it, or questions concerned with how we ought to think about discretion and its use. The generic focus is quite deliberate: my concern is discretionary behaviour itself, rather than its connection with discrete topics, such as discretion in criminal justice, discretion and regulation, or discretion and welfare (in fact readers will find these subjects well covered in this book). The collection is comprised of a series of original essays by writers drawn from both law and the social sciences and is intended for students and academics, in both law and the social sciences, who are interested in discretion and its control, or in decision-making behaviour generally. I have been particularly concerned to avoid academic parochialism and, in an effort to extend horizons, I have included the writings of American as well as British scholars. The emphasis which all the authors have given to matters of generic significance should transcend particular jurisdictional boundaries and preoccupations. It seems, unfortunately, that the insights gained by the contrasting perspectives of law and the social sciences too infrequently extend beyond disciplinary boundaries. This book is an effort to repair the lack of communication. One purpose of the multi-disciplinary approach is to show lawyers, in particular (if such demonstration still be necessary), that social scientists have much to contribute to enhancing their understanding of the nature of legal discretion.

Discretion has in the past sometimes been considered a desirable means of individualizing the application of the law, and of softening the rigours that from time to time arise from the dispassionate application of legal rules. However, it seems that many commentators, especially since the publication of Davis's book *Discretionary Justice*

(1969), have become more inclined to see discretion in a critical light, and more conscious of its disadvantages and its injustices. What the chapters in this book suggest from the public-policy point of view is that there is now less pessimism about the centrality and inevitability of legal discretion, less readiness to see it in pejorative terms. From a theoretical point of view, the chapters indicate that understanding of the complex processes by which people make decisions has been substantially advanced since the 1960s. Certainly, with the trend in modern legal systems towards greater reliance upon discretion and less reliance upon clearly defined rules, it seems unlikely that scholarly interest in the subject will decline.

The book is arranged in three parts. The first, consisting of three chapters, introduces the subject, explores the contrasting ways in which lawyers and social scientists approach it, and deals generally with issues in the rules and discretion debate. The second part is comprised of chapters by social scientists which explore the character of discretionary behaviour in legal life, emphasizing in particular the patterns and consistencies in legal decision-making. These chapters explain the nature of some of the social, and especially organizational, constraints which shape legal decisions. Finally, the three chapters in Part III suggest different ways of thinking about legal discretion and its implications for social policy, on the one hand, and scholarly analysis, on the other. In an effort to make the contributions as coherent as possible, and especially to assist students, each part is given a relatively detailed editorial introduction and commentary which surveys the particular issues and summarizes arguments. *Readers may wish to skip these introductory sections and concentrate wholly on the chapters which are themselves capable of being read as independent contributions in their own right.*

I have been helped in various ways in preparing this book. The project has been part of an interest in the problem of legal decision-making I have had for many years, and on which for part of that time I have been collaborating with Peter K. Manning. I began work on the present volume during a year as Visiting Fellow of Gonville and Caius College, Cambridge, where several years earlier, as a Tapp Research Fellow, I first had the opportunity of thinking about the issues addressed in this book. I am most grateful to the Master and Fellows of Caius for electing me to the Fellowship, and for the excellent facilities which the College made available to me. I also wish to thank Jeanette Price at the Oxford Centre for Socio-Legal Studies for the very considerable help she has given me in preparing the text for publication.

K.O.H.

Oxford, 1991

Contents

Contributors

M. P. BAUMGARTNER received her Ph.D. from Yale University in 1981 and is currently an Assistant Professor in the Department of Sociology at Rutgers University. She is the author of *The Moral Order of a Suburb* (Oxford University Press, 1988) and a number of articles in the sociology of law and social control. At the present time she is engaged in the study of conflict and its management in groups of children.

JOHN BELL is Professor of Public and Comparative Law at the University of Leeds. He has written on legal reasoning, notably in *Policy Arguments in Judicial Decisions* (Clarendon Press, 1983) and in *Cross on Statutory Interpretation* (2nd edn. with Sir G. Engle, Butterworths, 1987). He also edited (with J. Eekelaar) *Oxford Essays in Jurisprudence—Third Series* (Clarendon Press, 1987)

ROBERT M. EMERSON is Professor of Sociology at the University of California, Los Angeles. He has written extensively on ethnographic and field-research methods, and has published a number of articles that rely upon qualitative research to examine social control decision-making across a variety of settings. His publications include: 'On Last Resorts', *American Journal of Sociology* (1981); 'Holistic Effects in Social Control Decision-Making', *Law and Society Review* (1983); *Contemporary Field Research: A Collection of Readings* (Waveland, 1988); and 'Case Processing and Interorganizational Knowledge: Detecting the "Real Reasons" for Referrals', in *Social Problems* (1991).

MARTHA S. FELDMAN is an Associate Professor of Political Science in Public Policy at the University of Michigan, Ann Arbor, Michigan. Her research interests involve how people construct their social reality and how they act in a social context. Her particular focus has been on organizational decision-making and how various forms of information and communication are involved in that process. She is currently studying organizational routines as a form of intelligence that is organizational rather than individual. Her publications include *Order Without Design: Information Production and Policy Making, Reconstructing Reality in the Courtroom* (co-authored with W. Lance Bennett), and 'Information in Organizations as Signal and Symbol', *Administrative Science Quarterly* (1981) (co-authored with James G. March).

JOEL HANDLER is Professor of Law at the University of California, Los Angeles. He received degrees from Princeton University and Harvard Law School. Previously, he was the Vilas Research Professor and the George A. Wiley Professor at the University of Wisconsin Law School. He has been a Guggenheim Fellow and a member of the board of trustees and executive committee of the Law and Society Association, of which he is now President. His primary research interests are in the areas of poverty law and administration, social welfare programmes, race, social movements, public-interest law, legal services, and law-reform activities. He has published more than a dozen books on these subjects, including *The Conditions of Discretion: Autonomy, Community, Bureaucracy* (Russell Sage, 1986).

KEITH HAWKINS is Deputy Director of the Centre for Socio-Legal Studies at Oxford University and author of *Environment and Enforcement* (Clarendon Press, 1984). He has a long-standing interest in legal decision-making and has explored the topic in the criminal justice and regulatory arenas. He co-edits *Law and Policy* (Basil Blackwell), *Law in Social Context* (University of Pennsylvania Press), and *Oxford Socio-Legal Studies* (Oxford University Press).

NICOLA LACEY is Fellow and Tutor in Law at New College, Oxford. Her teaching and research interests are in legal theory, criminal law and justice, sex and race discrimination laws, and feminist social theory. Her publications include *State Punishment: Political Principles and Community Values* (Routledge, 1988) and *Reconstructing Criminal Law: Text and Materials* (with Celia Wells and Dirk Meure) (Weidenfeld and Nicolson, 1990).

RICHARD LEMPERT is Francis A. Allen Professor of Law and Professor of Sociology at the University of Michigan. He has served as editor of the *Law and Society Review*, Trustee of the Law and Society Association, and Chair of the National Research Council's Committee on Research on Law Enforcement and the Administration of Justice. He is also author, along with Joseph Sanders, of *An Invitation to Law and Social Science* (University of Pennsylvania Press, 1986).

PETER K. MANNING is Professor of Sociology and Psychiatry at Michigan State University; among his other appointments have been posts at Balliol College, and the Centre for Socio-Legal Studies at Oxford. He is author or editor of eleven books, the most recent of which is *Symbolic Communication* (MIT Press, 1988). He is currently working with Keith Hawkins on a book on *Legal Decision-Making*.

BLAIR PALEY is a graduate student in clinical psychology at the University of California at Los Angeles. She is currently investigating the social behaviour of pre-school children considered to be at risk for later behaviour problems. As an undergraduate at UCLA she majored in sociology while conducting research on the use of prosecutorial discretion.

ROY SAINSBURY is a research Fellow at the Social Policy Research Unit, University of York. His research work on social security administration has included studies of the computerization of the social security system, the operation of the housing benefit appeal system, and (currently) Medical Appeal Tribunals.

CARL E. SCHNEIDER is Professor of Law at the University of Michigan. He has written a series of articles which argue that family-law scholarship needs to be directed at sharper definitions, broader generalizations, and deeper theories and which attempt to implement those suggestions. In another series of articles, he has critically explored the role of rights-thinking in US law. He is currently completing a family-law casebook in which the ideas in both series play an important part.

PART I

Issues in the
Use of Discretion

THIS book is intended to explore in some detail, and from a variety of law and social science perspectives, the nature of legal discretion, and how it is shaped and constrained in actual practice. In the opening chapter, which introduces the book and its major themes, some of the analyses of discretion put forward recently are summarized. These are followed by a discussion of some of the ways in which social scientists have grappled with the problem of understanding and explaining decision-making behaviour. The legal system is an interesting and complex arena in which to study decision-making because of the special characteristics of legal rules and the nature of the legal mandate. It is important to know what part legal rules play in action by legal officials, and how they act to guide and constrain legal decision-making in relation to the host of other social, political, economic, and organizational constraints which either directly guide discretion or serve to frame the way in which it is exercised. The chapter makes the point that the use of rules involves a considerable degree of discretion, while the exercise of discretion is to a substantial extent guided by rules, though not necessarily by legal rules.

There follow two chapters on discretion by lawyers, one from each side of the Atlantic. In the first, Carl Schneider addresses discretion and rules from the point of view of a US academic lawyer, exploring their advantages and disadvantages in systematic fashion. Schneider's discussion focuses on judicial discretion (therefore on adjudication), and on US law. But his analysis is one that stresses the generic aspects of discretion, and in no sense is it as a result parochial or culture-bound. Indeed, Schneider draws some helpful comparisons between the place of discretion in common-law and civil-law systems as part of an argument that it is deeply and inevitably embedded in law. He observes that the nature of the common law seems to be particularly hospitable to the idea of discretion, and, to the extent that the common law may be regarded as continually seeking to preserve flexibility, judges enjoy an important role in using their discretion in adapting legal doctrines and in expressing conceptions of justice where rules seem not to.

Schneider is concerned with the tensions which exist between rules and discretion and how lawyers deal with them. His argument is not that rules are superior to discretion, or that discretion is superior to rules, but rather that they both have their advantages and disadvantages, and their correct mix depends entirely on the particular problem to be addressed and its context. Many lawyers are given to thinking in terms of rules and the apparent frailties of discretion. Yet they recognize also that discretion is sometimes necessary to blunt the application of a general rule. Discretion is attractive because rules sometimes do not work in intended ways, may promote injustice, may leave gaps, or may collide with other rules. One irony is that discretion is sometimes needed to allow a decision-maker to promote the purpose of a rule. Schneider makes the point that it is impossible to discern any general principle which informs us as to how to choose between rules or discretion, suggesting that such choice is usually dependent upon the particular context in which a decision has to be made.

The approach adopted by Schneider is not to try to propose some general principle for choosing between rules and discretion; indeed, he concludes that such a choice is 'complex and uncertain', heavily dependent on context, and that it is too simple to talk in terms of a choice between one or the other. This is because the choice, in the first place, is one between different mixes of discretion and rules, since neither rules nor discretion in practice exist in any pure form. Secondly, there are usually compelling advantages and disadvantages to both discretion and rules which will push decision-makers towards the compromise of a satisfactory mix between them. Schneider proposes a number of matters that need to be considered in choosing what particular mix of rules and discretion is appropriate in a particular situation. His concern is to address the advantages of rules while emphasizing that the problems of discretion may be overdone by the critics.

Four types of discretionary authority are identified. First is what Schneider terms 'khadi discretion', which is not a characteristic of Western legal systems. Here, the decision-maker decides each case individually, on the basis of *ad hoc* decisions involving legal, ethical, emotional, and political considerations. Secondly, there is 'rule-failure discretion'. This is found where discretionary authority is created in anticipation of cases that will be so complex, varied, and hard to anticipate that it is difficult to envisage rules that will guide decision-makers to the right result. 'Rule-building discretion', the third type, occurs when decision-makers are granted discretionary authority in the belief that they will themselves develop better rules with experience. This type, the embodiment of common-law adjudication, permits incremental adjustment which may be particularly important during times of rapid social change. Finally, there is 'rule-compromise discretion', which is found where the legislature or other rule-making body cannot agree on appropriate rules and consequently passes the responsibility on to individual decision-makers.

Among the disadvantages of discretion identified by Schneider is the fact that discretion usually makes it easier for decision-makers to act on the basis of improper considerations, and it encourages mistakes. Secondly, discretion permits the substitution of the decision-maker's own personal standards for public, legal standards. In its worst form it is important to recognize that discretion is power, with all its corrupting implications. To Schneider's discussion might be added a third disadvantage, one that seems to exercise both lawyers and members of the public: discretion is conducive to apparent inconsistencies of outcome which arise even if decisions are made according to approved procedures. Discretion does not necessarily result in apparently like cases being treated alike.

In the light of such disadvantages, the corresponding advantages of rules seem attractive. Rules, after all, can contribute to the legitimacy of a decision. Besides, rule-makers may often be better placed than individual decision-makers to know the interests of justice. Rules are also more likely to assist in attaining the goal of treating like cases alike and can serve some social purposes better than discretion. Their public character means that norms they reflect can be more clearly communicated than can individual decisions from which general principles have to be drawn. Similarly, rules serve the planning function better than discretionary decisions. People and institutions organize their lives and activities more effectively when they know what the relevant rules are. And, since rules are a way of institutionalizing experience, they may well be more efficient than discretion.

The legitimacy and importance of discretion are somewhat controversial matters. Like other authors in this book, Schneider sees discretion in practice as much more constrained than it might appear. From a policy point of view, the important question is whether the constraints acting on discretion serve the interests of justice and the broad legal purpose. Many of the various constraints that act upon legal discretion are neglected in the scholarly literature. Among those to which Schneider draws attention are the power to appoint—deciding who is to decide—which, as observers of appointments to the US Supreme Court will recognize, may lead to discretion being exercised in ways desired by the person or body making the appointment. Then there are various constraints of a formal kind, such as the approved procedures (for instance, restrictions on the use of evidence) by which a decision must be reached or announced (a requirement to give reasons for decisions is sometimes thought useful in concentrating the decision-maker's mind). If procedural rules can limit substantive discretion, policies and general principles are another means by which individual discretion may be constrained; this is true of policies embodied in the law itself, or of the policies which legal bureaucracies devise to guide or control the exercise of discretion by their 'field-' or 'street-level' bureaucrats (Lipsky 1980).

Procedural constraints are linked with mechanisms of accountability which to a variable extent serve to guide or control what legal decision-makers do. The possibility of criticism of decisions made by legal actors can restrain the untoward exercise of discretion. This may be particularly apt so far as judicial discretion is concerned, but it would seem very likely that other legal decision-makers are also constrained by the possibility of criticism. Similarly, rights granted to the subjects of decision, or the parties to a legal case, also limit what a decision-maker may actually choose to do. Formal disciplinary or budgetary controls which may be exerted against decision-makers who err in some major respect are another general constraint on discretion.

Many legal decisions are made by actors who are part of legal bureaucracies (see Part II) whose hierarchical organization serves to shape how decisions are made. This is most clearly apparent in legal decision-making in the structure of the courts, but also exists within other legal bureaucracies. Membership of an organization provides incentives and disincentives to people to make decisions in certain ways. These often take the form of an organizational inertia that discourages departures from earlier decisions. Another system of decision-making by precedent often tends to emerge to influence organizational actors who typically like to decide cases according to the ways 'normally' adopted in 'cases of this kind'. The human tendency to categorize events and problems in certain ways is an important source of rule-guided behaviour that leads to informal rules of decision growing up—customs, traditions, conventions, routine practices, and so on—which also govern or influence how decisions are made. Such an approach to the exercise of discretion has an appeal in its efficiency, for to exercise a broadly unconstrained discretion takes more time and effort. Similarly, no decision-maker acts entirely alone, and, to the extent that discretionary authority is shared, each decision-maker's scope for discretion is narrowed. Discretion is also constrained by the willingness of decision-makers to share authority with others, or to defer to the exercise of discretionary authority by others, and by the organizational necessity to co-ordinate decisions to achieve consistency. Inter-organizational constraints operate as well. For instance, the earlier exercise of discretion, whether by litigants, screening officials (those people who tend to provide the first point of contact with the legal system, such as regulatory inspectors, police officers, or social security staff), or others, constitutes a real limit on the exercise of discretion, for a subsequent decision-maker can act only on the basis of those cases supplied by others. Furthermore, the particular way in which a case is constructed by earlier participants in the process (see, e.g., Sanders 1987) has profound implications for how the matter will be understood and decided by a subsequent decision-maker.

A final set of constraints on the exercise of legal discretion is to be found in decision-makers' socialization and training. These influences generally lead to decisions being made that accord with the broad notions of rationality that obtain in a society, though this probably varies according to the particular decision-makers concerned. This may be truer of judges than of police officers, say, or other kinds of legal actors who exercise an authority that may be heavily influenced by their occupational subculture or broad organizational norms which may sometimes act against wider legal or social standards of correctness or propriety. Schneider regards legal training, in particular, as an important force shaping the norms and values of legal practitioners and judges.

Some of the themes introduced by Schneider are pursued by John Bell in a chapter that draws on the literature of continental European writers, a source unfortunately neglected by many Anglo-American socio-legal academics. Bell's chapter carefully maps out the nature and implications of discretion from the point of view of a jurisprudence scholar. However, it seeks to learn from social scientists' studies of legal discretion and is concerned with the relationship between norms of conduct, on the one hand, and legal values, on the other. Bell considers what a theory of law which had absorbed the findings of sociological studies of discretionary decision-making might look like. The chapter is, in effect, an argument for legal scholarship to give more emphasis to discretion, for Bell argues that the scope and context of the exercise of discretion as an exercise of social power is of prime concern, not simply its legal limits and definition. Discretion must be seen as central, not peripheral, to the institutions created and legitimated by law; to do this will then draw attention to the interrelationship of legal and other social values. Bell regards the empirical studies of legal decision-making as helping to clarify the important legitimating function of law. This view adds to his criticisms of the excessively circumscribed view of discretion held by many legal theorists, and leads him to question whether the extent of scholarly attention given to rules is justified.

Anglo-American thinking about law has been marked by two broad approaches. One shows a concern for what Bell calls 'ruled justice' in which law is a comprehensive and autonomous order. Emphasis here is given to adjudication. In this approach court decisions in resolving disputes form the core of a concept of law. In the sociology of law, on the other hand, law is regarded as a resource for legal actors, one to be mobilized in negotiating to attain their broad ends. This is particularly the case where the decision-maker holds a wide discretion, where rules have limited scope. This discretion is generally exercised outside courts, so adjudication is correspondingly of limited interest.

Particular attention is given in the chapter to the contribution of empirical studies on the regulation of pollution, which are premised on the assumption that law is not a discrete social phenomenon but one that interacts with other social phenomena. Law, in other words, is to be seen merely as only one of a number of forces affecting what happens in the world. Thus discretion exists within institutional power relationships in which the principal determinants for action are not legal. A legal theorist would regard the discretion exercised by the officers researched in the studies on the regulation of pollution as largely undirected by law, apart from a general obligation upon them to pursue the purposes of the legislation. The research reveals the frailties of rules which are blunt instruments for the attainment of sometimes complex policy goals. Some rules may be over-inclusive, penalizing too widely and demanding a degree of flexibility in their application; or they may be difficult to formulate precisely, or a hindrance to the conduct of the particular task, both of which demand informal adaptation to particular circumstances. And also apparent is one of the ironies of rules: sometimes precise rules must be ignored in the effort to attain the broad purposes of legislation. Courts occupy a relatively modest place in these studies of discretion; indeed, the use of discretion by legal actors here is broadly aimed at reducing the possibility that a dispute will actually end up in court, thereby serving to question the lawyer's traditional preoccupation with court decisions and adjudicated outcomes. It is clear from studies such as these that the institutional setting in which decision-making takes place is crucial to understanding the behaviour of those exercising legal discretion.

In Bell's definition of discretion a legal actor possesses a power to choose standards for action; there is a unilateral exercise of choice; and a power to choose conferred or legitimated by law. Choice itself involves the degree of self-determination possessed by the actor, the actor's freedom from external constraints, and the area over which choice is exercised. Choice may be both a matter of deciding whether to act and one of deciding how to act. The constraints on the exercise of discretion are not simply a matter of the objectives of discretion and the permitted range of its exercise, but of the rationality of its exercise. Furthermore, there will be practical institutional constraints which essentially determine the effective limits of a legal actor's power of choice, rather than the limits formally established in law.

Power and legitimacy are regarded by Bell as key issues. Power suffuses a wide array of social relationships, both legal and non-legal, and is an important component of discretion, since it is the authority conferred on an individual to act in ways which that individual chooses. The discretion-holder is able to affect people's positions unilaterally, be they recipients of welfare or industrialists engaged in pollution, and in a liberal society the unilateral exercise of power is of inevitable concern. But an analysis of discretion in law must move beyond the focus on the unilateral exercise of power by state officials. Legitimacy is important because the idea of legitimate choice is bound up in the concept of discretion. As Bell argues, law has to legitimate both the choice and the legal actor's power. The state legitimates by creating and endorsing the exercise of power, by providing authority and social recognition. From his jurisprudential perspective, Bell sees similarities in the conception of discretion held by legal sociologists. He notes that studies of the exercise of discretion tend not to distinguish between choices which are created by law and those which arise otherwise and are exploited.

Bell draws attention to some of the areas in the study of discretion where scholars tend to be silent. Lawyers are particularly concerned with the scope given judges as to the exercise of their discretion in the interpretation of legal texts. The indeterminacy of law permits choice, and varying degrees of choice are also involved in the actual interpretation of rules. But discretion sometimes involves a decision about objectives, or the resolution of competing objectives— about, in the broadest sense, the making of policy. And in this sense Bell suggests that discretion is more appropriately seen as a question of setting standards rather than as a matter of judgment. Policy-making is an issue whose importance, it might be added, is matched by its neglect in the literature of socio-legal studies. Again, in addressing the question of discretion which arises as the result of an absence of legal regulation, Bell notes (following Goodin 1986) that there is a difference in the way in which discretion is viewed, depending on whether we are talking about public law, in which officials are granted power to act, or private law, in which citizens generally need no particular authorization to act. It is only in the former case that the existence of discretion seems to be visible.

Bell concludes that for the jurisprudential scholar an important contribution of the microsociological studies of discretion is to prompt a re-evaluation of the relative importance of discretion *vis-à-vis* rules by examining the realities of the institutional context of law. Indeed, what these studies show, according to Bell, is that the hole in Dworkin's doughnut (Dworkin 1977*b*) is in fact interesting and important since it is central to the institutions of the law. Furthermore, the studies point up the relationship between law and other forms of constraint on the exercise of discretion. This is one of the major themes pursued in Part II of this book.

1. The Use of Legal Discretion: Perspectives from Law and Social Science

KEITH HAWKINS

DISCRETION is a central and inevitable part of the legal order. It is central to law because contemporary legal systems have come increasingly to rely on express grants of authority to legal and administrative officials to attain broad legislative purposes. It is inevitable because the translation of rule into action, the process by which abstraction becomes actuality, involves people in interpretation and choice. Law is fundamentally an interpretative enterprise in which discretionary behaviour is compelled by what Denis Galligan has neatly summarized as the 'vagaries of language, the diversity of circumstances, and the indeterminacy of official purposes' (1986a:1).

Discretion is the means by which law—the most consequential normative system in a society—is translated into action. One of the commonplaces of socio-legal studies is that the form such action takes may not necessarily be predictable from scrutiny of legal rules themselves. Discretion—which might be regarded as the space, as it were, between legal rules in which legal actors[1] may exercise choice—may be formally granted, or it may be assumed. It is in the everyday discretionary behaviour of judges, public officials, lawyers, and others that the legal system distributes its burdens and benefits, provides answers to questions, and solutions to problems.

Discretion is all-pervasive in legal systems, though its extent in any particular instance may vary enormously. It is, however, difficult to contemplate the making of a legal decision that does not have at least

I am grateful for comments on an earlier draft of this paper made by Robert Baldwin, Sally Lloyd-Bostock, and Peter Manning. Some of the ideas in this chapter are drawn from my longstanding work with Peter Manning on *Legal Decision-Making* (Hawkins and Manning, forthcoming). His own contribution over such a long period is now hard to isolate. But it is considerable and I most gratefully acknowledge it.

[1] I use the term 'legal actor' to refer not only to judges and lawyers, but also to those many other officials, such as the police, regulatory inspectors, probation officers, social security workers, and the like, whose work involves extensive decision-making in the implementation of a legal mandate.

a measure of discretion. As the role of the state has enlarged, dependence on bureaucracies of various kinds to advance the objectives of public order and welfare, matters of public or occupational health and safety, planning, the regulation of business, and so on, has increased. Legal systems rely heavily upon official grants of discretionary power for a variety of reasons: among them are the complexity of contemporary society, the sheer size and burden of the legislative task, and the growing dependence upon specialist, technical, or scientific knowledge and expertise. In the face of all of this, rules seem both inflexible and ill suited as a means of coping with uncertainty and change. Sometimes, of course, law-makers want to remain as silent as possible on controversial or complex matters of public policy; in these circumstances, awards of discretion to legal bureaucracies allow legislatures to duck or to fudge hard issues.

Considerable discretionary authority is vested in legal bureaucracies both to make and to implement policy. Indeed, discretionary power resides at all levels in such organizations, from the most senior officials at the centre who frame broad policy, to the most junior recruit at 'field' or 'street' level whose work as a 'screening' or 'gatekeeping' official means direct contact with the difficulties of the real world. This, the point at which the legal system touches the people or problems it is intended to address, is where the tensions, dilemmas, and sometimes contradictions embodied in the law are worked out in practice. It is here that discretionary power not only permits the realization of the law's broad purposes, but also allows or even encourages officials sometimes to distort the word or spirit of the law, sometimes to ignore them. And sometimes, of course, officials may assume a legal authority they do not in fact possess, or deny an authority which they do.

The purpose of this chapter is to introduce and take up some of the main ideas raised by the authors of the individual chapters in this book and also to explore some of the features in the use of discretion by legal actors. It begins by discussing legal writings dealing with the jurisprudence and justice of discretion, and goes on to address some of the important contributions to understanding decision-making made by social scientists. The chapter then embarks on two broad arguments. One is that it is important that legal discretion is understood better and that this requires that it be seen empirically, in its natural state, and in holistic perspective. The other line of argument is that the use of rules involves discretion, while the use of discretion involves rules.

The chapter considers perspectives from law and social science[2] (mainly sociology, so far as this book is concerned) in approaching decision-making by legal officials, and it addresses the relationship of rules and discretion and some of the ironies to be found there. This relationship is a particular concern of lawyers (see, e.g. Schneider, Chapter 2, and Bell, Chapter 3), though the book makes the argument that apparent contrasts are more blurred in reality than might be supposed. Discretion is heavily implicated in the use of rules: interpretative behaviour is involved in making sense of rules, and in making choices about the relevance and use of rules. At the same time, it is clear that rules enter the use of discretion: much of what is often thought to be the free and flexible application of discretion by legal actors is in fact guided and constrained by rules to a considerable extent. These rules, however, tend not to be legal, but social and organizational in character.[3] From a sociological view, the 'arbitrariness' or 'capriciousness' of discretion (as lawyers and others might see it) resides in the disjunction between expectations prompted by a reading of legal rules, on the one hand, and the patterned forms of behaviour engaged in by legal actors in their routine work, on the other. It is the lack of fit between the legal expectations about how a decision should be made and how it is socially determined in practice which may give rise to accusations of arbitrariness or irrationality.

The Jurisprudence and Justice of Discretion

Law and social science have tended to approach the problem of legal decision-making in distinctive ways. Legal philosophers have been most concerned with clarifying the concept of discretion, and exploring its relationship with rules and the extent to which rules authorize discretionary behaviour. This is because discretion makes sense for them only in relation to a set of standards or rules, 'when someone is in general charged with making decisions', Dworkin (1977*b*: 31) writes, 'subject to standards set by a particular authority'. Other lawyers, however, have been more preoccupied with discretion as a problem of legal and public policy, and accordingly with its potential for injustice (e.g. Davis 1969) or for social advancement (e.g. Handler 1986; this volume, Chapter 10).

---

[2] I use the term in a general way to embrace often very disparate work by sociologists, political scientists, economists, organizational theorists, and others.

[3] This is a theme of many of the chapters in this book, especially those in Part II.

The interest of many social scientists (and sociologists in particular) has, in contrast, been in analysing the law in action so as to further an understanding of how the words of law may—or may not—be translated into legal action. Social scientists tend to see discretion not so much in relation to legal rules, as in terms of choices that may sometimes be made in circumstances where there are no discernible rules or standards. They think in terms of decision-making, rather than discretion, and this leads to differences of emphasis. Many social scientists probably share with lawyers a concern for the problem of how law can best be made to serve its purposes (see, generally, Schneider, Chapter 2). But where lawyers think in terms of the role of legal rules in achieving outcomes, social scientists tend to think rather in terms of decision goals or decision processes.

Many writers have helped clarify various dimensions of discretion.[4] To Dworkin we owe the reminder that it is a relative concept, which takes its meaning from a context of rules or standards and existing only 'as an area left open by a surrounding belt of restriction' (1977*b*: 31). As Denis Galligan has argued, however, Dworkin's metaphor of the doughnut can misleadingly convey an impression of a clear division between discretion and its surrounding standards which is hard to discern where standards have gaps or are vague, abstract, or in conflict (1986*a*: 32). Dworkin goes on to observe that context confers three senses of discretion. One form of 'weak' discretion requires that some form of judgment or choice be exercised by the decision-maker, even though standards exist. Another form of 'weak' discretion is found where an official has the final authority for making a decision which thereafter cannot be altered or set aside by another. In contrast, 'strong' discretion exists where a decision-maker 'is simply not bound by standards set by the authority in question', a sense which speaks to the range of the standards and the decisions they purport to control (1977*b*: 32).[5]

Goodin (1986), pursuing the same analytical line, has suggested two further pairs of definitional contrasts in addition to his own variant of the strong—weak distinction. First, officials may be said to have 'formal' discretion when options are explicitly written into a

---

[4] The ground has recently been well covered by Denis Galligan (1986*a*). Defining discretion is a very complex exercise, partly owing to the many varied efforts in the literature: see, generally, Salem 1983.

[5] Among many helpful discussions of Dworkin are those by Bankowski and Nelken (1981), Galligan (1986*a*), and Goodin (1986).

rule. Where language is vague, however, and options are merely implicit in the statement of a rule, Goodin defines the resultant discretion as 'informal' (1986: 236). Secondly, officials whose decisions are subject to review and possible reversal by another official may be said to have 'provisional discretion', while those whose decisions are not subject to review may be said to have 'ultimate discretion' (ibid.: 236).

In Denis Galligan's substantial analysis (1986*a*) is to be found a receptiveness to social science thinking about discretion, though the work is also valuable for its jurisprudential contribution in clarifying the senses of discretion. Galligan points out (ibid.: 8 ff.) that in its broadest sense discretion denotes an area of autonomy within which one's decisions are to some extent a matter of personal judgment and autonomy. He adds that the idea of discretion 'suggests also that the judgments and assessments which one official makes will be regarded in a certain way by other officials' (ibid.: 8). These ideas Galligan regards as two principal variables. The 'central sense of discretionary power' is described as

powers delegated within a system of authority to an official or set of officials, where they have some significant scope for settling the reasons and standards according to which that power is to be exercised, and for applying them in the making of specific decisions. The process of settling the reasons and standards must be taken to include not just the more obvious cases of creating standards where none are given, but also individualizing and interpreting standards, and assessing the relative importance of conflicting standards. Central to this sense of discretion is the idea that within a defined area of power the official must reflect upon its purposes, and then settle the policies and strategies for achieving them. There may be discretion in identifying and interpreting purposes; there may also be discretion as to the policies, standards, and procedures to be followed in achieving these purposes. (ibid.: 21–2)

Another substantial strand of scholarship has been concerned about the relationship of discretion with conceptions of justice (see Schneider, Chapter 2, Sainsbury, Chapter 9, and Handler, Chapter 10). In the liberal state, law is to be applied consistently, openly, and dispassionately; rules are regarded as the most appropriate means to these ends. Discretion represents the opposite; it is subjective justice where rules are formal justice (Handler 1986: 169). This broad conception has spawned a series of by now familiar criticisms. First, while the flexibility of discretion can be valuable in individualizing the application of the law, its subjectivism can also be the cause of inconsistency in decision outcomes: apparently similar cases may not be treated in the same way by decision-makers. This criticism has most frequently been heard in the administration of criminal justice about judges in their sentencing decisions, or members of parole boards in their release practices. An obvious corollary, but a criticism much less remarked, is that discretion can impose similar outcomes upon apparently different cases (Hawkins 1980).

Secondly, apparent inconsistency is often cited as an example of arbitrary decision-making (e.g. Goodin 1986: 242 ff.). An arbitrary decision is one 'based upon improper criteria that do not relate in any rational way to organizational ends' (Jowell 1975: 14), such as friendship or race. A third set of criticisms have to do with the power that discretion grants to officials and the scope for its abuse. Control may be exerted in undesirable ways. For those affected by decisions, discretion can lead to uncertainty and insecurity and, in some legal settings, to intrusive behaviour by officials (Goodin 1986: 244 ff.). Fourthly, the procedures by which discretion is exercised prompt concern. Decision-makers are free to take into account a wide array of information, which may be of questionable accuracy, reliability, or relevance. This concern becomes the greater when discretion is exercised in private. Privacy not only obstructs the possibility of review and the general accountability of decision-makers; it also leads to a lack of understanding about how decisions are made, not only by those who are the subject of decision, but also by those who decide.

Prominent among those lawyers concerned with the justice of discretion has been Kenneth Culp Davis, whose influential book *Discretionary Justice* was first published in 1969. Discretion occurs, for Davis, whenever the effective limits on the power of a public official leave freedom to choose between possible courses of action or inaction (1969: 4). Davis's work was devoted to thinking about the fundamental justice of discretionary determinations by legal actors, and it delivered a sustained critique of the extent of discretion formally allowed and of the manner of its exercise. Davis's work gained added force from his recognition of 'the reality that justice to individual parties is adminis-tered more outside courts than in them [in] discretionary determina-tions . . .' (ibid.: 215).

Davis regarded discretion as the major source of injustice and confronted the basic question of how to reduce it. He started from the position that officials need some discretion, but became concerned with what he regarded as the substantial amount of unnecessary discretion in legal systems that threatened the proper application of policy. Davis's remedies were conceived in characteristically legal terms. He advocated the use of precise rules to 'confine' discretion when it was too broad: 'eliminating and limiting discretionary power . . . fixing the boundaries and keeping discretion within them' (ibid.: 55). He argued for discretion to be 'structured' so as to control its exercise in an orderly fashion (ibid.: 97 ff.). And he proposed that discretion be 'checked': that its exercise be scrutinized by another 'as a protection against arbitrariness' (ibid.: 142).

Davis at once increased academic interest in discretion and redirected conceptions of it away from the somewhat benevolent view then prevailing.[6] In doing so he created a new vocabulary of reform by arguing for the 'confining, structuring and checking' of discretionary power. His advocacy of these legal modes of control, however, is telling. Davis's writing can be seen as an expression of the civil rights and legal rights movements in the United States whose central strategy was the establishment and clarification of rights for citizens in their dealings with government. The reduction of bureaucratic discretion was crucial to the success of this strategy, with decision-makers made accountable to rules that should be consistently applied (Handler 1986: 194–5). Discretion becomes a problem for Davis when it is insufficiently governed by rules (see, further, Bankowski and Nelken 1981). His conception of discretion, furthermore, is one of individualistic activity: it is the discretion of individuals (rather than groups or organizations), and the discretion that affects private citizens. Davis's general conception was therefore imprinted with a limited, though forceful, approach and this may have created too pejorative an impression of discretion (see, generally, Baldwin and Hawkins 1984; Galligan 1986*a*: 167 ff.).

A very different analysis of discretion has been put forward more recently by Joel Handler. He is broadly concerned with social justice, rather than narrower conceptions of legal justice, though he shares Davis's awareness of the potential for injustice of discretionary systems. Handler adopts a more positive position about discretion than Davis, since its pliability can be turned to advantage. The idea of discretion means, writes Handler, 'inevitably that each situation is unique. . . .

---

[6] This is not to suggest that discretion had been overlooked in the US literature, nor to ignore the considerable contribution of many other scholars to thinking about discretion in the late 1950s and the 1960s, such as Francis Allen (1959), Philippe Nonet (1969), or Charles Reich (1963, 1964, 1965, 1966). The force and comprehensiveness of Davis's arguments, however, and the directness of his policy recommendations, were such as to assure the prominence of his ideas.

The recognition of uniqueness opens the opportunity to be flexible, experimental, and sensitive to the particular' (1986: 301). Handler analyses the failings of procedural due process and then, accepting discretion as necessary and desirable, specifies 'the conditions . . . for a normatively appropriate discretionary decision' (ibid.: 7). He argues for greater legal responsiveness in the social welfare state, but does not share Davis's faith in legal modes of control. Procedural due process has failed, he asserts, in part owing to the maldistribution of wealth and power, and in part because it is conceptually flawed, since it is founded upon a 'liberal legal conception of the individual and the state [that] does not describe the reality of the modern social welfare state' (1986: 7; see also Lacey, Chapter 11).

The individualistic focus of much legal writing is merely one of a number of contrasts in law and social science work on discretion. Whether legal scholars have been concerned to clarify conceptual issues or to devise methods for the control of discretion, they have largely tended to think about the phenomenon as if it were not only a property of individual behaviour, but also essentially rule-guided, as if legal decisions were the product of individual knowledge, reflection, and reasoning. The effective constraints on discretion also tend to be conceived of in legal terms; fetters are usually to be found in rules, reasons, review, or some other apparatus of accountability (e.g. Davis 1969; but see also Schneider, Chapter 2, and Lacey, Chapter 11). Lawyers do not usually contemplate the many other forces that work upon a legal decision-maker compelling or constraining action which reside in matters normative, economic, political, and organizational.[7] This limited focus arises partly because many lawyers, as Richard Lempert points out, have not shown much concern with the actual behaviour of legal actors. Rules, however, 'need not shape behaviour', as Lempert argues, 'for rules are not inexorably influential'.

Another focus of legal writings about discretion has been on the courts and on the formalities of decision-making by adjudication. This is particularly true in common-law systems, where, in Galanter's opinion, 'adjudication is the primary focus of legal scholarship and holds sway over legal thought vastly disproportionate to its prominence as a source of rules' (1986: 153). The chapter by Carl Schneider in this book deals with the exercise of judicial discretion in particular, but his discussion has a broader significance since his analysis is

[7] An important exception is Denis Galligan's searching and comprehensive analysis (1986*a*).

generic, and judicial discretion is treated as an exemplar of wider processes. Social scientists, in contrast, have been more concerned with law outside the courtroom, in recognition of the fact that 'Disputes and controls are, for the most part, experienced not in courts (or other forums sponsored by the state) but at the various institutional locations of our activities—home, neighborhood, school, workplace . . .' (ibid.: 206). Their focus has been on the behaviour of the police or regulatory officials, of prosecutors and defence counsel, or other kinds of decision-makers like members of panels or tribunals (see Lempert, Chapter 6, Emerson and Paley, Chapter 7, and Sainsbury, Chapter 9).

The contrasting approaches of law and social science have both, however, tended to underplay various important sources of influence. Where lawyers have usually shown little concern for the actual behaviour of those who exercise legal discretion, social scientists have frequently been guilty of discounting the part played by legal rules in shaping discretion. Their tendency to underplay the variable influence of law may to some extent be due to the fact that most studies of legal actors at work have been of officials who operate in settings relatively unstructured by legal rules. Research suggests, however, that officials' discretion can be more clearly imprinted by the nature and form of the legal rules they work with than at first thought (see, generally, McBarnet 1981), even if such influence is not necessarily exerted in ways that might be intended by legislatures or legal bureaucracies (Hawkins 1989). It is this kind of irony that suggests that closer empirical examination of legal decision-making is needed.

Understanding Decision-Making

Social scientists have not generally been concerned with decision-making in specifically legal contexts until quite recently. Much of the work on decision-making in general has been conducted from the perspectives of economics or psychology and concerned with problems in business, management, and public policy. Organization theory has produced much of the best-known writing; this has focused on decision-making within organizations as a form of administrative behaviour (H. A. Simon 1947). In the last twenty-five years, however, important work concerned specifically with legal decision-making has appeared. Some of it has been carried out by criminologists, some by sociologists or (in the United States in particular) by political scientists whose work is heavily influenced by sociology. Much of the sociological research has attempted to advance an understanding particularly of the negotiated decisions that are frequently made in various parts of the legal system outside the courtroom in settings which lend themselves to ethnographic work in the anthropological tradition.[8] There now seems to be a growing interest in the collective or organizational aspects of discretion, which are emphasized in Part II of this book.

While various approaches to the social scientific study of decision-making are evident in the literature, it is possible to discern two broad contrasts. One distinctive approach tends to be normative and starts from the premiss that decision-making is a fundamentally rational matter. The other is descriptive and concerned with understanding the natural processes of decision-making.[9]

Rational Decision Theory and its Variants

Much early social science work on decision-making was marked by various assumptions which led to a particular emphasis on the notion of rationality. Rational-choice theories of decision are concerned with the effective attainment of a particular objective or set of objectives and give rise to explanations that have an individualistic focus and presuppose a very orderly view of human behaviour. The approach has been extremely influential in areas as diverse as industrial and governmental decision-making, on the one hand (C. R. Miller 1990), and analysis of decision-making in criminal justice, on the other (see, e.g., Gottfredson and Gottfredson 1980).

Rational decision theory, derived originally from work in micro-

---

[8] There is now a large literature, particularly in the field of criminal justice, where there are many studies of policing, plea-bargaining (in the United States especially), and the work of supervisory officials such as probation officers.

[9] The rest of this section is not intended to be exhaustive but rather illustrative. It does not deal, for example, with political perspectives on decision-making. The politics of discretion have not for the most part been closely studied by socio-legal scholars (but see, e.g., Wilson 1980), though, given the amount of legal decision-making which involves organizational activity and the extent to which attempts may be made to influence how decisions are made where uncertainty or conflicts of value exist, it is clear that this is an important area for more work involving the study of power in the exercise of discretion. A perspective from politics on the use of power to advance, protect, or preserve some conception of the interests of groups or individuals contrasts with rational or bureaucratic conceptions of the use of discretion, where there is no place for political activity because their organizing assumptions are that decisions are made to attain the organization's goals using the best available information, or that decisions are made in accordance with legitimate organizational rules and procedures.

economics or statistical decision theory, is premised on the fundamental assumption that decisions are purposive choices made by informed, disinterested, and calculating actors working with a clear set of individual or organizational goals. Decision-making, in this view, is intentional and consequential activity carried out by a rational individual. Another of the guiding assumptions of rational-choice models is that decision-makers survey the likely outcomes of various courses of action that are possible and under consideration. Furthermore, consequences are assumed to be capable of being fully anticipated, and the decision-maker is then assumed to choose the alternative that promises most closely to attain the objectives of the decision. Once objectives are known (or reasonably inferred), such a model permits predictions to be made of the ways in which other decision-makers will choose. Decision-making is reduced here to a 'technical calculus' (C. R. Miller 1990: 165). In short, decision-making is seen as

intentional, consequential, and optimizing. That is, [it is assumed] that decisions are based on preferences (e.g., wants, needs, values, goals, interests, subjective utilities) and expectations about outcomes associated with different alternative actions. And [it is assumed] that the best possible alternative (in terms of its consequences for a decision-maker's preferences) is chosen. (March, 1988: 1–2)

Choice implies a set of alternatives. Under classical theories of rational choice it was assumed that the decision process involved a costless search among alternatives, irrespective of the limits on the human capacity to process large amounts of information. In his celebrated book *Administrative Behavior*, however, Herbert A. Simon (1947) modified the idea of rational choice, suggesting that rationality was in fact bounded, that people do not act in a purely rational way in making decisions. Bounded rationality recognizes limits on decision-makers' knowledge and ability: people do not have unlimited resources and capacity to search for and process information, but are assumed to work with only a limited number of logically possible alternatives. As a result, Simon argued, decision-makers would typically search among alternative decisions only until a satisfactory alternative, likely to be influenced by past decisions and practices, presented itself. The decision-maker 'satisfices', that is, takes the first satisfactory solution encountered. Bounded rationality, however, remains firmly rooted in the tradition of classical rationality, since 'it is simply a "rational" (that is efficient) adaptation to a set of empirical limitations' (C. R. Miller 1990: 167).

Rational decision theory has been influential in a number of the social science analyses of legal decision-making, especially those by criminologists concerned with criminal justice decisions (e.g. Gottfredson and Gottfredson 1980). For example, Leslie Wilkins defines as a rational decision 'that decision among those possible for the decision-maker which, in the light of the information available, maximizes the probability of the achievement of the purpose of the decision-maker in that specific and particular case' (1975: 70). In research terms the 'decision' is treated as a choice made by an individual based upon unproblematic 'factors' or 'criteria' which may be deduced from the creation of a putative relationship between observed input (various kinds of information) to a decision-maker and observed output (decision outcome). It seems to be assumed that an item of information revealed to be statistically related to output represents a matter taken into account by the decision-maker, and it becomes a 'factor' held to 'explain' the decision. The validity of this method resides in its capacity to predict the outcomes of further decisions, but it assumes an empirical association between a fact and an outcome and the decision-maker's cognitive awareness of such a fact. Furthermore, an ability to predict an outcome need not explain how that outcome was reached: there is no explanation or understanding of how input is translated into output.

The conceptual and methodological stances of this work reveal various preconceptions about the behaviour under study which are empirically questionable. Official objectives of the particular part of the legal system under study, or what decision-makers claim they are trying to do, are taken as given. Though rational-choice approaches tend to look for their explanations for legal decisions in formal policy, rules, criteria, or procedures, these cannot automatically be assumed to have guided the decision-maker to a particular outcome. It is often difficult, indeed, to conceive of a legal decision or a legal institution as having a single or clear set of purposes; purposes are often confused, unknown, or disputed (Hawkins 1986: 1181 ff.). Furthermore, decisions are seen as the work of autonomous individuals, exercising a discretion unconstrained by colleagues or context. They are treated as

simple, discrete and unproblematic, and not relatively complex, subtle, and part of, or the culmination of, a process, in which external constraints, such as organizational and occupational rules, norms, procedures, and resources also operate. Indeed, decisions may well appear to be simple, discrete matters because the structure of the legal process requires them to be presented, described . . . [or] sent forward for consideration in that form. (ibid.: 1187).

Rationalist work, with its emphasis on outcome rather than process, draws attention to discrepancy rather than regularity. And discrepancy, if made apparent, is regarded as pejorative, rather than as something intrinsically interesting.

Another difficulty particularly relevant to rational-choice explanations (though it bedevils other approaches also) is what might be termed the problem of recognition. How can we recognize *that* a decision has been made? And how can we know *how* a decision has been made (Manning, this volume, Chapter 8; 1986; Hawkins and Manning, forthcoming)? Peter Manning points out that observed or assumed decision outcomes may be produced in any number of ways, but the process of choice, and the nature of that choice, have to be inferred following what is taken to be a decision. If we want to know how the power to choose was exercised, we are accordingly reliant upon the accounts or the justifications of the decision-makers (Manning 1986). A real 'decision', must be distinguished, for instance, from the ratification of an earlier choice, or a conscious accounting for or rationalization of the decision in terms regarded as more legitimate by the decision-maker.

The usefulness of rational-choice theory in understanding legal discretion varies. Some individualistic decision-making behaviour by legal actors may be explicable in rational-choice terms, as when, for example, lawyers or claimants have to decide whether to settle out of court or litigate in personal injury claims (Ross 1970; Genn 1987). In this case the decision focus is particularly narrow and the lawyer's or claimant's objectives are presumably clear (getting the highest figure by way of compensation); nor is there much doubt also about the commercial objective of the defendant's insurance company, namely to incur as little cost as possible (see, generally, Phillips and Hawkins 1976). Other kinds of legal decision, however, tend to show up the explanatory limitations of rational choice models of decision-making. The clear set of decision goals and the well-informed actor they presuppose are conditions that probably obtain in relatively few settings.

Moreover, as Part II of this book shows, rational-choice theories are premised upon an individualistic conception of decision-making which does not often accord with reality. Discretion is often a collective enterprise. But legal actors may not have a clear set of objectives, and these may not be consistently held by disparate individuals. Decision-makers do not necessarily make the choice that is most likely to attain the formal—ostensible—objectives of the decision; they may frequently have regard to the possibly conflicting interests of others. Within legal bureaucracies, for example, it is not safe to assume that all members of an organization consistently hold the same conception of what their legal mandate is (even assuming their conception is clear), or consistently seek to attain the same goals. The logic of rational decision theory is to assume that decision-makers' conception of their interests are congruent with the interests of their organization, and that their decisions are not informed by matters of self-interest, economics, politics, and the like.[10]

A naturalist perspective

Rational decision theory has been challenged by studies which have stressed the natural processes by which decisions are made. Naturalism

[10] In explanations of decision-making that emphasize bureaucratic features, the substantive rationality of rational-choice theory is replaced by a conception of procedural rationality (H. A. Simon 1979). On this view of decision-making, decisions are seen not so much as deliberate choices, but more as outputs from bureaucracies which follow well-established procedures and patterns of behaviour (Allison 1971: 67). Many decisions made by organizational actors, however, tend not to be guided by calculation in an individual case, but are made merely by following some procedure already laid down by existing rules or by some routine established by existing practice. On this view, decision-making is less the exercise of individual choice, more an output of a bureaucratic process. Decisions are viewed in a more practical light, in contrast with classical rationality; 'satisficing' behaviour leads to adoption of a course of action that is satisfactory; outcomes are not fully explored; conflicts between different positions or alternatives are not fully resolved. Nevertheless, decision-making is still very much an orderly process. Objectives are attended to in sequence, which leads to a conception of organizations as adaptive mechanisms that develop operating procedures deemed appropriate for certain problems or situations which guide decision-making. Decision-makers are assumed to operate with less calculation than in classical rationality; their choices are influenced instead by regular policies and practices. The operation of self-interest in decision-making is defeated, in this view, through the operation of control devices such as rewards based on performance, or seniority, or rules ensuring fair treatment, or the possibility of a career advancement. Here, decisions are by no means consciously worked through in the way posited by the rational-choice approach, but instead tend to be relatively quickly done on the basis of existing practice, and with relatively little need for, or use of, information. To follow a precedent is not necessarily to select the most rational means of attaining a particular goal (see, generally, Pfeffer 1981*b*).

relies on descriptive analysis, and seeks to understand how decisions are actually arrived at unencumbered by any particular assumptions about what the nature of the behaviour is, or should be. This view is associated in the socio-legal field with sociologists in the traditions of interactionism or ethnomethodology such as Aaron Cicourel (1968) and Robert Emerson (1969, 1983). Such writers have enhanced our understanding of discretion in both an exterior sense, by showing how an appreciation of context and pattern is valuable in extending the focus beyond the individual case, and also in an interior sense, by exploring the significance of meaning to individual legal actors who must choose.

Naturalism questions the goal-directed conception of classical rationality. On the contrary, decision goals are seen as the consequences of efforts to explain or rationalize action which may be the product of routine or the influence of other actors, rather than as some overarching set of objectives which first informed the choice that came to be made. Naturalism suggests that actions are not necessarily the product of intention, or of conscious choice or planning, even though decision outcomes may to some extent be predictable. Actions are not seen as necessarily the result of the exercise of conscious choice. Instead, the notions of context and meaning are central to naturalist views of decision-making.

The approach stresses the *ad hoc*, particularistic nature of legal decision-making, the decision routines employed, and the relatively haphazard way in which information may be used in the process. Work in the naturalist tradition draws attention to the moral and symbolic content of decisions and the systems of belief and meaning held by decision-makers. This sort of work is concerned with such matters as the ways in which decision-makers make sense of their decision task, or the possible consequences of various courses of action, their adaptive behaviour, and the contexts in which they choose. It addresses how information may acquire meaning and relevance depending on the way it is framed and made sense of, an approach characterized by March's dictum that 'Interpretation, not choice, is what is distinctively human'. (1988: 15)

The use of the notion of frame which, when applied to interpretation, refers to the structure of knowledge, experience, values, and meanings which a decision-maker uses to make sense of the decision problem and the available information (see Hawkins 1986; Manning and Hawkins 1990) is particularly relevant here. Framing is a way of connecting criteria with outcome.[11] Naturalism is not an individualistic conception; rather it emphasizes a holistic view of discretion and decision-making as a collective process. In this it contrasts with the normative and instrumentalist tendencies in rationalist writing. Where writers in the rational tradition (e.g. Gottfredson and Gottfredson 1980) tend to be concerned with the substance of decisions ('factors' or 'criteria'), naturalism attends to the processes by which decisions are made and their contexts: organizational, social, political, or economic.[12] At the same time, naturalism also draws attention to an individual's or organization's need for survival. An organization is seen as responsive and adaptive to its environment, while its members are viewed as people with their own values, needs, expectations, and agendas, rather than as dispassionate individuals all working coherently together to achieve a set of formal organizational goals. Decisions are made, but do not necessarily reflect some conception of the formal aims of an organization so much as the interests of individuals in maintaining their own position. People both anticipate and adapt. They follow rules, but they also create rules, norms, patterns of behaving. They make decisions in ways that are situatedly rational, that is, rational in a particular context. On this view, there are not necessarily any broad, clear, taken-for-granted organizational or other goals whose attainment is sought through choice. Instead, decisions are seen very much as embedded in their own particular contexts, as the response of a decision-maker to a particular set of circumstances. In general, decisions are taken and action occurs, but these things do not happen as a result of conscious planning or choice (see, generally, Weick 1979). The remaining discussion in this chapter is written from the point of view of naturalism.

---

[11] Manning, for example, explains the complex behaviour that actually takes place by which legal actors produce decisions as a result of the processes of framing within a decision field.

[12] Chapter 7 by Emerson and Paley, and Chapter 8 by Manning (in particular), are firmly rooted in this approach. Some have complained that much naturalist work is too concerned with the banal, but Manning's chapter is especially interesting for moving the focus from routine and repetitive decisions to decision-making in conditions of crisis.

Elements of a Holistic Perspective

Case and policy decisions

If we wish to understand the nature of legal discretion empirically, it is important to take a systemic or holistic view of it. The individual case is usually taken as the unit of analysis in most social science studies of legal decision-making, though what is usually more appropriate, as the following section argues, is a broader focus which, *inter alia*, looks at the careers of cases within a decision-making system, and at interactions between cases or groups of cases. The concern for the individual case is not surprising, since legal actors and legal bureaucracies typically assemble problems for decision into individual 'cases', each relating to a particular and concrete matter and consisting of physically segregated units by which they may be handled.[13]

Even so, individual case determinations are themselves more complex than they might seem, even within an ostensible single decision point. As Lempert shows (Chapter 6), what may on the surface appear to be one simple discretionary decision quite often involves a rather more complex series of decisions. A legal decision may require a judgment first as to the nature of the problem for decision (questions concerned with 'what actually happened', or 'what the present position is', and so on), then whether the problem or event is addressed by, or constitutes a breach of, a rule. If a breach is found, or a rule applies, further decisions may be needed as to what action should be taken, and, if so, what precise action is required. Subsequent decisions are thus contingent upon earlier ones, suggesting that analytically it is possible to distinguish 'core' and subsequent 'contingent' discretion.

Discretion is also often regarded as a feature of decision-making by individuals. This, too, is not surprising, since individuals or panels of individuals are often allocated formal authority to make legal decisions. Decision-making in law is, however, to a greater extent than is apparent from much of the literature, a collective enterprise. Indeed, it is hard in reality to sustain the idea of the individual actor exercising discretion according to legal rules or standards alone, unencumbered by the decisions or influences of others. Some legal decisions are

---

[13] The domination of individualistic approaches to legal decision-making and their limitations is a theme of Chapter 7 by Emerson and Paley, and Chapter 8 by Manning; see also Emerson 1983.

explicitly designed to involve groups, like boards, tribunals, and juries. Where a discretionary outcome is the product of a number of decision-makers acting together, discretion is exercised, as it were, in parallel. In the event that differences between individual decision-makers cannot be reflected in a majority vote, they have to be negotiated into an outcome that can be presented as the group's decision. In resolving individual differences, expertise, experience, status, and personal charisma are important matters shaping discretion, since they confer an interpersonal authority to have cases decided in particular ways (see, further, Hawkins and Manning, forthcoming).

A focus on the individual case and the activities of individual decision-makers often does not portray the reality of legal discretion in another way. A good deal of decision-making in legal bureaucracies is concerned with matters of policy—deciding in general how to decide in specific cases. Policy-making involves making decisions about the objectives and meaning of the law, and about how these ideas are to be shaped into strategies to permit their implementation. This is 'the very heart of the discretionary process' (Galligan 1986a: 110). Policy is the means by which discretion is at once shaped and transferred down through an organizational hierarchy. Policy decisions speak abstractly to the future in varying degrees of generality and exist in the form of a series of statements often incorporating matters such as the objectives of decisions, criteria to be taken into account, information to be used, and procedures to be followed. Policy, like legal rules, acts therefore as one of the constraints in the context or field within which individual decisions have to be made (see Manning, Chapter 8).

A serial view of discretion

An argument was made above for a view of discretion as part of a sequence of decisions and occurring as part of a network of relationships in the legal system (see Emerson 1983; Emerson and Paley, this volume, Chapter 7). Substantial power is wielded by those making earlier determinations in the handling of cases, for discretion is exercised not only in parallel in legal systems, but also in series. A decision made at one point in the system may profoundly affect the way in which a subsequent decision is made, owing to the structural position of the individual at the point at which prior discretion is exercised (see Lempert, Chapter 6). It makes sense to see many legal decisions as comprised of a number of discretionary determinations following in sequence. Cases are processed over time by means of a referral system: the creation of any legal case and its subsequent career are shaped by decisions made in a dynamic, unfolding process. Once created, individual cases in the legal system are typically handed on from one decision-maker to another until they are resolved, discarded, or otherwise disposed of.

A serial perspective also draws attention to the fact that effective power to decide is frequently assumed by actors other than the person allocated formal authority to exercise discretion. What is described as a 'decision' reached is sometimes nothing more than a ratification of an earlier decision made in the handling of a case, even though that prior decision may appear in the guise of an opinion or a recommendation. The nature of a discretionary determination may change or be changed depending on where in the legal system authority to decide is located. In such circumstances, matters such as the flow of information from one point in the system to another become particularly important (see Emerson and Paley, Chapter 7, and Manning, Chapter 8). Since discretion is diffused among those supplying information, evaluations, and recommendations to the proximate or ultimate decision-makers, it is important to distinguish the real exercise of discretion from mere ratification. Some people who supply information or assessment may have such an enormous influence on the subsequent handling of a case that it becomes difficult to conceive of the visible, official point of decision being the place at which real discretion was exercised.

The diffusion of discretion means that decision-making power is dispersed in legal systems.[14] Power resides, *inter alia*, in the capacity

[14] A central problem in the use of discretion is how power and authority are exercised and to what constraints they are subject. If power in decision-making is a capacity to affect outcomes, to write rules can be to exercise power, but equally (as is clear from a number of the chapters) to exercise legal discretion is also to exercise power. Power has a structural aspect, arising in particular from the way in which the legal system is organized, the division of labour and hierarchical arrangements within legal organizations. It also has an interactional aspect: it seems to be generally accepted that power is a characteristic of social relationships, whether among individuals or organizations, and that it varies according to particular relationships or social contexts as well as over time.

Where power is exercised legitimately, it becomes an exercise of authority (Weber 1947; see also Bell; this volume, Chapter 3). Power in institutions may be transformed into authority when values and practices which are accepted and expected in a particular social context are regarded as legitimate within that context. So far as decision-making by legal actors is concerned, legitimacy is important, not least because it encourages compliance on the part of those who are the objects of decision. With of decision-makers to drop or divert cases. The primary concerns of decision-makers are often shaped by a concern to handle and manage a stream of cases seen in organizational context (Emerson 1983). Earlier decisions may serve to close off the scope of discretion afforded to subsequent decision-makers entirely or partially, either by excluding a subsequent decision-maker (by discarding the case) or by narrowing that decision-maker's range of choice. For instance, legal actors handling cases prior to trial take advantage of their structural position in various ways. The low visibility of many legal decisions (like arrest of disrespectful teenagers by the police), and the degree of credibility accorded the source of information used in formal decisions, are two illustrations (see Lempert, Chapter 6). Officials have their own views on the merits of particular cases and are often able to dispose of them informally in ways that accord with their sense of justice, or that allow them to make or honour bargains over other cases. This is largely how plea-bargaining works in the United States (e.g. Heumann 1978; Feeley 1979). Again, in trials or hearings, advocates can exert considerable control over what is and (equally importantly) what is not put before the adjudicator. On the other

time, the distribution of power within a social setting may be accepted and thereby legitimated, creating stable expectations of patterns of influence.

Acquisition and use of power are also matters of politics. To the extent that decisions are made in legal bureaucracies which involve the resolution of uncertainties or differences of position, such decision-making becomes a matter of organizational politics. The tie between politics and power involves a particular view of decision-making, and one which contrasts with theories of decision-making that are premised on rational conceptions or bureaucratic procedures. In both rational-choice and bureaucratic models of choice, writes Pfeffer,

> there is no place for and no presumed effect of political activity. Decisions are made to best achieve the organization's goals, either by relying on the best information and options that have been uncovered, or by using rules and procedures which have evolved in the organization. Political activity, by contrast, implies the conscious effort to muster and use force to overcome opposition in a choice situation. (1981*b*: 7)

Handler (Chapter 10) explores conceptions of power, using Lukes's work (1974) as a starting-point. This discussion is important for drawing attention to the fact that power may not only be exercised upon those taking part in decision-making but beyond, by excluding people or issues from decision-making altogether. An analysis of the problem of discretion must, on this view, therefore take into account the fact that some people may not be granted the opportunity of access to discretionary determinations. Handler goes on to point out, however, that, according to Lukes, this view fails to account for the fact that power may be exercised in such a way as to shape whether and how matters for decision are conceived of in the first place. Disputes here are pre-empted.

hand, Lempert (Chapter 6) shows how decisions can be made contrary to a legal mandate because no opportunity is provided for review in the legal structure.

Another form of power resides in opportunities afforded by the legal system to those who create, assemble, or supply material relevant to a decision to formal decision-makers. These people are able, artfully or unwittingly, to frame the contents of reports or other information to give prominence to a particular point of view (see Hawkins 1983 for examples). The use of language in documentary reports may often reveal where the effective source of power or influence in the making of a decision actually resides. Officials may frame how discretion may subsequently be exercised, not only by describing or presenting the case in a particular fashion, but also by making related decisions in a certain way. Thus, for instance, the penalty imposed by the authorities for prison misconduct may well profoundly influence a subsequent determination about the prisoner's release by the parole board (see Hawkins 1986: 1196 ff.). What has happened earlier in the processing of a case, or similar cases, has powerful indications for the present decision, as well as for future ones. Furthermore, from the point of view of the earlier decision-maker, one decision is not made independently, but in a way that takes account of the implications of other cases for the present one and vice versa (see Emerson 1983: 425; Emerson and Paley, this volume, Chapter 7).

The matters attended to by decision-makers and the nature of the constraints to which they feel subject may change as time passes and cases move in the sequence of handling decisions. It follows that decision-makers at different points in the handling system might be expected to have different priorities; indeed, there may be not only different sets of resource constraints operating, but also quite different value systems. When discretion is viewed in serial perspective, the nature of the links between different parts of the decision-making system, and how they are bound together, become apparent. The history of a case is especially important because the legal method compels the selective social reconstruction of the past. In recreating history, the method of law is to pare down or remove the uncertainties of the real world 'in the course of successive transformations over time from the original event or act to final adjudication' (Cicourel 1968: 28). What happens, to quote Cicourel's description of the juvenile justice system, is that

Each encounter or written report affects the juvenile and events considered illegal in such a way that the contingencies in which the participants interpret what is going on, the thinking or 'theorizing' employed, are progressively altered or eliminated or reified as the case is reviewed at different levels of the legal process and reaches a hearing or trial stage. (ibid.: p. xiv)

One implication for policy here is that, because discretion in effect exists in legal systems in a certain equilibrium which may be disturbed if a rule is changed at one point in an effort to limit or extend discretion, discretionary play in one part of the system may be transposed elsewhere. This suggests that those who would change rules, policies, or procedures must adopt a holistic approach in appraising the legal system and seek to anticipate more effectively the precise impact of different structures and forms of rules on discretionary behaviour.

Adjudication and negotiation

Decisions are produced in legal systems in a number of ways (see, generally, Galanter 1986), of which adjudication and negotiation are two core forms in three-party or two-party settings.[15] Those who are interested in what courts do tend, accordingly, to think about discretion in terms of adjudicative decision-making, while those who are interested in how law works are more concerned with the negotiation that characterizes most of the decision-making outside the courtroom, much of which serves to divert cases being litigated from ultimate adjudication. The central position accorded to adjudication and the work of the courts in legal scholarship about the uses of discretion is understandable, given that courts provide authoritative statements of what the law regards as legitimate conduct (see Bell, Chapter 3).

Adjudication is of particular interest to lawyers because, in settings where decisions are made by adjudication, such as courts, rules are the basis by which disputes are resolved. That is, it is only possible to resolve a matter by adjudication on the basis of a specific rule or standard that speaks generally to similar cases (Aubert 1984). Adjudicated decisions are based 'on those aspects identified as salient by applicable legal categories' (Galanter 1986: 158). Adjudication grants to an authoritative, independent individual or group possessed of special forms of knowledge (ibid.) the power to make a decision binding upon the parties to a dispute. It imposes a solution to a problem defined in

[15] There are, of course, many deviations from the pure forms that are discussed here; for a comprehensive survey, see Galanter 1986.

adversarial terms, that is, in contrasting and partisan ways; it therefore implies argument. Adjudication also implies participation in decision-making by the affected parties through the supply of information and adversarial debate, but such participation does not extend to the exercise of discretion itself. The outcomes of adjudicated decisions tend to be cast in uncompromising binary terms (win-all or lose-all; guilty or not guilty). This, allied with the logic of the surrounding structure of rules, also helps to give adjudicated outcomes some measure of predictability.

Another influence on outcome is the set of values that people bring to the decision-making task (Lempert, Chapter 6; see also Asquith 1983), and in this connection who adjudicates is of central importance to the kinds of decision that are made. One way of controlling how discretion is exercised, of course, is in the choice of who decides (a matter well appreciated by connoisseurs of the political skirmishing which inevitably attends proposed appointments to the US Supreme Court).[16] Lempert (Chapter 6) shows that changes in the appointments to the housing board he studied took place (with corresponding changes in the decisions reached) when those with power to appoint concluded that some decision-makers were too pro-tenant. The law itself may state some preferences in terms of its formal requirements for the sort of people who are to be appointed to adjudicate (see Schneider, Chapter 2).[17]

The focus of concern in almost all of the chapters in the present volume is not, however, the judge, the usual object of attention in many legal analyses of discretion, but those many other people who do not work in the courts. Matters are more complex outside the courtroom. Decisions are typically made by means of negotiation by officials who create, handle, and process cases, who often have a rather unspecific legal mandate, and whose activities are relatively loosely circumscribed by rules. Indeed, rules which act outside the courts tend to be framed in such a way as to foster the use of discretion

---

[16] Another way of controlling the exercise of discretion, whatever the decision-making form employed, is, of course, by training and socialization, which serve to inculcate appropriate decision-making values. Training involves the acquisition of norms and values central to the occupational task, and acts to frame the exercise of discretion in desired ways. Training serves, therefore, as an important means by which to advance or change bureaucratic or legal policy (see Schneider, Chapter 2).

[17] Requirements for certain sorts of training or experience may be set out, as in the case of the membership rules for the Parole Board for England and Wales in the Criminal Justice Act 1967.

to attain policy objectives (see Bell, Chapter 3). In bureaucracies, furthermore, discretion tends to be squeezed out to, or effectively assumed by, the periphery, where it may be exercised largely invisibly and immune from organizational control.

A very large proportion of legal or potentially legal cases are disposed of by negotiation. In many others negotiation precedes adjudication. When outcomes are reached by negotiation, discretion assumes a different character (see Handler, Chapter 10). While the rule structure may be much looser, people usually negotiate nevertheless within a broad framework of rules, or with a mandate conferred on them by law (see, generally, Hawkins 1984). Negotiation, however, is particularistic decision-making in the sense that what is usually at issue is the substantive problem in an individual case. The application of a rule in an adjudicated decision, in contrast, does not necessarily speak to the substance of the matter at hand. Negotiation relies upon bargaining, and to that extent any agreed outcome is tolerable to both sides in a dispute (Gulliver 1969: 17). The decision reached is usually a compromise, jointly arrived at, rather than an all-or-nothing adjudicated verdict. Negotiation therefore achieves at least a measure of mutual commitment to the decision reached. The incentive to arrive at a decision is not provided by the compulsion of the adjudicator (though the threat of an adjudicated decision being imposed on the problem is often enough to coerce the parties to negotiate), but the self-interest of both parties in reaching a quick, preferably amicable, and cheap resolution of their problem. Negotiation also implies participation in decision-making, but it does not involve parties arguing before a dispassionate third-party adjudicator who reaches a decision and then imposes it upon the parties. Instead, negotiation takes place in informal settings, to that extent less visible and less suited to the promotion of predictable outcomes, given the less apparent place of legal rules in the context of decision, and the emphasis upon reciprocity. Negotiation is pervasive in both private-law and public-law settings, though in some respects its character may differ as between them. For example, the bargaining that takes place in settlement of a claim (Genn 1987) may differ from the bargaining that may be involved where an official may be surrendering power formally to enforce the law in return for an offer of compliance (Hawkins 1984).

None of this is to suggest, however, that legal rules exert little or no influence upon decisions. Organizations and their members may not always be constrained by rules, but they also use rules as defences, as resources, or as matters about which to negotiate. To the extent that bargaining achieves its ends, it works partly because of constraints provided by cultural and occupational norms, and the like. But it works also because of the existence of legal rules that give rise to stable expectations about how the ultimate decision-makers are likely to act (if a dispute proceeds that far)[18], and the formal machinery that may ultimately be recruited to adjudicate on a dispute. The relationship between rules and discretion is, however, complex.

Discretion in Using Rules

In reality it is impossible to treat rules and discretion as discrete or opposing entities. Discretion suffuses the interpretation of rules, as well as their application. In thinking about the relationship between rules and discretion, it is important to distinguish between fact-finding and fact-defining decisions, on the one hand, and decisions about action, on the other. Rules themselves have to be defined as to their meaning and relevance. Even where the meaning of a rule seems clear, the facts upon which the application of a rule may depend have always to be interpreted. To claim that one is dispassionately following a rule is to take for granted the interpretative work—the choices— surrounding fact-finding, and to assume that the 'facts' assembled are relevant to the application of a particular rule.

Interpreting a rule involves, at the minimum, discovering its meaning, characterizing the present problem, and judging whether that problem is addressed by the rule.[19] And, even where a rule is granted meaning, there will still be scope for the further exercise of discretion by officials, not only as to its applicability, but also as to the accuracy or genuineness of information relevant to the exercise of discretion. The facts, writes Galligan,

can be ascertained only by imperfect means, relying on imperfect procedures— the evidence of others, one's own perceptions and understandings, and the classification of those perceptions; also, there are limits to the time that may be spent in the quest for factual accuracy. . . . any decision requires

[18] This is not to suggest that bargaining leads to decision outcomes that are not predictable in an aggregate sense (Baumgartner, Chapter 4) or cannot be predicted by someone with an inside knowledge of how particular legal actors routinely exercise their discretion.

[19] On the use of rules generally, see Twining and Miers 1982.

assessment and judgment, both in fixing the methods for eliciting the facts and in deciding how much evidence is sufficient. Understood in this special sense, there is some justification for talking of discretion in settling the facts. Similarly, in applying a standard to the facts, the decision-maker has to settle both the meaning of the standard and the characterization of the facts in terms of that meaning. (1986*a*: 34–5)

The form and complexity of a rule have important implications for the degree of discretion created. Schneider (Chapter 2) suggests that the simpler the rule the more likely it is that the principle embodied in it will be adhered to, while the more complex the rule the greater the discretion available to individual decision-makers in its interpretation and application. Similarly, complex systems of rules, though highly specific, may also have the effect of creating greater discretion in practice, as Long's (1981) study of US tax legislation suggests. This recalls Damaska's comment that 'there is a point beyond which increased complexity of law, especially in loosely-ordered normative systems, objectively increases rather than decreases the decision-maker's freedom' (1975: 528). On the other hand, a broad legal mandate, such as that typically granted to regulatory bureaucracies, will give rise to huge areas of administrative discretion. In such circumstances, as Bell (Chapter 3) suggests, rules are reference points about which a legal actor may organize the exercise of discretion. Pollution standards operate in this way, for example, when an inspector has to decide whether to act and what action to take when confronted with a discharge in excess of the consented amount (Hawkins 1984).

The particular way in which discretion will be exercised may not be predictable from the particular forms of rule. For instance, where the form of a rule or set of rules is devised to circumscribe or channel discretion, the objective may not actually be achieved. Sometimes the opposite effect will happen. Since discretion is adaptive in character, rules may serve to displace discretion to other sites for decision-making within a legal system, and thereby possibly to enlarge it, or create the conditions for its exercise in more private, less accountable, settings. A telling example of this effect is to be found in the efforts to curtail discretion selectively to release prisoners on parole in California by use of legislatively fixed, presumptive sentences which served to push effective power to dispose of serious criminal cases into the hands of those who engage in pre-trial bargaining (Hawkins 1980).

Furthermore, the form in which legal rules are cast may create discretion in such a way as sometimes to divert, or even to subvert, their broad purpose. This latter point can be illustrated with an example from health-and-safety regulation. Factory inspectors often have a choice about which safety law to prosecute. One set of rules may be drafted in specific terms and organized around relatively absolute duties, while others embody general principles and duties. An example of the former is s.14(i) of the Factories Act 1961, which imposes an absolute duty upon employers in its demand that dangerous machinery be guarded. In contrast is s.2(i) of the Health and Safety at Work Act 1974, which, for some factory inspectors, has a daunting indeterminacy in the duty it imposes upon employers, 'to ensure, so far as is reasonably practicable . . . health, safety and welfare at work . . .'. The qualifying phrase requires a calculation by the inspector of the risks, costs, and technical implications which may affect possible compliance, a matter that will ultimately fall to the court to decide if a prosecution is pursued and the charge is defended. As a result, inspectors are encouraged to prosecute violations of absolute rather than general duties by the easier proof required to show breach of an absolute duty and the correspondingly greater chance of a guilty plea and a successful outcome to the case. This systematic bias, in turn, has important policy implications in terms of the sorts of legal breaches, accidents, or risks that are treated most seriously and are publicly addressed by the courts: in this example the result is that safety matters are given disproportionate attention at the expense of occupational health problems, where deaths may in fact be far more numerous (Hawkins 1989).

Thinking about the relationships of rules and discretion draws attention to tensions, ironies, and contradictions. Rules are valuable to legal actors, not simply because they can offer secure guidance, but because any ambiguity, factual or normative, surrounding them gives leeway for the exercise of discretion, which grants flexibility in their application. Similarly, rules are important resources for legal actors, allowing, for instance, justification for decisions after the fact (Bittner 1967*a*). Indeed, discretion in general carries with it various functional benefits for legal systems, such as allowing the handling of the gap between rhetoric and reality in the legal system (McBarnet 1981), obscuring lack of consensus or ambiguities in policy (Prosser 1981), or foreclosing the use of costly formal procedures in the law (see Lacey, Chapter 11). Rules devised to attain some general purpose may give rise to conspicuous lack of justice when applied in a particular, concrete case, demanding a decision to mitigate or even to avoid their effects. Yet one of the consequences of a concern for discretion as a problem in socio-legal studies has been to view discretion critically as the reason for the lack of fit between the values and rules of the written law and the practices of legal actors (the 'gap' problem). Legal actors, however, do not necessarily behave in random or even inconsistent ways, but often predictably, though to say this does not deny that apparent inconsistency in decision-making also exists within the system.

Rules in Using Discretion

To explore the use of discretion empirically reveals an orderly process at work, since discretionary decisions are rarely as unconstrained as they might appear.[20] It is precisely these social constraints that lead to highly patterned outcomes of discretionary decisions in the aggregate and may prompt some to conclude that little or no effective discretion really exists (see Baumgartner, Chapter 4). Patterns in discretionary outcomes provide a marked contrast to the characteristic legal view of the use of discretion as individualized decision-making that is potentially capricious. While lawyers may conceive of a part of a legal system without rules as one of 'absolute discretion' (Raz 1979), it does not make sense from a social scientific point of view to speak of 'absolute' or 'unfettered' discretion, since to do so is to imply that discretion in the real world may be constrained only by legal rules, and to overlook the fact that it is also shaped by political, economic, social, and organizational forces outside the legal structure. It is important not to strip away these contexts since they exert considerable influence. Implicit social rules constrain discretion powerfully.

There are also, of course, many explicit social or organizational rules to assist in the exercise of discretion. Organizations, for instance, have their own routines (see Feldman, Chapter 5, and Manning, Chapter 8). Furthermore, organizations may well shape discretion in ways not necessarily anticipated by law by imposing their own constraints on the way in which their members exercise discretion. If, for example, they introduce decision-making procedures designed to make their staff more accountable, this can lead to adaptive behaviour

[20] This is a theme of many of the book's chapters. See, in particular, those by Schneider (Chapter 2), Baumgartner (Chapter 4), Feldman, (Chapter 5), Lempert (Chapter 6), Emerson and Paley (Chapter 7), and Manning (Chapter 8).

by individuals to minimize criticism from superiors. The effect of such controls can be to produce decisions which emphasize conformity to regular or expected organizational practices at the expense of an attempt to advance the bureaucracy's broad legal mandate. If organizations seek to make their staff more productive (as with the use of arrest or prosecution quotas by enforcement agencies, for example), individuals may spend their time generating the appropriate indices of output for organizational reward and neglecting other important activities.

Nevertheless, many advantages accrue for individuals from making decisions in compliance with a set of rules, legal or otherwise. In administrative agencies, for example, bureaucratic rules guide officials in making decisions or in providing protection from criticism in difficult cases. Because rules offer guidance, they are an important ingredient in the efficiency with which decisions can be made, since they permit ready repetition of the process of deciding without the need to treat all potentially relevant matters in a new case afresh. This aspect of rule-guided behaviour also leads to the emergence of other, informal, rules of thumb, where legal actors have to deal with a stream of cases presenting similar features. The result is that organizational actors often decide, not on some conception of the merits of a particular case, but according to general, established, rule-governed procedures (see below). Where legal decision-makers impose other constraints and forms of guidance on their own exercise of discretion in circumstances where the law grants them discretion, one consequence may be to persuade them that, from their own internal perspective, they possess less discretion than may, on an external view, be the case (Galligan 1986*a*: 12–13; see also Lempert, this volume, Chapter 6). The following discussion touches on a few of the more prominent occasions for rule-governed behaviour.

Routine and repetitive decisions

Discretion is often exercised in routine and repetitive ways (see Feldman, Chapter 5, Emerson and Paley, Chapter 7, and Manning, Chapter 8), and the frequency with which legal actors make decisions has important implications for the nature of their discretion. Those legal actors, however, who make decisions relatively infrequently are likely to approach the matter in a more complex way, taking more time and considering more information. The experience of having to make regular and repetitive decisions (such as those made by police officers or regulatory inspectors, social security officials, probation officers, or members of tribunals or panels) leads to the development of shorthand ways of classifying cases and appraising each one by focusing on the extent to which it presents typical features. The adoption of a simplified categorical approach supplants individualized consideration; instead, simple rules of thumb dictate what information is relevant and how each case should be dealt with. In the context of legal decision-making, it is clear that discretion is heavily influenced by conceptions of precedent, by understandings of the 'normal ways' of acting and deciding when confronted with certain kinds of problem or case or in certain kinds of situations (see, further, Sudnow 1965; Lloyd-Bostock 1991). Only those cases not regarded as fulfilling simple criteria—those designated as not 'normal'—prompt any special consideration (Sudnow 1965). For example, Emerson and Paley (Chapter 7) show how decision-makers often seek to cope with complexity by moulding cases into a binary type: 'good' or 'bad' (or 'serious' or 'light' Mather 1979: 27). When a case has been so categorized, the decision about disposal tends then to be straightforward: a 'good' case is routinely handled in a particular way. However, what Emerson and Paley show is how this apparently simple decision-making process is actually reached, and how complex the processes leading up to this simple categorization can actually be.

Patterns are easily discerned in the use of discretion by legal actors, and are the more readily visible where decisions are made routinely (see Baumgartner, Chapter 4). To the extent that decisions do not involve simplified routines for assessing information and reaching decisions, however, it is possible that they may be less predictable. Shorthand decision methods are employed partly because familiarity with the broad features in typical cases gives decision-makers confidence in being able to see similarities in other cases, and partly in the interest of saving the time and anxiety otherwise involved in addressing each new case afresh. Typification elides legal rules. It is a means of imposing order on a potentially disorderly process that opens the way to the application of organizational and other norms beyond, or instead of, legal norms (matters sometimes regarded as 'extra legal'), to permit ready disposal of a case. Hence typification reaches to a wider range of matters deemed relevant. As decision-makers gain experience, this process of typification becomes simpler and more routine (Rubinstein 1973; see, generally, Rock 1973). Indeed, it seems clear that certain kinds of highly repetitive decisions are made virtually automatically (Lloyd-Bostock 1991).

Repetitive decision-making builds up in the participants a stock of knowledge about the decision-making proclivities of others. Where discretion is exercised by those who know the decision-making behaviour of other actors well, such familiarity allows a high degree of mutual predictability of decision-making. This can make it possible for decision-makers to penetrate or look behind earlier decisions to understand the 'real meaning' of a decision, much as people sometimes 'read between the lines' to understand what is really being said. It also makes practices like plea-bargaining or settling out of court possible, enabling legal actors to make decisions in anticipation of what 'the other side' will do, or decisions in anticipation of what others to whom cases will be handed on will do (see Emerson and Paley, Chapter 7). The repetitive decision-maker who deals with others for whom decision-making about a matter with legal implications is an infrequent or even unique occurrence, however (the 'repeat-player' faced with a 'one-shotter' (Galanter 1974)), is at a considerable advantage, in terms of having decisions made in ways deemed desirable (see Lempert, Chapter 6).[21] The absence of a repeat-player from one side in an adversarial hearing will lead to considerable imbalance in the distribution of power.[22]

Time and precedent

Legal cases have both a history and a future. Discretion may be backward-looking, or reflective, and have a responsive or a reactive character. In other cases, however, it may have a strong anticipatory or predictive character. In fact, it is only because of a rich knowledge of the past that people may predict. Predictive decisions can be pre-emptive or prospective, made in anticipation of what another person or organization is likely to do in response to one's own actions. Emerson and Paley (Chapter 7) provide a way of thinking about the organizational handling of cases with their use of the concept of horizon, which draws attention to the different contexts in which cases must be processed in the legal handling system. Their chapter is concerned with discretion as a phenomenon that looks both forward

---

[21] Galanter (1974) also observes that it pays a recurrent litigant to expend resources to influence the making of relevant rules by lobbying, and so on.

[22] Handler (Chapter 10) is concerned with the distribution of advantage in bargaining arrangements leading to the making of legal decisions.

and back, showing how people decide on a course of action by reference both to past events as well as anticipated future events. Decision-makers contemplating court action, for example, have to anticipate questions that might arise concerning the nature or sufficiency of available evidence and decide on strategy accordingly. Similarly, pre-trial decisions about charge or plea are usually informed by knowledge of the sentencing proclivities of judges. Sometimes anticipatory behaviour may be used in an artful way by a decision-maker to attain a particular kind of preferred outcome, as when a clerk allocates certain kinds of case for trial to a judge whose sentencing practices are well known so as to ensure that the case is likely to receive what he or she would regard as the appropriate punishment (Lovegrove 1984).[23]

The past is particularly instructive, not only for judges in common-law systems, but also for officials in legal bureaucracies where regular working practices crystallize into organizational precedent. Precedent serves important functions. It grants access to a repertoire of accustomed ways of handling problems, and is another device to make the task of decision-making quicker and easier. Sainsbury (Chapter 9) quotes an example of an official who said that, after thirty years, 'you have a pretty good built-in computer telling you what assessments should be'. Where initial cases may be regarded as a marker for the handling of later cases, precedent reveals the relevance of a decision-making sequence for organizations. One decision usually carries implications for others, since decisions create expectations. As Martha Feldman (Chapter 5) points out, when people work in organizations, they do so under the weight of a whole series of expectations which others have of how they will make decisions, a matter contributing greatly to the regularities of discretion. Equally, legal officials may use a decision to inform an interested audience (for an example, see Hawkins 1986: 1196 ff.). Precedent also serves to instruct other decision-makers. As Lempert (Chapter 6) shows, officials tend to develop their own sense of precedent for their decision practices, a sense which hardens with the passage of time (Rubinstein 1973) and may culminate in suggesting to later decision-makers in effect that, for all practical purposes, they themselves possess relatively

---

[23] While the behaviour of known individuals may be rather predictable, that of outsiders to the legal system, like potential witnesses, tends to be rather unpredictable (Hawkins 1989).

little discretion in particular instances.[24] The practical consequence of this behaviour is that organizationally- or subjectively-created precedents can acquire the same binding force as legal rules. Furthermore, as Lempert points out, the forces contributing to the creation of precedent are not necessarily the same as those that keep it in effect. Finally, but not least, precedent acts as a refuge when the exercise of discretion is questioned.

Moral evaluation

Another set of rules has a strong moral component. Indeed, it is clear from a large number of studies that assessments of moral character made by legal decision-makers are one of the most pervasive and persistent features in shaping the exercise of discretion. For instance, moral disreputability tends to prompt more punitive responses by law enforcers (e.g. Emerson 1969; Hawkins 1984); and in the handling of cases, both criminal and civil, much turns on the credibility of the individuals caught up in the case, whether as complainants, defendants, or witnesses.[25] Credibility itself is a matter bound up with assessments of moral character, social class, educational attainment, and so on. The identity, status, or character of a person offering information or evaluation to a decision-maker may be extremely influential and may prompt a series of common-sense assessments about the trustworthiness, competence, or sincerity of the person concerned. For example, lawyers will do their best to make their own witnesses appear credible, by attributing to them, or giving them the opportunity to display, qualities which are socially valued. Therefore they will do their best in a trial to make their witnesses seem respectable, sincere, honest, and so on. Similarly, the lawyer on the other side will try to convey precisely the opposite impression (practising lawyers have all sorts of practical insights into the nature of legal discretion).

Important implications follow from this. Joel Handler shows how social workers appraise needy clients and how, in handling the uncertainties of the work and the demands placed upon them by clients, social workers develop 'practice ideologies'. These are based on the social construction of moral character and serve to screen out

---

[24] Lempert (Chapter 6) also provides evidence, however, which indicates that this is not necessarily a general effect. This suggests that the development of such precedent may be contingent on other matters, such as the relative frequency with which cases are encountered by decision-makers.

[25] Similarly, the credibility of the source of information used in decisions is very important: for examples, see Hawkins 1986; Manning 1988*d*.

incompatible information and resist change, thereby allowing the easier and more efficient exercise of discretion. Moral concerns tend to predominate in such screening decisions, and the kind of moral character ascribed to an individual determines the agency's obligations to the client. These processes are means by which an agency is able to admit clients who are important to its success as an organization and reject undesirables. They operate systematically and establish yet another set of regularities in discretionary outcomes. They are also another aspect of the power implicated in the exercise of discretion.

Conclusion

The chapters in this book show how economic, political, personal, or organizational realities all serve to constrain discretion, as well as legal rules. Baumgartner's analysis (Chapter 4) suggests that these forces act profoundly in systematic and predictable ways and provides compelling evidence of what Feldman has elsewhere (1989) called order without design. In behavioural terms, Lempert argues (Chapter 6), discretion is not the freedom to decide as the actor chooses, but the freedom to be influenced by factors other than the law. This leads to regularities in discretionary decisions which may be as predictable as those by adjudicators consciously applying specific and detailed legal rules. Indeed, these patterns are sufficiently clear for Baumgartner to call into question the reality of legal discretion.

The lawyer, whose interest is in the immediate case and the behaviour of the individual decision-maker, will want any case to be disposed of by principles that are legal, public, valid, and consistently applied. Baumgartner's analysis will not presumably be of much comfort. Lawyers will be concerned that regularities in the use of discretion do not necessarily fit well with legal conceptions of its proper exercise. Furthermore, even though legal actors may in the aggregate exercise their discretion in very patterned and predictable ways, this does not mean that there are no inconsistencies in particular decision outcomes, nor, necessarily, that there is consistency over time.

To understand better how law works, how the words of law are translated into action, it is essential to know how legal discretion is exercised. A better appreciation of the nature of discretion is also essential to refinement of legal debate, and to policy questions concerned with matters such as the development of more effective control on the discretion of legal and administrative officials. It should be clear, however, that producing a more sophisticated understanding of how discretion is used is a very complex task, because decision-making is itself extremely complex, and discretion is a dynamic and adaptable phenomenon. Its use is not always what it may seem, because the complexity of a particular decision process is almost always obscured. Nicola Lacey (Chapter 11) questions whether discretion can be exclusively seen (as lawyers typically regard it) as residing in a discrete event or mental act. She also questions whether it is always wise to think of discretion as bound up with legal grants of discretionary power, since some who, on the face of it, enjoy wide legal discretion in fact exercise little discretion by adopting decision routines, and those (such as clerks who receive phone calls to the police (Manning, 1988*d*)) who might be thought to possess little discretion in fact wield a considerable power both to exclude potential legal cases and to direct others for handling in particular ways. These forms of discretionary decisions are peculiarly unsuited to formal legal means of control (see Lacey). It has already been argued that to impose such controls may be counter-productive, since a change in rules may not lead to the change in the exercise of discretion desired, or may lead to change in an unanticipated direction.[26]

In researching or writing about the uses of discretion it is essential that organizing assumptions are constantly exposed. Certain values and ideological tenets are socially prized, and consequently taken for granted. It is easy to allow normatively valued conceptions to dominate, not only debate about discretion, but the ways in which people research it.[27] Indeed, there is a tendency in much of the literature on discretion to conflate the normative and the descriptive. Pfeffer has discussed some of the implications of organizing assumptions in research in the context of organization theory:

Efficiency, effectiveness and profit are normatively valued and legitimate, while conceptions of organizations as political systems are much less consistent

---

[26] There are also important policy questions surrounding discretion that speak directly to the question of its control. Empirical research can help here by revealing where, for instance, power to decide is actually located or how it is diffused. This may suggest whether it is desirable or practical to try to control the exercise of discretion in particular circumstances by controlling the behaviour of decision-makers or whether it may sometimes be more desirable to try to change the rules allocating discretion in the first place. This latter approach may restrict, but it may also alter the nature of the discretion to be exercised.

[27] Both Handler (Chapter 10) and Lacey (Chapter 11), for example, take issue with the paradigmatic view of legal liberalism.

with dominant ideology and values. Thus, research demonstrating the non-rationality of decision procedures in organizations or in individuals has been met with relative neglect. The theories of organizations found explicitly or implicitly stated in the principal textbooks and in scholarly research presume bureaucratically rational functional imperatives for management and organizations. (1981*b*: 15)

In much of the social science work about decision-making organized around a conception of rational choice, it is often not clear whether the writing is descriptive of actual practice, or prescriptive of preferred practice. There is a constant danger in socio-legal research on discretion, for example, of imputing goals and motives to legal actors derived from tacit or unexamined assumption or from the ostensible objectives of those parts of the legal system under study. This should emphasize the continuing need for empirical research on discretion, its use, and its consequences, that is as dispassionate and as true to its natural state as possible.

2. Discretion and Rules
A Lawyer's View

CARL E. SCHNEIDER

I N modern society the law regulates the complex behavior of millions of people. To do this efficiently—to do this at all—broadly applicable rules must be used. Yet such rules are bound to be incomplete, to be ambiguous, to fail in some cases, to be unfair in others. Some of the drawbacks of rules can be minimized by giving discretion to the administrators and judges who apply them. Yet doing so dilutes the advantages of rules and creates the risk that discretion may be abused. Working out the proper balance of these considerations is both necessary and perplexing in every area of law.

Scholars, lawyers, and judges are hardly unaware of these problems. Those who have most directly addressed the problem of discretion fall primarily into two groups. The first group comprises of those—principally sociologists[1] and political scientists, but also some lawyers—who examine discretionary decisions and ways of controlling discretionary decisions in various particular bureaucratic contexts, most extensively the police. The second group consists of the legal philosophers who have for decades, if not centuries, asked, 'Do judges in some cases have freedom in resolving legal issues to decide them more than one way, or are judges always legally bound to reach one conclusion rather than any others?' (Greenawalt 1975: 365). The former group thus directs its attention to highly context-specific questions, the latter to highly abstract questions.

This chapter falls into neither category. Rather, it looks at the problem of discretion and rules from a lawyer's point of view. In thinking about how the law can best serve its purposes, lawyers are repeatedly confronted with what may be crudely described as a tension between writing rules and giving someone (to the lawyer's

I am grateful to Lynn A. Baker, David L. Chambers, Edward H. Cooper, Keith Hawkins, Richard O. Lempert, Frederick F. Schauer, Eric Stein, and Kent D. Syverud for their generous and helpful comments on various incarnations of this chapter.

[1] For a particularly good example of this genre, one uncommonly self-conscious about the systematic issues raised by the tension between discretion and rules, see Lempert, Chapter 6, which also contains helpful citations to the social science literature on discretion.

mind, usually a judge) discretion. In this chapter I consider how that tension should be handled. I ask what kinds of advantages rules and discretion seem systematically to offer and what kinds of disadvantages they seem systematically to present. While I cannot pretend that my answers will be those of a typical lawyer (if only because there is probably no such person), I do hope that they will give the reader of this volume some insight into the kinds of issues the tension between discretion and rules seems to lawyers to raise and the ways lawyers commonly deal with them.

Even in the minds of lawyers, the tension between discretion and rules provokes conflicting impulses. Most lawyers have pledged their faith to the concept of rules and to the doctrine of due process; correspondingly, they are dubious about discretionary decisions. And, like the public, lawyers tend to think about 'law' as a system of rules. Where an area of law—like my own field of family law—seems poor in rules and rich in discretion, they begin to wonder whether it is really law.

But lawyers know that rules must be interpreted and that rules can lead to wrong results in particular cases. Thus lawyers know with special acuteness that discretion is necessary. In addition, lawyers are as susceptible as anyone else to a new social attitude toward the authority of rules. This new attitude is vividly evoked by Keynes, who, speaking of himself and the friends of his youth, said:

We entirely repudiated a personal liability on us to obey general rules. We claimed the right to judge every individual case on its merits, and the wisdom, experience and self-control to do so successfully. This was a very important part of our faith, violently and aggressively held, and for the outer world it was our most dangerous characteristic. We repudiated entirely customary morals, conventions and traditional wisdom . . . we recognized no moral obligation on us, no inner sanction, to conform or to obey. Before heaven we claimed to be our own judge in our own case. (1956: 252)

Professor P. S. Atiyah further illuminates this new attitude when he writes, 'Modern man is unwilling to accept the authority of a principle whose application seems unjust in a particular case, merely because there might be some beneficial long-term consequence which he is unable to identify or even perceive' (1980: 1270). Thus, despite their recognition of the primacy of rules, lawyers recognize that discretion is both invaluable and inevitable.

Because they are pulled so vigorously in both directions, lawyers as a group cannot be said to have a coherent attitude toward the problem of discretion and rules. Nor, I think, do lawyers systematically divide along the lines of any discernible principle in approaching the problem. Rather, a lawyer's view of the choice between discretion and rules is often context specific. Sometimes that choice is driven simply by the lawyer's view of what substantive use a judge is likely to make of any grant of discretion.

In this chapter I will not try to resolve the tension between discretion and rules. I do not believe that one can be systematically preferred to the other. Nor do I offer any formula to follow in choosing between discretion and rules. On the contrary. My general position is that the choice will be complex and uncertain and that it will depend on factors that will be difficult to assess and that will vary from circumstance to circumstance (so that it is not unreasonable for lawyers to look to particular contexts in evaluating discretion and rules). I will argue that, in the world in which we live, there typically is not a choice between discretion and rules, but rather a choice between different mixes of discretion and rules. The first reason for this is that discretion and rules rarely appear in unadulterated form in any large area of legal significance. Typically, I will suggest, there is no such thing as an important legal decision from which all elements of discretion have been removed. Yet I will also suggest that, typically, there is no such thing as an important legal decision in which judicial discretion is free to roam wholly unchecked.

The second reason we rarely face a choice between discretion and rules is that there are compelling advantages and compelling disadvantages to both discretion and rules. We will commonly want to secure the advantages of *both* discretion and rules while avoiding their disadvantages. Worse, it will usually be unclear just how to secure those advantages and to avoid the disadvantages in any particular situation. This will generally mean that we must grope toward some satisfactory mix of discretion and rules.

The purpose of this chapter, then, is primarily analytic. I want to show how the problem of discretion and rules looks to a lawyer. I want to present a systematic, if brief, chart of the things to consider in evaluating what mix of discretion and rules to prefer in any particular situation. In so far as my purpose strays beyond the analytic, it is to domesticate both discretion and rules, to suggest that the dangers of each tend to be exaggerated. Thus I will treat at special length the advantages rules offer. And I will go to special trouble to show that discretion is neither as uncommon in the American legal system as its critics suggest nor as unconstrained in its working as its critics fear.

Before beginning, we need a few brief working definitions. These definitions must be very rough ideal types, because, as I just said, part of my point will be that there is rarely if ever such a thing as a pure rule or pure discretion and that most cases are resolved through a complex mix of rules and discretion. For our purposes, then, the ideal type of a 'rule' is an authoritative, mandatory, binding, specific, and precise direction to a judge which instructs him how to decide a case or to resolve a legal issue.[2] And, for our purposes, discretion describes those 'cases as to which a judge, who has consulted all relevant legal materials, is left free by the law to decide one way or another' (Greenawalt 1975: 365).

On the continuum between rules and discretion are a number of intermediate categories. Some of these can be derived from the work of Professor Dworkin. For instance, he calls 'a "policy" that kind of standard that sets out a goal to be reached, generally an improvement in some economic, political, or social feature of the community . . .' (1977*b*: 22). He calls 'a "principle" a standard that is to be observed, not because it will advance or secure an economic, political, or social situation deemed desirable, but because it is a requirement of justice or fairness or some other dimension of morality' (ibid.: 22). He distinguishes policies and principles from rules: 'Rules are applicable in an all-or-nothing fashion. If the facts a rule stipulates are given, then either the rule is valid, in which case the answer it supplies must be accepted, or it is not, in which case it contributes nothing to the decision' (ibid.: 24). Policies and principles, on the other hand, 'do not set out legal consequences that follow automatically when the conditions provided are met' (ibid.: 25). Policies and principles, then, can be thought of as less directive than rules but more directive than confiding a decision to the discretion of the decision-maker.

There are also more directive versions of discretion. Professor Dworkin calls our working definition the 'strong' form of discretion. But he also specifies two 'weak' forms of discretion: 'Sometimes we use "discretion" in a weak sense, simply to say that for some reason the standards an official must apply cannot be applied mechanically but demand the use of judgment' (ibid.: 31). The other weak sense refers to occasions when 'some official has final authority to make a

[2] I am drawing here on Schauer 1991.

decision, which cannot be reviewed and reversed by any other official' (ibid.: 32).

There are conventionally thought to be two large categories of discretion—discretion to make rules and discretion to find facts and interpret them in terms of 'the law'. In American law, the former kind of discretion is formally and ultimately allotted to legislatures, but of course there are many areas of law in which American courts are expected to act as common-law courts and to be a primary source of rules (even though they must yield to any assertion of legislative authority) and many other areas in which they are expected to provide interstitial rules or to clarify legislative rules (often in quite consequential ways). The latter kind of discretion we may loosely call discretion to decide cases. In the United States this kind of discretion is primarily exercised by courts and administrative agencies. The distinction between discretion to write rules and discretion to decide cases is analytically helpful. But it must not be allowed to obscure the fact that there is a large blurred area between the two categories in which judges create rules in the process of finding facts and applying the law.

We will be concerned with both kinds of discretion. However, it is judicial and administrative discretion that is the principal source of much of the concern about discretion. When lawyers think about the problem of discretion, their paradigmatic question is how legislatures can write rules so as to limit the discretion of courts and agencies to decide cases. We will thus be most centrally concerned with the dangers and delights of judicial (and to a lesser extent) administrative discretion.

Discretion in Context

In an illuminating discussion, Dean Teitelbaum writes that

discretion is formally considered deviant. American sociology of law, which has largely devoted itself to discovering the operation of discretion at all levels of the justice system, typically draws a distinction between legal norms ('legal ideals') and the conduct of individuals and groups whose behavior should be governed by those norms ('legal reality'). Where a 'gap' between theoretical expectations about the operation of legal norms and observed behavior is observed, it is ordinarily interpreted from the perspective of a regime of rules: as a failure in statutory formulation or a failure to comply with the legal norm. Thus, for example, the significance of observed police behavior is often said to lie in its nonconformity with what we suppose legal rules to require of policemen, which should be remedied either by clarifying the law or by reforming police behavior. (Teitelbaum, forthcoming)

The 'gap' view of discretion is, of course, the one I have described as paradigmatic of the way lawyers most readily think of discretion. And, of course, that view reflects a real, indeed a central, problem with discretion. But, as Dean Teitelbaum implies, the 'gap' view is incomplete and therefore misleading. In fact, discretion plays a larger, richer part in Western law than that view suggests and than we unreflectively assume. In this section, I want to take a first step toward domesticating discretion and understanding its functions by using American examples to show how broad, how commonplace, how unremarkable the role of discretion in Western law is.

Although we tend not to think of it in this way, the most important allocation of discretion in our system is to the government from 'the people'. The allocation is phrased in the broadest and haziest terms, if it may be said to be phrased at all. It is, within constitutional bounds, an award of plenary authority. Although elected officials are in a sense 'instructed' by the voters at elections, and although they may consult public opinion polls, those instructions and polls are extraordinarily obscure guides to governmental decisions. And there is not even agreement as to whether officials are elected simply to reflect the views of the voters or to express their own best judgments. In short, elected officials exercise discretion in perhaps all meanings of that term and wield it in perhaps every central aspect of their work.

Of course, a principal part of the people's delegation of discretion to the government is specifically accorded to the legislature. And, of course, the legislature principally exercises that discretion in making laws. But it also commonly awards vast grants of discretion to administrative agencies. Sometimes this is discretion to make rules, as testified by acres of trees that died so that the CFR might live.[3] Sometimes it is discretion to adjudicate claims against the government and disputes among citizens, as the Social Security Administration, the Veterans' Administration, and the National Labor Relations Board, among many others, show every working day.

The executive branch acquires its own broad swaths of discretion as its share of the people's grant of authority. Part of that discretion is exercised in collaborating with the legislature in drafting, debating,

---

[3] The CFR is the Code of Federal Regulations, and in it are published the rules and regulations of federal agencies. I need hardly say that one set fills endless yards of bookshelf space.

and enacting laws. But discretion is also deployed in the ordinary process of administering the government and enforcing legislation. In the sociological literature, the police exemplify this kind of discretion. A brief look at the problem of discretion in police departments should help us appreciate the breadth of discretion an administrative agency exercises at all levels of its work.

Police-agency discretion begins at the administrative level. Very generally, for example, police administrators have considerable discretion to decide whether the department's policy should be to respond to complaints from citizens about crimes or rather to try to institute programs which will prevent crimes from being committed in the first place. Less grandly, they can decide how the department should be organized and run day to day. But police commissioners and senior officials cannot monopolize police discretion: individual police officers have substantial discretion in doing their work. (Indeed, one might say that a primary constraint on administrative discretion is that officers wield so much discretion of their own.) As Professor Reiss indicates,

Most police officers work most of the time without direct supervision. Their discretionary decisions, thus, are not generally open to review by superiors. . . . Even when evidence of activity is submitted, such as in an arrest report, the capacity to review discretion is limited. There is no simple way to determine the facts in police encounters with citizens, the alternatives available to make choices, and their behavior. (1974*b* 181).

Individual officers exercise this kind of discretion even where they are in principle most strictly constrained by procedural regulations: 'in practice, when enforcing the law, the police exercise enormous discretion to arrest. Field observation studies of police decisions to arrest demonstrate this point: in one such study, the police released roughly one-half of the persons they suspected of committing crimes . . .' (ibid.: 191). Nor is police authority or discretion limited to the task of enforcing the law, since police activities 'include intervention in conflicts between members of families, landlords and tenants, and employers and employees, as well as assistance in sickness, in tracing missing persons, and in dealing with the plight of animals or hazardous situations' (ibid.: 86).

The problem of controlling administrative discretion is a familiar one. What Americans call administrative law is centrally concerned with devising rules that allow governmental agencies the leeway they need for doing their work while deterring them from abusing their discretion. The Administrative Procedure Act grants courts considerable power to supervise administrative agencies in the hope of accomplishing those delicate ends. The law of police procedure has been constitutionalized in the hope that through such doctrines as the 'Miranda' rule[4] the discretion of police departments and officers can be checked.

Nevertheless, it is the discretion exercised in the judicial branch with which lawyers are traditionally most familiar and concerned. As I have already noted, great discretion is granted to judges in various kinds of law-making. For instance, many common-law substantive areas are presumptively confided to the courts, sometimes so much so that it is the legislature, not the judiciary, which acts interstitially. And courts often acquire considerable discretionary powers even in areas where the legislature is the prime mover, as Professor Chayes observes: 'In enacting fundamental social and economic legislation, Congress is often unwilling or unable to do more than express a kind of general policy objective or orientation. . . . the result is to leave a wide measure of discretion to the judicial delegate. The corrective power of Congress is also stringently limited in practice' (1976: 1314). A particularly vivid example is that centerpiece of US anti-trust law, the Sherman Anti-Trust Act. It contains two key provisions. The first makes illegal 'every contract, combination in the form of trust or otherwise, or conspiracy, in restraint of trade'. The second makes it illegal to 'monopolize or attempt to monopolize, or combine or conspire . . . to monopolize any part of the trade or commerce among the several states'. The meaning of these terse commands was left to the courts (and the executive) to supply.

Of course, judges also exercise great discretion in fact-finding, especially, but not exclusively, when there is no jury. Further, judges exercise (sometimes along with juries) a generous discretion in 'law application'—that vast borderland between 'fact' and 'law' that is created by doctrines like the 'reasonable man' standard in torts or the 'rule of reason' in anti-trust law.[5] Finally, considerable discretion is

---

[4] The 'Miranda' rule comes from *Miranda* v. *Arizona*, 384 US 436 (1966), and should be familiar to anyone who has ever seen an American movie or television program in which the police figure. It requires the police to tell suspects their rights when they are taken into custody, and it bars the use in court of statements made by defendants who have not been properly informed.

[5] I examine these areas of discretion at somewhat greater length in the next section of this chapter.

confided to judges in some kinds of remedy-giving. For example, both
the decision to grant injunctive relief and the shape of injunctive relief
are traditionally discretionary. Since an injunction can attempt to
regulate the relations of the parties into the future in considerable
complexity and since the role of injunctive relief has greatly expanded
in recent years, this source of discretion can be broad indeed.

But judicial discretion is exercised in contexts other than trials. For
instance, judges have wide discretion in what might be called semi-
administrative matters. In the criminal justice system, for instance, the

main forms of discretion that they exercise are by decisions to: (1) detain
defendants, grant bail or release them on their own recognisance; (2) dismiss
matters or bind over at preliminary hearing; (3) accept pleas of guilty or to
find guilty or not guilty in bench trials; (4) rule on matters of substance and
procedure during trial proceedings; (5) decide the fate of defendants found
guilty . . .' (Reiss, 1974*b*: 197–8).

Nor are judges the only actors in the judicial branch to make
discretionary decisions. Juries not only make some of the same kinds
of discretionary decisions judges do, but they are effectively less
subject to review when they make them. This is because juries
deliberate in secret, usually need not explain their decisions, and are
deferred to on the theory that they represent the voice of the community.
Lawyers too are endowed with weighty kinds of discretion. Most
prominently, prosecutors exercise discretion in such matters as deciding
whether to file or to drop charges and in plea-bargaining. But defense
counsel also commonly have discretion in preparing the defense, in
conducting the trial, in plea-bargaining, and in advising their clients.
Similarly, lawyers in civil suits generally have broad leeway in
framing and responding to complaints, conducting the trial, and
negotiating settlements. They have particularly conspicuous discretion
in pre-trial proceedings, especially in what is called discovery. In
discovery, a lawyer may use judicial power to compel an opponent to
produce records and submit to depositions. While ultimately the
court can supervise discovery, in practice that supervision is loose and
allows lawyers generous latitude. The lawyer's discretion in all these
respects is, of course, limited by his responsibility to the client. But
many of these areas of discretion (like the conduct of the trial) are
generally regarded (at least by lawyers) as within the lawyer's special
purview, and in others of those areas (like negotiating settlements)

the lawyer's professional expertise will often assure him considerable authority.

Finally, actors outside the formal legal system exercise discretion in ways that affect that system. For instance, the law has co-operated in making semi-legal institutions of such enterprises as arbitration, mediation, and conciliation, all of which accord some non-official person considerable authority to resolve disputes that might otherwise go to a court or government agency. Even ordinary citizens retain a good deal of discretion about the work of the criminal and civil justice systems, since these systems primarily depend for their workload on the initiative of citizens. And, in so far as citizens enter contracts, form associations, unite in partnerships, and create corporations, they exercise their discretion in the creation and conduct of publicly enforced private government.

The centrality of discretionary decisions in the American legal system can be put into perspective by comparing it to civil-law systems, for, by contrast with them, the common-law system seems almost designed to promote the exercise of discretion.[6] For one thing, the common law seems intently concerned with preserving doctrinal flexibility. Dean Levi expressed a standard common-law view when he wrote,

The categories used in the legal process must be left ambiguous in order to permit the infusion of new ideas. And this is true even where legislation or a constitution is involved. The words used by the legislature or the constitutional convention must come to have new meanings . . . In this manner the laws come to express the ideas of the community and even when written in general terms, in statute or constitution, are molded for the specific case. (1949: 4)

A consequence of this approach is that, despite the doctrine of *stare decisis* (the doctrine that courts must follow the relevant precedents in making decisions) judges often have real discretion in shaping and reshaping legal doctrines. Common-law decision-making seems not just designed to secure doctrinal flexibility. It also conduces to allowing judges to 'do justice' in a particular case where a rule seems not to. The common-law judges' discretion is preserved out of what sometimes seems a preference for making fine distinctions so that justice can be done in each case. And the classic common-law judge

---

[6] I am not, of course, denying that there are many important sources of discretion in civil-law systems. Indeed, I try to suggest in this chapter that there are many kinds of discretion which no system can escape and many kinds which no system would want to escape.

has mastered the art of detecting distinctions between cases which duller eyes might miss.

The common law's emphasis on discretion to do justice in individual cases was enhanced when the common-law courts and the courts of equity were combined, since equity was in several ways an importantly discretionary body of law. Equity was designed from the beginning to respond to instances in which common-law rules proved too rigid. Equity's standards for decision were extraordinarily discretionary; early equity judges decided cases as 'reason and conscience' demanded. Equity expanded the scope of judicial discretion to ensure flexibility in the decision of individual cases and in remedial relief. While, as readers of *Bleak House* know, equity (particularly in England) itself became sclerotic, its ultimate contribution has been to broaden judicial discretion, since the common law has incorporated many of its more flexible doctrines, remedies, and attitudes. Discretion pervades the common-law system in still other ways: Much fact-finding and law application are done by the jury, a lay group which does not consider enough cases to develop its own rules and which cannot be effectively reviewed. As I wrote earlier, the jury meets in private, its findings of fact are reviewable only under a standard that defers generously to the jury's conclusions, and it generally need not explain how it understood or applied the law. The consequence of this is that juries can ignore the judge's instructions about the law. While courts hardly encourage jury nullification, they deliberately risk it in the interests of promoting the jury's discretion. One reason for doing so is to allow for the injection of 'community values' into the legal process. As Professor Damaska writes, 'It is this openness to ordinary community judgments that may well be more deeply engrained or more canonical in Anglo-American legal culture than the more visible arabesques of pleading, or the exquisite refinements of evidentiary rules' (1986: 42).

When in a common-law system fact-finding is confided to a judge, he is accorded more discretion than his civil-law counterpart. The common-law trial judge is essentially expected to 'find' facts after a single event—the trial—and his conclusions may, as I have said, be reversed only if they are egregiously ill founded. In civil-law systems, in contrast, the trial court assembles a factual record which is then passed on to the appellate court, which can review that record *de novo*.

Furthermore, common-law judges are much less subject than civil-law judges to systematic, hierarchical supervision. In civil-law systems, the judge is a bureaucrat who hopes to make a career by moving up the hierarchy of judicial jobs. In common-law systems, the judge is brought in laterally after achieving some stature in another branch of the legal profession. Once anointed, the judge may not particularly expect a promotion, which will often depend on the vagaries of politics. While the common-law system is hierarchical in the sense that a lower court's rulings may be reversed on appeal, it is less hierarchical in career terms, so that the common-law judge's discretion is less subject to the psychological and professional pressures which may affect the civil-law judge.

One scholar has argued that the discretionary powers of Anglo-American judges are in fact expanding. Professor Atiyah writes,

It is my thesis that the balance between principle and pragmatism in the judicial process has shifted markedly since the beginning of the last century. In the first half of the nineteenth century, I suggest the courts were inclined to resolve the conflict by adhering to principle. They were less concerned with doing justice in the particular case and more concerned with the impact of their decision in the future. In modern times, by contrast, I suggest that the courts have become highly pragmatic and a great deal less principled. Nor has the change been carried through by the courts alone. At virtually every point it has been assisted by legislation. (1980: 1251)

As Professor Atiyah explains, 'Rules of procedure and evidence tend increasingly to be subject to discretion rather than fixed rule; and even where there are rules they tend increasingly to be of a prima facie nature, rules liable to be displaced where the court feels they may work injustice' (ibid.: 1255). Professor Atiyah associates this change with a change in the prominence of two of the law's functions. Law 'provides a means of settling disputes by fair and peaceful procedures . . .'. But 'the judicial process is part of a complex set of arrangements designed to provide incentives and disincentives for various types of behavior' (1980: 1249). Professor Atiyah suggests that the former function has acquired a much more prominent position relative to the latter function than it used to have. And, since the latter works through rules and the former through 'pragmatism', the scope of discretion has grown greatly.

Professor Schauer confirms the growing power of discretion and places it in the context of the history of American legal thought. He detects

a tradition in American law and legal theory that not only connects [Ronald] Dworkin in interesting ways with the work of theorists as diverse as Lon

Fuller and Duncan Kennedy, but also has important points of contact with American Legal Realism and the aristotelian conception of equity. The tradition starts with an intuitively appealing goal—getting *this case* just right. But that goal and the tradition embracing it are in tension with the very idea of a rule, for implicit in rule-based adjudication is a tolerance for some proportion of wrong results, results other than the results that would be reached, all things other than the rule considered, for the case at hand. In many of the most important areas of American adjudication, the tolerance for the wrong answer has evaporated, often for good reason, and the current paradigm for adjudication in the American legal culture may already have departed from rule-bound decisionmaking. This new paradigm instead stresses the importance not of deciding the case according to the rule, but of tailoring the rule to fit the case. Instead of bowing to the inevitable resistance of rules, the new paradigm exalts reasons without the mediating rigidity of rules, thus avoiding the occasional embarrassment generated by rules. And because this new jurisprudence treats what looks like rules as continuously subject to molding in order best to maintain the purposes behind those rules in the face of a changing world, we can say that what emerges is a jurisprudence not of rules but of reasons. (1987: 847)

If the scope of discretion in American law has been increasing in recent years, one explanation lies in the rise of what Professor Chayes has called 'public law' litigation (1976: 1281). That litigation involves unusually complex issues of public policy, issues which often cannot be resolved without imposing on judges broadly discretionary duties. It includes 'school desegregation, employment discrimination, and prisoners' or inmates' rights cases' as well as 'antitrust, securities fraud and other aspects of the conduct of corporate business, bankruptcy and reorganizations, union governance, consumer fraud, housing discrimination, electoral reapportionment, [and] environmental man-agement' cases (ibid.: 1284). Public-law litigation may be contrasted with what Professor Robert Mnookin calls 'traditional adjudication', which a civil suit by a person injured by another person's negligence exemplifies. Traditional adjudication, he suggests, 'require[s] deter-mination of some event and [is] thus "act-oriented"'. It 'usually requires the determination of *past* acts and facts'. It does not involve 'appraisals of future relationships where the "loser's" future behavior can be an important ingredient'. It relies heavily on precedent. And parties to traditional adjudication all 'have a right to participate in the adjudicatory process' (Mnookin 1975: 251–3). In contrast to this kind of litigation, public-law litigation necessitates exercises of judicial discretion: it is not 'act-oriented'; it looks in large part to future, not past, events; it features interdependent, outcome-affecting factors; it often finds precedent an unhelpful guide to decision; and it frequently excludes affected parties.

Let me fill out these points slightly. Public-law litigation it is not 'act-oriented' in anything like the sense that Professor Mnookin intends by that phrase. Instead, it is often oriented to the complex behavior of complex institutions. In public-law adjudication, '[t]he fact inquiry is not historical and adjudicative but predictive and legislative', (Chayes 1976: 1302) and the decree that concludes that litigation often 'seeks to adjust future behavior, not to compensate for past wrong' (ibid.: 1298). The public-law decree 'provides for a complex, on-going regime of performance rather than a simple, one-shot, one-way transfer', (ibid.: 1298) and that regime regulates 'an elaborate and organic network of interparty relationships' (ibid.: 1299). In public law, 'the judge will not, as in the traditional model, be able to derive his responses directly from the liability determination, since . . . the substantive law will point out only the general direction to be pursued and a few salient landmarks to be sought out or avoided' (ibid.: 1299–300). And, finally, public-law remedies 'often hav[e] important consequences for many persons including absentees' (ibid.: 1302). (Indeed, a large part of the conventional objection to public-law litigation is exactly that many of the parties who have an interest in the litigation are unrepresented in it, including the public at large.) In all these ways, then, public-law litigation requires judges to make much more complex and uncertain judgments with less guidance from rules than the model of traditional adjudication seems to countenance, and thus it obliges them to call more fully on judicial discretion.

In this section, I have argued that discretion is intricately and inextricably woven into the warp and woof of American law. This argument, of course, does not prove that discretion is always desirable or always harmless. But it should raise doubts about whether discretion is simply an inconvenient power legal actors have that problematically creates gaps between what the law should be and what the law is. It should suggest that discretion is integral to the American (and perhaps any) legal system, that it serves crucial and irreplaceable functions. In the next section we will pursue this possibility by looking more closely at the attractions of discretion.

The Advantages of Discretion

Why is discretion so ubiquitous in Anglo-American law? What functions does it serve? What basic ideas in Western jurisprudence does it promote? What costs would eliminating it impose? What, in sum, are the advantages of discretion?

The first attraction of discretion is a negative one—rules can have disadvantages or can malfunction. Sometimes rule-makers fail to anticipate all the problems a rule is written to solve. Discretion can fill gaps in rules. Sometimes two or more rules simultaneously apply but dictate conflicting results. Discretion can permit the decision-maker to resolve the conflict in ways that best accommodate all the interests involved. Sometimes a rule will, applied to a particular case, produce a result that conflicts with the rule's purpose. Discretion can allow the decision-maker to promote the rule's purpose. Sometimes a rule will, applied to a particular case, produce a result that conflicts with our understanding of what justice demands. Discretion can let the decision-maker do justice. And sometimes the circumstances in which a rule must be applied will be so complex that no effective rule can be written. Discretion frees the decision-maker to deal with that complexity.

The advantages of discretion can be put in a more positive form by asking what the sources of discretion are. If we can understand how and why discretionary authority is created, we can better understand its attractions. Often there is a direct and deliberate grant of discretion (of varying levels of completeness) to a decision-maker. We will identify four ideal types of directly and deliberately created discretionary authority. The first of these is distinguishable from the others by its distance from the ordinary principles of 'law' as it is understood in Western industrialized countries. The rest of them are distinguishable by the reason for the grant of discretionary authority. They are not, however, mutually exclusive; discretion may be granted for more than one reason.

The first kind of directly and deliberately created discretionary authority can be called 'khadi-discretion'. This kind of discretion is the most complete and the most foreign to our legal system. It is created where it is thought that decision-makers can be found who are wise, who understand the principles of justice, and who already know or are well placed to discover the relevant facts, sometimes through acquaintance with the parties or through personal enquiry of people who know them. Of course, my name for this kind of discretion is taken from Max Weber's concept of khadi-justice. As Professor Kronman cogently summarizes Weber's understanding of it, khadi-justice is

adjudication of a purely *ad hoc* sort in which cases are decided on an individual basis and in accordance with an indiscriminate mixture of legal, ethical, emotional and political considerations. Khadi-justice is irrational in the sense that it is peculiarly ruleless; it makes no effort to base decisions on general principles, but seeks, instead, to decide each case on its own merits and in light of the unique considerations that distinguish it from every other case. . . . The characterization of khadi-justice as a substantive form of law-making highlights another of its qualities, namely, its failure to distinguish in a principled fashion between legal and extra-legal (ethical or political) grounds for decision. It is the expansiveness of this form of adjudication—its willingness to take into account all sorts of considerations, non-legal as well as legal—which gives it its substantive character; the idea of a limited and self-contained 'legal' point of view is foreign to all true khadi-justice. (1983: 76–7)

King Solomon's child-custody decision exemplifies khadi-justice. The litigants cite no law to Solomon, and he does not appear to consult any rules, procedural or substantive. His principle of decision cannot be reliably determined even after the decision: did he award the child to its natural mother, to the woman who most loved the child, or to the woman with the best moral character? What impressed all Israel about the decision was not that Solomon understood the law, but 'that the wisdom of God was in him, to do judgment'. Even his technique was apparently a classic khadi technique: 'when stories are told of really clever *qadis* they often involve the *qadi* trapping one of the parties in a display of his true character' (Rosen 1980–81: 231).

The second kind of direct and deliberate grant of discretionary authority is more characteristic of Western legal systems. It may be called 'rule-failure discretion'. It is created where it is believed that cases will arise in circumstances so varied, so complex, and so unpredictable that satisfactory rules that will accurately guide decision-makers to correct results in a sufficiently large number of cases cannot be written. Rule-failure discretion differs from khadi-discretion in several ways. The first is in the motive for its creation. Discretionary authority is accorded the khadi partly because of the khadi's special personal qualities and status. While Western judges are expected to have a 'judicial temperament', discretion is generally not accorded them because of that quality. On the contrary, that quality is supposed to restrain them from abusing their discretion. A judicial temperament is thought necessary because discretion must be exercised; judicial temperament does not justify the exercise of discretion. A second difference between the two kinds of justice is that, unlike the khadi, the Western judge is not expected to bring his own knowledge of the parties and their situation to bear. On the contrary, if he knows the parties, he is expected to excuse himself from the case. A third difference is that, while khadi-justice is 'peculiarly ruleless', Western justice is ordinarily embarrassed to be ruleless. Finally, unlike the khadi, the Western judge is generally expected to eschew 'non-legal' sources of authority. Even a judge with broad discretion is expected to consult only 'legal' sources, doctrines, and policies. He should look as much as possible to the law for norms and should not rely on his personal preferences or political allegiances.[7]

I have been distinguishing rule-failure discretion from khadi-discretion. But both variations draw on discretion's classic advantage— that it provides flexibility, that it allows the decision-maker to do justice in the individual case. Professor Cooper's praise of Rule 52(a) of the Federal Rules of Civil Procedure—'findings of fact . . . shall not be set aside unless clearly erroneous, and due regard shall be given to the opportunity of the trial court to judge of the credibility of the witnesses'—nicely exemplifies this virtue of discretion. Professor Cooper attributes that rule's 'enormous success' to 'the fact that the "clearly erroneous" phrase has no intrinsic meaning. It is elastic, capacious, malleable, and above all variable. Because it means nothing, it can mean anything and everything that it ought to mean. It cannot be defined, unless the definition might enumerate a nearly infinite number of shadings along the spectrum of working review standards' (1988: 645). Professor Cooper continues,

Rule 52(a) has been successful because the clearly erroneous standard of review does not establish a single test. Appellate courts have been left free to adapt the measure of review to the shifting needs of different cases, different laws, and different times. This success reflects the rule-making process at its best. A general tone is set, no attempt is made to anticipate and meet the exigencies of countless multitudes of cases, and practice develops along lines that are not often articulated but are often wise. (ibid.: 670)

---

[7] I am not arguing that US law is without its impulses to khadi-justice. For example, some of the popular and even scholarly justifications for according the US Supreme Court broadly discretionary authority sometimes seem to draw on elements of the justifications for khadi-justice.

A direct and deliberate grant of discretionary authority can be made for a third and related reason. 'Rule-building discretion' arises where the rule-maker could devise tolerably effective rules, but concludes that better rules would be developed (or that the same rules could be developed more efficiently) if the decision-makers were allowed to develop rules for themselves as they go along. The rule-maker might believe, in other words, that a decision-maker would, out of his experience with individual cases over long periods of time, acquire a better understanding than anyone else could of the generic problems being dealt with and of the concrete circumstances in which such problems present themselves. The decision-maker's experience may be both a valuable source of ideas for rules and a valuable check on the imagination of rule-writers. This is the theory of common-law adjudication—that, as courts repeatedly immerse themselves in and decide concrete cases, the cases will gradually sort themselves into patterns, principles for solving them will eventually emerge, and rules (based on experience) will finally be written.

Judicial discretion of this kind may be specially useful during times of rapid and great social change. Under such circumstances, rules are hard to write because (1) the rapidity of change makes them controversial, (2) the direction and extent of change are uncertain, and (3) rules must be replaced frequently. Discretion can alleviate these problems by allowing courts to adjust incrementally to changing social ideas instead of being confined to legislative standards that are not readily altered.

Another advantage of giving judges such discretion is that it allows them to take their community's standards into account. Of course, this advantage is attended by risks. But judges might desirably consider such standards on two theories. First, it may sometimes be appropriate to evaluate and resolve disputes on the basis of, or at least with a good and sympathetic understanding of, the social and normative environment in which the litigants acted and in which they will have to live. A variety of factors might make this preferable. Such an understanding might promote a more accurate interpretation of the litigants' behavior. It could help keep the law in touch with the people the law seeks to regulate and assist, with the social circumstances in which they live, and with norms that ought to affect the interpretation of the law. A second justification for allowing community standards to affect judicial decisions is that the community has an interest in those decisions, since they affect the community. American, and (to a lesser extent) English, law recognizes this interest by confiding important legal decisions to juries. We may also sometimes find it appropriate to recognize that interest when judges make decisions.

There are some obvious difficulties with consulting local standards, of course. The first is a practical one: it will often be hard to know just what local standards are. And the larger and more complex the local community is, the more diverse and undiscoverable local standards may be. The second is the conventional objection that local standards may conflict with broader (and, it is usually assumed, better) social understandings:

Domestic relations disputes, because they are so much a matter of community interest and deal with relations which engage every member of the community, may be especially likely to call forth deeply held local values which vary sharply from legal norms regarding divorce and familial relations. . . . Indeed, these dangers seem peculiarly great in precisely those settings where one could identify common values most readily: communities which are relatively homogeneous or where those with social authority share a single, strongly-held set of religious or other values. (Teitelbaum and DuPaix 1988: 1125–6)

Discretion presents a futher, related advantage: it allows the court to take into account the parties' own preferences. As Dean Levi wrote years ago (and not for the first time even then),

[T]he litigants . . . are bound by something they helped to make. Moreover, the examples or analogies urged by the parties bring into the law the common ideas of the society. The ideas have their day in court, and they will have their day again. This is what makes the hearing fair, rather than any idea that the judge is completely impartial, for of course he cannot be completely so. (1949: 5)

The fourth and last form of a direct and deliberate grant of discretionary authority may be called 'rule-compromise discretion'. Sometimes the members of the governmental body responsible for instructing the decision-maker cannot agree on rules or even guidelines, and they will then deliberately choose to pass responsibility to the decision-maker. In other words, according discretion to courts, administrative agencies, or regulatory authorities can be a form of deliberate legislative compromise. Less deliberately, legislative inaction may have the effect of tacitly giving courts authority to decide cases without legislative direction.

We have been surveying the reasons a rule-maker might adduce for according a decision-maker discretion. But discretionary authority may also be created indirectly and undeliberately. It often grows out of the institutional structure of decision. For example, where a decision-maker is not subject to review, the decision-maker has discretion in one of Professor Dworkin's 'weak senses' (1977*b*: 32). As Justice Jackson put it, 'We are not final because we are infallible, but we are infallible only because we are final' (*Brown* v. *Allen*, 1953: 540). In any kind of adjudication, of course, this kind of discretion will eventually be exercised: someone must make the final decision.

But it is not just the last decision-maker in the hierarchy who acquires considerable discretionary authority from 'structural' sources. Indeed, the first decision-maker often has very considerable discretion (not least because he is often effectively the last decision-maker). First, someone must find facts, and fact-finding is inevitably a partly discretionary process, since it requires making complicated judgments whose components cannot be foretold and resolved in advance. Deciding what actually happened always involves some discretionary judgments about what evidence to hear, what evidence to regard as relevant, and what evidence to regard as reliable, to say nothing about drawing final conclusions about what actually happened. In most hierarchical situations, it will be impractical to keep regathering evidence, so that many discretionary decisions about facts will be effectively unreviewable. In much litigation, this fact-finding authority is enhanced by the usual understanding that the trial court's opportunity to see and hear the parties and the witnesses gives its conclusions special reliability.

A second reason the first decision-maker often has great discretion (in many ways greater discretion than the last decision-maker) is that someone must decide what the relevant rules are, and in the first instance this must effectively be the fact-finder, since it is impossible to know what facts are relevant until the rules to which the facts are relevant have been identified. While a decision about the law can more easily be reviewed and reversed than a decision about the facts, the trial judge's conclusions about the law will often have large, practical effects. They can, for instance, influence the way the parties conceive of and litigate the issues in the case. They can affect what evidence is collected and what evidence is left unexplored. And, since the costs of an appeal and of a new trial can often be prohibitively great, the trial judge's rulings about the law often are effectively irreversible (as to the particular case).

A third source of the initial decision-makers's discretionary authority arises from his power to decide how to apply the rule to the facts.

As Professor Cooper writes, 'It is now common to recognize that there is a third category, law application, that has the characteristics of both law-making and fact-finding' (1988: 658). This process involves difficult and complicated decisions which inevitably involve the exercise of judgment and hence create scope for discretion. These decisions require the decision-maker to exercise the discretion of both an interpreter of law and a finder of facts. Further, because these decisions are complicated and because it can be hard to tell whether they are decisions about the law (and therefore reviewable by an appellate court) or about the facts (and therefore reviewable by an appellate court only if the trial court has seriously erred), they are not easily reversed on appeal. Finally, since, as regularly happens in litigation of any real complexity, multiplicitous and uncertain facts must be applied to broadly written rules, the scope for discretion is obviously substantial.

The argument that discretion is an inherent part of deciding cases may be stated in a still stronger way. The power to decide what the relevant rules are and then to apply the rule to the facts can be described as the power to interpret law. It is sometimes said that language is so imprecise and interpretation so uncertain that even rules cannot cabin discretion. This is not the place to enter into the vast jurisprudential debate that assertion raises.[8] However, in the last section of this chapter I will express some doubts about this strongest statement of the scope of judicial and administrative discretion by cataloguing the powerful forces that constrain discretion.

Let me now conclude this exploration of the advantages of discretion by briefly summarizing them. Discretion allows decisions to be tailored to the particular circumstances of each particular case. Discretion gives decision-makers flexibility to do justice. It does so partly by allowing them to consider all the individual circumstances that ought to affect a decision but that could not be anticipated by rules. It also does so by allowing decision-makers to watch how well their decisions work and to adjust future decisions to respond to the new information. Finally, discretion conduces to better decisions by discouraging overly bureaucratic ways of thinking and by making the decision-maker's job attractive to able people.

One study of the criminal-justice system summarizes the advantages of discretion with special passion:

---

[8] For an admirable treatment of these issues, see Schauer 1991.

The solace of standardized rules and procedures is largely illusory. Rigid rules tend to ossify individual responsibility and discourage individualistic thinking. Those who would shrink discretion obey the precept: 'Treat likes alike.' However, the overriding lesson of experience in our criminal justice operation is that every case is different. The major worry is that the people out there dealing with the problems will lose their appreciation of the differences between the cases and will begin reacting to them as repetitive. There is nothing quite like a good set of rules *cum* guidelines to bring common elements to the fore and obscure differences. If nothing else, our experience with mandatory minimums in drug sentencing should have taught the sterility of the reduced factor method of response. The learned fact should be that crimes and criminals emerge from a rich variety of circumstances. Separately and in combination, the variants can never be fully anticipated or assessed; yet they are often critical to forming the just response. (Uviller 1984: 32)

On the one hand, this brief summary of the advantages of discretion is curiously negative. It suggests that, were rules as capable of clear statement as the basic laws of mathematics and were people's minds as mechanical and predictable as calculators, legal decision-makers would not need and would not be given discretion. More positively, however, this summary is intended to make clear that we do not live in such a world. Rules cannot be written that will always work as their authors would have wanted them to, and decision-makers work in institutional settings which necessarily give them scope for judgment. In sum, however much we may acknowledge the primacy of rules in a system of law, we cannot deny the large and essential service discretion performs, even in a world of rules.

The Advantages of Rules

What, then, are the drawbacks of discretion? Why do we speak of the primacy of rules? The most prominent drawbacks of discretion hardly need elaboration. Discretion makes it easier than rules usually do for decision-makers to consult illegitimate considerations, and it does nothing to keep them from making 'mistakes'. Less prominently, discretion may have untoward psychological effects on decision-makers. Discretion is a kind of power, and power corrupts. Discretionary power seems conducive to an arrogance and carelessness in dealing with other people's lives that judges already have too many incentives to succumb to.

But the drawbacks of discretion can be more meaningfully phrased in terms of the advantages rules offer. I will consider a number of these advantages. The first is that rules can contribute to the legitimacy of a decision. To put the point almost schematically, in a democracy, power flows from the people. The closer a decision is to the people, the more secure its basis in a source of legitimacy. Several factors make it likely that legislative rules will be 'closer' than administrative or judicial decisions. All legislators (except those in the House of Lords) are elected; no judges in England are elected, and many in the United States are not. Legislators generally campaign on the basis of their views about issues; judges (when they run for election) generally do not. It is thought legitimate to vote against a legislator because you dislike his decisions; it is often thought improper even to ask a judge how he would vote on a kind of case his court seemed likely to confront.

The most commonly feared drawback of discretion is closely related to this function of rules. That drawback is the risk that a judge will so far depart from the sources of his authority as to substitute his own standards for public ones. There is no doubt that this happens. But, if we are trying to decide what mix of discretion and rules should govern an area of law, what we need to know is how often it happens. Unfortunately, critics of discretion often provide little evidence with which to answer that question, and what they do present is often anecdotal and outdated. Their listeners are thus left to their own dark imaginings. These critics deserve our sympathy, since systematic evidence about how often judges abuse their discretion in this way is hard to collect and analyse. On the other hand, there is some evidence that judges try to do what is expected of them. Writing generally about legal decision-making, Professor Lempert and Professor Sanders conclude that

rules of decision as well as methods of presentation apparently make a difference in the way evidence is used. . . . At times such ideas are debunked by lawyers and nonlawyers alike on the theory that lay people will decide cases as they see fit and that nothing will alter this. This 'perfidy' theory of human behavior finds little support in the previous data. Decision rules structure the problem the fact finder must resolve, and so alter the ways in which cases are decided. (1986: 75)

There is some more specific evidence for this position in my own field of family law. One of the most startling examples comes from Professor Mnookin's fascinating study of the judicial reaction to *Bellotti* v. *Baird*.[9] In that case, the Supreme Court held that a minor

[9] 443 US 622 (1979).

who wished to have an abortion without parental consent had to be allowed to show a judge either that she was capable of making the decision on her own or that an abortion would be in her best interest. Professor Mnookin investigated what happened when such rules were instituted in Massachusetts, a state many of whose judges are Catholic males, many of whom presumably oppose abortion. He found that judges virtually never denied minors an abortion (1985: 149–264). Similarly, Professor Weitzman, who is not notably sympathetic to the work of courts handling divorces, writes that courts (which had long followed older principles) have adapted to new views about women by not disadvantaging working mothers in custody disputes (1985: 239).

There is also some evidence about the judicial and administrative use of 'improper' standards in the law of child abuse and neglect. Professor Garrison writes, 'The laxity of traditional standards has undeniably permitted intervention in some cases in which there were no discernible problems in family function, but these egregious abuses of discretion appear to be the exception rather than the rule' (1987: 1791). And Professor Wald finds 'little reason to believe that such cases constitute even a significant proportion of interventions in most states' (1980: 676).

In some of the circumstances in which judges are conventionally taken to be substituting private standards for public ones, they may in fact simply be reflecting widely held social views. As has been acutely observed,

> There is substantial evidence that courts applying the best interest standard [in child-custody disputes] do so in a way that is favorable to mothers, and fathers typically do not prevail in custody disputes unless they are able to demonstrate that the mother has some serious disability. These results are often attributed to the insidious biases of judges. Another explanation is that judges in awarding custody to mothers are continuing to track a powerful social norm which, in fact, has not suffered significant erosion. There is ample evidence today that mothers continue to assume the major responsibilities of caring for children. (Scott, Reppucci, and Aber 1988: 1076–7)

Of course, the legislature might wish to change the law so that judges no longer draw on this 'powerful social norm'. But for us the point is that the judges who are drawing on it may not be substituting their private standards for public ones. Rather, they may be giving meaning to a broad legal standard (that custody disputes should be decided in whatever way serves the child's best interests) by consulting a deeply held social consensus.

In any event, our concerns about substituting private for public standards should probably be more acute in some situations than in others. The more the question presented may speak to the irrational sides of human nature, the greater the risks of discretionary error presumably are. As Professor Schauer writes,

The Supreme Court's decision [in *Palmore* v. *Sidoti*[10]] that the fact of an interracial marriage could *not* be taken into account is a typical example of the fear of error through bias. Although there may be cases, perhaps including this one, in which a conscientious and sensitive decisionmaker would make the optimal decision by taking this factor into account there are likely even more cases in which a decisionmaker, empowered to consider the racial identity of any of the participants, will because of racial hostility make a significantly suboptimal decision. (1991: 259)

On the other hand, there will often be no special risks of bias. Where those risks are not present, the likelihood of discretionary error will be diminished, as will the incentive for avoiding discretionary decisions. The less the risk of bias, the greater the need to ask whether substituting rules for discretion would be more costly than running the risk of bias. In other words, the knowledge that bias and 'private' standards can sometimes distort decisions ought to lead us to assess the likelihood and severity of that risk in the particular circumstances of each kind of decision. But that knowledge should not drive us toward an automatic preference for rules, however slight their advantage and however great their cost, and away from discretionary decisions, where their costs are slight and their advantage great.

In short, in deciding what mix of discretion and rules to prefer, we ought not to ask whether private standards will *ever* be substituted for public ones. Only the most draconian rule could entirely prevent judges from manipulating the many kinds of discretion they exercise so as to smuggle in their private standards. Rather, we should ask how great is the risk that judges will abuse their discretion, what are the best means of diminishing that risk, and what are the costs of those means. These are all questions which cannot be answered a priori, since the answers will depend on a range of highly various circumstances. And these are questions which will be difficult to answer even in a specific context. But they are the right questions to ask.

[10] 466 US 429 (1984).

The best means of diminishing the risk that discretion will be abused will often be the most direct means. Often, the 'private' standards we may most want to avoid will be easily identified. In those cases, the best course may be the simplest—expressly to prohibit judges from using the improper standards. While this technique cannot wholly prevent judges from using improper standards, used with sufficient precision and clarity it can probably markedly reduce the incidence of impropriety. This means of reducing the risk that judges will substitute private for public standards has the advantage of imposing relatively low costs. The standards to be prohibited can often be readily articulated. Any other standards already in place need not be tampered with. And the many costs of trying to deprive judges of discretion completely need not be endured. Only the standards to be avoided are prohibited; judges need not be deprived of otherwise desirable discretion in order to deter them from consulting improper standards.

The second advantage of rules is that (despite what we have said about the advantages of allowing decision-makers discretion to do justice in individual cases) rule-makers may often be better situated than decision-makers to decide what justice is and how to achieve it both in an individual case and in general. Rule-makers typically have more time than decision-makers to study a problem, which can allow them to take more of the elements of the problem into account and to think about them more reflectively. Rule-makers may have more resources for gathering information, and legislative rule-makers need not be inhibited by the rules of evidence and procedure which limit courts. Legislative rule-makers may also be better able to bring together the whole range of social groups interested in the resolution of a problem and thus to acquire a fuller range of information about the problem and to secure a better degree of acquiescence in the solution.

Nor does one always get the best view of a problem by looking at a particular controversy in which it presents itself. This is the point of many criticisms of the common-law method of developing rules. For instance, a judge viewing a particular case may be distracted from a just decision by the special but irrelevant circumstances of the particular litigants. Sometimes these may be plainly irrelevant factors, like racial prejudice. But many chance characteristics of the litigants or their circumstances may influence a decision in a way that, on a longer view, we would think wrong. For example, many people would argue that the marital misbehavior of a spouse which does not directly and evidently affect a child has too often diverted courts from consulting only the child's best interest when they decide which parent should have custody of that child.

In thinking about which institution will make the better decisions and thus about how discretion should be allotted among institutions, one crucial but often overlooked factor should be kept in mind—the quality of the decision-maker. As Professor Cooper wrote with shocking frankness in discussing discretion and interlocutory appeals:[11]

> The nature and quality of the federal district judges is the single most important factor to be counted. The better the judges are, the less need there is for frequent interlocutory appeal—they will make fewer mistakes, and more often correct their own mistakes before serious harm is done. . . . Should trial judges prove to be much like appellate judges in ability and temperament, it is possible to rely on them to play a significant role in determining the need for interlocutory appeals. . . . To the extent that we do not trust trial judges, on the other hand, we will be driven to rely more on clear rules or on discretionary devices that are controlled by the courts of appeals. (1984: 158–9)[11]

Nor can we stop with evaluating the quality of trial judges. We must also worry about the quality of the higher courts that review their decisions and of the bar which argues before both benches. Professor Cooper's comments are again relevant and wise:

> The timing of appeals may have to depend on rules that are clear, simple, and rigid if it is not possible to rely on the learning, wisdom, and character of the lawyers who take appeals. Complex or discretionary rules carry high costs at the hands of an ignorant or supine bar. . . . Complex rules can be tailored to special needs, however, if lawyers can be trained to understand them. (ibid.: 161)

We may summarize this advantage of rules by saying that rule-makers will sometimes, perhaps often, be better situated than decision-makers to establish the principles by which a dispute should be resolved. But this will not always be the case. Once again, then, we see that the proper mix of rules and discretion can be found only by looking at the full facts of the particular context in which the rule-makers and decision-makers will be acting.

---

[11] Professor Cooper notes a further problem with thinking about the relationship between discretion and judicial quality: the quality of the decision-maker may depend in part on the extent of the discretion. People of ability are unlikely to take jobs which allow them little scope for discretion; people of less ability may prefer jobs which do not tax their ability to exercise discretion. Yet it is not clear that according judges discretion will be enough to attract able people to the bench.

The third advantage of rules relates to our basic assumption that like cases should be treated alike. As Professor Mnookin writes, 'Indeterminate standards . . . pose an obviously greater risk of violating the fundamental precept that like cases should be treated alike' (1975: 263). One way to try to ensure that they are is by employing rules instead of allowing each decision-maker to decide case by case what principles to apply to what fact situations and how to apply them. Rules suppress differences of opinion about what works to serve what purpose, about how to balance factors, and about what justice requires; such differences of opinion could otherwise lead to different results in similar cases. Rules also serve as record-keeping devices, devices that are more efficient and therefore more likely to be used effectively than an elaborate system of precedent. Finally, rules provide an often superior way of co-ordinating the decisions of multiple decision-makers and one decision-maker over time. But will it always be true that a rule will be more conducive than discretion to treating like cases similarly? The answer to this question depends in part on the complexity of the rule. The simpler the rule and the more capacious its categories, the greater the extent to which different cases will be decided under a single principle. Yet the more complex the rule and the more differentiated its categories, the greater the discretion judges are likely to have in applying it.

One important function of the treat-like-cases-alike principle is giving litigants the sense that they have been treated fairly. But will rules or discretion better give litigants that sense? Rules have the advantage of telling litigants clearly that the standard under which their case is to be decided has the authority of legitimacy. Discretionary decisions, in contrast, are more readily open to the objection that they merely reflect the judge's personal and arbitrary preferences, that they arise out of some untoward favoritism for the winner or some prejudice against the loser. But, even if litigants accept the legitimacy of the source of the standard applied, they may still believe the standard to be unjust. And, even if litigants accept the standard's desirability, they may reject the way it is applied. Losers are likely to see differences between cases that look significant to them but that look trivial to others. Because litigants are usually able to see only the strengths of their own case, it is unlikely that any plausible set of rules can prevent this from happening. It is likely, though, that mechanical rules of the kind that prevent the court from looking at the particular facts of a case would produce an acute sense of injustice, often on the theory that different cases were being treated alike. Litigants seem likely to feel that cases involving important consequences ought to be decided with the fullest possible attention to all the facts and all the equities. Attempts to substitute flat rules for such enquiries seem most unlikely to satisfy the litigants' sense of justice (Schneider 1991).

The fourth and fifth advantages of rules arise out of the relatively 'public' nature of rules and the relatively 'private' nature of discretion. Generally speaking, rules will in some useful sense be public in both formulation and dissemination. Where rules are formulated by a legislature, hearings are held, committee reports are issued, and bills are debated. Where rules are formulated by an administrative agency, drafts are issued, public comments are invited, and the rules are promulgated in some public way. Even where rules are formulated by a court in the process of adjudication, the court hears a public argument and issues a public explanation of the rule and the reasons for adopting it. In all three of these cases the proceedings may have been reported in the press and followed and debated by interested publics.

In addition, rules must usually be disseminated in some importantly public way. First, many rules are intended to instruct people how to act. Such rules cannot have their intended effect unless people know before they act what the rule is. Secondly, many rules are intended to instruct legal actors how to make particular kinds of decisions. Such rules cannot have their intended effect unless the actors know before their decision what the rule is. (Of course, many rules are intended to have both effects, and thus are 'publicized' for both reasons.) At the least, then, even where a rule does not receive genuinely public attention, it will have been formulated in advance of a decision and will generally be accessible to anyone who knows and cares to look.

By contrast, discretion looks private. Most discretionary decisions are not formulated publicly because they are usually made by the legal institutions whose deliberations are least public—courts and administrative agencies. While discretionary decisions are often publicly announced and explained, they are generally less widely and intensively disseminated, in part because they give less guidance than rules both to interested publics and to legal actors. More basically, while standards for the exercise of discretion may be written and circulated before a decision is made, a discretionary decision is precisely one whose outcome cannot be described in advance. It is precisely one that is confided to a decision-maker, and thus no exact prior instructions need be given. In sum, while most rules are publicly formulated and disseminated, discretionary decisions cannot readily be.

This contrast between the public nature of rules and the private nature of discretion helps us see that the fourth advantage of rules is that they can serve the 'planning function' better than discretionary decisions. The people and institutions affected by a decision need to know in advance how a case will be decided so that they may plan their lives and work in accordance with the law. But, as Professor Mnookin writes, 'Inherent in the application of a broad . . . principle is the risk of retroactive application of a norm of which the parties affected will have had no advance notice' (1975: 262–3). On the whole, rules give better warning than discretionary decisions because they are likelier to provide clear and complete information about what a court or agency will do. (One important reason common-law adjudication is not an intolerable affront to the planning function is that rules are eventually adduced and articulated.)

Yet even this apparently clear advantage of rules cannot be stated without enquiring into the particular decisions which the choice between discretion and rules may affect. People will not always need to know what the law is before they act. For example, most husbands and wives are probably not interested in the law governing child-custody disputes on divorce. Most couples do not expect to be divorced, and many of them would find it impractical and perhaps even wrong to shape their marital behavior and their care for their children with an eye to gaining an advantage in divorce litigation. There are, however, undoubtedly some exceptions. Anna Karenina, for instance, thought during her marriage about the chances of losing custody of her son because of her adultery. And, even if parties do not need to know custody law in order to plan, that knowledge may still offer them psychological repose. A mother might feel better during her marriage if she knew that the law would ensure her custody of her child even after a divorce. (And, on divorce, her husband might accommodate himself to the disappointment more easily if he had known all along that he had little chance of gaining custody.)

But even if people sometimes do not need to know the law in order to plan their behavior before they become involved in a legal dispute, they will surely want to know it after they become involved. Yet even this undoubtedly legitimate interest will not always dictate an answer to the choice between discretion and rules. For example, it is often said that litigants ought to be told as clearly as possible how a court will decide a case so that they can be guided in their settlement negotiations. On the other hand, the less certain the result a court would reach, the greater the practical scope for bargaining. Discretion, in other words, tends to give the parties greater freedom in negotiation. We might, for all the usual reasons given for freedom of contract (yet keeping in mind the usual reasons for being cautious about the consequences of that kind of freedom), prefer a discretionary standard which accorded parties that greater freedom while still giving a court the authority to resolve their dispute if they could not do so themselves.

The fifth attraction of rules also grows out of the contrast between the public quality of rules and the private quality of discretion. This attraction is that rules can serve social purposes that discretionary decisions generally serve less well. Rules are often an announcement about how people should behave, an announcement that attempts to affect behavior. Rules frequently (although not inevitably) communicate this information more clearly and emphatically and are more easily recognized as commands than a series of individual decisions from which general principles have to be drawn. On the other hand, this attraction of rules will present itself less forcefully where the law's primary purpose is not to influence behavior. The largest category of such situations is probably where that purpose is to settle disputes, rather than to guide social behavior.

The sixth and final attraction of rules is that they are, on average, more efficient than discretion, for rules are a way of institutionalizing experience. A rule is ordinarily a distillation of a long process of thinking about how a particular kind of case should be handled. Decision-makers exercising discretion, unless they consult some rules or guidelines, risk having to go through the entire process for each decision. Rules can relieve decision-makers of that burdensome and repetitive enquiry (and can reduce the risk that the decision-maker will make a mis-step in retracing the process).

Rules also promote efficiency by telling decision-makers which facts and arguments will be relevant, thus allowing them to exclude from their consideration the many arguments and facts that will be irrelevant. And rules not only make the work of decision-makers easier; they also help litigants and their attorneys by alerting them to the facts and arguments the decision-maker will want to hear and by warning them not to expend their efforts on irrelevant arguments. In short, as Whitehead said,

It is a profoundly erroneous truism, repeated by all copy-books and by eminent people when they are making speeches, that we should cultivate the habit of thinking of what we are doing. The precise opposite is the case. Civilization advances by extending the number of important operations which we can perform without thinking about them. Operations of thought are like cavalry charges in a battle—they are strictly limited in number, they require fresh horses, and must only be made at decisive moments. (Whitehead 1948: 41–2)

On the other hand, rules are not invariably more efficient than discretion. Writing rules can itself cost time and effort. Elaborate and cumbersome rules can impose onerous costs on decision-makers and on litigants. When people complain about bureaucracy, it is often such costs which provoke their displeasure. Not only can rules thus be inefficient; discretion can be efficient. Discretion can be inexpensive where the decision-maker's choices are not momentous—where, that is, the decision-maker has relatively few alternatives and cannot easily make a seriously wrong choice. Thus it may be efficient to accord discretion to the decision-maker who is a 'repeat player' who regularly applies a narrow set of policies to standard fact patterns. On the other hand, circumstances of this last kind are likely to be circumstances in which rules (or strong guidelines) can be developed which are more efficient than discretion. (Indeed, such a decision-maker is likely to develop such rules informally even if they are not imposed formally (see Lempert, Chapter 6)). Where, in contrast, the decision-maker regularly applies diverse and conflicting policies to widely differing situations, the efficiency advantage of rules may be relatively slight. First, in that circumstance, the decision-maker will not often have to retrace steps, since a different path will be followed for almost every decision. Secondly, in that circumstance, the rule-maker will be hard put to identify all the possible situations in advance and to write rules for them (and only for them).

Essentially, these observations take us back to the sources of discretion which I enumerated earlier. Each of those sources (khadi-, rule-failure, rule-building, rule-compromise, and structural discretion) can be said to describe a respect in which there is no way to write a rule that efficiently accomplishes what the rule-maker would like to accomplish. The more severe that problem, the greater the comparative efficiency of discretion.

In this section, I have been at pains to show that it cannot safely be assumed that rules will be superior to discretion, or even that all the advantages of rules will prevail in a given situation. I have emphasized that the correct mix of discretion and rules must be determined situation by situation. But I hope that this emphasis has not obscured the fundamental point of the section—that there are powerful, often overwhelming, arguments for rules.

This survey of the virtues of rules suggests that, when a good rule can be written, it is much to be preferred to a grant of discretion. Compared to discretion, rules offer advantages in terms of legitimacy, wisdom, fairness, and efficiency. But, as this survey has also sought to show at each step of its way, we can never safely assume that each advantage fully presents itself in any particular situation. All the defects to which rules are heir work to dilute those advantages and to drive us toward some mix of rules and discretion.

A Thousand Limitations: The Constraints on Discretion

I have just recited the arguments in favor of rules. So central are rules to our idea of what law is, and so basic are the advantages of rules, that I need not dwell further on their legitimacy and importance.[12] However, the legitimacy and importance of discretion are less widely accepted. I have argued that discretion is much more deeply and widely embedded in law than the casual observer might suppose. But something more needs to be said in defense of discretion. In this section I will argue that our legal system can tolerate so much discretion in part because limitations on discretion are as inevitable and abundant as the sources of discretion, and because discretionary decisions are rarely as unfettered as they look.

Discretion can be and regularly is constrained in multitudinous ways. 'Complete freedom—unfettered and undirected—there never is. A thousand limitations—the product some of statute, some of precedent, some of vague tradition or of an immemorial technique—encompass and hedge us even when we think of ourselves as ranging freely and at large. . . . Narrow at best is any freedom that is allotted to us' (Cardozo 1924: 61). Let us briefly survey some of those thousand limitations on discretion.

Discretion is limited in the first instance because someone must choose the people who will exercise discretion. That power is commonly used to select people who may be expected to exercise discretion with

---

[12] The reader who wishes to pursue the subject further would do well to consult Schauer 1991.

restraint or to exercise it in ways the appointer prefers. Americans are most accustomed to this limitation in the Presidential appointment of Supreme Court justices. Though Presidents have occasionally been unpleasantly surprised, they have gotten what they wanted more often than is conventionally supposed. Of the present members of the Court, only Justice Brennan and, in some but not all areas, Justice Blackmun have voted in ways that would have astonished the Presidents who appointed them.

Lifelong tenure of course reduces the usefulness of the selection power in reducing discretion, but most state-court judges do not have lifelong tenure. On the contrary, many of them must be regularly reselected. Of course, the effectiveness of this technique is greatest where one is selecting a decision-maker who will be making only one kind of decision. Where the decision-maker has to make many kinds of decisions, it will often be difficult to know all his views in advance and to find someone who has *all* the right views. Still, the task of making such choices is made easier by the human tendency to think about sets of problems in systematic ways. Thus someone who thinks 'correctly' about one problem is likely (although not certain) to think 'correctly' about related problems.

Decision-makers' exercise of discretion is further inhibited by their socialization and training. Decision-makers, after all, do not live or work in a vacuum; they are inevitably products of their environment, and their environment is, to some extent, an environment of shared social norms. Some of these social norms will speak directly to the substantive issues to be decided. Some others of these social norms will speak to the way any issue may be decided. As Professor Dworkin writes, 'Almost any situation in which a person acts . . . makes relevant certain standards of rationality, fairness, and effectiveness' (1977*b*: 33). Most decision-makers in an industrialized Western democracy, and certainly governmental decision-makers, are widely felt to be obliged to make decisions that are rational within the standards of their society and that accord with its basic institutions. Among the social norms which will inhibit decision-makers' exercise of discretion are all the reasons for being skeptical of discretion which we are exploring in this chapter. That some uses of discretion may not be strongly inhibited by social norms and that decision-makers will sometimes resist inhibitory norms do not mean that those norms are generally ineffective brakes on discretion.

Judges will be affected not only by their socialization as twentieth-century Westerners, but also by their specifically legal training and the norms that training inculcates. In the United States, a system of national law schools offering intensive training (particularly in the first year) helps give those norms a measure of universality and stability. These law schools explicitly try to train a student to 'think like a lawyer'. Law classes are essentially sessions in which students are repeatedly made to practise legal analysis. The professor asks the students question after question. Each one is designed to show the students what kinds of questions to ask about a text and what kinds of answers are appropriate and inappropriate. After a year of this routine, students have begun to internalize many of the legal system's assumptions and to speak its language.

When students graduate, their training becomes less formal, but it hardly ends. Recent graduates will often begin what is effectively an apprenticeship with the law firm which first hires them. And the recent graduate's day-to-day work of dealing with judges and with lawyers from other firms offers another kind of practical education in the mores of the law.

Judges are usually given relatively little formal training. But the lawyers who become judges will usually have had abundant opportunities to watch judges work. From that experience, from talking and working with veteran judges, and from dealing with the lawyers who practise before them, new judges learn a set of professional norms, some formally articulated, some simply assumed.

Through their training, then, lawyers and judges acquire habits of thought that limit the range of arguments that they will find acceptable and the kinds of decisions that they will be willing to advocate and reach. They learn substantive norms that tell them what kinds of principles are legitimate and illegitimate. They learn 'procedural' norms that tell them what kinds of evidence and procedures are permissible. They learn ethical norms that help deter them from exercising their discretion in self-serving ways.

I have been arguing that decision-makers' discretion is constrained by their socialization and training. Generally speaking, that socialization and training will reduce the extent to which decision-makers apply 'private' standards instead of 'public' ones. And that socialization and training will generally equip decision-makers with a common language, with shared assumptions, and with standard ways of reasoning, all of which make it easier to predict how they will act and what kinds of instructions will produce what kinds of responses.

However, socialization and training can have the defects of their virtues. They can themselves create 'private' standards which unduly reflect the interest of the decision-maker's own profession and institution. Thus some critics of judicial discretion fear that judges will serve the guild interests of lawyers and will promote the political power of the judiciary. Similarly, some critics of police discretion note that the police have strong institutional interests and strong cultural values of their own that may conflict with broader 'public' interests and values. More generally, students of bureaucracy commonly observe that large organizations can resist outside or even hierarchical control exactly because the organization's employees have internalized institutional norms, attitudes, and practices which they will not gladly abandon.

Next, the lessons of a judge's socialization and training are often reaffirmed, and the judge's exercise of discretion is further inhibited, by the criticism which judges (and other decision-makers) receive. Some of this criticism is scholarly. But judges are much more likely to hear and to feel the strictures of the local bar and of their colleagues on the bench. 'The inscrutable force of professional opinion', Justice Cardozo wrote, 'presses upon us like the atmosphere, though we are heedless of its weight' (1924: 61). Nor is criticism of judges confined to the legal profession: sufficiently prominent and consequential decisions may be attacked by politicians, journalists, and members of other interested publics, including the public at large. Judges even hear from their friends and family.

Another kind of limitation on discretion grows out of the decision-maker's internal dynamics. That is, courts and agencies will often be constrained by their institutional structure and imperatives and by the psychology of those who staff them. Efficiency concerns, simple laziness, a wish to avoid responsibility, and even a desire to escape the boredom of constantly repeating the reasoning necessary to decide a case can drive decision-makers toward relying on their own earlier decisions in factually similar cases rather than embarking on fresh discretionary frolics. In other words, decision-makers usually have strong incentives to develop their own rules, their own common law, their own constraints on discretion, even if such restrictions are not forced on them from the outside. The more work a court must do, the less time it will have for the work of exercising unfettered discretion. Such a court may then exercise discretion in deciding how to decide cases, but it will have an incentive to construct principles of decision that are easily applied and to follow those principles as routinely as possible. Such a court will thereby have constrained (although not entirely prevented) its own exercise of discretion in the future.[13]

These same kinds of pressures can limit discretion in another important way, for they can lead one decision-maker to defer to some other decision-maker, often another officially constituted decision-maker. For instance, we have already seen how American appellate courts have adopted a series of rules and practices (of which Rule 52a is a particularly prominent example) designed to limit the range of questions which appellate courts have to address by confiding discretion to decide those questions largely to trial courts. But legal agents may also limit their own discretion by deferring to less official institutions. In the United States it has become an increasingly official practice for courts to allow criminal defendants to negotiate a guilty plea and a sentence with the prosecutor's office. Less officially still, courts regularly approve without real scrutiny all kinds of settlements between divorcing spouses, even though the doctrine of the law is that courts must examine and approve such settlements to ensure that vulnerable spouses and helpless children are not injured.

A related constraint on discretion is the institution's need to co-ordinate the activities of several decision-makers or to co-ordinate the same decision-maker's decisions over time. Because of the strength in American law of the principle that like cases should be treated alike, this pressure to co-ordinate is widely felt. Administrative agencies face the problem of co-ordination in a particularly acute form, since they will often need to co-ordinate the decisions of numerous employees, many of whom may be making decisions of considerable importance. But even courts need to co-ordinate their decisions. To some degree this is done hierarchically: it is a primary function of appellate courts to resolve differences in legal interpretation among the lower courts within their jurisdiction. To some degree, though, the lower courts are expected to co-ordinate their decisions among themselves. Thus the ruling of one trial court has precedential value for (although it does not bind) another trial court in the same jurisdiction.

Furthermore, all people try to make sense of the world by categorizing the events and problems they encounter. Judges and agency officials are no different. Such categories can in effect become rules of decision which govern, or at least influence, how issues are resolved. These

---

[13] For a particularly illuminating description of this and other institutional and psychological constraints on discretion, see Lempert, Chapter 6.

categories work to constrain discretion because they limit the range of ways in which judges think about cases. These categories are themselves limited. Although they can arise out of a judge's general experience with the world, that experience is constrained by the fact that judges are generally drawn from a fairly narrow social spectrum. In addition, these categories will be influenced by a judge's experience of deciding cases. To some degree, judges will find that experience limiting. To take a simple example, a judge who regularly awarded custody to alcoholics and as regularly found the parties returning to court with more problems might be discouraged from awarding custody to alcoholics in the future.

Discretion is constrained not only by the internal dynamics of the decision-making entity, but also by the larger institutional context in which the entity acts. No governmental agency acts entirely alone and, in so far as power is shared, each agency's scope of discretion is limited. An obvious and generally important example of this constraint is the legislature's authority to enact statutes which courts must follow. But this constraint appears in other forms.

Sometimes, for instance, this constraint works 'jurisdictionally'. For example, courts conventionally lack authority to decide many kinds of family disputes, even if those disputes nominally involve the common-place judicial task of enforcing a contract.[14] These cases are implicitly, and sometimes explicitly, rationalized on the theory that 'family government is recognized by law as being as complete in itself as the State government is in itself. . .' (*North Carolina* v. *Rhodes* 1868: 458).[15] Thus, the extent to which a court may exercise its discretion to order a family's life is limited by this 'jurisdictional' principle.

This kind of restraint on discretion also operates where a decision-maker has 'jurisdiction' to regulate an area of life but shares that responsibility with another governmental actor. For instance, a department of social services can alter a child-custody battle by initiating proceedings to terminate one candidate's parental rights, and its failure to do so will limit (although not eliminate) a court's authority to deny a non-custodial parent visiting rights. That department of

---

[14] e.g., *Kilgrow* v. *Kilgrow*, 107 So.2d 885 (1958). There the court found that it lacked the authority to resolve a parental dispute over whether a child should attend a public or a parochial school, even though the parents had entered into a pre-nuptial agreement settling the question.

[15] 61 NC 445 (1868).

social services can also limit judicial discretion by issuing a strongly negative or positive report on a potential custodian.

Sometimes this kind of constraint works by giving other branches power to retaliate against the judiciary. At its most extreme, this power involves impeaching judges or depriving courts of jurisdiction. But it can also operate at a less dramatic level. For instance, legislatures can sometimes attempt to put pressure on courts by lowering judicial appropriations or refusing to approve the appointment of new judges.

Courts share authority not just with other governmental agencies, but even with the litigants themselves. At the most basic level, litigants' decisions determine what disputes will be brought to a court. This sounds obvious and trivial, but the importance of the litigants' decisions is suggested by the fact that, even in an area as intensively legalized as disputes over child custody on divorce, only about 10 per cent of the cases are actually litigated (Melli, Erlangen, and Chambliss 1988: 1142). Once cases have been initiated, the parties will have considerable control over what kinds of legal arguments a court is asked to resolve and what kind of evidence it hears. Both the introduction and the omission of important facts cabin a court's decisions.

Litigants place other limits on judicial discretion. Sometimes litigants will have something the court wants, like the ability to settle a case. Sometimes litigants will be able to resist a judicial order. This problem is particularly acute in areas like family law or much 'public-law' litigation, where the court seeks to affect the future behavior of the parties and where it must thus often depend on co-operation from the litigants. The unfortunate Morgan–Foretich case is only a lurid example of a much larger problem.[16]

The constraints on discretion which we have canvassed thus far can have powerful effects, but they generally are not directly designed as constraints on discretion. A more deliberate attempt to restrain discretion is to be found in the hierarchical organization of most decision-makers, notably including the judiciary. Because this is also

---

[16] In that case, the mother was ordered to allow the father to visit the child. The mother claimed that the father had sexually abused the child. She sent the child into hiding and refused to reveal its whereabouts. She was imprisoned for contempt of court and was released only after Congress passed a law limiting the length of time a person could be imprisoned on such grounds. Glimpses of that unhappy litigation may be had in *Morgan* v. *Foretich*, 846 F.2d 941 (1988); *Morgan* v. *Foretich*, 564 A.2d 407 (DC App.) (1988); *Morgan* v. *Foretich*, 564 A.2nd 1 (DC App.) (1989). On the enforcement problem, see Schneider 1985: 1056.

one of the most familiar limits on discretion,[17] we need say little about it. Intermediate appellate courts review trial-court procedures, opinions, and holdings; supreme courts review intermediate courts. This power of course allows appellate courts to correct what they take to be errors. More significantly, the aversion to being reversed often deters lower courts from erring in the first place. In extreme cases of judicial misbehavior, disciplinary proceedings may be brought or judges may be impeached. And judges who wish to be elevated to a higher court will often feel constrained to please whoever has the power to make promotions. Of course, because of their more bureaucratic structure, administrative agencies constrain discretion through the tools of hierarchy even more vigorously and thoroughly than courts.

Another way of restraining the exercise of discretion common to both courts and bureaucracies is to require that decision-makers follow a set of procedures. Some procedures limit discretion by telling a court or agency how to conduct its proceedings. These procedures may limit the evidence that may be received, specify who may make arguments, state who must receive notice of the proceedings, identify the litigant who speaks first, and so on. The underlying idea is that, if a decision-maker has followed the right procedure, the right decision is likelier to follow. In other words, procedural rules limit substantive discretion.

Other procedures limit discretion by telling the decision-maker what procedures to follow in deciding a case. One such procedural requirement is the obligation to justify decisions, particularly to justify them in writing. The process of explaining affects the decision-maker, if only because writing clarifies thought and makes it harder for the writer to avoid noticing abuses of discretion. It also opens the decision-maker to criticism from the parties and the public and to review from hierarchical superiors.

A yet more direct way of limiting discretion is to provide the decision-maker with policies and principles to guide him in making his decision. Decision-makers are commonly furnished with a statement at least of the purposes and goals the decision is ultimately intended to serve. A classic example is the rule that, in a dispute over which parent should have custody of a child after a divorce, the court should use the child's best interest as its only criterion. It has often been noted that this standard by itself does not decide cases. But, while this

---

[17] 'Hierarchy is probably the oldest axiom of organization: see Exodus 19: 25.' Kaufman 1977: 50 n. 61.

standard does vest a judge with discretion, it also constrains that discretion. For example, even if the guideline does not tell us exactly what is in the best interests of children, there will be many results virtually everyone would agree are *not* in those best interests, as where a court choosing between two otherwise equally qualified parents awarded custody to the parent who habitually beat the child. And, for example, the best-interest guideline eliminates some plausible altern- ative bases for making custody decisions. Thus a judge is directed not to consult the interests of the would-be custodians in making a decision. In any event, decision-makers are also often given (or will construct) a statement of second-level considerations which are intended to promote those purposes and goals.

Perhaps the most obvious way of limiting a decision-maker's discretion is to provide him with rules written at some level of detail that attempt to tell him what decision to reach where a particular set of facts exists. This limitation is in some senses the polar opposite of discretion, since we often say that, where a decision-maker applies a rule, he has no discretion. But, as I have been arguing, even a rule will often not deprive the decision-maker of all his discretion, since applying and interpreting the rule will regularly involve judgments of several kinds. In this section, we have been concerned with how far the whole range of powers of decision-makers can be constrained. In that context, then, rules can be seen as a limit on discretion, and not simply as an alternative to it.

Finally, a decision-maker's discretion is limited where one or more of the parties before him is endowed with rights. Rights transfer partial and sometimes complete responsibility for a decision from a governmental body to an individual. If there is a constitutional right to enter into binding surrogate-mother contracts, for example, the power to exercise discretion in custody disputes between a natural father and a surrogate mother is limited.

In this section, then, I have tried to counter the conventional distrust of discretion by showing that discretion is subject to more numerous and severe constraints than is commonly supposed. I am not saying, of course, that these constraints necessarily free discretion of danger. But I am saying that, in deciding what mix of discretion and rules to prefer, one cannot stop one's investigation with the discovery that an actor has discretion. Rather, one must ask what kinds of cultural, social, political, psychological, institutional, and doctrinal forces may moderate that discretion.

Conclusion

It has been wisely said that when we walk toward one blessing, we walk away from another. In this chapter I have tried to show that this is true of the choices we face in deciding what mix of discretion and rules should govern the making of legal decisions. I have argued that rules have a primacy in law because of their capacity to provide superior legitimacy, wisdom, fairness, and efficiency. But I have also tried to demonstrate that rules regularly fail to deliver on those promises and that the imperatives of institutional decision-making bar us from eliminating discretion from law.

I have also sought to argue that the necessity of discretion is not as grim as it is often thought to be. As we have seen, discretion is so much a part of Western law that its extent often goes quite unnoticed. And, as we have seen, discretion offers advantages that are otherwise unobtainable.

All this leaves us in an irreducibly equivocal position, for it is not possible to say a priori what mixture of rules and discretion will best serve in any particular situation. Rather, that choice must be made case by case, with an eye to all the social, psychological, institutional, and political forces that will shape the way a legal decision is made. In fine, the only rule governing the choice is the rule of discretion.

3. Discretionary Decision-Making: A Jurisprudential View

JOHN BELL

As Denis Galligan (1986*a*:1) has noted, discretion has not been a central topic of jurisprudential writing, though it has been a major focus of interest for legal sociology. While legal theory in the area of administrative law has paid significant attention to the issue of analysing discretion, it has tended to be with heavy emphasis on the judicial control of administrative action (see, especially, Venezia 1959). There has been only a limited effort to integrate the findings of sociological studies of discretionary decision-making into legal theoretical writing about the nature of law. This article offers merely a few pointers to the kind of theory of law which could emerge from such an integration.

Within Anglo-American legal theory, in particular, two lines of thought have dominated writing about the nature of law: the view I shall call 'ruled justice' and the view which takes adjudication as its centrepiece. 'Ruled justice' views law as a set of social norms of greater or lesser specificity designed to guide and control the behaviour of citizens. Law is a self-contained, comprehensive, and autonomous order of a distinct kind within society (Galanter 1980:11). On the adjudication view, law and legal discourse come into their own in the resolution of disputes, so that the institutions and reasons for court decisions form the 'core' of a concept of law. By contrast the paradigm of law in works of legal sociology seems to revolve around the idea of law as a 'resource' for legal actors, against the background of which they react and negotiate to create a world to their liking (Comaroff and Roberts 1981: 11–17, 244–6). This paradigm is most apt in situations of discretion where the discretion-holder exercises significant choice in the way he relates to other actors. Such discretion occurs in areas where rules play only a limited part, and legal reasons for acting are not to the fore. In this way, the model of 'ruled justice' is called into question (see below). Most discretion of this kind occurs outside courts, and so adjudication is of limited interest.

The Contribution of Empirical Studies

The specific contribution of empirical studies of discretion towards a theory of law lies partly in their assumption about law and partly in their results. Such studies take for granted that law is not a discrete social phenomenon, but that it has its importance in its interaction with other social factors. Law is only one element affecting the way the world works. The results confirm this view by noting the way discretion exists within institutional power relationships in which the principal determinants for action are not legal.

Let us take the example of studies on pollution regulation and enforcement (see Richardson, Ogus, and Burrows 1983; Hawkins 1984; Hawkins and Thomas 1984; Allars, 1985). These have as their centrepiece the work of enforcement officers in the application of pollution regulations. Viewed simply as a legal theorist would see it, the officers have to interpret and apply the legal standards to the facts, they have discretions whether to dispense a particular person from some aspects of this legal regulation, and they have a discretion whether to prosecute. Whereas the former discretion is explicit in the legal texts, the second arises from the fact that the agency has the power to prosecute. Apart from a general obligation to pursue the purposes of the legislation, the law provides few other directions as to how the discretions are to be exercised.

The studies reveal the difficulty of using rules to achieve policy objectives in that rules may be over-inclusive, penalizing too much conduct, so that formal or informal relaxation is needed. Rules may also be difficult to formulate with adequate precision to fit the varying types of situation, so that informal adjustments are necessary. In the case of an ongoing policy objective, the all-or-nothing approach of rules is inadequate to meet the need to achieve a continuing improvement in performance by polluters. If the objectives are to be achieved, these effects of rules have to be modified in practice by the use of discretion by officials, if necessary contrary to the express provisions of the legal rules.

The importance of officials and organizations is the central feature of empirical studies. They are created in order to implement legal policies, but do so primarily through negotiation, using the law as a background and final sanction, while trying to negotiate targets with polluters, determine what is an 'acceptable' level of pollution in the context (including the means of the polluter), and deciding whether to prosecute for breaches or to achieve their objectives by warnings or other means. The institutions provide the framework within which the officers work. Legal rules and standards are treated as privileged statements of the policy, but it is the overall objective which matters most. In controlling pollution, the influence of the rules is mediated through institutional structures and values (Richardson, Ogus, and Burrows 1983: 190). The greater constraints are not the legal rules, but the self-perception of officials as to their role, strongly influenced by the expectations of their superiors, the polluters, and the public as to how the legal rules will be used (ibid.: 152 ff.). As Richardson states: 'The most immediately relevant interpretation of these [legal] restrictions was that made by the individual officer himself, but his own interpretation of professional expectations and bureaucratic demands, for example, depended in part on his understanding of the definitions applied by his seniors' (ibid.: 190). Indeed, as Hawkins (1984: 188) notes, the law may be perceived as a hindrance and an inconvenience to carrying out the task, rather than providing the reasons for action. In such sociologically informed studies, it is part of the method, but confirmed by the findings, that the right place to study the law is in the institutional context within which it operates, and that this is especially so in the area of discretion.

As far as the court-centred legal theorists are concerned, the empirical studies likewise pose a challenge. The concentration on the way legal standards, and also fact-gathering through monitoring about whether something amounts to 'pollution', are subject to negotiation and arrangement between officials and polluters brings into question the notion of 'dispute' which is pivotal in any court-centred view of the functon of law. If discretion can serve to obviate the way in which disputes arise, and if the court dispute is part of a continuing relationship between the parties, rather than a discrete instance, then the importance of the court decision in the whole process may be reduced. Predictions of the attitudes of courts may lead to the kind of despair which Hawkins notes, but may also set part of the framework for bargaining. But in none of the studies does the court play a central role of influence.

There is also an implication in Hawkins's work which challenges the dispute model. He argues that it presupposes a rationalistic model of decision-making, with discrete inputs and outputs (Hawkins 1986: 1179–95; also Baldwin and Hawkins 1984). The empirical studies sustain what he describes as a 'naturalistic' model of decision-making, where there may often not be identifiable moments of decision, but rather subtle, shifting, and dynamic processes which end up with results. 'Facts' and 'solutions' may come out of them, but may not be specifically identifiable. Rather they arise 'naturally' out of the way in which decision-making is approached. Because of the way in which the decision-making is approached, for example by constant interaction and negotiation, no real dispute may arise. This analysis reinforces the importance of the institutional setting for understanding legal decision-making:

Frame, then, is a feature of overriding importance in understanding decision behaviour. It is the means by which meaning and relevance are given to information, for information as such does not automatically prompt a particular decision, and it involves organizing, selecting, and omitting 'facts'—as well, of course, as interpreting them. (Hawkins 1986: 1195)

Such studies emphasize the importance of legal rules and powers as resources, and confirm the results in other sociological studies of law. For example, Comaroff and Roberts (1981: 5) demonstrate the way in which factual and normative ambiguities function to provide social actors with flexibility in the reinterpretation of social situations. The legal classification serves to provide the individual with reference points when an opportune moment arises, rather than direct resolutions to problems.

These studies raise a number of issues for a theory of law. First, what does discretion involve? They emphasize the function of discretion as central to power relationships which the law engenders and delimits. Secondly, how important is discretion within law? They suggest that the flexibilities which discretion permits, rather than legal rules are central to the operation of law. Thirdly, what legal theory do we develop? They suggest that law has to be understood not in terms of a discrete set of normative standards, but primarily within an institutional context.

What Discretion Involves

For the purpose of this chapter, discretion will be taken to involve (1) a power to choose standards for action on the part of an actor, (2) which choice is made unilaterally by one legal subject in relation to another, and (3) which choice is conferred or legitimated by the law. Each of these points is contestable, but I hope they draw attention to issues of central jurisprudential interest in this topic. The central feature of this characterization is the power relationship which the law endorses or creates through the institutions of discretion in law.

Discretion as choice

Almost any definition of discretion starts with the notion of choice (see, e.g., Venezia 1959: 132; Davis 1969: 4; Bockel 1978: 355; Galligan 1986*a*: 2). The central aspect of this notion of choice is, as Venezia (1959: 132) put it, the degree of self-determination which the actor possesses as a consequence of the responsibility which he has for achieving the success of a particular enterprise. Tied closely in with this aspect is the freedom the actor has from external constraints. A final feature which my definition focuses upon is the area over which choice is exercised.

The importance of choice is well brought out by Galligan, who suggests that a central sense of discretion involves 'significant scope for settling the reasons and standards according to which . . . power is to be exercised, and for applying them in the making of specific decisions' (1986*a*: 21). As Bockel (1978: 357) points out, this choice may be exercised over the merits of acting at all, or over the content of a decision. The actor has choice over either or both of these areas and decides the appropriate reasons for acting. While the content of the decision may be predetermined by law, a discretion would exist where a person has a choice whether to initiate the legal process or not, as in the case of a prosecutorial discretion.

Bockel's refinement helps to reinforce the point that the existence of a power to choose is not incompatible with constraints. After all, classical definitions of discretion would suggest that the function of law is to set the boundaries within which discretion is to work (see A. Hauriou, cited at Bockel 1978: 355). The choice can be legitimately exercised within a framework. What is important, as Galligan's definition suggests, is that the choice is exercised over a significant aspect of an issue. At the very least, a discretion will be granted to achieve a specific goal or goals. As Goodin suggests, 'an official may be said to have discretion if and only if he is empowered to pursue some social goal(s) in the context of individual cases in such a way as he judges to be best calculated, in the circumstances, to promote those goals' (1986: 233). The specific goal, and perhaps also specific modalities for achieving it or for avoiding interfering with other goals, will delimit the scope of any discretion.

The constraints for discretion will not simply concern the objectives to be pursued and the range of permitted choice. There will also be constraints of a formal kind on the rationality of the exercise of discretion. A decision must be rationally justified and related to the purposes for which the power is conferred. It is this aspect which most taxes public lawyers in their consideration of discretion. In addition, there will be institutional constraints of a practical kind. Since discretion has to operate within an institutional context, the range of effective choice open to a decision-maker may be less than would appear from a simple reading of the formal rule. The conferring of discretion within an institutional context is often deliberate. The institutional setting is known to provide a context and limits to the decision-making, and the real extent of the freedom of choice conferred can only be assessed by looking at the institutional framework to which the discretion belongs (Turk 1980: 153). It is for this reason that the definition offered by Davis (1969: 4) focuses on the 'effective limits' on the power of choice, rather than on the limits formally set out in the legal text.

Given this analysis of discretion as choice within a framework of constraints, I find difficulty with Dworkin's dichotomy (1977*b*: 31–9, 67–71) between strong discretion, involving setting one's own standards for decision in an unlimited way, and weak discretion, which simply involves judgment in interpreting and applying standards. As I have stated elsewhere (Bell 1983: 28), what is at issue is the extent of the creative function of the judge or of other persons on whom discretion is conferred. Having genuine freedom of action within a significant range of options suffices to identify politically important power, even if there is not unlimited choice.

If choice involves a degree of self-determination within a framework of constraints, one does have to pay attention to the kinds of review to which a decision is subject. If a reviewing authority can decide in every case that the decision is wrong and can substitute its view for that of the original decision-holder, then we are really in Dworkin's archetypal 'weak' discretion: a freedom to make the right decision in interpreting and applying the rules. Where, however, the reviewing authority will make an alternative decision only in the marginal case where the original decision is irrational or aberrant, then the original decision-maker is less controlled and has a more authoritative exercise of power. Such a distinction is appropriate when considering the place of interpretation within a definition of discretion.

Discretion as power

The authorization to determine one's own reasons for acting in relation to dealings with others is one of the principal reasons for the interest which discretion attracts. It enables the discretion-holder to affect unilaterally the position of other persons in society, be they the recipients of welfare or industrialists engaged in pollution. The interest of the legal sociologist lies in the way the power is exercised, the public lawyer is concerned with the way the power is controlled by law, and the legal theorist is concerned about the way in which power is distributed in society.

The analysis of discretion as power is nothing new (see, e.g., M. J. Adler and S. Asquith, in Adler and Asquith 1981*a*: ch. 1; Z. Bankowski and D. Nelken, in ibid.: ch. 12; R. E. Goodin 1986: *passim*). It underlines, expressly or implicitly, our concerns with discretion. The archetypal power relationships are those between officials of the state and citizens, and these form the focus not merely of empirical research on discretionary decision-making, but also of two of the major legal-theoretical works on discretion, namely Galligan and Venezia. However, the power to make such unilateral choices is not confined to the public realm, but can also be found in relationships of doctor and patient, teacher and pupil, parent and child. Venezia himself points this out by a comparison between the discretionary power of an employer to dismiss an employee and the exercise of power by public authorities.

Galligan's analysis (1986*a*: 86–7) proposes a distinction between the public-law model of discretion and the private-law model. In the latter, law has the role of providing stable facilities for private relationships (essentially of a reciprocal and agreed kind) in which actions of the executive are essentially limited to the implementation of rules. In this world, discretion has a limited place and struggles to achieve the status of legitimacy. By contrast, in the public-law model, the social order requires more positive interventionist measures, and discretion is an integral part of achieving these policy goals, and thus it has greater legitimacy in the ideology of the political system. Much as this analysis has undoubted value, I would suggest that the key difference Galligan's analysis isolates is not so much about the role of discretion in law, as the appropriateness of discretionary power in the hands of state officials. In that power relationships may exist outside the realm of state action, the restriction of state discretion may well have the consequence of expanding the scope of private discretions. This is well seen in the area of deregulation, where the state may take the role of underwriting the power exercised by self-regulating, private organizations. It is not clear that the discretion exercised in such circumstances is significantly different from that exercised by state officials. There are arguments for extending Galligan's 'public' model to cover these or other private activities (see Wolf 1986: 224–5; Collins 1987: 94–100). Galligan's models may help us to analyse our attitudes to discretion of state officials, but they need expansion to see if these do indeed reflect a different set of attitudes to the existence of discretion as a way of implementing social policies, rather than a debate about its location.

My argument is essentially this: in a liberal society concerned with the flourishing of all citizens under conditions of freedom and equality, we are inevitably drawn to consider the appropriateness of power exercised unilaterally whether this be by officials of the state or by fellow citizens, such as dominant market traders, parents, or professionals. The issues are much the same (Ackerman 1980: ch. 1). Is the professional doctor to exercise power in an unlimited way in relation to the object of welfare, the patient? This question resembles many concerning the activities of social workers employed by the state. Even if liberal theory has been long preoccupied with the role of the state, it does not seem to me that an adequate analysis of discretion in law can content itself with a focus on the unilateral power relationships exercised by state officials.

Discretion conferred or legitimated by law

As Richardson, Ogus, and Burrows point out, 'discretion is not merely choice; it conveys a sense of legitimate choice, a decision reached within the confines of certain restrictions' (1983: 20–1). The legitimation of choice and power by law is central to any study of discretion. It is, however, necessary to identify the areas in which this legitimation occurs.

If we expand the public-law view of the place of discretion which Galligan expresses, then it is easier to see that the state may legitimate social power either by creating it or by endorsing its exercise and providing social recognition and authority. Where the law creates a specific discretion, then the legitimation is easy to see. But the incorporation of social situations of power like parent and child, doctor and patient, etc., within legal regulation also gives a degree of state endorsement of the power relationship, even if the legal regulation often is about setting limits on that legitimation, imposing controls, or withdrawing recognition in certain events.[1] As Bankowski and Nelken (Adler and Asquith 1981*a*: 256) point out, one function of law may be to transform power into authority, and the legal technique of creating or legitimating the choice of standards in dealing between people which occurs in discretion may have this effect. The importance of such legal legitimation will depend very much on what other reasons (e.g. natural love and affection, or professionalism) exist as justifications for according authority to a power-holder.

Depending on current views, the existence of certain types of discretion in the hands of officials may be more-or-less welcome, and the same applies to discretion in the hands of private individuals. It is not the location alone which satisfies the liberal's concern about the abuse of power. For example, it could be argued that, where power is exercised for reasons of self-interest by private individuals, then the liberal should be more concerned than if it is exercised paternalistically by state officials.

The Place of Discretion in Law

The classical approach of legal theorists is to concentrate on law as a system of rules or other standards providing legal reasons for action on the part of citizens and officials. Discretions appear as either the consequence of the conferment of power or as the result of some absence or indeterminacy of the legal materials. Discretion is the 'hole in the doughnut' (Dworkin 1977*b*: 31). The legal sociologist approaches the matter of discretion in not too different a manner. Studies on the law in general and the exercise of discretion in particular tend to blur the line between choices which are the consequence of deliberate legal creation and those which arise inadvertently and are seized upon opportunistically by citizens. In the Comaroff and Roberts study, it is the exploitation of indeterminacy in the definition and application of legal rules which is the focus of attention, without much concern for whether the law has created this or whether it has just arisen

---

[1] Cf. the view of Adler and Asquith (1981*a*: 12), who suggest that the power relations in discretionary relationships between state officials and the public must be seen as reflections of structured power relations in society in general.

accidentally. In the pollution studies, the discretions specifically provided for in the law are studied together with the leeways of interpretation and other situations of choice of a less deliberate kind.

In view of what has been said about the definition of discretion, which is reinforced by empirical studies, it is necessary to pay some attention first to what areas belong to discretion in law, and, secondly, to the centrality of discretion in law. Is the attention given to rules fully justified?

The content of discretion in law

While the area of deliberately created discretions poses no real conceptual difficulty, the areas of apparently unintended discretion in both legal interpretation and in the absence of legal regulation are cause for comment.

Legal interpretation and discretion. As vividly described by Comaroff and Roberts (1981: 231–9), the scope for choice left open by indeterminacy in legal regulation provides the opportunity for power to be exercised by the individuals in society. For this reason, much attention has been paid by the present author and others to the exercise of judicial discretion in the interpretation of legal texts. At the same time, authors, such as Dworkin (1977a), and Coval and Smith (1977), have argued that the kind of choice exercised in the interpretation of legal norms may be authoritative in the sense of being final, but it is only 'weak discretion', since there are legally provided standards against which the correctness of an interpretation can be judged. In a slightly different way, the point is made by the courts as well. For instance, the German Constitutional Court distinguishes between the correct interpretation of 'indeterminate legal concepts', which is subject to strict control in the courts, and 'discretion', which is not.[2] For there to be discretion in the sense of social power, there needs to be a sense of unquestioned or mainly unchallenged authority to make a decision. It conveys a sense of responsibility and not merely judgment on the part of the person concerned (Mayer and Kopp 1985: 154).

While there is some value in the distinction drawn, it is subject to a number of difficulties. Firstly, as Betti (1971: 149–50) points out, discretion is a rich concept involving varying degrees of choice in

---

[2] See BVerfG 1960:11, 168, 191–2; Jesch 1957: 163; Ule 1985.

interpreting legal texts or applying them. 'Sovereign discretion' involves freedom to choose ends and means over a wide range of options, while 'administrative discretion' covers such choices within the framework of a particular policy to be achieved, and 'technical discretion' involves choices of the means alone to be used. Turning more specifically to interpretation, this may involve 'supplementary discretion', the filling out of a rule to adapt it to specific facts, or mere 'evaluation', the judgment of whether the rule applies. Where the legal standard is fairly precise, then little room will be left for more than 'evaluation' and this fits well into the notion of 'weak discretion'. An incomplete standard or incompleteness in its content may give rise to greater degrees of choice, which may not amount to sovereign discretion, or 'strong discretion' in Dworkin's narrow sense, but may involve significant amounts of standard-setting. The more the decision-maker has to assess appropriate objectives or to reconcile ones in competition, and the more he has to consider not merely the technical feasibility of particular means for achieving goals, but also the side-effects they may have, and thus the desirability of pursuing them, then the more appropriate is the label 'discretion as standard-setting', rather than 'discretion as judgment'. To exclude 'evaluation' or pure interpretation from the central focus of discretion is not to suggest that it is unimportant. Much of importance occurs in the way people use and misuse the law. The focus of attention in considering this area is not so much on the way in which the law creates or legitimates the exercise of power, but on how people place themselves in situations in which legal reasons for action become significant elements in the outcome of their dealings with other people. The focus is not so much with what law does, as on what people do in interaction with the law.

Discretion as the consequence of no legal regulation. The attention paid in much discretion literature to discretion exercised by state officials says something about constitutional theory and about perceptions of the functions of law. Especially in systems which hold that the state has no power except that which the law of the land grants it, law is often seen as in essence the conferring of power to state officials to act in specific circumstances and the laying down of standards by which such action is judged legitimate. Private citizens, on the other hand, need no such authorization to act. The law may confer on them specific discretionary powers, but it may equally well leave them unrestricted in their choice of action. To take Goodin's example (1986: 233), I have a choice what colour to paint my house because the law, subject to any specific planning regulations, prescribes nothing on house colourings. By analogy with Bentham, one might describe these as 'bare discretions'. Must a theory of discretion in law incorporate such situations?

Although it may be said that law claims to be all encompassing in the social situations it embraces (Raz 1975: 151–2), our major concern is with situations in which the law takes a specific stance in the regulation of a relationship. It is easy to see such a positive role for the law and state legitimation of power when the law creates the situation in which power is to be exercised. Where the law does nothing and might be expected to do nothing, such as where I intend to inflict my lack of colour sense on my neighbours, then we are less happy with the suggestion that this is legal discretion. Goodin suggests that 'only when there is some prima-facie expectation that the decision will be subject to constraints of a rule-like form is the absence of constraints a matter for comment' (1986: 233–4). Such a suggestion leaves us in the position of deeming discretion to exist whenever our political culture would expect situations of power to be controlled strictly by law and they are not. This, however, attributes to the law a higher degree of deliberation than really exists. Of course, there may be situations where legal non-regulation is a deliberate part of a strategy to reinforce existing social power-holders. In other cases, the law may not act because it has had no call to act, may have been unable to act, or may simply not have bothered. It will be sufficient to confine the notion of discretion in law to situations of deliberate legal regulation.

Legal discretion may be said to arise in two kinds of case: first where the law creates a power situation, and, secondly, where the law legitimates a power situation which already exists. The former is unproblematic. The second may occur in relation to either officials or private individuals. The law may not create the situation of power, and its reasons for acting may well not predominate in the thinking of the actors, but it provides social recognition and legitimation for the use of power in such situations, albeit within certain constraints. By legitimating the activity of the discretion-holder, the law may affect the attitudes of concerned third parties, even if it has little bearing on the attitudes of the principal parties of the power relationship.

To sum up, discretion in law is about those situations in which the law creates or transforms into legal institutions situations of unilateral power. The social endorsement which this entails is of particular concern to the liberal keen to ensure the free flourishing of individuals and wary of effective restrictions on it. A bare discretion may sometimes be of interest, where the law's inaction amounts to the same thing as social endorsement. But this is not necessarily the case, and that would justify leaving this area to one side in a jurisprudential analysis of discretion. Whereas a full sociological description of a situation will include all kinds of discretion, legal theory may legitimately concern itself with the subset of situations described by the notion of discretion in law.

Discretion and institutions

Perhaps the greatest contribution of the empirical research on discretion to an understanding of discretion in law comes from the way in which the explanation of discretionary decision-making is situated within the context of social institutions.[3] To return to the example of pollution control, the behaviour of officials and the way in which disputes arose or decisions came to be made is viewed in the context of the operation of an inspectorate. The institutional context helps not merely to explain behaviour; it also helps to locate the importance of discretionary decisions within the actual functioning of the law.

As Chambliss and Seidman point out in relation to bureaucracies in general, 'laws that create and circumscribe the boundaries of bureaucracies place limitations on the activities of role occupants but they do not determine them' (1982: 287). All the same, the freedom thus created is limited in that the bureaucracy creates its interests and ideology within a wider social framework. In other words the importance of legal control must be assessed by setting the institution within the context of broader social controls (ibid.: 288–9). While compliance with objectives and restrictions imposed by law may be part of the action of holders of discretion, there is also the desire to deploy their resources for the full achievement of objectives. In this latter, 'engineering' aspect, as Selznick (1969: 94) calls it, the constraints of law are less important than the overall efficient performance of tasks defined frequently from non-legal perspectives.

---

[3] 'Institution' in this context should be understood as referring to a social organization, rather than to a complex series of interrelated legal norms: on this latter, see MacCormick 1974: 102, 105–7.

This approach, supported in the empirical literature, has two consequences. First, far from being the uninteresting 'hole' in the legal regulation, discretion is the centrepiece of the institutional edifice to which the legal rules play a subservient role of setting the boundaries. What is most important is not that the legal rules are in place, but that they designate the appropriate social institution to perform the task of discretion. Secondly, the importance of legal controls must be viewed in relation to the other social controls which operate in a particular area. Lawyers, like Dicey (1959: 188, cf. 411–12), have a habit of treating legally uncontrolled discretion as 'arbitrary' and to disapprove of it. Yet the empirical studies show that other constraints of a very effective kind may exist both within the institution exercising discretion and on the institution from external sources. In fact, practising lawyers are quite familiar with such a point of view and will argue that they should not exercise control over discretion because of the existence of political or other control.[4] When account is taken of this importance of discretion to the real operation of law and to determining what law does, then discretion should occupy a more central place in the presentation of law.

Discretion is concerned, as Türk (1980: 161) points out, with the functional autonomy of the decision-maker, such that an actor can satisfactorily deploy his own needs, interests, goals, and qualifications through choice between an adequate range of alternative courses of action. This functional autonomy is, however, defined institutionally. By plotting all the constraints, legal and otherwise, within the institutional context, we come to understand the full scope of the autonomy which the individual possesses. If we are concerned about discretion as the exercise of social power, then it is the context and scope of this power which should concern us, and not simply its legal limits and definition. All the same, it is worthwhile to distinguish the role of discretion as powers of choice deliberately granted or legitimated in the hands of a decision-maker, and those choices and freedoms to manœuvre which arise out of the indeterminacies or inadequacies of legal regulation. In the former, the law is granting authority to choices which are made, while, in the second, the decision-maker is more opportunistically taking advantage of the situation to achieve his objectives.

---

[4] See *R* v. *Environment Secretary, ex parte Nottinghamshire CC* [1986] AC 240 at pp. 250–1.

Discretion and Legal Theory

As J. W. Harris (1979: 23) has written,

When jurisprudential writers concern themselves with macroscopic questions about aspects of societies under law other than the functioning of courts, their conclusions tend to be distorted by their preoccupation with the specifically 'legal' aspects of such societies. In other words, when they are supposed to be discussing universals about 'legal systems', in the sense of institutional structures, they tend to over-emphasize 'legal systems' in the sense of normative fields of meaning, or 'legal systems', in the sense of collections of doctrine. (1979: 23)

His criticism is highly pertinent to the analysis of discretion in legal theory. Although there is no single way in which law is viewed by legal theorists which can be contrasted with the views of legal sociologists, the legal theory underlying the approach of the empirical studies of discretion provides reasons to question some contemporary approaches in legal theory, particularly the idea of 'ruled justice' and 'law as dispute settlement'.

Discretion and 'ruled justice'

The approach of 'ruled justice' or the model of rules, as Galligan (1986*a*: 56) calls it, contains a number of elements. Salient among these in the literature are the way in which law commands authority and the way in which it provides reasons for action for legal subjects.

In the first sense, legal justice provides authority for social decisions which conform to certain criteria of validity. 'The law', as Raz says, 'presents itself as a body of authoritative standards and requires all those to whom they apply to acknowledge their authority' (1979: 33). In presenting the law in this light, legal theorists seek to explain (1) the derivation of the authority of particular legal standards from a basic criterion of validity (Hart 1961: ch. 6; Kelsen 1967: 193–201; Harris 1979: ch. IV; Raz 1979: chs. 3 and 8); (2) the logical status of propositions of law, and (3) the coherence of the law as a system of standards (MacCormick 1978: chs. 7 and 8; Harris, 1979: 81–3). In that the rules of law are disinterestedly applied to particular circumstances, the decision-maker is able to claim an authority for his decisions which does not depend on his personal authority. An extreme version would be to characterize this behaviour as 'bureaucratic' in the sense that the decision and the decision-maker are mere conduits between the legal rule and the social situation to which it is applied (Weber, 1968: i. 979; Galligan 1986: 62–3). Such a characterization, as I have shown elsewhere (Bell 1987: 40–2) fits ill with the nature of bureaucratic activity, especially with the discretionary tasks which are integral to it. The ability to set standards for one's dealings with another means that personal responsibility is undertaken and that the authority of the decision-maker must come in part from the respect which he personally, or the institution to which he belongs, commands (ibid.: 42). While this does not deny there is value in the explanations offered by legal theorists of the derivation of legal authority for decisions, it does call into question the sufficiency of such explanations for the authority of legal decisions. Empirical studies of discretion provide explanations for the authority of officials enforcing, say, pollution regulations which go well beyond the respect due to the legal standards which they are applying.

A second view would see the law as providing determinative (or exclusionary) reasons for action by citizens (Raz 1980: 229). This is not to suggest a simple causal connection between the law and the behaviour of citizens. Few legal theorists have ever proposed the view that legal reasons are dominant in determining actions by citizens. As Bankowski and Nelken suggest, such a view may well have been more propagated by legal sociologists as a straw man to be knocked down, rather than held seriously by legal theorists (Adler and Asquith 1981a: 254). Although it is acknowledged that a citizen may well act because of non-legal reasons, these are only acceptable to the extent that they are legally recognized (Raz 1979: 33). Stated in this abstract form, not all legal standards need be normative (ibid.: ch. VIII, esp. 145), but it does insist that law provides a comprehensive, self-contained way of viewing conduct within society. Legal reasons for action are offered as guides, and the state system encourages conformity to them. Whether one adopts the perspective of Holmes's bad man for whom prudential reasons dominate (1897: 459–61), or Finnis's good citizen for whom moral reasons dominate (1980: 14–15; 1987: 67–9), legal reasons are expected to be important reasons for action (Raz 1975: 154).

Even expressed in this rather more sophisticated way, the idea has its limitations when applied to discretion. It becomes clear that reasons drawn from legal sources and other reasons are closely intertwined. Honoré suggests that 'the main function of a legal system is to strengthen the motives which citizens have to obey certain prescriptions in certain situations' (1977: 104). This defines the function, rather than the form of laws, and emphasizes the way in which legal reasons for action are intended to be supplementary, and even parasitic upon, other reasons for action. This is clearly so in the area of discretion where the principal reasons for action are not directly provided by the law.

A discretion-centred approach would involve an Honoré-style concern for seeing the less direct ways in which the law encourages certain types of behaviour. It would focus on the way in which legal reasons for action combine with non-legal reasons for action and serve to legitimate them. The key feature is not the specificity and separate identity of legal norms, but their interaction with and duplication of non-legal reasons for action. In the area of discretion, law is not so much providing legal reasons why an act should be done, but providing legal reasons why others should view such an act as authoritative and effective.

Above and beyond this, the method of connection between rules and discretion is important. The rules help to create an institution within which individuals operate and relate to each other. The institution concerned is not simply of the abstract, normative kind described by MacCormick (1974), but a concrete human institution from which the legal rules and powers take their legal and non-legal sense. It is within this context that reasons for action are determined, and thus where the importance of legal reasons for action can be assessed. Furthermore, if one takes Hawkins's insights (above) into account, one can also locate in this approach the way legal reasons fit into the processes in which transactions are handled, even if there is not a specific moment of 'decision'.

Discretion and 'dispute settlement'

Adjudication provides the other focus of much contemporary juris-prudential literature, especially in the United States. On this view, law has its focal meaning and life at the point where legal discourse is at its purest and most distinctive, in court. Even though many citizens may not rely on legal reasons for determining their conduct, officials, particularly judges, are expected to rely on them as central. Thus, in the reasons for judicial decisions, we might expect to find the arche-types for the kind and importance of legal reasons for action and for the special contribution of law to society. (Though this is not to suggest that the judicial role is confined to dispute settlement (see Bell 1987: 40–2.)

Judicial reasons for decisions. Studies of legal reasoning, in fact, show the way in which legal and other reasons interact, thus confirming the general thrust of empirical studies of law. Even assuming that there are easy cases for legal decision (cf. Hutchinson and Wakefield 1982), jurisprudential writing on fact-finding (e.g. Frank 1949) and on hard cases in determining legal rules (Dworkin 1977*b*: ch. 4; MacCormick 1978; Bell 1983) demonstrates the connection between legal and other forms of reasoning. In finding facts, the skills of common-sense judgment, understanding of human nature, and so on, play a predominant part. In deciding both whether a case is indeed a 'hard' case and how it is to be resolved, the judge employs justifications drawn from political morality and social utility as part of the legal resolution of the dispute. Within such a perspective, the place of non-legal reasons in discretionary decision-making is exemplified in the exercise of judicial standard-setting. As a result, the focus moves away from the criteria of validity and the distinction between specifically legal and other norms to the political role which judicial institutions perform (Dworkin 1977*b*: ch. 4; Bell 1983: ch. 2).

Attention paid to the place of discretionary standards in law (as opposed to the kinds of discretion involved in legal interpretation) would merely strengthen the case for such studies on the connection between legal and other forms of reasoning and decision-making.

Disputes and their place in law. A more problematic issue raised by empirical studies of discretionary decision-making is the place which traditional legal theory assigns to the dispute resolution function of law. The empirical studies give rise to two reflections. The first is whether dispute settlement is indeed at the centre of the social function of law. It is true that many sociological studies of law, particularly in tribal societies, have focused on the way in which disputes are handled (Roberts 1979: 198–206; Comaroff and Roberts 1981: 5–17). Dispute settlement procedures are supposed to identify legal rules and to be a focus of the way law contributes to the pacifying of a community. Yet the empirical studies of discretionary decision-making seem to suggest this has significant limits for an understanding of law. In the pollution studies, for example, the role of disputes before courts was, by and large, marginal, if not an irritant to the law enforcers as well as to those prosecuted (Hawkins 1984: 188). It is not obvious from these that judicial standard-setting is a predominant feature in determining how even officials decide what is appropriate conduct or not. The central place accorded to courts by both jurisprudents and legal sociologists might seem to be unjustified. But such a conclusion would follow only if we took the jurisprudents and sociologists to be suggesting that what goes on in court does determine behaviour outside in any direct way. At least when the jurisprudential studies are analysed, they are not offering predictions of behaviour in society, merely trying to define more closely what is the legal perspective on social behaviour. As Jerome Frank (1949) pointed out, there is a wealth of features both inside and outside courts and legal rules pronounced by them which will determine how people will actually behave. It is because courts provide authoritative statements of what the law regards as legitimate conduct that they and their decisions attract so much attention. Empirical studies of discretion merely offer salutary warnings about the limits of the importance which can be attributed to what goes on in court.

The empirical studies also call into question the notion of a 'dispute' which the courts can resolve. In that discretions operate often in long-standing interactions between discretion-holders and those subject to them, the positions adopted at the moment of a 'dispute' are often the result of long processes of negotiation between individuals, rules, and others. Likewise, 'decisions' may not be clearly identifiable moments, but may be the result of the cumulative operation of these processes. While this may not require us to go so far as to accept the view that we cannot study disputes without a full theory of social formation which explains how they arise (cf. Cain and Kulcsar 1982), it does suggest that we need at least to understand the institutional processes and context in which disputes arise and from which they take their importance. The institutional approach of many empirical studies would thus seem fully justified.

Law and legitimation

The foregoing might seem to suggest that, whether legal theorists focus on law as rules or law as dispute settlement, empirical studies of law demonstrate that their insights are partial and unimportant. Certainly this would be the case if legal theorists are to be taken to be describing the influence of law on society. What has been noted above, however, is that legal theorists are offering a description of what is the legal point of view on social activity. It is clear that legal theorists may not concentrate enough on the institutional aspects of law, and may focus on standards alone too much, but this latter approach has value if the function of law is to provide a scheme of legitimation for the behaviour of officials and citizens under law.

To take discretionary decision-making as a more central phenomenon in law involves seeing a major function of the law as not merely the creator of power-relations, but frequently the legitimator and regulator of existing situations of power. Especially in the latter situation, the principal reasons for action will be connected with the internal dynamics of the relationship in which the law pays a limited part. The function of law in legitimating conduct is twofold: it offers the discretion-holder additional reasons for action in order to secure social legitimation in the way he exercises power, and, to the subject of discretion and to outsiders, it provides reasons for accepting the power of the discretion-holder as legitimate authority. In this way, the law affects, not necessarily determinatively nor by giving directions, the reasons for actions and attitudes among the community. Where discretionary power relations are created by law, this effect is even more evident. This is not to deny that law will have practical effects in the real world, but such effects are contingent upon the attitudes of social actors. As many legal theorists have accepted, effectiveness and validity are not the same thing.

Seen in this way, law provides a scheme of values which explain why the power and actions of individuals in society should be regarded as legitimate. As Maihofer (1970: 20–1) suggests, law seen as encapsulating a (legal) ideology serves to socialize and to regulate conduct and conflicts between individuals. As 'ruled justice' it sets out a legal point of view on the legitimacy of social behaviour. When focused on adjudication, it serves to legitimate both the outcomes of court procedures and the conduct of adjudicators in reaching those solutions. Only to the extent that individuals are prepared to endorse the legal point of view or to use it as a determinative guide to their behaviour will it have any impact on the way people behave.

Law as a scheme of values is both supportive and critical in relation to what goes on in the community. In so far as conformity to law or achieving its approbation is valuable in society and to individuals, then it has a place in the reasons influencing the conduct of officials and citizens. The values it expresses will serve to rationalize and raise support for specific programmes under which discretion is conferred or legitimated in the hands of particular individuals.[5] The success of law in this endeavour will inevitably vary according both to the society in question and to the area of law involved.

Compared with the traditional model of 'ruled justice', such an approach envisages a more complex relationship between legal values and norms of conduct, but one fully compatible with the idea of 'ruled justice' as a characterization of conduct from the legal point of view. The approach focuses more on the way in which law provides an authoritative perception or perceptions[6] of the nature of social relationships and how they can be accepted as legitimate. Achieving specific objectives, especially through the threat of sanctions, is consequential. Law in its terminology and values is not simply concerned with getting things done, but also with having them perceived as what ought to be done.

Compared with the focus on dispute settlement, the legitimation approach can explain the centrality of court institutions as authoritative exponents of the legal point of view and as a public forum in which that perception of reality is authoritatively stated and applied to the concrete world of specific social relationships. The concern about the kinds of standard which judges apply relates both to their political role and to the connection between the legal and other perceptions of social conduct. Although disputes may have a limited place in social relationships, they have a privileged place in the application of the legal ideology. It is in court that the legal ideology is most purely applied, and the empirical studies of discretion show how much less this is the case in non-court situations.

Even if such a legitimation approach does make sense of the 'ruled-justice' and 'law-as-dispute-settlement' approaches, what value has this as an object of study? After all, do not the empirical studies suggest that such a legal point of view is of marginal significance in explaining what actually happens in societies under law? Surely, if law is treated as a system of ideological values, it makes even less claim to importance than if it were a model of rules?

---

[5] Luhmann 1967: 531, 551. Ideology in this sense is not a false consciousness, but merely a scheme of values adopted to explain or to direct the law. It forms the bridge between positive law (the 'lawyer's law' in the lawbooks) and ideal law (the values which the notion of law has in the minds of people): cf. Campbell 1976: 11–12.

[6] The law may admit of a number of diverging readings of a particular situation; see Goodrich 1987: 187.

A parallel can be drawn with another scheme of values: morals. Moral values set standards for conduct and legitimation which we know in practice to be often ignored or not the primary motivation for actions. Yet the moral code has a value as an object of study both for what it says about our ideals and for the reasons it proffers for our actions. In a similar way, law as a system of values reveals something about the ideals and objectives of a society and the reasons for action and attitudes which it offers to individuals. In that standards are not set in the abstract, but in relation to specific institutional arrangements, so a study of legitimation involves the location of values in their institutional setting. Equally, a model of law which took discretion and legitimation seriously would have to relate legal standards and other reasons for action at work in situations of discretionary power.

Conclusion

The importance of discretion in law very much emphasizes the point that law as a set of standards cannot be a closed-off subject of study. While traditional legal theory does admit the openness of the legal normative order (Tammelo 1959; Raz 1979: ch. 4), the idea of law as legitimating power makes this more clear in the situations where discretionary decision-making takes place. It is not merely that other standards are at work in discretionary situations, provide the context for legal standards, and call into question the relevance of the latter as reasons for action. The whole force of the legal point of view as a source of legitimation depends on its relationship to other viewpoints adopted in a particular society. Once discretion is not seen as peripheral to the operation of law, but as central to the institutions which the law creates and legitimates, then the interaction between law and other schemes of values becomes of central importance.

The contribution of empirical studies of discretionary decision-making is thus to render more plausible the centrality of a legitimation view of law's function, and to limit the claims which legal theorists can make about the role of law in social arrangements. Law is best viewed not so much as a discrete set of normative directions, but as a scheme of legitimating values operating within specific institutional frameworks in conjunction with other social schemes of value. Legal values as a coherent system are worthy of study, but attention needs to be paid to their connection with other political and social values.

To some extent, such messages are really contained in the premisses of the empirical studies, but the results contribute much to give credence to them. Legal theory is not abolished by legal sociology, but it is called upon to reassess its claims and approach. In doing so, it can then contribute more to our understanding of law as a whole.

PART II

Social Processes in the Use of Legal Discretion

ONE of the ironies of discretionary behaviour is that it prompts seemingly contradictory images in much of the scholarly literature. One view of discretion, usually associated with its practitioners, emphasizes its individualistic character, its ability to respond to the needs or deserts of each particular case. Legal decision-makers often claim that they judge matters 'on the merits of the individual case', according to the rules and values that seem relevant to a particular matter. This *ad hoc* approach creates a problem, however, that exercises lawyers in particular: it can lead to seeming disparities in the outcomes which flow from discretionary decisions made upon apparently similar evidence. This is the stuff, for example, of the persistent critiques of current sentencing practice. Rules are usually invoked by those who value consistency as the most suitable means of controlling the vagaries created by the inconsistency of individuals.

The other image is much less developed in the literature. It is one gradually emerging from the accumulated evidence of social scientific analyses of discretion. These emphasize the orderliness and rationality of discretionary behaviour and draw attention to its patterns and regularities. The chapters in this part of the book address the apparent contradiction and show how discretion can appear at once particularistic and patterned.

Some social scientists now argue for a view of discretion that sees it not as capricious, but as rather predictable behaviour. Patterns in discretionary behaviour emerge very clearly when presented in aggregated analysis, as M. P. Baumgartner shows. Her chapter is a provocative piece which assembles a formidable array of evidence from the sociological and anthropological literature and emphasizes the considerable regularities in decision outcomes. This leads the author to argue that discretion, in the sense of an individualized decision, is in fact a 'myth'. In challenging the individualistic conception of discretion she questions the extent to which it can be claimed that legal actors are exercising any real measure of choice, or are tailoring their discretion to the demands of any particular case.

Baumgartner's argument reflects the preponderance of the socio-legal evidence, and is largely based on studies of the administration of criminal justice; but it is almost certainly equally relevant to civil justice. The chapters which follow Baumgartner's then show how the apparent contradiction between individualized and predictable decision-making is possible by exploring some of the social constraints which operate upon legal actors so as to produce, in the aggregate (if not necessarily in individual cases), predictable decision outcomes, thereby creating the irony of decisions which individually may seem unpredictable—and which may, indeed, seem capricious to some— while conforming to broader, more predictable patterns.

Baumgartner starts from what she regards as the traditional conception that discretion is dictated by individual judgment and conscience, leading to a flexible justice which, though tailored to the exigencies of each case, is also responsible for a significant degree of unpredictability, sometimes leading to disparities in decision outcome in which like cases are not treated alike. On this same conception, a legal system without discretion would be rigid, but at the same time orderly, consistent, and predictable. What Baumgartner focuses on are social rather than legal rules—the 'social principles that structure discretionary decision-making'—that lead to it being substantially predictable. This amounts to a very different view of discretion from the stereotypical legal conception, one which does not see it as involving decisions freshly made on every occasion in which it is exercised, but as shaped by forces that are not to be found primarily in legal rules so much as in the social context of legal cases. A view of discretion as a product of social rather than governmental laws means that decisions are predictable by reference to sociological insights, rather than by reference to the rules of law.

The distinction between formal and sociological predictability is an important one, leading Baumgartner to argue that the social laws determining discretion lead to greater predictability of outcome than adherence to legal rules. This is because social laws are general and unchanging, whereas legal codes are ephemeral and vary from jurisdiction to jurisdiction. However, the uniformity arising from social constraints on discretion (in contrast with the uniformity associated with legal rules), is not generally considered to be legitimate. Both those who use discretion and those who are the subjects of discretionary decisions often seem to be unaware of the social rules governing its use, hence the frequency with which legal officials insist that their decisions are tailored to the unique features of every case that they handle.

The social characteristics and identities of those involved in legal decisions, including third parties, are central to how decisions are made about handling a particular case. They provide an order and logic in settings of what may seem to be unconstrained discretion. Baumgartner's chapter explores these various pervasive characteristics, showing how familiar social indicators such as age, gender, wealth, and education are related to the exercise of discretion in predictable ways. Furthermore, says Baumgartner, their influence extends to every stage in the legal process, leading to a striking uniformity in the ways in which cases are dealt with. The author painstakingly assembles a large amount of empirical evidence from a wide variety of studies which allows her to state a number of law-like social scientifically derived propositions about the relationship of social characteristics and decision outcomes.

Baumgartner concentrates her analysis upon three variables: intimacy, respectability, and social status, though, as she points out, other similar variables are also closely associated with the way in which discretion is exercised, and she might have repeated the analysis on them as well. For instance, relational distance is an important feature: in a wide variety of criminal cases, the greater degree of personal intimacy, the greater the tendency of officials to treat people leniently. This remains the case across both cases and jurisdictions, and is true both of Western industrial societies and others. Similarly, conceptions of moral respectability are also clearly linked with the ways in which discretion is exercised. Those who have previously had encounters with the criminal justice system tend to be dealt with more severely: it is well known, for example, that those who present the wrong cues to legal officials (by way of dress, demeanour, and so on) are likely to be dealt with more severely than those who exhibit deference. Social status is also important in the exercise of discretion. Low-status offenders are treated more harshly by police, prosecutors, judges, and juries than those of higher status; offenders against high-status victims are treated more harshly than those against low-status victims.

One of the most important points about Baumgartner's analysis is the way in which she is able to show that social characteristics transcend decision-making roles. That is, those who make different decisions in different segments of the criminal justice system display very similar decision-making tendencies. As a result, Baumgartner claims that, with knowledge of these sociological laws and of the relevant social characteristics of individuals embroiled in the legal process, it is not difficult to anticipate case outcomes. Officials may consciously experience the need for unique judgment in every case, she says, but their behaviour conforms to sociological laws that transcend particular incidents.

There are important implications in this analysis. The different characteristics possessed by people and the way in which they act to influence the use of discretion mean that individuals are not equal before the law. According to Baumgartner, this leads to discretion amounting in practice to discrimination, to the systematic advantaging of certain people over others. She is pessimistic about the prospects for changing this position, observing that the social constraints upon the exercise of discretion have remained largely impervious to reform by changes in legal rules or administrative policy. Indeed, Baumgartner acknowledges that discretion is inevitable in legal systems, by reason of their decentralized structures and reliance upon interpretative behaviour. As a result she sees systematic discrimination as inevitable and concludes that law will always be discriminatory to some extent, a problem she regards, with Donald Black (1989a), as ultimately capable of remedy only with an end to reliance on law itself.

Baumgartner's chapter is valuable because it presents an aggregate picture of the use of discretion, one that helps us think about discretion in a different way, and it draws attention to the cumulative consequences of individual outcomes. It is also important, however, to know how an individual decision was reached, and to understand how vagaries, deviant cases, arise, for aggregate pictures obscure detail and detail is essential in understanding the nature of legal discretion. In Baumgartner's analysis there is little room for the individual judgment or the personal whim of the legal actor, but people exercise discretion in observance of sociological laws which transcend time and jurisdiction. What uncertainty remains about the handling of cases, she says, simply marks the boundary beyond which sociological knowledge does not yet extend and points the direction for future research.

Yet we know that legal actors do make choices, and that sometimes they differ as to their preferred outcomes, a matter which Baumgartner would explain by reference to different social properties operating in each case. People, however, still complain about huge disparities in the decisions made about similar cases; decision-makers still choose and act in very different ways. Lawyers and others are very conscious that in their experience there is palpably something which they can recognize as discretion operating. In the sentencing of criminal offences (to take an example of legal decision-making in which the formal law customarily grants wide discretion to judges) there still seems to be disparity in individual decisions made about seemingly similar offenders. (It must be noted, however, that such designations are fraught with hazards—an onlooker tends to be impressed with the beguiling certitudes of the independent observer and must resist the temptation to leap to conclusions about the similarity or dissimilarity of subjects or decision outcomes without finding out whether the decision-makers themselves also saw similarity or difference. This is why it is so important to note Peter Manning's call (Chapter 8) for naturalistic research which attempts to understand the precise decision context for each individual decision.)

How can the regularities identified by Baumgartner be explained in light of this? The remaining chapters in Part II explore the patterned nature of legal discretion arising from social constraints. They have a common theme in emphasizing the social context for much individual legal decision-making provided by organizations, and contribute, in effect, to understanding and explaining the existence of the patterns identified by Baumgartner.

Martha Feldman's chapter addresses the tension between general rules and the demands of an individual case. Feldman is concerned with the social constraints on discretionary behaviour, particularly those arising from organizational life. Since a great deal of legal decision-making is carried out within an organizational context, it is important to see what can be learnt from organizational theorists, when thinking about the exercise of legal discretion.

Feldman reveals some of the social forces which shape discretion by drawing on the literature of organization theory to connect decision-making and social processes. In contrast with the implicit views of many legal writers on discretion who seem reluctant to take a holistic view of the phenomenon, but to regard it as a property of the behaviour of discrete individuals, Feldman regards decision-making as a social, rather than an individual process. Her approach, in keeping with that of many social scientists, has regard to the organizational dimensions, the systemic nature, implications, and consequences of discretionary behaviour. Her chapter accordingly explores the social control of discretionary behaviour in ways which contrast with the preference of many lawyers for resort to rules or procedural controls on decision-making.

Feldman's starting-point is a definition of discretion as the legitimate right to make choices based on one's authoritative assessment of a situation. Discretion is inevitable in bureaucratic settings because choices have to be made and legal actors cannot depend upon a structure of rules or a directive issued by a superior officer to make decisions for them. Such choices are often unsupervised. The fact that many of the decisions made by police officers or regulatory inspectors, for example, have to be made on the spot in often isolated settings in effect grants a substantial degree of autonomy to such front-line decision-makers who screen cases for access to the legal system (Hawkins and Manning, forthcoming). Often, general rules give little guidance as to how decisions have actually to be made, and it may well be impossible to write rules that will speak to all (or even some) possible contingencies. As Feldman points out, the practice of writing more detailed rules to try to counter this problem can be counter-productive (see, e.g., Long 1981; cf. Davis 1969) because the greater complexity arising from the profusion of rules ironically may actually confer greater freedom of choice upon a decision-maker.

Nevertheless, legal bureaucracies are concerned to maintain as high a degree of control over the discretionary practices of their staffs as possible (see, generally, Kaufmann 1960), and sometimes rely on output measures as a substitute for direct supervision. In the legal field, however, such indices of 'legal productivity' as the number of arrests or cases prosecuted are not necessarily a good indicator of the quality of the decisions reached, and may, indeed, serve to distort (often in undesirable ways) the manner in which discretion is actually exercised. Feldman notes that two remedies to the problem would be to select the right people (those who share the goals of the organization, and are able to make connections between their actions and the outcomes that result from them), and to motivate people by the appropriate use of sanctions and rewards to work towards the goals of the organization.

Bureaucratic discretion is both efficient and at the same time given to individual injustices, Feldman argues. Rules work well in bureaucracies possessed of limited resources when they can be employed to make decisions about a large number of cases quickly; they do this by addressing a relatively small number of relevant characteristics and defining others as irrelevant. However, such bureaucratically 'irrelevant' features may be centrally important in individual cases; to overlook them both can be a cause of injustice in the individual case and may also serve to work against or undermine the broad goals of the organization. The question then arises as to how bureaucracies can be organized so that the exercise of discretion is confined to the proper individual features in each case (what Feldman calls 'the appropriate idiosyncracies'). There are two questions here: the relevant special concerns; and how appropriate decision-making behaviour can be induced.

Feldman notes, however, that it is often difficult to say what the special features of any case are because it is can be hard to know how to attain a given end, or whether it has been attained. One of the common problems with legal decision-making is that, though the broad objective of a particular piece of legislation or a legal rule seems to be clear (for example, cleaner rivers or safer factories), there is no agreement on how to attain the goal efficiently or effectively. We want to reduce or eliminate the use of asbestos, because it is harmful, but how may this best be achieved? Nor is there agreement on the degree to which we should seek to attain legislative goals. We may agree as to the necessity of compliance, but how is it to be attained, and how much compliance is desirable, given that costs increase as legally enforceable standards get stricter? Goals in legal bureaucracies are often difficult to attain, even if problems of meaning, interpretation, and resolution of policy objectives are reasonably settled. Other problems remain. For instance, people sometimes adapt to legal requirements in unpredictable ways. New safety laws may be introduced in an effort to reduce the number of injuries and deaths arising from occupational accidents by requiring that dangerous machines be guarded in certain ways. Yet such a provision may actually achieve the opposite effect if workpeople, as a result of being impeded by guards put in place in fulfilment of legal requirements to comply, take avoiding action which turns out to be even more dangerous.

The concluding part of John Bell's discussion in Part I is concerned with questioning conventional ideas of ruled justice and conceptions of law as dispute settlement. In dealing with the latter, Bell argues that law is especially important in relation to discretion both in offering a rationale for decision and for providing good reason to those who are the subjects of the decision why they should treat decision-makers as exercising a legitimate authority. On this view law is a scheme of values which explain why the power and actions of certain individuals should be regarded as legitimate. This is one reason why such emphasis is given by lawyers to courts and to adjudication, for this is where the most public, formal, and authoritative statements of the law are to be found. Social scientists have not awarded the courts such a central place in their efforts to study the nature of discretion. They have been more concerned with its exercise in less conspicuous areas of legal life by officials whose work as legal actors brings them into direct contact with people. As Richard Lempert argues in his chapter in this part, the characteristic approach in most of the empirical studies has been not to display too great a concern for legal rules in recognition both of the social contexts which compel discretion and shape its exercise and of the fact that legal actors as a practical matter also have the discretion to ignore rules that deny them discretion. How visible their actions are and the degree to which they may be held accountable serve to restrict their discretion. Judges, as Lempert points out, are in a more visible position compared with many other legal actors, and usually subject to formal reversal.

Lempert, who is both lawyer and sociologist, takes up the nature of adjudicative discretion, the primary concern of lawyers and those who regard discretion as the capacity afforded by a structure of legal rules to choose otherwise. His chapter points to the insights that can be gained from analysis of discretionary practices over time. It poses a series of contrasts between an analytical and a behavioural perspective on the nature of discretion. One way of reading Lempert's chapter is as a critique from a behavioural point of view, of some jurisprudential conceptions of discretion.

Lempert distinguishes between discretion first as a quality of rules, secondly as a quality of behaviour, and thirdly (a phenomenological conception that has been little explored) as a sense that people have of their freedom to act. He argues that, while the first conception of discretion has been studied by lawyers in particular, social scientists may more appropriately study the latter two. Discretion as a quality of behaviour seems to be treated by social scientists as synonymous with decision-making which is not necessarily conducted by reference to rules.

Lempert studied a board dealing with public housing eviction cases in Hawaii. His chapter is, therefore, concerned with decision-making by a panel (in this case of five citizen volunteers). Taking a number of cases heard by the public housing eviction board as examples, Lempert shows that discretion assumes very different appearances and is granted different emphases when viewed either legally and analytically or behaviourally. He shows that the conception of discretion as the freedom to choose from a range of legally permissible options is in practice routinely constrained by adjudicators themselves into a relatively narrow range of options. Lempert is, however, careful to point out that both his and other studies do not address the behaviour of appellate courts, the institutions that have received most attention from jurisprudence scholars. What may limit the application of his conclusions to the appellate courts, Lempert suggests, is an interesting structural matter, namely that, since they control their dockets, appellate courts are not routinely confronted with a stream of similar cases. The latter encourages repetitive, relatively unexamined decision-making (what Lempert calls 'shallow case logics'), leading to a retreat from discretion.

In addressing the adjudicative discretion of his public housing eviction board, Lempert considers the interrelated questions of discretion as a quality of behaviour and the sense that adjudicators have of their discretion. Looking at the ways in which the decision-makers exercised discretion, and the forces that shaped it both in particular cases, and over time (using observation of hearings, interviews, and documentary research), he shows how discretion may be moulded by external forces and how it may be systematically transformed. Lempert pursues the idea, raised in Part I by Schneider, of discretion which may arise as a result of the structural position of the legal decision-maker, leading to a conception of discretion as an unreviewable exercise of judgment. According to Lempert, this is commonly found among certain kinds of legal actors, especially 'street-level bureaucrats'. A major reason for making an exercise of discretion unreviewable is recognition of the fact that a reviewing body will be unlikely to exercise better judgment. In another illustration of discretion as a function of structural position Lempert suggests that legal actors can exploit their position in the legal system by effectively framing the way in which a case is evaluated. He shows that the discretion that was effectively exercised was the result of the particular view taken of the merits of the case by the person prosecuting, who, also by virtue of the structural position accorded him by law as prosecutor, was able to influence the conduct of the proceedings by shaping the course the discussion took.

Lempert also shows that what may seem to be a simple exercise of discretion may often turn out to involve a number of determinations, each contingent upon earlier ones, some of which may not clearly be sanctioned by the written law, so much as by decision-makers' routine practices. He also points out that the salience of the decisions made varies according to the standpoint of the particular person concerned. What the two parties in his example are concerned with is how prior discretionary questions are handled (whether a violation of the lease has been found and whether the tenant will be allowed to stay). The third matter (the conditions under which the tenant will be allowed to stay) is treated as subsidiary. For the decision-makers, however, the first question (is there a violation or not?) is the crucial matter and separable from the decisions which may follow it. These are contingent upon it and tend to be treated together. Analytically, the two contingent questions are separable and seem different in terms of the distinctions drawn by Dworkin (1977*b*) between 'strong' and 'weak' discretion. But Lempert argues that from a behavioural point of view these distinctions make no sense. To emphasize the point, he notes that from an analytical perspective the decision as to whether there has been a violation of the lease may be quite difficult. Yet, from a behavioural point of view, the matter can seem simple;

indeed, in his example the matter was not even discussed and it appeared to be taken for granted that there was no violation.

Legal actors are frequently accorded wide discretion by the law, but Lempert argues that substantial leeway is not especially important in precisely those areas where it is imagined to be important, namely, in deciding actual cases. The significance of wide discretion arises in the way in which decision-makers decide how to categorize cases and determine how such groups of cases should be decided. Even though Lempert's board changed its policy very substantially over time, it never allowed itself much room for the play of discretion. The important discretion, in Lempert's view, is the discretion to make rules to constrain routine discretion. Indeed, wide discretion can add to the complexities of a case for decision-makers who frequently may simplify matters in arriving at a decision: Lempert draws attention to the irony of a case where the law granted considerable discretion as to how to dispose of the matter once a violation had been found, but where the decision-making board did not regard itself as having a great deal of choice.

The ways in which the discretion of legal actors is constrained by organizations is also the subject of particular attention in the chapter by Emerson and Paley. Their empirical focus is on one of the hidden decisions in the criminal justice process: the decision whether or not to file complaints received from the police in a public prosecutor's office. The authors seek to escape from an excessively narrow and mechanistic treatment of legal decision-making. They observe that decisions made with full discretion can be patterned and rational, although the regularities that are observable by no means come about as a result of the operation of legal rules. Many analyses of discretion dichotomize 'rules' and 'discretion', assuming the more of one, the less of the other. For Emerson and Paley such an approach is questionable because rule use involves interpretation unspecified by the rules themselves. Such interpretation is a variable process also subject to discretion: the decision as to what constitutes relevant facts or a situation to which rules apply itself implies the use of discretion. And discretion is also involved in the determination that a particular decision problem falls within a prior precedent. A major consequence of the application of the rules–discretion dichotomy is that discretion tends to be treated as a residual category, as something that is not governed by rules, with little attention being paid to the complexities of how discretionary decisions are actually made. The rules–discretion dichotomy also ignores the context in which decisions are made. For Emerson and Paley the exercise of legal discretion is a complex matter and one heavily dependent on its particular contexts.

However, Emerson and Paley are concerned that the contexts of discretionary decision-making in the real world are too often overlooked. To illustrate the significance of context they adopt the idea of the organizational horizon: the context as known and understood by decision-makers when dealing with a decision task. This notion is central to the way in which cases are handled by legal decision-makers, prompting them to make assumptions about the real meaning of matters in any case to be dealt with and leading to further assumptions about the potential behaviour of others who may subsequently encounter the case. Past context and future contingency are, however, not fixed, but matters whose relevance shifts. One implication of this argument is that decisions made in accordance with rules are not something simply done in an abstract and formal fashion, but rules are also applied in the light of their anticipated consequences. The use of the concept of horizon allows Emerson and Paley to explore aspects of the social and organizational contexts in which decisions are made, the central part played by legal institutions in shaping the character of cases, and how they are treated by decision-makers. The organizational horizon is a resource for the decision-maker helping establish the rationality of a particular exercise of discretion. The horizons of context which face a decision-maker are intimately bound up with the practical business of reaching a decision; they both arise from decision practices and facilitate the making of further decisions. These horizons are not immutable things but tend to shift, Emerson and Paley point out, as cases move through organizational processing. Changes of place and of decision-maker occur in the sequence of decisions which comprise the legal handling system and serve to change the character of the decision-makers' horizons. Knowledge of institutional practices and processes comes to involve and highlight distinctively organizational horizons.

One implication of the approach adopted by Emerson and Paley is to challenge an assumption evident in much of the research into legal decision-making. Many lawyers and social scientists take as the appropriate unit for analysis the individual case (e.g. Gottfredson and Gottfredson 1980; cf. Hawkins 1986). This poses problems. First, in some legal settings, cases are handled by decision-makers as part of a wider case-set or caseload (Emerson 1983). As Emerson and Paley point out, these actors learn at the outset that the allocation and availability of resources is of crucial significance in setting constraints for the exercise of discretion. What a decision made in one case implies for other cases can be profoundly important. That is, the routine handling of other cases forms part of the context for deciding about the present case. Secondly, cases tend to be regarded as collections of unproblematic facts which comprise the raw material for decision. But facts are assembled (sometimes artfully) by those involved in the earlier handling and processing of legal cases. To view legal cases as discrete entities comprised of unproblematic congeries of facts ignores these features. The business of creating files of material—'facts', records, accounts, assessments, and the like—often involves not only the construction, but the selective reconstruction of reality.

The authors conclude that it is not possible to analyse 'a case' independently of the immediate institutional context in which it arises and is processed, since a case is the unit in which processing work is done. As they say, the very term 'case' implies an institutional definition. A case furthermore embodies the stock of knowledge available in any decision-making setting which informs decision-makers as to the typical kinds of case or person involved, and so on. A case is, in short, understood in the legal system by reference to known institutional practices (Emerson 1983, 1991).

The chapter by Emerson and Paley also draws attention to the connection between discretion and time. It shows how an organizational horizon is comprised of two major components: an organizational history and an organizational future. The argument is not that the organizational horizon determines subsequent exercises of discretion, but that it provides an initial frame, creating presumptions about how to handle matters in reaching a subsequent decision. Such presumptions may be subsequently overturned. An organizational history informs the decision-maker how and why a case has appeared. Assumptions are made about the practical concerns of screening officials which have led to the handing-on of the case for further decision, and account is taken of the way in which these decision-makers routinely exercise their discretion. An organizational future which is known or can be anticipated involves a weighing-up of the various decisions available to the decision-maker and their implications. That these implications are also capable of anticipation draws attention to decision-makers' familiarity with the routine decision practices of those whose exercise of discretion will act subsequently on the case. The point is that, as Emerson and Paley make clear, cases are not dealt with as isolated entities, but as part of wider organizational processes and knowledge which is at once local and variable. Different sorts of knowledge become relevant as cases are handled and passed on through the system, being dealt with by different decision-makers.

The final chapter in Part II is by Peter Manning. In its critique of individualistic explanations of decision-making and its advocacy of research in the naturalist tradition it continues both the lines of thinking and the methodological approach adopted by Emerson and Paley. But where the other chapters have explained routine and repetitive uses of discretion, Manning is concerned with decision-making about untoward or critical events. It is a challenging task to explain the nature of decision-making which deals with rare events. The focus of Manning's analysis is how patterns of organizational decision-making are shaped in response to major events: disasters, scandals, and the like. These events amount to crises that prompt what Manning calls 'big-bang' decisions: decisions as to how an organization should handle or respond to such events. The chapter proposes a way of integrating thinking about the exercise of discretion at both a general and an individual level. It also addresses the nature of the social, political, and economic contexts of discretion and the ways in which they shape how discretion in an individual case is exercised. Manning's approach is to distinguish the notion of decision from the processes of reflecting and acting, arguing that a legal decision must be seen as no more than an account for a public outcome of deciding ascribed to legal actors.

In Manning's chapter frame analysis is fruitfully combined with semiotics to explore and explain the exercise of legal discretion in a regulatory organization. The chapter shifts the focus of analytical attention away from the act of deciding as such and towards the problem of understanding changes in the character of the field within which decisions are made, since, in the context of understanding how legal organizations respond to crises, Manning argues, the 'raw event' is relatively insignificant. Manning shares with Emerson and Paley a starting-point critical of case-focused legal thinking about discretion which overlooks the context in which it is exercised. Manning, however, broadens the idea of context to include the 'political–economic surround' as well as 'the organizational context, and the cognitive framing of decisions'. These are all important in developing a full and sensitive analysis of legal discretion.

The chapter may also be read as a conceptual and methodological study in which an argument is made for a particular approach to discussion of the phenomenon of discretion, one which avoids the problems of inadequate conceptualization. Manning also seeks to emphasize the importance of a naturalistic appreciation of the character of discretion, that is, one that seeks to remain true to the features and nature of the social world studied. Central to Manning's criticisms of the limitations of the individualistic conception of decision-making is a naturalistic perspective which relies on the concepts of frame, field, context, surround, and code. This approach is able to link the social world of meaning with the formal legal world. Naturalistic studies, which require finely detailed field observations, consider the constraints, hidden as well as explicit, that act upon decision-makers in the context of the various social forces that are at play in the decision-process. The behaviour of the individual decision-maker is again placed in an organizational context. The concepts of frame and field are the focal points of Manning's analysis. He describes the process of framing in some detail, showing how a structure of knowledge, values, and meanings is brought to the exercise of discretion by organizational decision-makers. The field of decisions is bounded by its surround, which consists of matters known to the decision-maker, but excluded from the frame. When an event such as a disaster occurs, the frame which indicates 'business as usual' in a legal organization such as a regulatory bureaucracy is replaced by one which indicates the existence of a 'crisis'.

Using semiotics, Manning discusses how acts and events are translated from the ordinary world into the legal world. Like other contributors he pursues a holistic view of discretion, arguing that any decision is unintelligible outside the context of the symbols and meaning with which it is associated. To explore what discretion looks like in legal organizations confronting catastrophic events, Manning takes the example of the context of decision-making about nuclear accidents. He suggests that when decision-makers confront crises the character of discretion probably changes. Manning is concerned, like Feldman, with the functions of routine in organizations, showing how it both produces order and resists change. For instance, in regulatory bureaucracies the nature of decisions made is also shaped by the fact that regulatory agencies and those regulated are part of a culture, one of whose central assumptions is that matters are 'safe' unless compelling evidence to the contrary is produced. Analysis of routine is a means by which to probe into the nature of discretion in organizational decision-making in times of crisis, for, if routines significantly inform the making of decisions in normal circumstances in organizations, then how routine operates in a time of crisis affords a better understanding of discretion.

Manning also demonstrates the connections between the critical event and the structure of the organization responding to it, suggesting that it may not matter greatly whether the organization is of a centralized or decentralized type (many legal bureaucracies, such as the police and regulatory inspectorates are of a substantially decentralized structure). Centralization of decision-making takes place naturally, a consequence in part, no doubt, of the way in which organizational actors' sense of time is affected by crisis. Manning points to the paradox that while it might be assumed that information would be processed with much greater care and refinement in time of crisis, decision-makers' sense of time shifts towards replacing the 'business as usual' attitude with 'emergency' activities.

What the public is led to understand by the term 'accident' is heavily dependent upon the capacity of regulatory and other organizations to define an event authoritatively as such. The public implications of an event are crucial to the notion of what an accident is. Indeed, it may not be until an untoward event becomes public knowledge that decision-makers treat the event as a crisis. This leads Manning to conclude that decisions are accounts ascribed by and to legal actors, and it is only after the fact that one can make systematic sense of the deciding that went on. Public accounts of decisions made in a time of crisis hinge on the issue of blameworthiness, which Manning takes to be the distinguishing characteristic that sets natural events apart from human disasters: it is this which determines that something is an 'accident'.

Manning's chapter, then, introduces the idea of the framing of decisions as a means of understanding discretion, the effect of which is to limit and to channel the exercise of discretion in certain directions and to close off other possible outcomes. He concludes that reframing may alter the scope of discretion. By adopting a 'rhetoric of emergency' those in positions of authority in organizations may recast the decision frame and grant themselves wider discretion.

4. The Myth of Discretion

M. P. BAUMGARTNER

IN the traditional view, legal officials who exercise discretion in the performance of their duties act 'according to the dictates of their own judgment and conscience, uncontrolled by the judgment and conscience of others' (H. C. Black 1968: 553). As individuals, they consider the unique features of the cases they handle and choose responses that reflect the special circumstances they encounter as well as their distinctive characters and inclinations. The result is a flexible justice in which outcomes are tailored case by case, but also one in which a significant measure of unpredictability prevails. In following their own sense of what is best in each instance, officials often treat technically similar cases in dissimilar ways. This is the inevitable consequence of allowing people to introduce their subjective moral standards into decisions about when and how to apply the law.

Behind this interpretation of discretion lies a conception of what legal systems would be like without it: more rigid, perhaps even oppressively so, but at the same time more orderly and consistent (see, e.g., Pound 1908; Breitel 1960; Lamiell 1979; Radelet 1986: ch. 5). Legal decision-making would be a more standardized affair, largely involving the mechanical matching of rules to incidents, and legal outcomes could be anticipated from knowledge of the relevant statutes and precedents alone. In this view, then, there would be a great deal of predictability in law if there were no discretion to undermine it, a predictability that gives way to idiosyncrasy, variation, and caprice to the extent that officials are empowered to follow their own instincts in disposing of their cases.

Such an understanding of discretion is both time-honored and widespread. This chapter argues, however, that it has been rendered obsolete by developments in the social sciences and is in pressing need of revision. To a large extent, it is simply inaccurate and represents a myth about how discretion operates. Evidence gathered in recent years reveals that the exercise of discretion by legal officials is in fact far from unpredictable. To the contrary, it follows clear and specifiable principles and is remarkably patterned and consistent. The decisions officials make when left to their own devices are not mysteriously rooted in the unknown peculiarities of individual cases, but can be anticipated with considerable accuracy from general formulations. They are not fashioned anew in every encounter, but arise from forces that transcend particular incidents. The constraints which govern discretionary decision-making are not to be found primarily in statutes, though, but rather in the social context of legal cases. The consciences that prompt officials to behave as they do turn out to be social instruments, responsive to the characteristics of all of the parties involved in legal encounters. While governmental laws may not structure the realm of discretion, then, social laws do, and, while discretionary outcomes may not be *formally* predictable, they are instead *sociologically* so.

Indeed, not only are discretionary outcomes highly predictable, but in an important sense they are more so than ones arising from strict adherence to statutes could ever be. Legal codes vary across jurisdictions, changing with the passage of time and geographical distance. The sociological laws that determine the use of discretion, however, are general and unchanging. They apply throughout history, in all locations, at all stages of a legal system, and in the handling of all kinds of crime. Thus, they may actually be said to impose a greater degree of regularity on legal decisions than any single code could possibly do.

Unlike uniformity associated with the strict and automatic applications of written rules, that grounded in social factors is not generally considered legitimate nor widely recognized to exist. Both the people who are vested with discretion and those who are subject to it often appear unaware of the social laws governing its use. Officials may feel and may insist that they tailor their decisions to the unique features of every case they handle, and citizens may concur. Asked to explain their actions, police officers, prosecutors, and judges may refer to a host of purely situational contingencies. Regardless of how people perceive the matter, however, social regularities are evident in what they do, and socially similar cases tend to be resolved in similar ways across all jurisdictions and stages of the legal process. It is therefore unnecessary—and possibly misleading—to invoke the conscious experiences of officials in order to account for their conduct.

Research shows that various features of the social context of a case are relevant to the way in which it is handled. Particularly well documented is the importance of the social characteristics of alleged offenders, and, to a lesser extent, those of victim-complainants (see, especially, D. Black 1976; see also Horwitz 1990). Also significant, however, are the social identities of third parties who become involved, whether as allies who side with one of the principals in a partisan fashion or as legal officials themselves. In order to explain why cases are resolved as they are, it is necessary to take all of these social influences into account. Together, they provide the order, logic, and regularity underlying the most seemingly unfettered uses of discretion.

The Predictability of Discretionary Behavior

The social identities that people bring to their legal involvements are defined by a number of characteristics. One comprehensive scheme lists five general kinds of variation that can affect legal outcomes: differences in social stratification, morphology, culture, organization, and non-legal social control (D. Black 1976). More concretely, people differ in such matters as their age, sex, wealth, education, group memberships, personal networks, ethnicity, religion, and respectability. All of these influence the exercise of discretion in predictable ways, although some have been accorded more attention than others in the theoretical and empirical literature of legal sociology. Their significance extends to every stage of the legal process, where they tend to have similar effects and to impose remarkable uniformity on the ways in which officials dispose of their cases.

OFFENDERS AND VICTIMS

Most legal matters—both criminal and civil—involve confrontations between two or more citizens which have come to official attention. Who the concerned citizens are is highly predictive of how legal personnel will handle their conflicts. Cases that are technically indistinguishable are likely to turn out very differently when the parties involved have different social backgrounds. This is not a matter of chance or whim, but rather of sociological regularity.

Relational distance

One of the most powerful and best documented of the social factors that constrain legal decision-making is 'relational distance', or the extent to which the adversaries in a case were personally tied to each other before their disagreement (see D. Black 1970; 1976: 40–8). In general, the greater their prior intimacy, the more indifferent and lenient legal officials will be. Police officers, for example, are less likely

to recognize disputes between intimates as crimes, and less likely to
arrest offenders in such matters; prosecutors are less likely to press
charges; grand juries are less likely to indict; judges and trial juries are
less likely to convict; and judges are less likely to sentence harshly.

What is particularly striking in the present context is that intimacy
has the same effect on the decision-making of people who occupy very
different places in the legal system and who cope with very different
sorts of job demands. It operates in the reaction to very different kinds
of offense, with different definitional and evidentiary standards. And
it operates not just in modern industrial societies, but in all others,
both historical and contemporary, even though the conscious decision-
making calculus of people in these widely divergent places may well
not be the same.

Examples drawn from studies that have explored the effects of
intimacy illustrate the range of contexts across which the principle
applies. An investigation of legal responses to rape in Boston, for
instance, shows that the prior relationship existing between a rapist
and his victim is highly predictive of the reactions of diverse people,
including police officers, medical personnel, prosecutors, and judges.
Thus, the police define some rape cases as 'strong' and others as
'weak', and show a great deal more enthusiasm for pursuing the
former (Holmstrom and Burgess 1983: 41). To them, a case is strong
when the offender is a stranger. Hospital personnel who treat rape
victims similarly distinguish 'legitimate' cases from others, and, for
them as well, a prior relationship between the parties affects the
validity of the charge. One doctor flatly announced that 'any girl who
knows the guy isn't raped' (ibid.: 73). At the prosecutorial level, a
previous tie between victim and assailant is seen as a serious 'problem'
with a case; the stronger the tie, the worse the problem. In one case, a
trial was already underway when 'it came out that the girls [including
the victim] had not just happened to meet the defendants [as the
prosecutor had thought]. They had made arrangements ahead of
time to meet them. The DA reacted strongly . . . He said, "It's an out-
and-out case of fornication." ' (ibid.: 147). Charges against one of the
defendants were accordingly dismissed. However, the other defendant
had already pleaded guilty to abuse of a female child (since the victim
was 15). The prosecutor then 'argued in court on [his] behalf and
recommended probation', a recommendation immediately accepted
by the judge. More generally, prosecutors and defense attorneys often
struggle in court over how to characterize the prior connection

between victims and assailants; prosecutors seek to establish distance, defense attorneys intimacy, doing so because they recognize the significance of this issue for the outcome of their cases (ibid.: 176–7; 202–4). Although in the Boston study virtually all charges between acquaintances dropped out of the legal arena long before adjudication, other investigations indicate that who wins these struggles can determine trial verdicts. One survey of members of the general public—the sorts of people who sit on juries—presented the subjects with several vignettes and asked whether the sexual assaults described in them constituted rapes: 'If any relationship is known to exist between the victim and the accused, no matter how casual, the proportion of those who consider the event rape drops to less than 50 per cent' (Klemmack and Klemmack 1976: 144). Presumably, police officers, physicians, prosecutors, and members of the general public operate under different constraints and take different factors into account in their decision-making. Furthermore, each group encompasses a large number of individuals and is disparate in many ways. Even so, the same social principle predicts how all these people react to rape and underlies a great deal of uniformity in their behavior.

Homicide is another crime for which people who know their victims are treated more leniently than strangers. It is, in its own way, a particularly instructive one, since legal officials often explain their reluctance to punish intimate offenders by arguing that victims in these cases are unlikely to co-operate with authorities in securing convictions and so may waste any effort expended on their behalf. Another reason sometimes given is that formal legal proceedings can jeopardize the possibility of reconciliation between the parties, something seen as a greater loss if the pre-existent bond has been close. Where homicide is concerned, however, neither of these claims has much relevance. Victims are in no position to offer or refuse their co-operation or to change their minds about pressing charges, nor do they have any future relationship with their killers to preserve. None the less, the relational distance between the parties predicts how discretion is exercised in homicide cases just as powerfully as in matters of other kinds.

A study of homicide dispositions in Houston, Texas, reveals just how significant the tie between murderer and victim is (Lundsgaarde 1977). Police officers, prosecutors, grand juries, trial juries, and judges all treat homicides between intimates as considerably less serious matters than ones between strangers. In the processing of a sample of two hundred murders that occurred in 1969, the cumulative effect of decisions favoring individuals known to their victims is striking: only a minority of those who killed relatives (39 per cent) suffered any legal penalty at all for what they did, compared to 47 per cent of those who killed associates and 64 per cent of those who killed strangers. The single most likely outcome in familial homicides was for either prosecutor or grand jury to decline to take further action against the murderer. (When the offender was a stranger, the typical resolution was a prison sentence.) Cases involving relatives that did go to trial more often resulted in acquittal than those involving strangers, and, when there were convictions, punishments tended to be more lenient. People who killed a family member were more often given probation and less often sent to prison than other murderers. If incarcerated, they were generally sent away for a shorter term: the average prison sentence imposed on relatives was eight years, on friends and associates ten years, and on strangers twenty-eight years. Furthermore, 9 per cent of the people who killed strangers were condemned to death, but not one of those who killed family members or friends suffered the same fate.

It is worth noting that legal officials show comparative leniency toward people who murder their relatives even in technically quite serious cases. Thus, the Houston sample included one instance in which a woman who was angry with her husband because he would not leave a bar with her went off, got a pistol, came back, and shot the man as he sat drinking. Despite the presence of witnesses, the defendant was found not guilty after trial. Another woman shot her sleeping husband in the aftermath of an earlier quarrel. She was convicted and sentenced to probation for three years. Neither of these murderers was in immediate fear for her own safety at the time of the crime, and both apparently acted with a great deal of intentionality. Yet neither of them was punished severely by the standards of the treatment typically accorded those who kill police officers or gas-station attendants (ibid.: 188–9).

Wherever offenders and victims vary in the strength of their prior relationship, the exercise of discretion tends to vary accordingly. A recent study followed a sample of felony arrests through the New York criminal justice system and found that intimacy between defendants and victims predicted outcomes not only in rape and homicide cases, but also in those involving assault, robbery, burglary, grand larceny, and auto theft (Vera Institute of Justice 1981). Victims who knew offenders often chose not to testify against them, usually to the great relief of legal officials, but, even when they were eager to proceed, the authorities were not: 'Judges and prosecutors, and in some instances police officers, were outspoken in their reluctance to prosecute as full-scale felonies some cases that erupted from quarrels between friends or lovers' (ibid.: 135). In general, the study revealed a dual system of justice, in which officials of various kinds use their discretion to distinguish between 'real' and 'technical' crimes:

Serious stranger-to-stranger felonies—'real felonies' in the language of the study—are treated seriously and convictions result in stiff sentences; in contrast, 'technical felonies' among family, friends, and lovers are usually downgraded, at times leading to dismissal and often resulting in reduced charges and light sentences. (Feeley 1983: p. xiii)

A comparative unwillingness to take aggressive action against intimate offenders is evident throughout the system, in the decisions of numerous officials confronting a wide variety of crimes.

Many other studies concur in finding legal agents reluctant to proceed against intimate offenders. These include studies of the police (e.g. D. Black 1970, 1971, 1980; D. A. Smith and Visher 1981), prosecutors (e.g. F. Miller 1970; Hall 1975: 318; Stanko 1981–82: 234–5), court clerks (Yngvesson 1988), and judges (e.g. Feeley 1979: 132, 161–2), as they process different kinds of offenses in diverse jurisdictions. Furthermore, the effects of relational distance are not restricted to contemporary settings. In sixteenth-century Spain, for example, a governing body in Castile asked the king to order that 'all lawsuits between relatives within the fourth degree be settled and determined through compromise arbitration' and thus removed from the courts altogether (Kagan 1981: 19). In eighteenth-century colonial New York, crimes of interpersonal violence—which arose mostly from personal disagreements between friends, neighbors, and other acquaintances—were the least likely of all frequent crimes to result in formal legal outcomes (Greenberg 1974: 96). They had low rates of both conviction and acquittal; many simply disappeared from the system. Legal officials pursued them less aggressively than cases involving theft, public disorder, or contempt of authority, in which intimacy was less likely to be a confounding factor (ibid.). A similar tendency to treat property offenses more harshly than those of interpersonal violence—where it appears that the latter involved close acquaintances more often than the former—has been documented for the nineteenth-century American south (Ayers 1984: 75, 111). It is also evident in the practices of nineteenth- and early twentieth-century French juries, which more often convicted property offenders than violent ones, as well as individuals who murdered strangers more often than those who killed intimates (Donovan 1981). Despite the many obvious differences that distinguished the legal officials of these various times and places, then, all consistently and predictably exercised their discretion to sanction offending strangers more often than offending intimates.

Respectability

Other social factors also predict the outcome of discretionary decisions. One of the most significant of these is the moral respectability of the citizens whose cases come to the attention of legal officials (D. Black, 1976: ch. 6). People who bring unblemished reputations to their encounters with law generally fare better than those who are already morally stigmatized, whether they appear as complainants or defendants. As with relational distance, this pattern applies to all stages of the legal process and is evident in the discretionary decisions of many different kinds of people operating under diverse circumstances.

Few studies have considered simultaneously the effects of victim and offender respectability on legal outcomes, although both are known to be substantial. Better documented is the importance of the offender's reputation. Officials of all kinds take aggressive action more often against accused individuals who have previously been in trouble with the law, for example, than against those who are first-time violators. Thus, the police are more likely to arrest people with prior records, when they know about them, and to pursue the cases against them vigorously (see, e.g., Werthman and Piliavin 1967: 72–3; Cicourel 1968; Spradley 1970: 176–80; Holmstrom and Burgess 1983: 43). One study concluded that 'nothing makes [the police] more enthusiastic about a case than to find out the assailant has other charges against him or a prison record' (Holmstrom and Burgess 1983: 43). Another study found that the police are sensitive not only to the existence of a prior record but to the precise nature of the earlier misbehavior. They distinguish various categories of offenders, including 'fresh meat' (first-time violators), 'dirt bags' (continual petty thieves and fighters), 'pukes' (those who have served prison time for felonies), and 'animals' (those believed to lack all morals and to be indiscriminately violent). As the seriousness of a citizen's previous misconduct goes up in police eyes, so does the importance of vigorous legal control (Timmer 1981). Similarly, research has found that pollution-control officers more often proceed formally against repeat violators than against firms with no past history of environmental offenses: the former are deemed more blameworthy than the latter (Hawkins 1984: 164–6). Criminal prosecutors are also more likely to bring serious charges against repeat offenders (see, e.g., Swigert and Farrell 1976; Mather 1979; Myers and Hagan 1979), and judges and juries are more likely to convict them and to sentence them harshly (see, e.g., Tiffany, Avichai, and Peters 1975; Pope 1978; Feeley 1979: 132, 142; Vera Institute of Justice 1981). Finally, parole boards are less likely to award early release from prison to inmates with extensive records or a history of misconduct while incarcerated (Hawkins 1983).

Even without formal prior records, citizens may appear unrespectable and suffer legal disabilities as a result. Offenders whose clothing, hair-style, and posture strike officials as unsavory, for example, as well as those generally known to be trouble-makers, are more often subjected to aggressive legal action (see, e.g., Werthman and Piliavin 1967; Feeley 1979: 163). Those who show disrespect or contempt for authority—most importantly, by being rude and unco-operative toward legal officials themselves—are more vulnerable than those who display deference (see, e.g., Piliavin and Briar 1964; LaFave 1965: 146–7; Cicourel 1968; D. Black 1971; Manning 1977: 242–6; D. Black 1980: 169–72; Hawkins 1984: 166–8; Smith and Klein 1984). Any moral stigma, such as that associated with drug addiction, alcoholism, or homosexuality, increases the likely strength of the legal reaction toward offenders. On the other hand, officials appear more reluctant to proceed formally against people known to have engaged in especially meritorious behavior in the past, including those with a history of great personal sacrifice or those with outstanding records of military or community service (see, e.g., Maynard 1982; Holmstrom and Burgess 1983: 199).

Just as important in predicting the exercise of discretion is the respectability of the victims who turn to the law for help. Officials at every stage of the criminal process proceed more vigorously against those who offend respectable victims than against those accused by the morally compromised. The police, for example, are very sensitive to whether victims have 'clean hands'; when they do not, and are themselves engaged in crime at the time of their victimization, the police are reluctant to record their complaints or to arrest the people who have offended them (LaFave 1965: 124). A concern with the respectability of victims is evident across a wide variety of offense types. In regard to domestic assault, one observational study of the police recorded instances in which officers lost interest in a victim upon learning that she had just been released from a mental hospital, mocked a homosexual complainant by affecting a lisp, and were 'extremely abusive' toward a victim who was living with a man outside of matrimony, 'openly criticizing her marital status' (D. Black 1980: 173, 115–16). In another matter, they defined a theft as the victim's just deserts for his own misconduct:

A black man who had been in bed with a married woman rushed out the back door when the woman's husband came home unexpectedly, only to find that her children had removed the tools from his truck while he was in the house. When the man complained to the police . . . they told him that 'this was the price he had to pay for his indiscretion'. (ibid.: 1980: 173)

The police also assess the respectability of rape victims along several dimensions and respond accordingly. They pursue rapists less vigorously when their victims are drunk at the time of the crime, have psychiatric histories, have been hitchhiking, or are known to be sexually experienced although unmarried. They are least likely to take action when the victims are prostitutes (Holmstrom and Burgess 1983: 42–3). In one instance noted during a study of rape dispositions, two officers were assigned to a case. The older of the two, an eleven-year veteran sergeant, was suspicious of the victim from the start, but the younger, a rookie, was highly sympathetic and supportive. During the trial, the victim admitted that she had met the offenders as a prostitute and had complained when they took back at gunpoint the money they had given her:

Hearing this testimony, the seasoned veteran got a now-we-really-know look on his face. The effect on the younger officer was more dramatic. He was visibly upset as she testified and said, 'Oh no.' It was clear that her words had changed his feelings. His sympathies had gone over to the other side. (Holmstrom and Burgess 1983: 49–50)

The respectability of the victim also affects the willingness of police officers to proceed formally even in the case of homicide: 'If the police find the body of a skid-row vagrant and the circumstances indicate that he died violently, such as by a beating or stabbing, the routine classification of the case in at least one American city is "death by misadventure"' (D. Black 1989*a*: 6–7) Other legal officials are governed by the same social principle. Prosecutors, like police officers, treat offenses against respectable victims as more serious, and do so for all sorts of crime. A study of district attorneys has concluded that 'the character and credibility of the victim is a key factor in determining prosecutorial strategies, one at least as important as "objective" evidence about the crime or characteristics of the defendant' (Stanko 1981–2: 226). Prosecutors are less likely to proceed aggressively when the victim is a prostitute or a pimp, a homosexual, or an alcoholic. In one case observed during this investigation, district attorneys showed a disinclination to prosecute an attempted murder case against members of a Chinese gang who had fired shots at other members in an internecine dispute. They described one of the victims as a 'complainant who's got a rap sheet all over the place' and who would be 'torn to pieces' on the witness stand (ibid.: 235–6). In another instance, a district attorney, after speaking to the victims, decided to bring first-degree robbery charges against three men who had taken $80 from a young couple at knifepoint: 'About two minutes after the case was sent to the typist, the male complainant returned to the DA and stated that he was in the area to buy heroin [at the time of the robbery]. He did not want his girlfriend to know about the buy. The DA recalled the papers and reduced the charge to a misdemeanor' (ibid.: 236–7). Other studies have documented the same pattern (see, e.g., Williams 1976; Holmstrom and Burgess 1983: 144).

Further along in the criminal process, judges and jurors also favor victims of greater respectability. Those who offend people with good reputations are more likely to be convicted (see, e.g., Reskin and Visher 1986). In rape cases, conviction occurs more often when the victim is either sexually inexperienced or involved in a monogamous relationship, and when she is not 'discredited in some way (through family problems, welfare, alcohol or drug use, prison record, or psychiatric history)' (Holmstrom and Burgess 1983: 249–50). In homicide cases, judges and jurors often appear to agree with a defense attorney who was heard to remark that 'no property needs stealing but a lot of people need killing'—at least in regard to the second of his contentions (Lundsgaarde 1977: 42). Another attorney has elaborated: 'The best defense in a murder case is the fact that the deceased should have been killed regardless of how it happened'; in a particularly successful instance, this attorney claimed, 'The jury was ready to dig up the deceased and shoot him all over again' (Percy Foreman, quoted in M. Smith 1966). A recent study confirmed that

a victim's character, reputation, personal disposition, or personality can be resurrected for presentation before a judge and jury . . . A victim characterized as dumb, illiterate, and quarrelsome is unlikely to find much sympathy from jurors who are instructed that the victim's character may be considered an important factor in reducing the penalty for the convicted murderer. (Lundsgaarde 1977: 154)

One especially informative study examined the reactions of simulated jurors to a case of negligent homicide resulting from drunken driving (Landy and Aronson 1969). Research subjects were given descriptions of the crime that varied in how they portrayed both the victims and the offenders, although the technical elements were always the same. Sometimes the victims were 'attractive' and sometimes 'unattractive'; the dependants might be 'attractive', 'unattractive', or 'neutral'. An attractive victim, for example, was a noted architect active in community service who, at the time of his death, 'was on his way to the Lincoln Orphanage, of which he was a founding member, with Christmas gifts'. An unattractive victim was 'a notorious gangster . . . best known for his alleged responsibility in the Riverview massacre of five men . . . He had been out of jail on bond, awaiting trial on a double indictment of mail fraud and income tax evasion.' More attractive defendants were similarly more respectable, and unattractive ones less so. The subjects were asked to specify an appropriate term of imprisonment for the defendants. It was found that 'both the character of the defendant and the character of the victim are important variables in the severity of the sentence imposed' (ibid.: 151). The sentence was most severe where unattractive defendants were coupled with attractive victims (ibid.: 150).

Like relational distance, respectability predicts legal outcomes not just in contemporary settings but in others as well. In the church courts of fifteenth-century London, for example, 'canon law had decreed that a person could be accused by ill fame alone; and a person's ill fame . . . took on the garb of a prosecutor' (Wunderli 1981: 40). Early European anti-vagrancy laws explicitly mandated progressively more severe sanctions for repeat offenders (Chambliss 1964). In eighteenth-century England, jurors assessed the character and reputation of both defendants and complainants in rendering their verdicts; unrespectable offenders were treated more harshly, as were those who injured respectable victims. The most severe outcome—the death sentence—was far more likely for 'old offenders' with bad reputations (Beattie 1986: 126, 448; see also Hay 1975). Following their condemnation, convicted persons might petition for a pardon or a commutation of their sentence, and at this stage too their respectability mattered (see Hay 1975: 44–5). In the colony of New York during the same historical period, the courts similarly 'tended to punish second-time offenders far more harshly than those making their initial appearance at the bar' (Greenberg 1974: 210). The judges were also interested in the informal reputations of the citizens whose cases they handled, apart from any previous contact with the law. A person known as an upstanding citizen was likely to be treated leniently when accused of a crime, while someone who, like one defendant, was known as 'a very Low Notorious Wicked Woman of Evil Life Conversation and Behavior' was likely to be treated with considerable severity (ibid.: 113). As in England, capital punishment was a special risk for the chronically deviant, people who, like Mary Daily, had already been accused in court on five previous occasions when she was sentenced to hang for burglary in 1771 (ibid.: 116–17). A final example of the effects of reputation can be found among the Comanche Indians of North America, a highly militaristic people who 'tended to attribute moral rightness to the braver man' (Hoebel 1940: 194). In the early days of reservation life after their defeat by Euro-Americans, these previously stateless people began to use adjudication to handle offenses for the first time, applying traditional standards in a new context. In one case, a dispute over land ownership was resolved when the Comanche judge asked about the war records of the opposing parties. Informed that one man had rescued a felled comrade in the face of enemy fire, while the other had no such bravery to report, he promptly decided in favor of the former (ibid.).

Respectability, then, determines how officials exercise discretion in a wide variety of contexts. It predicts the behavior of police officers, prosecutors, judges, and juries in contemporary society, as well as the behavior of their counterparts in other settings. It affects the processing of people accused of homicide, assault, rape, theft, and many other offenses. It has a similar effect on decision-makers who are quite different from one another. Along with relational distance and other social variables, it shapes legal outcomes in highly predictable ways.

Social status

Yet another factor that determines how discretion is exercised is the social status of the parties involved in legal encounters (see D. Black 1976: ch. 2; see also Chambliss and Seidman 1971; Horwitz 1990). Wealth and prominence have a consistent and patterned effect on official decision-making: offenses against high-status victims result in more extensive legal intervention and more severe sanctions than offenses against people of low social standing, and, when the status of victims is held constant, lower-ranking offenders are treated more harshly than higher-ranking ones. The overall result is that low-status people who offend high-status people face the greatest legal severity, followed in order by high-status people who offend other high-status people, low-status people who offend other low-status people, and high status people who offend status inferiors (D. Black 1976: 28–9). This effect may be obscured in studies which fail to consider the relative status of both victim and offender; such research may find no evidence of status differences in the disposition of cases or may even suggest that high-status defendants are at a disadvantage. When the overall status configuration of a case is taken into account, however, the pattern just described becomes apparent and can be documented in decisions occurring at different stages of the legal system, in the processing of different kinds of offense, and in different societies.

In the contemporary United States, the effects of social status are evident throughout the legal process, beginning with the discretionary decisions of police officers. Thus, studies have found that the police are generally more sympathetic to white and middle-class victims than they are to victims who are black or lower class. They more often comply with the wishes of higher-status complainants (see D. Black 1980: 136; Smith and Klein 1984), write up more offenses against them as crimes (see D. Black 1970), and make more arrests on their behalf (see D. A. Smith, Visher, and Davidson 1984). They also take more time and trouble with their problems in other ways. In responding to domestic disputes, for instance, they are more likely to engage in active mediation when the parties are white and middle class than when they are black and poor. In the latter case, the police 'are more inclined to stand by passively, doing little or nothing of a positive nature' (D. Black 1980: 136; see also ibid.: 142–7). Domestic violence involving high-status people is accordingly more likely to elicit helping behavior from the police, whereas the same violence among poor blacks is more often dismissed as unimportant—even, as one investigator found, as simply a custom of black neighborhoods, 'like shooting craps' (Banton 1964: 173).

Where there are no victims involved, the exercise of police discretion can be predicted from knowledge of offender characteristics alone. Traffic enforcement is one kind of police work in which complainants rarely play a role, and in this context differences among drivers by themselves affect whether or not officers decide to write tickets or take other formal action. Black and lower-class drivers are at greater risk in this regard than higher-status people are, both when it comes to receiving tickets (D. Black 1980: 32–6) and to being arrested for drunken driving (Hollinger 1984). Similarly, the police proceed more aggressively against younger drivers than older ones. One study found that, 'Even when no particular violation can be charged against a teenager, Massachusetts policemen frequently write traffic tickets . . . Registry files contain many tickets citing no violation but simply stating "improper operator", "drag racing", "obscene language", "noisy", or "driving to a riot"' (Gardiner 1969: 151).

Social status predicts the decisions not only of rank-and-file patrol officers but of detectives as well, who typically devote more investigative effort to crimes involving high-status victims. Thus, burglaries committed against affluent suburbanites are seen as more serious and investigated more vigorously than ones that take place in poor urban neighborhoods (Sanders 1977: 95–6). On the other hand, when the victims are poor and black, detectives more often question whether an offense has occurred at all and, in any event, tend to invest less in solving the crime (see Skolnick 1966: 174–5; Black 1980: 14–18). To the extent that detectives fail to investigate victimizations against the poor, they grant effective pardons to those who commit them.

Like the police, prosecutors too respond to social status and exercise their discretion accordingly. Thus, they typically take more aggressive action on behalf of high-status victims, prosecuting those who offend them more often and under more serious charges. Cases are seen to possess more 'prosecutive merit' when victims are 'older, white, male, and employed' (Myers and Hagan 1979: 448). Victims characterized by 'residence in a good neighborhood' and 'a respectable job or occupation' are also advantaged in this respect (Stanko 1981–2: 230). Offenses against them are defined as more serious. In one case recorded during a study of prosecution in the city of New York, a district attorney decided to press first-degree robbery charges against a purse-snatcher, identifying a tree branch as the dangerous weapon technically necessary to justify his action. He then remarked, 'I only wrote up one rob[bery] before with a tree branch [as a weapon] and that was because the victim was John F. Kennedy Jr. These are the cases that try themselves' (ibid.: 231). When a victim lacks social standing, however, prosecutors are more likely to see problems with the case. In another study, a prosecutor explained to an investigator that a rape of a black woman by several black men was 'a typical Roxbury rape'—Roxbury is a poor black neighborhood in Boston—and that 'you can't get a conviction [with blacks] even if you have a good case' (Holmstrom and Burgess 1983: 144). Offenses against poor blacks seem to strike prosecutors as lesser threats to social order and are accordingly prosecuted less vigorously (LaFree 1980).

When the social status of the victim is held constant, that of the offender predicts prosecutorial decision-making. All else the same, low-status offenders are more likely to be charged in the first place, and to be charged on more numerous and more serious counts, than higher-status persons are. This creates special risks for blacks (see Petersilia 1985), the unemployed (see, e.g., Boris 1979), and members of other economically disadvantaged groups.

Judges and juries also proceed more aggressively against defendants of lower status and against those who offend higher-status victims. They are more likely to convict such people and, having done so, to sentence them harshly. A recent study of the disposition of rape cases in Boston found, for example, that conviction was nearly six times more frequent in cases of inter-racial rape (virtually all of which involved black offenders and white victims) than in cases of intra-racial rape. Considering only the race of the victim, the researchers discovered that white victims were over four times more likely than black victims to see their assailants convicted (Holmstrom and Burgess 1983: 247–9). More generally, related research has shown that high-status people of all kinds tend to deliver courtroom testimony in a linguistic style different from that employed by lower-status people, and that this style makes what they say seem more credible (O'Barr 1982). This translates into a special advantage for high-status people confronted by lower-status adversaries, and they are accordingly more likely to win their cases.

At the sentencing stage, the relative social status of the parties remains an important predictor of outcomes. The most severe sentences are meted out to low-status people who offend those of high status; the least severe sentences are awarded under the opposite social conditions. This pattern is best documented for the imposition of the death penalty, a particularly harsh and dramatic punishment that has attracted much public and scholarly attention. In the contemporary United States, where blacks are economically disadvantaged relative to whites, capital punishment is chosen most often for blacks who kill whites, and then, in decreasing order, for whites who kill whites, blacks who kill blacks, and whites who kill blacks (see Bowers and Pierce 1980). The differences in magnitude are great. A study of death sentences in four US states has found, for example, that, in the least discriminatory of the four, blacks who kill whites are nearly fifteen times more likely to receive the death penalty than blacks who kill blacks; in the most discriminatory state, blacks who kill whites are almost ninety times more likely to be sentenced to die (data from Bowers and Pierce 1980, calculated in D. Black 1989a: 10). At the same time, white killers of blacks are virtually never condemned to death (Bowers and Pierce 1980). The pattern has apparently existed for as long as records have been kept (see Garfinkel 1949; Green 1964).

In the past, US judges and juries used capital punishment as a response to rape as well as to homicide, and, when they did so, race had the same effect on the handling of both offense types. One study has found, for example, that in Florida, between 1940 and 1964, not a single white rapist of a black woman was sentenced to die, whereas 54 per cent of blacks convicted of raping white women received the death penalty (Florida Civil Liberties Union 1964). While rapists are no longer executed in the United States, social status continues to affect their sentencing. Blacks who rape whites are still punished more severely than other rapists (LaFree 1980).

Further evidence of the role of status comes from studies of non-capital sentencing. Although most such investigations ignore the social identity of the victim and are thus of limited value, others confirm that the social status of the parties is an important predictor of sentencing decisions. The length of prison terms in Texas, for example, appears sensitive to the race of both victim and offender. For primarily intra-racial crimes like homicide and assault, blacks receive shorter sentences than whites. This is consistent with the principle that crimes involving high-status offenders and high-status victims are punished more severely than those involving two low-status people. For crimes such as burglary that more often cross racial lines, however, sentences are longer for black offenders (Bullock 1961). Virtually the same patterns have been found in sentencing behavior in Georgia. There, too, blacks receive shorter prison terms for assaults (which usually involve black victims) and longer ones for robberies (in which the victims are commonly white) (Myers and Talarico 1986).

Like intimacy and respectability, social status affects the exercise of discretion not only at various stages of the legal system and in the handling of a diversity of offenses, but also across societies from different parts of the world and different historical periods. In general, the more stratified a society is, the more extreme the inequities in its legal decision-making. This, in such highly unequal settings as the empires of ancient Rome, Manchu China, Inca Peru, and Aztec Mexico, low-status people faced particularly great difficulties in confronting more privileged adversaries (see, respectively, Garnsey 1968; van der Sprenkel 1962; Moore 1958; Offner 1983). In Rome, officials were expected to deny low-status people the right to bring legal actions against status superiors and to favor the party of higher rank in cases that did come to trial. In matters of personal injury, for example, officials were empowered to convert an ordinary accusation into one for 'grave' injury, with correspondingly greater penalties; in practice, they did this when lower-status people harmed their status superiors—when plebeians injured their masters, and when children injured their parents (Garnsey 1968: 150–3). In Manchu China and Inca Peru, violence against higher-status people was also punished more aggressively than violence against equals or status inferiors (van der Sprenkel 1962: 27; Moore 1958: 82).

Social status had a similar effect on the discretionary decision-making of officials in colonial New England. In seventeenth-century New Haven, for example, trial outcomes were highly sensitive to the relative social standing of complainants and offenders. In criminal matters, convictions were especially likely when high-status victims accused low-status defendants. For cases of this kind heard between 1639 and 1665, the conviction rate was 99 per cent. Those of lower status were also sentenced more harshly after being found guilty, the more so the lower in rank they were (Baumgartner 1978: 166–70).

A century and a half later in South Carolina, officials used their discretion in similar ways. In this setting, black slaves were prosecuted primarily for crimes against whites and only rarely for crimes against fellow blacks: 'violence among slaves was slightly regarded', and 'whites . . . could not conceptualize the rape of a slave by a fellow slave' (Hindus 1980: 143, 144). Blacks were convicted at twice the rate of whites and were punished more severely, which is not surprising in light of the fact that they almost always faced higher-status adversaries. The extreme disadvantage of blacks accused by whites is revealed in the following instances:

One slave was convicted of rape despite the fact that the court described the alleged victim as an imbecile incapable of reasoning. Her testimony would not have been admitted had the defendant been white. . . . One slave was ordered whipped 'because under no circumstances a Negro ought to raise a stick at a white person'. . . . What is intriguing about the order of punishment was that the court had explicitly declared the charge 'not proven', yet had ordered the whipping anyway! Another slave was acquitted of theft, then given eighteen lashes for taking 'a liberty a Negro ought not to take'. (ibid.: 152, 153–4)

Nineteenth-century Trinidad provides additional illustrations of the ways in which social status affects legal discretion. In this setting as in others, offenses against status superiors were treated considerably more harshly than those against equals or subordinates. In fact, low-status people were punished more severely for offending élites by interfering with their property or showing 'a disinclination to work' than for committing acts of violence against their peers (Trotman 1986: 138). At the same time, members of low-status groups 'could be whipped, kicked, and beaten to death with impunity' by higher-status offenders: 'There was no recourse to the law, since the courts invariably released the aggressor with ridiculous fines or warnings' (ibid.: 140). In one representative case, an indentured servant named Sahti

was admitted to the hospital suffering from the effects of a beating she had received from F. Henderson, the son of the estate proprietor. Sahti died fourteen days after the assault, and the postmortem examination revealed cerebral hemorrhage. . . . Yet the coroner's verdict was death from natural causes, and the charge of manslaughter against Henderson was withdrawn. (ibid.: 140)

Still further examples from other societies could be given, since the relationship between law and social status has been well documented. The general principle is always the same, however: legal officials respond differently to citizens of different status, using their discretion in patterned and predictable ways. This applies across settings separated from one another by geography and history, across stages of the legal system, and across categories of offense. Like intimacy and respectability, social status determines how discretion is exercised wherever discretion exists. The more one knows about the rank of parties embroiled in a legal confrontation anywhere, the less mystery there is about how officials will decide the case.

Intimacy, respectability, and status are not the only characteristics of offenders and victims that predict how discretion is exercised. Other things matter, too, such as the degree to which the parties are integrated into their communities, the number and kind of groups to which they belong, whether or not either is a formal organization, the ethnicity of the parties, their religious affiliation, and numerous additional factors (see, especially, D. Black 1976). Enough has been said, however, to show how legal decision-making is always sensitive to the identities of the people whose cases are being processed, and sensitive in ways that are similar across settings. It is not just the original victims and offenders, though, who become involved in legal matters. So do supporters (often) and legal officials (always), and the social characteristics of these people also determine the exercise of discretion.

SUPPORTERS

Legal decision-making is influenced not only by the social characteristics of the parties to a case, but also by those of supporters who come to their assistance. Supporters bring their own sociological advantages and liabilities with them when they take the side of a person caught up in a legal matter. The more involved they are, the more their strengths and weaknesses help shape discretionary legal outcomes. In general, the social characteristics that increase chances for legal victory in a complainant or defendant are desirable in an ally, making that individual's support more valuable. Someone likely to lose a case as a principal, on the other hand, makes a less effective supporter; in extreme cases, such a person may actually do more harm than good to the cause he or she seeks to champion.

When a legal dispute is viewed as a confrontation not just between two individuals but rather between two sides, the ability to predict how officials will react is strengthened and the extent of social regularity in official decision-making is further revealed. In sufficient numbers and given sufficient influence, supporters can transform a case from a sociologically weak one to one that is sociologically strong;

this dynamic accounts for many seemingly anomalous decisions in which less-advantaged citizens prevail over more-advantaged ones, doing so because the support they receive more than compensates for their personal vulnerability. An absence of allies, or the socially questionable characteristics of those who do come forward, have the opposite transformative effect. Officials, then, are sensitive to the overall social configuration of a case, balancing the characteristics of supporters on one side against those of supporters on the other, and measuring the principals in the light of the assistance they can generate.

As with all of the social factors that constrain discretionary decision-making, so with the characteristics of supporters: they have the same effects across societies, offense types, and stages of the legal process. In all contexts, supporters of high rank and unblemished reputation are strong legal assets, the more numerous the better. Those of low standing and compromised respectability contribute much less and may even become handicaps. An inability to attract support can also weaken a case, particularly if there is a great deal of support on the other side. All kinds of officials in all kinds of places defer to strong and prestigious sponsorship of a citizen's cause.

In ancient Rome, to provide one illustration, the social identities of a person's witnesses were of the greatest importance to his or her case. Sources from the time indicate that 'where witnesses were called, the judge reckoned their social position and character as relevant as the quality of their evidence . . . a witness with *dignitas, existimatio* and *auctoritas* was especially acceptable. These are three upper-class virtues: social standing, good reputation, and prestige' (Garnsey 1968: 152). Even a low-status person confronting a higher-status adversary might overcome his or her considerable disadvantage if fortunate enough to attract the assistance of a powerful patron.

In the ecclesiastical courts of medieval England, the right kind of support was also very helpful. The cases against many defendants there were dismissed outright by the judges hearing them upon the request of a third party such as a 'proctor/lawyer, a curate, a friend, a spouse, an alderman, or some person with influence at court' (Wunderli 1981: 44). In one instance, 'Elizabeth Crow . . . was dismissed from court without further trial at the request of her alderman, Sir Thomas Wyndowt' (ibid.: 44). In another, a notorious prostitute boasted of having influential friends at court who could 'fix' any case against her (ibid.: 45).

Some centuries later, in the secular courts of seventeenth- and eighteenth-century England, respectable and high-status support continued to confer a legal advantage. The social characteristics of principals and witnesses on both sides were carefully weighed against each other by judges and juries alike. At issue were verdicts, sentences, and, at a later stage of the process, royal pardons for those condemned to die. Defendants who could produce character witnesses with status equal or superior to that of their accusers were much better off than those who could not. Aware of the importance of character evidence, defendants made every effort to bring it with them to court: 'to have no witnesses at all was almost certain to be disastrous' (Beattie 1986: 448). But the witnesses had to be of adequate status and respectability: in one case, an individual was confronted by a man of 'some substance who identified him as the robber who had stopped him on a highway between Kingston and London and had taken his silver watch and spurs, a gold ring, and money'. The defendant produced eight witnesses, three of whom gave him an alibi. The judge was dissatisfied, however, asking 'not for a better factual defense but for better character witnesses: "Have you any of the substantial inhabitants of [your community] to your character?" he wanted to know.' The defendant did not, and was convicted and hanged (ibid.: 442). In a case involving a more fortunate man, a judge granted a reprieve when 'Gentlemen of distinction in the country [represented] the witnesses against him to be persons of no credit' (ibid.: 444). Worst off were people who, far from having high-status support, actually suffered from high-status condemnation. Thus, a judge said of one man that 'I should have been inclined to have saved his life, so far as it lay in my power to do so, had not the Gentlemen present assured me that he was so incorrigible a Villain as to be past all hope of amendment . . . [which] induced me to leave him to the Severity of the Law' (ibid.: 444). People condemned to death by the courts could continue to hope for royal pardons, provided that such dignitaries as local gentry and 'parish notables—the clergymen, church-wardens, overseers, the constable'— lent their support (ibid.: 445; see, generally, ibid.: 444–6; see also Hay 1975).

In the New England colonies of about the same period, similar social dynamics were at work. One study of witchcraft prosecution in this setting has documented the importance of high-status support or hostility for those accused as witches. Initial suspicions of witchcraft typically arose among low-status members of the community against one of their own number, but many (perhaps most) such cases were not persuasive to the local magistrates and grand juries. Only when 'persons of higher rank and larger influence joined the fray' were cases likely to proceed to indictment; '*some* representation at higher-status levels was requisite to move witchcraft charges into the courts' (Demos 1982: 291; emphasis in original). No case was likely to result in conviction and execution as long as important people like ministers were sceptical of the defendant's guilt (see, generally, ibid.: 285–92).

In other parts of the world, supporter characteristics affect the exercise of discretion in the same ways. Among the Tswana of southern Africa, for example, individuals strive to bolster their cases through the recruitment of allies, being especially sure to seek the assistance of 'men of political influence, prestige and skill in litigation' (Comaroff and Roberts 1981: 111). Such support is a considerable asset when cases appear in court, increasing the chances that a person will prevail even in the face of powerful opposition (ibid.: 112–13, 125–30). In Lebanon officials also defer to high-status sponsorship of the citizens whose cases they handle. Particularly desirable allies are the influence brokers, or 'waasta-makers', who emerge from the ranks of large landowners and wealthy businessmen. Such individuals, through their status and personal connections to legal personnel, help to secure immunity to prosecution, lenient outcomes in trials, and reductions in court-ordered sentences for those whose causes they advocate (see Witty 1980: 95–104). The importance of support can also be seen in the decisions of Moroccan judges. These individuals actively seek information and advice about people and cases before them from community 'notables'—'those persons who, by general reputation, familial background, or position, are generally regarded as the standard-bearers of the distinctive customs and highest values of their religion' (Rosen 1980–1: 238). What these people have to say is often decisive; their support can assure a favorable outcome and their disapproval a negative one (ibid.: 238–9).

In the contemporary United States, patterns of support also predict legal decisions. Police officers, for example, are less likely to make arrests when respectable citizens come forward to vouch for offenders and to guarantee that they will be no further trouble (see D. Black 1980: 175–6). At later stages of the judicial process, prosecutors and judges are similarly more favorable toward those who are well supported: 'If concerned family members or friends come to court, officials may take this as an indication of stabilizing forces in the defendant's life and may "down-grade" the worth of the case. Parents, clergymen, teachers, counselors, and employers also promote this move' (Feeley 1979: 164). Complainants do better if their version of affairs is endorsed by an arresting officer who is held in high esteem by his or her colleagues, as opposed to one who is less respected:

> At times the character of the arresting officer enters into the assessment of a case. When interpreting an officer's arrest report, prosecutors may adjust their response in light of their assessment of the particular officer's character . . . they have a high regard for some officers and an extreme distaste for others, and adjust the reading of their reports accordingly. (ibid.: 165)

Sentencing decisions, like decisions to arrest or to prosecute, are responsive to the support that offenders and victims are able to generate from others. At the end of the process, as at the beginning, those with the staunch support of respectable and high-status allies are treated more leniently by legal officials.

Once patterns of support are taken into account, then, the exercise of discretion appears even less capricious and idiosyncratic than it otherwise might. A further dimension of regularity and sociological constraint is revealed—one evident in the behavior of officials as they deal with diverse matters in societies of all kinds. Once again, the social principles that structure discretionary decision-making transcend particular settings and apply generally. The more social information is available about a case, the more accurately it is possible to predict how discretion will be used in handling it.

LEGAL OFFICIALS

One further kind of sociological determinant structures discretionary decision-making and makes official behavior even more predictable. This is the social background of the legal personnel themselves. It is a comparatively little-explored factor in legal sociology, but one which reduces yet further any remaining aura of mystery about the uses of discretion.

The degree to which officials are personally connected to the parties involved in a case, for example, strongly predicts how they will react. If they are tied more closely to one of the principals than the other, they are likely to favor that individual over his or her opponent. In many societies, this pattern produces concern about the perceived injustice that can arise under such conditions, as well as an attendant expectation that officials who have a relationship with one of the parties in a case will withdraw from handling it. It none the less sometimes happens—more so in some settings than in others—that officials find themselves dealing with a friend or colleague who is embroiled in conflict with someone else, and, when this happens, decisions sympathetic to the associate are likely to follow (see D. Black 1989*b*). One example can be found in the behavior of police officers in the contemporary United States, who treat fellow officers more favorably than civilians, whether as victims or offenders. When police officers are the offended parties, their colleagues are especially likely to rush to their assistance and to proceed vigorously against the people they accuse. On the other hand, when the officers are the alleged wrongdoers, official action against them is less likely. This is true even in regard to their off-duty conduct. A study of police control of domestic violence, for example, found that, when officers' wives complain against their husbands, those who respond to the call, as well as their superiors in the department, are likely to make extensive efforts to convince the victims not to press the matter formally (D. Black 1980: 174).

In cases in which legal officials are relationally equidistant from both of the parties, they are less likely to favor one of them from the start. The way in which they use their discretion, however, is still affected by considerations of intimacy: the closer they are to both parties, the less likely they are to proceed aggressively against either (D. Black and Baumgartner 1983: 113–14; D. Black 1989*b*; Horwitz 1990). Officials who are intimate with both sides are more inclined to encourage informal, conciliatory resolutions and to forgo the full exercise of their authority. Thus, judges and juries in close-knit communities who are well acquainted with the parties in dispute tend to acquit more often and to sentence more leniently than those in more impersonal settings who are strangers to the people they process (see the evidence assembled in Horwitz 1990).

Another relevant feature of the social background of officials is their social status. The higher this is in comparison to that of the parties to a case, the more authoritative the officials are likely to be in the exercise of their discretion (D. Black and Baumgartner 1983: 113). As a result, higher-status legal agents tend to be more severe in their dispositions than lower-status ones. In contemporary US practice, this means that officials who are female, black, and who come from working-class backgrounds are more lenient than their male, white, and middle-class counterparts. Female police officers, for example, make fewer arrests than men do, even though their departments often equate higher arrest rates with superior police performance (see Milton 1972; L. J. Sherman 1975). Women have been found to foster a less aggressive style of policing, to exhibit 'unbecoming conduct' less often, to be the subject of fewer citizen complaints, and to defuse violence more successfully while meeting with less resistance from suspects (see Milton 1972; Bloch and Anderson 1974; L. J. Sherman 1975). They engage in more conciliation, such as in the handling of domestic disputes, where they are more likely to spend time talking to the parties and calming them down (see Milton 1972: e.g. 65, 78). This behavior, and its consequences, have drawn the notice of male officers in some departments. In one case, an older patrolman in Indianapolis remarked to an investigator that: 'There are some families that when they get going will call you back two or three times a night. But I notice that when the women go, that is the last time we hear from them' (Milton 1972: 65). Similar differences have been noted in the behavior of male and female guards in male prisons. There, men are more likely to control inmates through the threat of formal punishment (such as isolation, loss of privileges, and loss of good-time credit) and through physical violence, while women more often proceed in a lenient, conciliatory style:

Women guards also use a strategy that is seldom used by men: the development of friendly, pleasant relationships with prisoners as a way of generating voluntary compliance. Some women play a mothering, nurturing role *vis-à-vis* inmates, a role that is in direct contrast to the macho, competitive role typical of men guards. (Zimmer 1987: 421)

Women rely on 'skills of communication and persuasion and the ability to generate voluntary compliance from others' (ibid.: 423).

Additional evidence on the ways in which the status characteristics of officials shape the exercise of their discretion comes from the study of judicial decision-making. Although judges as a group generally enjoy high status in American society, they differ among themselves in the extent of that status based upon their racial, ethnic, and religious backgrounds and their social class of origin. These factors in turn help predict their judicial behavior. An early study, for example, found that appellate judges with higher-status characteristics are comparatively more severe—thus favoring the defense less often— than their colleagues. Judges who are members of the Republican Party (a political party generally comprised of higher-status individuals than those found in the rival Democratic Party), those who are Protestants (especially those who are members of higher-income denominations), and, to a lesser extent, those who attended more expensive law schools, are all more severe toward defendants (Nagel 1962). These findings have emerged in other studies as well (Ulmer 1973; Goldman 1975). Beyond this, there is evidence that judges with more seniority and those who are 'judicial leaders' with national-level responsibilities are more severe in their decisions (Cook 1973; Goldman 1975).

A related investigation compared sentencing outcomes in the two American cities of Pittsburgh, Pennsylvania, and Minneapolis, Minnesota. In the former, methods of judicial selection produce a pool of judges who are commonly drawn from ethnic minority and lower-income groups and who have associated extensively with similar people throughout their careers. In Minneapolis, by contrast, judges are typically members of 'middle-class Northern-European Protestant backgrounds' who have had few contacts with individuals from lower-income populations (Levin 1974). In Pittsburgh, judges favor informal trials and sentence more leniently; in Minneapolis, they preside over court in a more magisterial fashion and sentence more harshly, especially when defendants who plead not guilty are convicted after trial (ibid.).

Race also appears to predict the use of judicial discretion. An investigation of decisions made by judges in the courts of a large north-eastern city found that black judges are less likely to convict defendants than white ones are. The likelihood of conviction (though not of harsh sentencing) varies systematically with the race of both judge and defendant: those most often convicted are black defendants before white judges, followed in decreasing order by black defendants before black judges, white defendants before white judges, and, lastly, white defendants before black judges (Uhlman 1979).

The status characteristics of jurors predict their discretionary decision-making as well. Studies have indicated that higher-status jury members more often favor conviction than their lower-status counterparts. Thus, jurors with more education, those with higher occupational status, and those who live in affluent suburbs all appear more prone to convict (Reed 1965; R. J. Simon 1967; Hastie, Penrod, and Pennington 1983: 129). White jurors are also harsher than black ones, especially in their treatment of black defendants (Bernard 1979). At the same time, juries typically include at least some members whose social status is inferior to that of a judge, and juries as a whole tend to be more lenient than judges are (see Kalven and Zeisel 1966: chs. 5–6). High-status jurors cannot convict a defendant alone, as judges can, but must persuade their lower-status colleagues to go along with them in order to do so. When they fail in their efforts, the accused goes free.

There is a great deal more to be learnt about the ways in which the social characteristics of legal personnel shape the exercise of their discretion. Already, however, it is apparent that the social backgrounds of officials are important determinants of how they use their authority, and that similar social characteristics predict similar decision-making tendencies in people who occupy very different roles in the justice system. It turns out, then, that one police officer or judge is not simply interchangeable with another, as legal ideology would have it, at least not unless the two share the same social characteristics and stand in the same social relationship to the parties in dispute. At the same time, differences among officials are not simply random and unpredictable, as traditional notions of discretion would have it. Rather, they are highly patterned and follow specifiable social principles, arising as they do from observable differences in the social circumstances of officials' lives. The characteristics of legal personnel thus add a further dimension of sociological constraint to the use of discretion, and knowledge about them makes it even easier to anticipate case outcomes.

Discretion and Discrimination

Across all social settings, the same principles predict and explain discretionary legal decision-making. They apply in societies widely separated by time and distance, and they determine outcomes at different stages of the justice system and in the handling of different kinds of offense. Officials may consciously experience the need for unique judgment in each and every matter that comes before them, but in fact their behavior conforms to sociological laws that transcend particular incidents. Knowing these laws makes it possible to anticipate legal decisions. This is true not just in the aggregate but on a case-by-case basis, where simultaneously taking into account the social characteristics of offenders, victims, witnesses, and officials enables an observer to specify which dispositions are likely to occur. This is not to say that legal officials lack choice in the exercise of their discretion, but rather that their choices are socially patterned and socially predictable. And, in fact, the more legal sociology advances, the more predictable the use of discretion becomes. Thus, with every new achievement in the field, the less what happens in any instance seems to hinge on chance factors of circumstance or personal whim, and the more obviously patterned it is revealed to be. What uncertainty remains about the handling of cases simply marks the boundary beyond which sociological knowledge does not yet extend and points the direction for future research.

All of this requires not only a new conception of discretion, but also a new appreciation of its consequences. The traditional view that saw discretionary decision-making as a very personal, situational, and idiosyncratic affair implied an image of random judgment in which the fate of all citizens alike hinged on largely unknowable factors. Uncertainty of case outcomes fell equitably across the citizenry; some people—perhaps many people—might end up being treated more favorably than stipulated by the written law, but for reasons of chance, emotion, or caprice that no one could take for granted and that might as well have worked against them or on behalf of someone else. The sociological reality of discretion reveals something quite different. How individuals fare in the legal system turns out not to be mysterious, and, what is more, not random. People enter the legal process with very different prospects, depending upon their own social characteristics as well as those of their opponents, supporters, and the officials who deal with them. Officials may answer to the dictates of their conscience, but their conscience consistently comes to different conclusions depending on the social circumstances of a case. Left to their own devices, agents of the law routinely favor some sorts of people over others. Discretion, in practice, amounts to what is commonly known as discrimination. The less discretion there is in law enforcement, the more case outcomes will be sensitive to formal rules and technical criteria alone; the more discretion there is, the more completely case outcomes will be determined by social factors that vary from case to case, and the more systematically advantaged some people will be relative to others.

In this context, it must be recognized that legal rules may themselves be understood as the products of discretion—that of the legislators or interpreting judges who create them—and are formulated according to the same social principles that govern all other discretionary legal behavior. This means that law-makers are influenced by their own social characteristics, those of the constituencies to whom they must answer, and those of the likely targets of any law whose passage they contemplate. Virtually everything already said in the present paper about the social patterning of discretion applies in this context as well, with the notable exception that legislators are rarely called upon to deal with the case-by-case variation law enforcers routinely confront and so generally frame their rules in broad terms that do not explicitly acknowledge the relevance of the diverse social circumstances under which the rules might be invoked. Discretion at later stages of the legal process amounts to the degree to which actors in a legal system are able to substitute or add their own judgment to that already exercised by others at earlier stages. If they have no ability to do so, they have no discretion; if they can do so readily, their discretion is considerable.

When law-makers and law-enforcers are socially similar and operate in similar social contexts, one can predict few occasions on which their respective judgments would be at variance. Accordingly, the decisions of legal officials will conform closely to the letter of the written law, in so far as this gives explicit guidance. When the social situations of law-makers and law-enforcers differ, however, differences in judgment are likely to arise. This seems most often to come about in either of two ways. First, the two groups may differ in the typical background characteristics of their members, such as in regard to social class, income, education, ethnicity, or sex. Probably the most common and most important difference is a second one, and that is the greater amount of detailed social information about specific cases typically possessed by members of the latter group. This, in turn, predicts a degree of social discrimination in law-enforcement not likely to have been envisioned or mandated by those who initially formulated the rules. When the judgment of those who must enforce the law diverges from the judgment of those who drafted it, the relative social status and amount of support enjoyed by the two groups has a great deal of impact on whose judgment prevails, with higher-status and better-supported law-makers more likely to see their rules applied in practice. Even comparatively low-status and isolated legal officials, however, tend to take advantage of every opportunity—officially sanctioned or otherwise—to adjust their behavior to the social contexts in which they operate. Across cases, this can extend to the manufacture or suppression of evidence, the reconstruction of facts (as, for example, when the murder of a sleeping victim is found to have occurred in self-defense), or the outright refusal to apply relevant legal rules. In practice, it is extremely difficult to coerce legal officials into behaving in ways that ignore or violate the social logic dictated by all of the circumstances of a case, no matter what the formal rules may or may not say on the subject. Because law-enforcers tend to be sensitive to a wide variety of situational social contingencies that are unknown to law-makers or do not affect them in the same way, they tend to introduce more systematic social discrimination into law than legislators do. The more discretion those who enforce the law manage to exercise, the more social factors shape case outcomes.

Efforts to curtail the attendant social discrimination in the application of rules have faced notorious difficulties. Only real changes in the social characteristics of citizens, supporters, legal personnel, and cases have had much effect; the underlying principles that constrain official responses have remained basically impervious to reform efforts. Consider, for example, the sentencing decisions of judges and juries in capital cases in the contemporary United States. In recent years there has been a great deal of concern about the unequal risks of execution faced by killers of different kinds—risks that condemn poor, black murderers of affluent white victims to death at much higher rates than white murderers of whites or, even more so, black murderers of blacks. This concern has resulted in federal Supreme Court directives to eliminate race and class bias in capital sentencing, as well as a host of new laws designed to bring this about. Safeguards have been incorporated into the sentencing process intended to ensure that only strictly legal factors influence who is condemned to die, and officials have been made aware of past discrimination and counseled to avoid it in their own behavior. Discretion remains, however, in the hands of prosecutors, judges, and juries, and status inequalities persist in American society. Empirical evidence reveals that race and class bias in capital sentencing continues unabated (see Bowers and Pierce 1980). The same kinds of people run the same elevated risks of execution; the same kinds of people enjoy relative immunity.

Another example of the strong and persistent association between discretion and discrimination can be seen in the legal response to domestic violence. As discussed above, officials in all societies use their discretion to exclude a disproportionate number of conflicts between intimates from the legal arena. The more intimate the parties, the more reluctant officials are to exercise their authority against offenders, so that family members who victimize each other are particularly immune to formal punishment. Recently this practice has come under sharp attack in the United States, especially in regard to the considerable unwillingness of police officers to arrest men who assault their wives. The critique has been fueled by research findings suggesting that arrest in domestic violence cases may actually deter future attacks (Sherman and Berk 1984). Directives have been issued in many police departments instructing officers to make arrests in domestic violence cases just as they would in cases of comparable violence between strangers. For all of this, rank-and-file police officers remain reluctant to arrest violent husbands and often continue to handle them in informal ways. Their discretionary decisions in the field largely ignore administrative exhortations to overlook the intimacy that characterizes cases of domestic violence.

Intimacy between the parties and the reputation of victims also continue to predict how US officials exercise discretion in rape cases, efforts to change this fact notwithstanding. Statutes in almost every US state have been rewritten in recent years to make the conviction of intimate rapists easier and to reduce the importance of victim respectability. Still, prosecutors remain hesitant to proceed in cases of so-called acquaintance rape (where the parties involved knew each other prior to the attack), often citing the unwillingness of juries to convict. Juries, for their part, are indeed commonly unwilling to decide against men who rape intimates; they also remain highly sensitive to the 'moral character' of victims (see Mansnerus 1989).

Experimental results further reveal how difficult it is to reduce social discrimination in the use of discretion. One study employed experimental techniques to assess variation in the credibility of trial testimony. It found that witnesses whose speech patterns were characteristic of high-status people—men, the educated, the middle class—were seen as more believable by the sorts of people who serve on juries (O'Barr 1982). The researchers then explored whether or not having judges inform the mock jurors about the known effects of witness speech style, while counseling them not to discriminate against witnesses on the basis of their speech, would reduce disparities in the assessment of credibility. It did not. Subjects who had been instructed by judges to disregard the speech style of witnesses were just as likely as those who had not to perceive people who spoke in a typically low-status fashion as 'less convincing, less believable, less competent, less intelligent, and less trustworthy' (ibid.: 93–6).

Only when the social context changes are officials likely to change their discretionary behavior. As previously low-status citizens gain in standing, for example, or as previously intimate relationships entail greater social distance, or as previously isolated people gain powerful support, or as the social characteristics of the officials themselves undergo a transformation, cases are processed differently by police officers, prosecutors, judges, and juries. The social principles structuring legal decision-making remain the same; only the social particulars of the incidents vary. To the extent that past social differences persist and that officials are aware of them—on this latter point, see D. Black 1989*a*: 64–7—discretionary legal outcomes are unaltered.

For as long as citizens and officials are socially diverse, then, and for as long as the latter manage to exercise discretion, a degree of systematic discrimination in law-enforcement seems inevitable. It cannot be wished away, and, furthermore, its precise forms are largely predictable. The question then arises whether and to what extent discretion could be eliminated as a way of reducing legal inequities (assuming, of course, that people want to reduce them, an assumption which may be unwarranted in some instances). Many commentators have in fact argued that discretion should be curtailed in the interests of legal consistency (see, e.g., Goldstein 1960; Davis 1969). Here, however, there is considerable reason to believe that, just as discrimination is inherent in discretion, so too is some measure of discretion inherent in law. While it may be possible to reduce or restrict it, discretion may be too basic an element of legal systems to root out completely. All law is to some extent decentralized in actual practice, requiring scattered officials to respond to incidents on their own and without supervision. This necessarily creates opportunities for the use of discretion, authorized or otherwise. More fundamentally, it appears that the application of laws must always involve some amount of interpretation, as for example in deciding how to operationalize such crucial elements of contemporary American cases as a 'credible threat', 'probable cause', the 'intent' of an offender, 'reasonable doubt' or a 'reasonable man', 'excessive' force, and a host of other equally ambiguous or evaluative notions. It may well be, then, that the simple mechanical matching of rules to incidents is an impossibility and that there must always be some judgment involved in applying abstract standards to actual cases. Certainly many analysts of legal decision-making have come to this conclusion (see, e.g., Pound 1908; Levi 1949; Breitel 1960; Bittner 1970: 4).

If discretion can never be totally abolished from law, then, and if social discrimination inevitably arises from discretion, it follows that law will always be discriminatory to some extent. Wherever it exists, there will be legally advantaged and disadvantaged people, selected according to principles that are already becoming known. An end to social inequities in the handling of legal cases may well require nothing less than an end to law itself, or what has been called the 'delegalization of society' (D. Black 1989*a*: ch. 5). It is by no means obvious, however, when and how such a revolutionary transformation would come about. Nor is it necessarily the case that non-legal forms of social control, which would assume greater prominence in a lawless society, are actually any less subject to social influence; in fact, they appear not to be (see, e.g., studies of non-legal social control by Koch 1974; Merry 1982; Baumgartner 1984 1988; Boehm 1984; Cooney 1988; and Morrill 1989, among others). Moral life is part of social life, and the sociological principles that govern discretionary decision-making in law are just a dimension of a larger order and regularity that pervade the human response to wrongdoing, wherever it occurs and whatever shape it takes.

5. Social Limits to Discretion: An Organizational Perspective

MARTHA S. FELDMAN

THIS chapter is about the social constraints on discretionary behavior. It contrasts with some of the other chapters in this book in that its basis is organizational rather than legal. The actors considered are bureaucrats rather than judges. The fundamental issues are, however, similar. How does one allow discretion in decision-making without also allowing capricious decision-making? How can decisions be responsive to the relevant features of a context without being *ad hoc*, unsystematic, or incomprehensible?

In any context there are individual as well as social constraints to discretion. Individuals have ways of thinking and values that constrain their decisions. In the literature on discretion, however, one of the primary concerns has been the lack of control over behavior that is subject only to the internal constraints of the individual and that is not subject either to formal rules and sanctions or to direct supervision. This concern stems from the belief that without such constraints autonomy is absolute. The literature from organization theory, however, provides a way of thinking about the intersection between decision-making and social processes that allows us to understand that such decision-making is subject to social control.

The literature on organizational decision-making that I summarize in the early part of this chapter suggests why decision-making, in general, is a social rather than an individual process. It follows that the social context is able to provide some ways of controlling discretionary behavior. I present and discuss three social processes that can control such behavior. I do not make specific recommendations about the implementation of these social control processes. While the literature on organizations and decision-making within organizations provides a way of thinking about the social control of discretionary behavior, the means of implementing control must be tailored to specific contexts. I leave the implementation of these ideas in the legal context to those who are experts in that field.

Defining Discretion

The Weberian bureaucracy is one in which there is no need for discretion. Functions are 'strictly delimited' and formalized in written rules (Weber 1946). The organization operates like a machine. The machine has no need for its parts to make choices about the functions they perform. Later students of bureaucracy, however, have recognized that discretion is an inevitable part of bureaucratic action (Wilson 1968; Nadel and Rourke 1975; Lipsky 1980). Some lament the fact and see it as a source of injustice (Davis 1969, 1976). Many have discussed the reasons for the existence of discretion (Nadel and Rourke 1975; Lipsky 1980; Burke 1986). No one has suggested a means of eliminating it.

For the purposes of this chapter discretion is defined as the legitimate right to make choices based on one's authoritative assessment of a situation. As such, discretion is an exercise of authority (Friedrich 1973). Authority, according to Carl Friedrich in his essay 'Authority, Reason and Discretion', involves the ability to give reasons for choices made. Thus, according to this definition, discretion is exercised when a person whose job it is to do so makes choices based on an assessment that is or can be justified by reasons.

This definition of discretion is consistent with the notion of decision-making within a structure of rules. The rules set the limits of the authority of the person making decisions. Within these limits, the person is authorized to make decisions. This definition does not imply that all of the authorized decisions made by a person are correct, only that a person is authorized to make a class of decision. For instance, teachers are authorized to give grades; police officers are authorized to make arrests; judges are authorized to make judicial rulings; policy analysts are authorized to gather information. Specific grades, arrests, rulings, and information may be found to be errors. Despite these errors, the actors maintain their authority to make decisions of the relevant type.[1]

When teachers grade papers, they exercise discretion; when police officers make an arrest or not, they exercise discretion; when policy analysts decide to do further research on an issue, they exercise discretion. Discretion does not occur in any of these instances if the specific action has been directly requested by the employee's superior.

---

[1] Of course, individual actors found to make too many errors or particularly egregious errors may have their authority revoked.

Thus, if a principal were to tell the teacher what grade to give, if the police sergeant were to direct the officer to arrest a specific person or if the policy analyst's supervisor were to request that she do more research on a given topic, they would not be exercising discretion in performing these actions. In most cases some of the actions taken by members of bureaucracies involve discretion, while other actions of the same sort are simply carrying out the orders of a bureaucratic superior.

This definition of discretion does not distinguish between the 'strong' and 'weak' forms of discretion described by Dworkin (1977*b*). When his distinction is translated to an organizational setting, the difference between weak (in which standards cannot be applied mechnically)[2] and strong (in which the official is not bound by standards set by the authority in question) discretion is the difference between situations constrained by formal rules and situations apparently unconstrained. The lack of constraint may be more apparent than real in the organizational setting, since informal rules and norms are often relevant. Because of the constraining nature of informal rules and norms in organizations, I do not distinguish between the weak and strong forms of discretion.

Reasons for Discretion

Discretion is a necessary part of many bureaucratic jobs. Discretion is necessary when choices have to be made and the workers cannot depend upon a supervisor or rules to make decisions for them. The work of 'street-level bureaucrats' illustrates particularly well why discretion is necessary. Street-level bureaucrats as defined by Michael Lipsky (1980) are people who represent the bureaucracy directly to clients and who exercise discretion in so doing. Teachers, police officers, and social workers are examples of street-level bureaucrats. These people must exercise discretion in the course of doing their work, in part, because they do not work under the direct observation of their supervisors. They are often geographically distant from their supervisors and the location of their work is often unpredictable. They have, at times, to make decisions on the spot, and this means making decisions on their own.

---

[2] A second form of 'weak' discretion according to Dworkin occurs when a decision made by an official cannot be reviewed or reversed by another official. This use of the term discretion is not relevant to the argument in this chapter.

Rules can often make up for the lack of direct supervision. Often, however, the cases that street-level bureaucrats deal with are sufficiently complex and individual that general rules give little guidance. Creating rules to cover all possible contingencies would be a mind-boggling task. If the goal of such rule-writing is to eliminate discretion, the activity may be counter-productive. A profusion of rules can lead to greater freedom because several rules may apply to any situation and the bureaucrat must choose which rules are appropriate in the present one.

Rules may actually be an impediment to supervision. They may be so voluminous and contradictory that they can only be enforced or invoked selectively . . . Police behavior is so highly specified by statutes and regulations that policemen are expected to invoke the law selectively. They could not possibly make arrests for all the infractions they observe during their working day . . . Similarly, federal civil-rights compliance officers have so many mandated responsibilities in comparison to their resources that they have been free to determine their own priorities. (Lipsky 1980: 14)

Measures of outcome or productivity are another substitute for direct supervision. Many bureaucratic tasks can be monitored simply by measuring total daily output. However, many tasks involving discretion are poorly assessed by such measures (ibid.: 48 ff.). The number of arrests is not a good measure of the quality of police work nor are student test scores a good measure of teaching ability. These measures are related to the work of policing and teaching. However, in both cases emphasis on the output measure distorts the true nature of the job. Emphasis on arrests, for instance, would encourage police officers to focus on cases in which arrests are more likely rather than on cases that may be more difficult and to arrest when there may be other, better resolutions. Emphasis on test scores would encourage teachers to focus narrowly on the test material and on the students who are most likely to improve their scores.

Discretion is also necessary when professionals such as doctors or lawyers are hired by bureaucracies. They are expected to make choices on the basis of their professional training. The case of professionals in bureaucracies provides a curious twist to the Weberian ideal. These bureaucrats perform their delimited function *by* exercising discretion. It has been noted that this combination creates difficulties not only for the theory of bureaucracy but also for the practice (Blau and Scott 1962). When there is a conflict, professionals tend to value

their professional judgment over their bureaucratic duties and affiliation. Lipsky, for example, tells of the ways that doctors have dealt
with the outpatient policies of the Veterans Administration Hospitals.
When the hospitals had a policy allowing no outpatients, the doctors
circumvented this policy by classifying their 'outpatients' as people in
need of 'continuing care'. When the hospitals changed their policies,
the number of continuing-care patients decreased in direct proportion
with the increase in the number of outpatients. Thus, the doctors
found a way to do what, as professionals, they considered appropriate
rather than abiding by the policies of the administrators that were
meant to limit the demands on the bureaucracy (Lipsky 1980).

Discretion as Decision-Making

Discretion is an act of choice. Consequently, understandings of
discretion are influenced by changes in the understanding of decision-
making. The formal study of decision-making has changed much over
the last forty years. At the beginning of this period the description of
decision-making was consistent with the Weberian description of
bureaucracy. It was generally quite linear and involved very little
uncertainty. That is, there was a clear causal and sequential connection
between the beginning of the process which involves the recognition
of a problem and the end of the process which involves the implementation of a solution. The dominant image is that of a production
line with clearly marked stages. Raw materials in the form of problems,
goals, and information are processed in a standard way to produce the
final product: a solution. Further investigation has revealed that there
is little that is either linear or certain about the process of making
decisions. The more recent descriptions provide new ways of understanding discretion. The following is a brief overview of the initial
understanding and the most relevant changes in the field of decision-
making.

The rational actor model (also called the classical rational model)
encompasses the fundamental notions of a simple decision process
(Downs 1957; Allison 1971). These notions serve as the basis for both
professional and lay ideas about proper decision-making. The model
is straightforward. There are five steps that are necessary. First, a
problem is recognized. Secondly, goals are established for the solution
to the problem. These first two steps are often combined because the
goal is often to solve the problem. Goals, however, may also make

specific demands on the solution. For instance, the goal may include a deadline, a limit on resources, or some other restriction on the type of solution. Thirdly, alternative solutions are proposed. Fourthly, information is gathered to assess these alternatives. Alternatives are assessed according to the likelihood and the efficiency with which they will attain the stated goals. Finally, a choice is made of the alternative that 'maximizes efficiency'. That is, the alternative is chosen that is the most consistent with attaining the goals.

A simple example of this choice process is the decision to rent an apartment. The problem is the need to move or to find a new place to live. The goal is likely to be to find an apartment that costs no more than a certain amount. There may be other goals as well that concern the location, size, and so forth. The alternatives are all the available apartments. The information required to assess the alternatives depends on the goals. In our example cost would be a necessary piece of information; location and size may also be necessary. All alternatives are assessed, and the apartment that best fulfils the goals is chosen.

While this appears to be an eminently reasonable approach to decision-making, researchers and practitioners have increasingly suggested that decision-making often does not fit this description. Three major issues have been examined with respect to this model, resulting in the suggestion that, while the model is attractive, it is applicable only to a very limited number of situations. The three issues are the ability to process sufficient information to fulfil the needs of the model, the existence of a unitary decision maker, and the specification of goals prior to making decisions.

The first major alteration of this model occurred in the late 1950s. Herbert Simon and James G. March pointed out that the amount of information required by this model was too great to be fulfilled in most situations. They claimed that individuals and organizations are limited in their cognitive abilities to process information (H. A. Simon 1956; March and Simon 1958). The rational model requires that *all* alternatives be considered and that they be assessed using *all* relevant information. This is a considerable strain on the available attention and memory of individuals and organizations. Thus, information may not be processed because people forget about it and do not have the time to attend to it.

More recently students of psychology have suggested that not only the capacity to think but also how people think create obstacles for the unbiased processing of information required by this model (Nisbett and Ross 1980; Kahneman, Slovic, and Tversky 1982). This research suggests that alternatives and information are ignored because people are not aware that they might be relevant. Thus, even if information is readily available, they may not think to use it because they do not think about the issue in a way that makes that information relevant.

The understanding of individual and organizational limits to information processing led to the proposal of a new model of decision-making. This new model was based on an acknowledgment that some uncertainty cannot be resolved and yet decisions must be made. The premiss of the model was 'bounded rationality' rather than the more comprehensive notion of rationality required by the previous model. According to this model people pursue goals, but they do not make choices by maximizing (or optimizing) the likelihood or efficiency of reaching their goals. Instead they 'satisfice' or reach an acceptable level of goal attainment rather than an optimal level (H. A. Simon 1956; March and Simon 1958).

We can modify the previous example to illustrate this new way of thinking about decision-making. Unless people live in a very small village or in a place with a very limited supply of housing, they generally do not gather information about all the currently available apartments. Indeed, doing so may be counter-productive because the search could take so long that perfectly acceptable apartments considered at the beginning may no longer be available by the time all apartments have been considered. The satisficing model suggests that people establish a set of criteria (e.g. cost, location, size, and so forth) and, then, look sequentially at the available apartments. When they find an apartment that meets the criteria, they rent it.[3]

The relatively straightforward conceptual change in moving from classical rationality to bounded rationality had far-reaching effects. The acceptance of uncertainty changed the nature of the inferences we could make about observed behavior and the predictions we could make about future behavior. No longer could rationality be used as an explanation. Only when all information is considered will all rational actors come to the same conclusions. If the conclusions are thoroughly dependent upon the available information, then rationality varies from actor to actor. Economists have adopted the notion of 'subjective utility' to replace the simpler notion of utility that can exist only with perfect information (Cooter and Ulen 1988; Ulen 1990). Organization

---

[3] Of course, it is possible that the search may convince the searcher to reassess the criteria because the criteria are either too easy or too hard to meet.

theorists have directed much attention to the issues involved in searching for appropriate information (Cyert and March 1963; H. A. Simon 1969; Galbraith 1973; Feldman and March 1981; March and Sevon 1984).

The next major alteration of the rational and bounded rational models took place as people began to question the assumption that there was agreement on goals and, ultimately, agreement on the means to achieving the goals. This concern is particularly relevant to decision-making in which more than one person is involved. The rational and bounded rational models when applied to organizations assume that they act as if they were individuals without conflict about goals or means. This is often expressed by the phrase that decisions are made as if by a unitary actor.[4] Political decision-making provides a particularly stark contradiction to this assumption (Allison 1971; Halperin 1974). Business firms have also been used to illustrate the phenomena of multiple and conflicting goals (Cyert and March 1963). Instead of a unitary actor, one finds that decisions are often made by multiple actors who have quite different notions about the goals to be pursued and about the appropriate means of pursuing them.

The consequences of these conflicts over goals and means is a manner of decision-making distinct from the rational models (Lindblom 1959; Cyert and March 1963). The careful, if limited, calculation of means to ends required by the rational models is impossible. Yet, action is still necessary. Consequently, agreement on action becomes more important than agreement on goals. Agreement often occurs through compromise, bargaining, and voting (Allison 1971; Halperin 1974; Steinbruner 1974). Through these means agreement on action may occur even when there is absolute disagreement on ends (Lindblom 1959). Incremental and marginal changes are more likely than major changes.

The apartment example can again be used to illustrate this form of decision-making. Imagine, first, that there are several people looking for an apartment in which they plan to live together. They may have different notions about the relative importance of such goals as cost and location. One may be willing to pay a higher price for a better location while another may not find location that important. Even if there is agreement that location is important, there may be several

---

[4] Questions have also been raised about the assumption that individuals meet this definition of a unitary actor (Kahneman and Treisman 1983).

different interpretations of a good location. For instance, one may be concerned with how quiet the neighborhood is, another may be concerned with what kind of shops are nearby, and another may be most concerned with proximity to the workplace. It may be impossible for the group to come to some agreement about these goals. The choice of an apartment may be made, instead, by looking at what is available and choosing among them by a process of discussion, negotiation, bargaining, or even voting. Thus, the choice can be made without a prior agreement about goals.

The final area of the rational models that has been questioned is the role of goals in the pursuit of action. The problem of multiple actors and multiple goals raises the issue, but the questioning has been much deeper. Are goals targets for action or are they constraints within which actions must be taken (H. A. Simon 1964)? Are goals stipulated prior to taking action or inferred from actions taken (March 1978; Weick 1979)? Is routine behavior goal oriented in any meaningful sense of the word (Feldman 1988)? Are decisions actions in pursuit of an end or are they acts of learning or interpretation (March and Olsen 1976; Cohen 1985 1987; Feldman 1989)? As the questioning continues, the meaning of goals and the relation of goals to decision-making become less and less clear. The question is no longer 'what's the right way to get from here to there?' but 'where are we?' (March and Olsen 1976; Weick 1979).

This last form of decision-making breaks down what is left of the sequential order of the rational model. In this form not only are goals not agreed upon before a decision is made; they may not even be considered. Imagine the following as an alternative scenario for moving to a new apartment. One person hears of an available apartment and discusses it with other people with whom he is friendly. Some of these people think moving to this apartment with some friends would be nice, and some of them are able to move. Those who both think it would be nice and are able to move sign the lease and take the apartment.

The rational and bounded rational models are based on the ability to calculate a right answer. In the rational model the answer is absolutely right. The alternative chosen is the one best suited to fulfilling the goals. In the bounded rational model the answer is conditionally right. The alternative chosen is the one best suited to the goals according to the available information. More or different information may lead to a different conclusion. Thus, according to these models, people pursue different actions because they are more-or-less capable of correct calculations, because they have different goals, or because they have different information. People with the same goals and the same information, given an adequate ability to calculate, will respond in the same ways.

The lessons of rational decision-making suggest two means of control of discretionary behavior. One is selection. The process of hiring people should ensure that people hired have a sufficient capacity to calculate that they are able to make reasonable and appropriate connections between the actions they take and the ends that result. Furthermore, people should be selected who have goals that are congruent with those of the organization hiring them. The second means is through motivation or the use of sanctions and rewards to help ensure that the goals of the individual are congruent with the goals of the organization or system.[5]

These means of control are certainly important. They are, however, not the only ones. Indeed, intelligent people with similar or compatible goals often interpret situations differently and produce different outcomes. This is, in part, because both goals and information may be ambiguous. That is, there may be many interpretations of what an organization or policy or law is trying to achieve and what information is relevant to these goals. If we take seriously the ambiguity of goals and information, we must also pay attention to the social context that promotes or inhibits differing understandings of the decision-making situation and the consequences of action. The modifications to the rational perspective on decision-making suggest that we may be able to exert control through means that influence the process of interpreting contexts. In a later section of this chapter I discuss three such means: formal training, informal socialization, and routines.

Functions of Bureaucratic Discretion

The exercise of discretion involves taking into consideration the idiosyncratic features of specific cases. As such, discretion introduces the possibility of inequality and injustice into bureaucratic action

---

[5] This second means may be thought of as teaching, since one is teaching someone to value a specific goal or outcome. It is different, however, from the sort of teaching that will be discussed shortly that changes the way people interpret a goal or outcome. In the strict rational model, we do not have the ambiguity of goals and outcome that necessitates the latter form of education.

and, at the same time, alleviates a basic deficiency in the bureaucratic disposition of cases. Bureaucracies, by their nature, are unsuited to dealing with individually distinct cases (Weber 1946; Hummel 1987). Rules are established for the 'general case' and, to the extent that the idiosyncrasies of a particular case can be ignored, the rules expedite the processing of these cases. Bureaucracies are, at least in theory, particularly well suited to processing quickly many cases for which the relevant characteristics can be easily codified and other characteristics can be considered irrelevant. Registering thousands of students for courses in the large state universities of the United States is an example of the kind of task to which bureaucracies are particularly well suited. The relevant features of these students are very straightforward: their student identification numbers, year in school, the courses they would like to take, and whether these courses are full or still have openings. All other features of the students (e.g. how important it is to take a certain course; whether they missed registering earlier for a course that is now closed because they were ill or out of the country; that they really should be registering as a senior with a higher priority claim to courses, rather than a junior, because they have finished coursework that does not yet show on the official record, and so forth) are, for the purposes of this process, irrelevant. While idiosyncrasies are not rare, they can be ignored in the vast majority of cases. The result is a great deal of efficiency. For example, at one such university forty-eight bureaucrats (forty of whom are temporary) register approximately twenty-five thousand students in a two-week period. Each student registers for three or four courses from over five thousand offerings. This averages to approximately one thousand courses per employee per week. This pace hardly allows for consideration of idiosyncrasies.

In any such process some clients are displeased with the outcome. In any such process, some outcomes are inappropriate. The trade-off is between the number of cases processed, the amount of resources available for processing them, and the appropriateness of the disposition of each case. For a fixed amount of resources many more cases can be processed if their idiosyncrasies can be ignored.

Not only do such processes use fewer resources than those that take into consideration the idiosyncrasies of cases; they are also more equal. Each case is given exactly the same consideration as every other case. Again we have the Weberian ideal. The same rules are applied to all cases. In some cases, however, idiosyncrasies are important. The bureaucratic process that cannot respond to them is rigid and, often, incapable of achieving ends for which the process was established (Hummel 1987). For example, a teacher who gives exactly the same amount and type of attention to each student is unlikely to be very effective at helping students overcome their particular learning problems. As a result, the teacher will be less effective at teaching the skills the students need to learn. In this case, we would prefer students not to be treated the same.

The dissimilar treatment of people is often perceived as appropriate. It can, however, result in injustice. One instance in which this occurs is when the idiosyncrasies attended to are not relevant to the established goal of the process. For instance, when teachers pay more attention to cute children than to plain ones, they are attending to idiosyncrasies that are irrelevant to the child's ability to learn. This results in an unjust situation in which cute children are able to learn more than plain ones because they are given more attention.

Thus, the exercise of discretion is necessary for the pursuit of bureaucratic goals and it inevitably introduces the possibility of injustice. An important question for the study of discretion is, then, how to limit the exercise of discretion to the appropriate idiosyncrasies of each case. It is to this question that we now turn.

Limiting Discretion

Limiting discretion to the relevant idiosyncrasies of a case involves two questions. First, what are the relevant idiosyncrasies; secondly, how can we encourage appropriate behavior? In the following sections I raise issues relevant to each of these questions. I suggest that we know more about the latter question than the former.

Relevant idiosyncracies

What idiosyncrasies of a case are relevant to the goals of a bureaucratic process is a question not easily answered. There are at least two reasons why this is true. One is that it is often difficult to know how to attain a given end. The other is that we do not always know whether we have attained the specified goal. The following paragraphs deal with each of these separately.

The goal of teaching is for children to learn; the goal of traffic patrols is to reduce traffic accidents; the goal of policy analysts is to provide decision-relevant information to policy-makers; the goal of hospital workers is to make people healthier. We can specify these goals and we can agree about them without having very clear ideas or much agreement about how to accomplish them or even what they mean. Though many of us have been both students and teachers, there is little consensus about what makes people learn. Some methods of teaching reading work for some children; other methods work for others; nothing seems to work for some and anything seems to work for others. Even a relatively straightforward goal like reducing traffic accidents may be very difficult to accomplish. Do more patrol cars on the road decrease accidents by making people slow down or increase accidents by making them more nervous? Similar difficulties arise for policy analysts, hospital workers, and many other employees of bureaucracies. This difficulty has been referred to as the ambiguity of understanding and it is characterized by the fact that 'it is hard to see the connections between organizational actions and their consequences' (March and Olsen 1976: 12).

Part of the reason that it is hard to see the connections between actions and results is that the goals themselves are often not clearly specified or specifiable (Hawkins 1984). It is not always clear how to teach children, in part, because it is not clear of what learning consists. There are persistent disagreements about what constitutes learning or being healthy or providing decision-relevant information. In such instances it is hard to know whether the goal has been achieved because it is hard to know what constitutes achieving the goal. Has a policy analyst failed because policy-makers do not use the information provided them; has a doctor failed when her patients continue unhealthy habits; has a teacher failed when his students prefer socializing to reading? When has the task been performed; when has the goal been attained? This problem with goals has been referred to as the ambiguity of history (March and Olsen 1976). Whether a goal has been achieved is often a matter of interpretation about which reasonable people may disagree.

The difficulties in resolving goal ambiguity are often ignored in our efforts to determine behavior that is appropriate to these goals. While there is ambiguity about both goals and behavior, attention tends to focus more on whether the behavior is appropriate than on how it relates to the goal that it is supposed to achieve. For instance, we have some fairly clear ideas about appropriate behavior for teachers: they should spend time in the classroom imparting information to students; they should evaluate the students' progress in some way; they should not discriminate among students on the basis of race, gender, or religion. These ideas limit what teachers do, despite the fact that we do not have very clear evidence about how they relate to learning. Thus, one way to deal with goal ambiguity is to focus on the procedures for making a decision or for taking action rather than on the substance of the decision or the relation of the action to a goal.

Encouraging appropriate behavior

How we determine what is appropriate behavior is a question for philosophers, sociologists, social psychologists, and students of jurisprudence. How we encourage some behaviors and discourage others in a bureaucratic context, however, is a question of organizational behavior. There is, of course, no single answer. Laws, regulations, organizational rules, and managerial dictates all specify appropriate behaviors and some of them specify sanctions for inappropriate behavior. For reasons discussed above, however, these mechanisms are not sufficient in the case of discretionary behavior. There are organizational processes that supplement these mechanisms and constrain the exercise of discretion. In the following, I discuss three of these processes: formal training, informal socialization, and organizational routines. These three are not entirely distinct, but they are sufficiently different that they warrant separate treatment.

Formal training.   For many jobs, formal training or pre-job socialization provides a repertoire of behaviors that are shared by co-workers and supervisors (Larson 1977; Sproull 1981). 'Prejob socialization produces personnel who enter an organization with particular beliefs. These include . . . for professionals at any rate, beliefs about appropriate ways to perform and evaluate specific work practices' (Sproull 1981: 209). Practitioners learn to value particular skills and means of doing their work and to believe that what they have learnt constitutes the right way to do their work. For instance, doctors learn to value particular techniques of diagnosis; teachers learn to value means of evaluating students' progress; police officers believe in the ways they have been taught to handle a weapon and in what they have learnt about how and when to make an arrest. While this training may be modified in practice, it provides a base from which the modifications occur. Perhaps more importantly, it also provides a base of expectations about accepted practice. Deviations from this practice may be questioned by co-workers, supervisors, or clients. Thus, deviation involves both a decision to deviate and the ability to justify the decision. These may each be barriers to change.

Formal training helps to impart values that influence perceptions of appropriateness. These values are about the roles to be played and the tasks to be performed. Training, for example, often assumes and reinforces particular relations between the provider and the client. Social workers learn to value client confidentiality. Police officers learn to see their clients as potential sources of information (Manning 1980).

Training also influences the definition of tasks. Policy analysts are taught to be neutral providers of facts, to reduce subjective bias, and not to be political 'hired guns' (Meltsner 1976; Feldman 1989). The training of police officers emphasizes keeping the peace and not taking justice into their own hands (Skolnick 1966). Again, these values may change with experience. Many values, however, will persist, and others will be a constant source of tension within the job.

Formal training not only imparts values and information but also serves as an important part of the selection process for jobs (Kaufman 1960). Training programs have entrance requirements that filter the applicants, retaining those who are deemed most likely to do well. The training itself weeds out people who do not have or cannot develop certain skills and who cannot function in the particular circumstances of the program. Thus, doctors must show evidence of being able to diagnose disease and, at least in certain phases of their training, they must also be able to perform for many hours with little sleep. Police officers must be able to obey orders, even those with which they do not agree (Van Maanen 1973). Policy analysts must be familiar with a variety of methods of analysing and presenting information (Meltsner 1976; Sugden and Williams 1978; Gramlich 1981). Lawyers must be able to read many cases, find the points of law in them, and relate these points to those in other cases. These requirements may or may not be important once the person is on the job. However, obtaining the job generally depends on doing well in the training program. Those who cannot perform are filtered out of the pool of applicants for jobs. Thus, the training process serves to ensure that people with the same jobs will have similar values, behavioral patterns, and preconceptions (Cohen and March 1974; Kanter 1977).

Informal socialization. Notions about the right way to perform a job certainly do not stop forming when formal training stops. Indeed many of the situations one confronts on the job are not covered by formal training. Others are covered but not in very realistic ways. In addition, people in particular organizations develop modes of operation that are peculiar to that setting. The newcomer to the organization will learn the modes of operation from members who have been a part of the organization longer.

Rookie police officers, for example, learn from their partners to categorize the type of people they deal with. 'By watching, listening, and mimicking, the neophyte policeman learns how to deal with the objects of his occupation—the traffic violator, the hippie, the drunk, the brass, and the criminal justice complex itself' (Van Maanen 1973: 412).

Teachers and social workers learn what short cuts are acceptable for dealing with demands made on an overloaded system. For example, Weatherly and Lipsky showed how teachers and education specialists reponded to a law passed in Massachusetts that mandated major changes in 'the education of students with any kind of physical, emotional, and/or mental handicap' (1977: 172). The professionals were not opposed to the changes, but they did not have the resources to carry them out. Referrals of students to special programs were a particular drain on resources. As a result school-system employees learnt to employ 'a variety of unofficial rationing techniques to hold down the number of referrals' (ibid.: 186). These techniques included teachers ignoring problems, principals dissuading parents of the need for a referral, administrators failing to follow through on referrals made by teachers, and administrators telling teachers to cut back on referrals.

In many jobs people learn what is an acceptable rate of work. Automobile workers learn to unite against management pressures to speed up car productions (Widick 1979). For example, when the Vega line in Lordstown, Ohio, was taken over by a new management group, the change was described by an employee in the following way: 'There's lots of variety in the paint shop, . . . You clip on the color hose, bleed out the old color and squirt. Clip, bleed, squirt, think. Clip, bleed, squirt, yawn. Clip, bleed, squirt, scratch your nose. Only now the Gee-Mads [the new management group] have taken away the time to scratch your nose' (Garson 1979: 212). Garson explains, 'The job had been boring and unbearable before. When it remained boring and became a bit more unbearable there was a 97 percent vote to strike' (ibid.: 212).

In other jobs people learn that unbridled ambition is expected (Dean 1976). The book that John Dean wrote after serving as General Counsel for the Nixon administration and while he was serving time for crimes related to the Watergate incident provides many examples of informal socialization. For instance, on his first day of work at the White House, Dean arrived early because he was excited. As he got out of his car he heard another employee walking by. 'He waved a greeting at me and hurried off, mumbling like the Mad Hatter that he was late. He would see me later, he called. It was not yet eight in the morning. *Late*, I thought. I had been worried about getting there too early. No one had told me when the work day started' (Dean 1976: 25).

Informal socialization occurs in a number of ways. Sometimes people adopt values because they are rewarded for doing so or because they are expected to do so. Sometimes people adopt values because they identify with people who have those values or because they imitate people with those values. Finally, sometimes people rationalize their actions in such a way that they adopt values consistent with their actions. The first four dynamics—reinforcement, response to expectations, identification, and imitation—are probably quite familiar. The fifth is less often discussed, but still quite common. People come to find unexpected meaning in their jobs or in the way they perform a task. For instance, Tom Wolfe describes how 'flak-catchers' (bureaucrats hearing complaints) in the Office of Economic Opportunity came to value their own fear and to give out large amounts of money to those who induced great fear in them.

If you were outrageous enough, if you could shake up the bureaucrats so bad that their eyeballs froze into iceballs and their mouths twisted up into smiles of sheer physical panic, into shit-eating grins, so to speak—then they knew you were the real goods. They knew you were the right studs to give the poverty grants and community organizing jobs to. Otherwise, they didn't know. (Wolfe 1970: 118)

Of course, most rationalizations are not so dramatic.

These informal socialization processes supplement formal training and formal expectations. They often constitute the way that the formal rules are implemented. They limit the range of acceptable action taken by organization members, in specific instances. They may be consistent or inconsistent with the formal training. One of the challenges to encouraging appropriate behavior is to learn to channel the effects of informal socialization to those that promote the desired behaviors.

Routines.   So far in this chapter I have been discussing ways in which the social context influences an individual's way of thinking about or evaluating the discretionary task. In this section I present another feature of the social context that is more strictly behavioral. Patterns of behavior predominant in an organization may restrict and constrain discretionary behavior even when the participants neither plan the pattern nor value their parts in it (Feldman 1989).

Routines provide a means of limiting the acceptable range of behavior within an organization. By routines, I refer to the patterns of behavior engaged in by more than one person in response to a common stimulus (Feldman 1988*b*). Examples of organizational routines include budgeting, hiring personnel, and providing information. These routines do not always result in the outcome they ostensibly pursue. Hiring routines do not always result in hiring anyone; routines in response to a request for a report do not always produce reports. This is the reason for defining the routine in terms of stimulus instead of outcome.

Such routines are constituted of patterns of behavior. The patterns specify both sequence and roles: in what order tasks are performed and by whom. For example, in a hiring routine there may be different people in charge of processing applications, choosing people to interview from among the applications, interviewing, and making the decision. Each of these tasks must be done roughly in the order listed above and by the people designated to perform the tasks.[6] People performing tasks later in the sequence are dependent on the people who perform earlier tasks. In some routines people must perform tasks simultaneously or interactively. For example, when policy analysts write policy papers that must be approved by many offices in the bureaucracy, analysts from these offices meet to negotiate what is written in the paper. They engage a routine that involves both the simultaneous and interactive performance of tasks such as coming to meetings and discussing sections of reports and the sequential performance of tasks such as gathering information, analysing it, and incorporating it into a report.

Whether the tasks in routines are performed in sequence, simultaneously, or interactively, there is a quality of interdependence to the process. Work done by some comes to naught or cannot be done if

---

[6]   I am aware that hiring sometimes takes place in an order quite unlike the one used in this example. The use of this example is not to describe hiring, *per se*, but to describe routines.

others do not perform their tasks. Indeed, where interaction is required there is a very high degree of interdependence. Even the definition of tasks depends upon the involvement of others.

This interdependence is particularly profound within organizational routines because of the repetition of the pattern and the expectation of participants in the routine that the pattern will be repeated. This creates a situation in which the task interdependence is reinforced. Not only must I perform my task for you to perform yours, but also you must act as if I am going to perform my task. An example of this occurred when I was studying policy analysts in the US Department of Energy. I was interested in the flow of information and I initially assumed that the person who initiated an interaction was important. I soon found, however, that there were many instances in which this was not true. In these instances the need for interaction was recognized by all parties and the act of initiating depended primarily on who had time to do it first. For example, if an action took place and two people knew they had to co-ordinate their responses to it, the first one who had time would call the other. This call would be made knowing that the other person would call soon anyway. Thus, who initiated the interaction was irrelevant to what took place during the interaction. This kind of interaction is important because of the power it has to perpetuate the routine. In this simple case of initiating an interaction, if Person A always initiates, then the smooth operation of the routine depends upon her actions. If she leaves the organization, the operation of the routine depends upon her successor continuing to initiate the inter-action. However, if either Person A or Person B initiates the interaction, then, when either of them leaves the organization, the routine continues unchanged.

This category of limitation does not apply to all jobs. Some are performed relatively autonomously and there is little interdependence. However, many bureaucratic jobs do require people to co-ordinate their work. At the simplest level this occurs because people have overlapping responsibilities so that work continues when someone is sick or on vacation. Thus, file clerks may work out means of keeping track of paperwork so that other people in the office can pick up where one has left off (Suchman 1983). More complex versions of this co-ordination occur where people work on projects together. These projects may involve narcotics agents setting up an arrest, teachers co-teaching a course, policy analysts writing a paper, or any number of other projects.

Effects on Discretionary Behavior

In much writing about discretion the assumption has been made that certain boundaries are set by formal rules and supervisory authority and that the actor's behavior is subject to no further limits (Davis 1976; Lipsky 1980). In some senses this is true, but it is not the whole story. Police officers are free to stop those people who appear suspicious (i.e. for whom there is 'probable cause'); teachers are free to pay more or less attention to whichever students they choose; policy analysts are free to develop more information on some topics and less on others. However, police officers are influenced by the categories they learn from their fellow officers to classify types of people; teachers are guided by training that emphasizes which students need more attention to learn the needed skill; a policy analyst's choice of which topics to develop expertise in depends, in part, on what the other analysts they work with expect them to know. Thus, the exercise of discretion has organizational or social context limits that supplement formal authority.

The limits are not absolute or determinate. They do not prescribe specific behaviors. Limits are interpreted differently by different people. People do not always agree about whether the limits have been transgressed. Thus, the limits cannot be enforced through sanctions, and they cannot be expressed in formal rules.

Formal limits to discretion are necessarily outside the discretionary situation. In responding to formal authority one is concerned with how the immediate situation will look to someone outside the context of it. This concern may result in ploys aimed at constraining the interpretation of the context by people who may be judging the actor's behavior. For instance, file clerks construct ways of doing their work so that, when the task is completed, it looks as if they followed the formal, written procedure (Suchman 1983). Police officers or social workers may find that they construct documentation of a case so that it fits an accepted order rather than documenting the events as they occur.

Organizational or social context limits, however, are strong in ways that formal authority is not. These limits are immediate. They are present within the situation in which they are relevant. When the limits are internal, the concern changes from 'how will this look to someone outside the context' to 'how do I play my role in this situation'. Thus, the police officer becomes concerned with how a police officer would act in this situation. The judge becomes concerned with acting judicially. Training, socialization, and routines establish practices that are reinforced not only by the expectations of others, but also by the internalized expectations of the person in the role.

Social context limits are probabilistic limits rather than absolute limits. They establish what is generally considered to be appropriate behavior; they do not determine what people will do or even what they will be sanctioned for doing. People do behave inappropriately. The inappropriate behavior of doctors, police officers, teachers, and judges is a matter of grave concern, and it is the reason that we strive to understand more about discretion. I suggest, however, that our concern should be with decreasing the likelihood of inappropriate behavior rather than with obliterating it. For this purpose social context limits are well suited.

The difference between the formal limits and the social context limits to discretion can be likened to the difference between a wall and a rushing stream of water. The wall is firm, clearly delineated, and it hurts when you run into it. The rushing stream has none of these characteristics. It moves; its speed varies; it is more powerful in the middle than on the edges. It does not always hurt to go into the stream; indeed it may at times be pleasurable. The wall, however, can be assaulted and broken down while the stream rushes on creating a path for itself against the mightiest resistance. The analogy is not perfect, but it makes the point. The stream and the social context have influence not because of their absolute strength but because of their insidious natures and their sheer persistence.

The social processes considered here influence the determination of relevant idiosyncrasies by influencing the determination of appropriate beliefs and behaviors. Potentially, they provide powerful tools for controlling the use of discretion and for stemming injustice as a result of discretion. However, in order to use them effectively we must be willing to choose to reinforce specific behaviors and values and we must use training, socialization, and routines to do so. To choose the desired behaviors and values, we must try to understand more about how behaviors are related to desired goals. To use organizational processes to reinforce the desired behaviors and values we must try to understand more about the relation of these processes to behaviors. Neither quest is a trivial undertaking.

6. Discretion in a Behavioral Perspective: The Case of a Public Housing Eviction Board

RICHARD LEMPERT

THE discretion that law grants may be examined as a quality of rules, as a quality of behavior, or as a sense that people have of their freedom to act.[1] Thus legal rules give discretion, people exercise discretion, and individuals contemplating or reflecting on action may feel as if their actions are or were discretionary. Discretion as a quality of rules is a topic much mooted by legal philosophers and lawyers writing from an analytic perspective (Hart and Sacks 1958; Rosenberg 1970–1; Greenawalt 1975; Dworkin 1977*b*; Post 1984; Fletcher 1984; Barak 1989). Discretion in its other two senses is more appropriately studied by social scientists. While the phenomenology of legal discretion has received little empirical attention, discretionary behavior has been the focus of considerable research by social scientists and empirically oriented lawyers studying the legal system. (See, e.g., Goldstein 1960; Schubert 1963; Sudnow 1965; Skolnick 1966; Davis 1969; Alschuler 1975; Heumann 1978; Kagan 1978; Emerson 1983; Hawkins 1984; Pepinsky 1984.)

Most philosophers who write on legal discretion are thinking primarily of judicial discretion and in particular of law-making discretion or discretion to determine the legal implications of an act. From the philosophical discussion two principles emerge. The first is the idea that legal discretion is authorized choice. Thus Hart and Sacks write, discretion is 'the power to choose between two or more courses of action each of which is thought of as permissible' (1958: 162).

Work on this chapter was supported by Grant #SES–8617981 from the Law and Social Science Program of the National Science Foundation and by the Cook Funds of the University of Michigan Law School. The co-operation of the Hawaii Housing Authority was essential to this research. I would like to thank the many people associated with the HHA who facilitated my investigation. I would also like to thank Keith Hawkins, Robert Post, Fred Schauer, and Carl Schneider for their perceptive and useful comments on an earlier draft of this chapter. All findings and opinions expressed in this chapter are mine and should not be attributed to the National Science Foundation, the University of Michigan Law school, or the Hawaii Housing Authority.

[1] I am indebted to Robert Post for clearly stating this point in a letter commenting on an earlier version of this manuscript.

Dworkin says that a judge has discretion if 'he simply is not bound by the authority in question' (1977*b*: 32). And for Greenawalt who has written one of the clearest and most helpful articles on the topic, 'discretion exists if there is more than one decision that will be considered proper by those to whom the decision-maker is responsible, and whatever external standards may be applicable either cannot be discovered by the decision-maker or do not yield clear answers to the questions that must be decided' (1975: 368).

The second principle is that adjudicative discretion is more than simply the matter of being unbound by authority and in this sense free to choose from among a number of alternatives: it involves choosing within a context set by law. Law, in other words, both constrains as well as frees. It frees the adjudicator because it provides no uniquely correct decision in the circumstances, but it constrains the adjudicator because not every possible decision is permissible (Barak 1989: 19). Without a freedom and constraint that are both rooted in law, there is no adjudicative discretion. Dworkin offers a nice image. 'Discretion', he says, 'like the hole in a doughnut, does not exist except as an area left open by a surrounding belt of restriction' (1977*b*: 31). When the discretion is adjudicative that doughnut is law (cf. Post 1984). If the legal system does not allow the judge to choose, the judge is not exercising discretion but is instead flouting the law, and his decision might properly be reversed. Conversely, if the law places no constraints on the judge's choices, the judge is not exercising a legal discretion at all, but is acting within a realm where law does not apply. Thus, a judge may choose to wear blue pants or green pants or even no pants under his robe; but we would not call his decision an exercise of adjudicative (or legal) discretion.

In discussing discretion, philosophers often point—either hypothetically or actually—to the exercise of discretion, but their concern is typically with the nature of rules and the ways in which or the degree to which rules authorize discretionary behavior, not with the behavior that occurs. One result is that, when one thinks of judicial discretion, one thinks of unpatterned judicial behavior. If a range of actions is permissible, there is no *a priori* reason to expect that one action within that range will be preferred to another. However, discretion is not only a property of legal rules; it is also a property of behavior. As a property of rules discretion need not shape behavior, for rules are not inexorably influential. Judges and others may choose to act where they have no rule-given discretion, and, conversely, if they have discretion, they may not fully consider the range of choices discretion allows. Thus, as a property of behavior, discretion need not reflect the leeway that discretion-conferring rules allow. If law is no guide, other social forces may be, and they may give rise to patterns of behavior that look, and in a sociological sense are, more rule-bound than behavior that is in theory rigorously structured by law. Indeed, discretion may invite social influences as a vacuum invites its own destruction. When law only loosely regulates decisions, other forces may arise that tighten that regulation.

For behaviorally oriented social scientists, judicial discretion has not been the central or even the most important locus of discretion in the legal system. While there are empirical studies of judicial law-making (Schubert 1963; Danelski 1966; Casper 1976) and judicial sentencing (e.g. Cook 1973; Partridge and Eldridge 1974; Hagan, Nagel, and Albonetti 1980; Uhlman and Walker 1980), these tend to focus more on the correlates and predictors of discretionary decision-making than on the manner in which discretion is exercised or the forces that channel discretion. Those interested in the latter issue and the way they culminate in 'discretionary justice' tend to focus on social control agents that are closer than the courts to those who are subjects of legal control. Predominant among these are: the police (e.g. Goldstein 1960; Skolnick 1967; Davis 1969; Reiss 1971; Black 1980), lawyers (e.g. Sudnow 1965; Skolnick 1966; Alschuler 1975; Heumann 1978) and regulatory inspectors of various sorts (Ross and Thomas 1981; Bardach and Kagan 1982; Hawkins 1984).

Those who study how officials exercise discretion often do not focus on legal rules, for discretion is seen as the result of social situations that both shape the exercise of discretion and make its exercise inevitable. Discretion exists not only where an agent is given authority to choose by statute or regulation, but also where that authority is expressly denied. Skolnick's cops, for example, are exercising discretion when they guarantee a burglar lenient treatment if he will improve their clearance rate by confessing to numbers of crimes for which he has not been arrested (1966: 176–9), and Ross's and Thomas's housing inspectors are exercising discretion when they pretend to possess authority they do not have (1981). The behaviorists, in other words, understand that legal actors always have discretion to ignore rules that deny them discretion. Whether this discretion is exercised depends both on the actor's role conception and on the degree to which the actor's conduct is visible and vulnerable to sanctions or reversal. The situation of judges on these dimensions is in most respects less conducive to ignoring clear legal commands than the situations of the other major actors in the law's social control hierarchy.

Both philosophers and social scientists give the impression that, where discretion exists, behavior is not controlled by rules. For the philosophers this is an analytic truth since, if a rule did constrain behavior, there would be no discretion. Social science studies give this impression, not only because they focus on situational pressures that shape behavior, but also because the rules they most predominantly discuss are frequently legal rules from which behavior deviates. However, as some (e.g. Sudnow 1965; Ross 1970) have recognized, one way in which actors can manage discretion is by establishing rules that as a behavioral matter take away much of the discretion that law or situation has allowed.

The Empirical Study

This chapter is about the adjudicative discretion which Hawaiian state law gives a public housing eviction board. It is concerned not only with discretion as a quality of behavior but also with the sense that adjudicators have of their discretion. The two are related, for an adjudicator's sense of discretion can shape the way discretion is exercised. Not only are adjudicators likely to respect the law where it appears to limit their discretion, but, despite legal discretion, adjudicators may establish norms that lead them to feel that they have no discretion in particular cases. In this chapter I shall look at a variety of ways in which the eviction board I observed has exercised discretion, and I shall try to identify forces that shaped the board's discretion in particular cases and changed the pattern of discretionary decisions over time.

The eviction board I studied hears the cases of almost all tenants whom the Hawaiian Housing Authority (HHA) seeks to evict from its public housing projects on the island of Oahu.[2] The board was authorized by state law in 1949 and established in 1957. However, I shall focus on the board as it existed from 1960 on, which is when a board composed of three authority officials was replaced by one composed of five citizen volunteers.

[2] Occasionally, when a quorum of the board cannot be mustered, the HHA will appoint a hearing officer to try cases. Also some tenants when threatened with eviction leave before the board can hear their cases.

My investigation into the HHA's eviction board occurred in two stages. The first stage, which involved three months of field research during the summer of 1969, examined the eviction board from its inception until that time.[3] The second stage, which involved field-work during the summer of 1987, examined the eviction board from 1966 until that point. During both stages I received the full co-operation of the HHA. I was able to interview the great majority of those people, except for tenants, who had been involved in the Authority's eviction process since 1960. These interviews included eviction-board members, Authority officials, including those responsible for prosecuting the Authority's cases before the board, project managers, and private legal-aid attorneys who had defended tenants before the board. I sat in on more than thirty eviction hearings, all those held during the two summers of my field-work. I read the full transcripts of more than a hundred additional hearings, most involving cases from the early 1960s. I perused Authority records for any official documents or other materials relating to evictions. I collected and coded information from the records of more than 1,400 eviction actions. And I read all the Federal and state statutes and regulations relating to the eviction process that I could identify.

I found that, during the eighteen years between my two visits, some aspects of the eviction process had remained the same, but others had changed—sometimes dramatically. The board's status, jurisdiction, and powers were officially the same. In both 1969 and 1987 the board was composed of citizen volunteers who were paid only a nominal sum ($10 a member a meeting in 1987) for their services. Although the board members were appointed by the Authority, they were independent of it. The board's chair was a board member, and neither the board nor its chair had to answer to the Authority for its decisions. The Authority was required to bring before the board any tenant it sought to evict, and the tenant had a right to a 'full and fair hearing', which included the rights to know in advance why the Authority sought to evict, to present witnesses or documentary evidence, to cross-examine opposing witnesses, and to be represented by counsel.[4] At both points in time the board had the power to acquit

[3] Field-work in Hawaii is a tough assignment, but someone has to do it.
[4] In the early 1960s the Hawaii Housing Authority was apparently unique among US public housing authorities in the degree to which it extended these due process protections to tenants it sought to evict. In the 1970s federal rules extended in somewhat different form similar protections to tenants in all federally aided projects across the United States.

tenants, in which case the tenants had to be allowed to remain; to evict tenants, in which case the Authority was granted a writ of possession without further litigation; or conditionally to evict tenants, in which case an eviction order would be issued but its execution would be held in abeyance and eventually cancelled so long as the tenant complied with the conditions specified.[5]

The types of cases the board heard and its procedures for hearing these cases also looked much the same in 1969 and 1987. In both years and every year in between actions brought for non-payment of rent dominated the docket. This was the sole charge in about three-quarters of the cases, and it was charged together with some other offense in an additional 5 per cent of the actions. Other cases the boards heard involved what I call 'trouble behavior'. This includes such things as income falsification,[6] fighting, parking more than one car or a car that does not run, keeping pets, and allowing unauthorized guests to occupy units.

Hearings were held around the same long table in the same conference room in 1969 and 1987, and in many ways they looked similar. Lawyers were seldom present, rules of evidence were relaxed; conversation was informal; tenants who did not spontaneously excuse themselves would be invited to tell their stories, and board members would not only question tenants but might advise them on how to deal with their problem or lecture them on their moral deficiencies. The hearings ordinarily lasted as long as the parties had something to say. Most took between twenty and thirty minutes, but a number took somewhat longer, and cases lasting an hour or more occurred.[7]

[5] These orders, called 'conditional deferrals' or simply 'conditions', were most common in cases brought for non-payment of rent, and the usual condition was that the tenant pay back the rent owing by a certain date and pay all rent when due for a certain period of time. A 1980 amendment to the statute establishing the eviction board could be read as removing the board's discretionary authority to issue conditional eviction orders where the HHA proved a lease violation, but a 1982 statement by the lawyer who then handled the Authority's eviction cases did not interpret the law that way nor, in a training session held that year, was the board told that this was what it meant.

[6] In both 1969 and 1987 the rent in most of the HHA's projects was set at a percentage of a family's annual income and there were income limits on eligibility for placement in the projects. In 1969 but not in 1987 there were also income limits on continued occupancy.

[7] The longer cases are ordinarily trouble-behavior cases, in which the Authority presents a number of witnesses and in which tenants are disproportionately likely to be represented by attorneys (Lempert and Monsma 1988). The hearings of twenty or thirty minutes common in open-and-shut non-payment cases may seem short but are in fact longer than the typical hearing in at least some housing (Lazerson 1982), small claims (Conley and O'Barr 1990), and misdemeanor courts (Mileski 1971).

Decisions were reached by the board in a brief discussion following the close of the case, and the tenant and manager were immediately informed about what the board had decided.

In other respects, however, there were marked differences in the situations I observed in 1969 and 1987. Many of these were not observable from the hearing but rather concerned the Authority's project management and its officials' views of the appropriate scope of board discretion. In 1969 considerable discretion was granted project managers with respect to rent collection on the projects. Managers were free to 'work with' tenants in financial difficulty, and it was largely up to the manager to decide if and when to bring a tenant before the eviction board. Thus, when non-payment tenants were brought up for eviction, they commonly had three, four, or more months rent owing. In 1987, thanks to computers, the central management staff knew as soon as the project managers which tenants were behind on their rent, and project managers had to justify decisions not to seek eviction when tenants were more than six weeks in arrears. Thus many non-payment tenants who faced the board in 1987 owed two months rent or less, and a number of them owed nothing because they had cleared their debts after being subpoenaed.[8] In 1969 the latter group would have had their cases cancelled.

In 1969 the Authority's central office officials, including its Supervising Public Housing Manager (SPHM), who was in charge of presenting cases to the eviction board, saw the board's independence as a virtue,[9] did not question the board's discretion to withhold eviction despite finding a lease violation, and regarded the conditional deferral as an appropriate decision when tenants owed rent.[10]

In 1987, by contrast, top Authority officials regarded the board as an awkwardly independent cog in the Authority's efforts to maintain peaceful, smooth running projects. While the board's power conditionally

---

[8] Cases were also more rapidly processed in 1987 because two full-time staff positions—a secretary and a lawyer—were devoted to the management of the eviction process. In 1969 the eviction process was managed by the Supervising Public Housing Manager (SPHM) and a secretary, each of whom had numerous other responsibilities that they regarded as more central to their roles.

[9] The law establishing the eviction board allowed the Authority to staff it with Authority officials, and it was so staffed before 1960. The authority's central-office official decided to reconstitute it as an independent body staffed by community volunteers because, I was told, they did not want a 'kangaroo court'.

[10] Project managers did not share these views. Four of the five managers felt strongly that, if they could prove a lease violation, they had the right to an eviction regardless of the credibility of a tenant's promise to reform.

to defer was recognized, its discretion to do so was not respected, and during the preceding seven years steps had been taken to minimize the occasions on which such discretion would be exercised. In 1979 a training session had been held for the board at which the Authority's rent-collection needs were emphasized. In 1982 the board chairs had been sent to 'judge's school' in Reno, Nevada, in the hope of promoting more legalistic decision-making, and in the same year another training session was held for all board members. Also beginning about 1980 fixed terms were established for board members. Several members were not reappointed because they were regarded as too pro-tenant, and new appointments were made with an eye to whether they would appreciate the Authority's point of view.[11]

Some changes between 1969 and 1987 were visible just from observing hearings. The most obvious was that the board in 1987 consisted of fourteen members rather than five. In 1970 two tenants were added to the eviction board to create a seven-member panel and in October 1979 a second seven-member panel was created, with its own chair, so that eviction actions could be heard every week rather than every other week, thus allowing the Authority to process cases more rapidly for eviction. As the panels never got together except for one or two parties a year, the situation was one of two seven-member eviction boards rather than one fourteen-member board.[12] Another difference was that the Authority's cases were presented by an attorney, whom I shall call the DAG,[13] rather than by the SPHM. However, in many respects the attorney proceeded at the hearing in much the same manner as the SPHM had in 1969. Both acted

---

[11] In 1987 more board members worked in real-estate property management than in any other occupation. In 1969 a majority of board members either had a social work background or did extensive volunteer work for the poor.

[12] I shall refer to each panel as the 'eviction baord'. In the data I collected panel identity is not significantly related to case outcome.

[13] DAG stands for Deputy Attorney-General. The Authority's prosecutor from 1982 on was a Deputy Attorney-General assigned by the Hawaii State Attorney General's Office to the HHA. Although the DAG remained technically a member of the Attorney General's Office and not of the HHA, for all practical purposes the DAG was an employee, reporting in 1987 to the SPHM and through her to the Director of Housing Management (DHM). The Authority had in 1979 appointed a full-time eviction specialist to prosecute cases and handle the other legal and quasi-legal work necessary to a smooth-running eviction process. The first such specialist was an Authority employee who was not a lawyer. His two successors were DAGs. As far as I can determine, the presence of a full-time eviction specialist was an important influence on the eviction process, but the fact that the specialist was a lawyer was not (Lempert 1989).

informally. They avoided legal jargon except at the outset when the cause of action was explained, and they conversed with the tenant to make sure that his or her story came out. The SPHM, however, tended to leave the presentation of the Authority's case to the project manager, while the DAG presented the details of the manager's report himself and relied on the project manager for confirmation and further information.

A more subtle difference between the hearings of 1969 and 1987 was that the board members in 1987 seemed less sympathetic to the tenants than they had in 1969. In 1987 the board members were less prone to delve into ways that the tenant might solve his or her problems and almost never questioned the adequacy of the project manager's efforts to 'work with' the tenant.

Finally, the possibility of an appeal to the Authority's Board of Commissioners was often mentioned during the 1987 hearings—both before and after the board's decision was rendered—but was seldom if ever mentioned in 1969. During his case presentation or summation the DAG emphasized the possibility of an appeal to remind the board members that, even if they voted to evict, the tenant would not necessarily be forced to leave.[14] After an eviction decision, the tenant was told how to appeal and what he or she would have to do to be successful. In 1969 such explanations were seldom necessary, for tenants were almost always allowed to stay.

From the Authority's point of view the stress placed on the appeal process was made possible by a 1980 amendment to the Act establishing the eviction board which provided that appeals had to be based on 'new facts or evidence pertinent to the case which could not have been presented and were not available for presentation' to the eviction board.[15] Before the law was amended the Commissioners had to hear appeals *de novo*, and any system that encouraged appeals would have been untenable. Indeed the burden of deciding whether an appeal presented new facts and evidence was eventually deemed excessive, and in 1984 this responsibility was delegated to the HHA's Executive Director. The result was that after 1984 appeals almost never reached

---

[14] The attorney was also fond of reminding the board that evicting an apparently needy family would free an apartment for a family that would follow project rules and was presumptively just as needy.

[15] Chapter 360 § 3 Hawaii Revised Statutes, as amended May 1980. The usual 'new fact or evidence' that tenants alleged on appeal was that since the hearing they had repaid all the rent that was owing. The 1980 Amendments made some other changes in the law establishing the eviction board, but these need not concern us.

the Commissioners unless it was a foregone conclusion that they would be allowed. Indeed, the Commissioners typically did not hear appeals but instead ratified 'stipulated agreements' negotiated between the housing staff and the tenant which noted as a new fact that the tenant had fully corrected the problem giving rise to the board's eviction order (usually by paying an outstanding rent debt) and stipulated that, in exchange for the withholding of the eviction order, the tenant agreed to comply fully with all lease provisions for a period of one year and to waive all rights to a hearing should any lease provision be violated within that time.

The changes that occurred between 1969 and 1987 did not, of course, occur at the same time. Yet, for purposes of investigating changes in the board's exercise of discretion, there are two watershed years. The first is 1975, which marks a dramatic change in the leadership of the Authority as well as the commencement of a lawsuit that at one time appeared to threaten the existence of the eviction board.[16] Before 1975 cases were handled as they had been in 1969 or, for that matter, in 1961, and the outcomes were the same. The second is 1979. This is when a secretary was assigned full time to handle the paperwork of evictions, and a full-time specialist was hired to process and prosecute eviction cases. It also marks the appointment of the second eviction panel, which was formed by dividing the old panel into two and adding three new appointees to one group and four to another. After the appointment of the second panel, the eviction process came to look much as it looked when I observed it in 1987. The period between 1975 and 1979 was not so much a period of gradual change as a period of upheaval and uncertainty (Lempert, 1990; Lempert and Monsma 1988). Hence we shall not focus on these years when we discuss the transformation of discretion.

With this information as background, we are now ready to examine the discretion the board exercised. First, I shall discuss several

[16] The specific changes need not concern us here, for their relevant consequences have been described. They involved the conversion of the HHA Executive Directorship from a Civil Service to a gubernatorial appointed position and the retirement of the long-time head of HHA—who had come up through the housing-management ranks—and his replacement by a more business-oriented head who had no prior housing experience. These changes in turn reflect vast new responsibilities—including the task of building and selling middle-income housing—that had been given to the HHA in the 1970s and a local scandal that developed over the way these responsibilities were handled. The case that almost scuttled the eviction board also has little to do with this chapter. It is entitled *Tileia* v. *Chang* and is described in Lempert and Monsma (1988).

varieties of discretion that are illustrated by board decision making. Then we shall see that discretion may not only be influenced by external forces, but may be systematically transformed.

Varieties of Discretion

The case of the house that burnt

In the 1960s, before the income limits for continued occupancy in federally aided low-income housing had been abolished, a family with eight children, let us call them the Teofilos,[17] exceeded the income limits and contracted to build a home. The day before the Teofilos were supposed to move, and after the grace period which federal law gave them to find a home had expired, their new house burnt to the ground. The Authority was not anxious to press the case for eviction, but felt that federal law required that action. The eviction board refused to issue the order. On several occasions it remanded the case to see if anything could be worked out and to give the Teofilos more time to find a home. One member who was involved in real estate went so far as to search for housing for the family in his own time. The board knew what the law required, but its members wished to avoid the force of the law. Indeed, in discussing what to do with the Teofilos, one member said he would not evict, no matter what the law required. Eventually the case was resolved when the Authority transferred the family to no-income-limit housing it operated for the Navy. Doing this breached both policy and regulations, for the family had no Navy connection and was too large for the unit available, but the Authority apparently felt that it was less important to conform to these rules than to federal housing regulations.

The board was able to exercise discretion effectively in this case because its actions were not reviewable. The board was given no legal authority to do anything other than evict, but it could effectively refuse to evict because the law establishing it did not provide an avenue by which the Authority could appeal to a court or other higher tribunal, and the same law did not allow the Authority to secure a writ of possession except by prevailing before its eviction board. The board was well aware of its power and that, but for it, the family would have been without decent shelter.

What is most striking about this case is that it is apparently unique.

---

[17] All names used in this chapter have been changed.

While I could not look at every case the board heard over thirty years, my perusal of several years of case transcripts did not turn up any other case in which the board knowingly did something it was not empowered by law to do. Furthermore, I did not see such a case during the two summers I sat in on board hearings, nor did I hear of such a case in my interviews with Authority officials, board members, or project managers. The latter's silence is quite telling, for they freely complained about board decisions that in their view exceeded the board's proper authority.

The board's more usual attitude in over-income cases is expressed by the chair's statement to a couple with seven children, one of whom was a mute. This family had been unable to find a house because the private rental market provided little housing for moderate-income families with more than a few children: 'I regret very much to inform you of the decision we came to arbitrarily; it's one that we have no other recourse [*sic*] on account of the qualifications of the law governing a case such as yours. We have to order eviction because there is no way we can do otherwise.' The difference in the attitude expressed here and the attitude expressed in the case I first described cannot be explained by board composition since many of the same people sat on both cases. It is explained, I believe, by the extraordinary nature of the tragedy that befell the first family. Almost all over-income cases the board heard involved families who had been successful by middle-class standards and who could not find suitable housing because of the tight nature of the housing market that confronted large families. The first case involved a family that had solved the housing problem in the most culturally approved fashion—buying a home—only to have their house unexpectedly taken from them.

It appears from both the philosophical and sociological literature that discretion in the sense of unreviewability is relatively common, since it is easy to provide examples of adjudicators who have discretion to make decisions that are unreviewable and continually use that discretion (see, e.g., Rosenberg 1970–1). Consideration of the Hawaiian data suggests that there is a further important distinction to be made. Typically, when an adjudicator like a multi-judge court has unreviewable discretion, it also has discretion in the rule-oriented sense that the authority to exercise judgment is entrusted to it; that is, it is authorized to choose from a wide range of outcomes, any one of which is permissible. Indeed, a major reason for making an exercise of discretion unreviewable is that it is unlikely that a reviewing agency will be able to exercise better judgment. The eviction board's members did not have discretion in this sense. The law did not allow them to exercise judgment about whether families that were over the income limits should be evicted once the statutory grace period had expired. They were mandated to evict in these circumstances. Their only discretion was whether to comply with their mandate. This discretion was effectively allotted them only because the Authority could not appeal from their decision.

It is a mistake to think that the law authorizes this type of discretionary decision-making.[18] Rather the law establishes structural or legal conditions[19] which ensure that a particular adjudicator's decisions will be complied with while not providing a way effectively to remedy errors through appeal. Such conditions give decision-makers the power to force actions that do not comport with legal norms, although as a matter of law they lack the authority.

What the law can do for judges, other structural features do for other decision-makers. Thus the cop on the beat who has stopped two youths in 'the wrong neighborhood' may arrest the one who 'gives him lip' and let off the one who is respectful (Werthman and Piliavin 1967; D. Black 1971). The cop can do this, not because the law provides that disrespect or being in the wrong neighborhood is a crime, but because the officer's power *vis-à-vis* youths is such that they must comply with his decisions, and the officer's 'credibility advantage' coupled with the low visibility of the encounter means that, if he later concocts an account of the encounter legally sufficient to justify arrest, he rather than the youth will be believed. The eviction board that spared the Teofilos was much like the cop, except that its flouting of the law was more visible. However, the Authority shared the board's sense that the Teofilos had done nothing that was unreasonable, and it was pressing for eviction only because it could be held accountable if it did not enforce federal income limits. Had the Authority been

---

[18] The jury is perhaps the best example of a legal decision-maker that gains considerable discretionary power from the fact that its decisions are not reviewable. The power is not accorded the jury by law but is rather a matter of the jury's structural position. See *Bushell's Case* 124 Eng. Rep. 1006 (1670), and *Sparf and Hanson* v. *United States* 156 US 51 (1895).

[19] An example of a structural condition is the fact that in the United States there is no higher court than the Supreme Court and hence no appeal, except through a cumbersome amendment process, from its constitutional decisions. An example of a legal condition is a restriction on interlocutory appeal which allows a trial court to harm a party through a mistaken ruling in a way that a higher court cannot, even by reversing the decision made by the inferior court, fully undo.

unsympathetic to the Teofilos, it might have found a way to impel the board to conform to the law.

Discretion in the sense of unreviewability is common at the street or factory level (Lipsky 1980; Bardach and Kagan 1982), and it might seem that it is common among adjudicators also. Looking at court decisions from the outside, there appear to be many situations in which adjudicators are able to enforce their will only because their decisions are unreviewable. But consider the matter from the adjudicator's point of view. The members of the eviction board in the Case of the House that Burnt could and, in effect, did say, 'The law required me to evict, but I exercised my discretion,' meaning discretion in the sense of the power of unreviewability. Usually, however, it will appear to the adjudicator whose decision sticks because of unreviewability that his discretionary action (which just happens to be unreviewable) is in accord with a legal mandate to exercise judgment and is not an exercise of lawless power. The Teofilo case may be unique in my data because adjudicative discretion that exists only because unreviewability confers a power is, at least phenomenologically, rare.[20]

The case of the beans that burnt

This case involved a Korean woman, whom I will call Mrs Park, who lived in one of the Authority's high-rise buildings for the elderly. On three separate occasions over two years, while boiling down beans with ginseng for an ethnic dish she enjoyed, Mrs Park had forgotten she had beans cooking and left the apartment. On each occasion the beans boiled dry and then burnt, sending smoke into the halls. After the third such incident the project manager sought to evict Mrs Park because he thought that she was likely to forget again and that an overheated pot or burning beans might in some way spark a fire. He cited the woman for violating lease covenants relating to (*a*) not damaging the dwelling unit or causing insurance premiums to increase, (*b*) keeping the unit in a safe and sanitary condition, (*c*) using facilities only in a reasonable manner, and (*d*) conducting oneself so as not to disturb the neighbors' peaceful enjoyment of their accommodations

---

[20] Some project managers, on the other hand, knowingly denied tenants their right to an eviction hearing by bluffing them out (Lempert 1989). They knew their actions, which involved misleading notices and, on occasion, blatant lies, were unauthorized denials of rights given to tenants by Authority policy. The managers, however, saw bluffing as a way of recapturing from the board a discretion—to decide when tenants could not be 'saved'—that was rightfully theirs. The bluff system began in the mid-1960s and endured for about a decade.

and maintaining the housing project in a decent, safe, and sanitary condition.

When I discussed this case with the Authority's prosecutor the day it was to be heard, we both expected Mrs Park to be growing feeble minded as well as old and increasingly incapable of living alone. At the hearing, however, a different picture emerged. Mrs Park came to the hearing with a lawyer, a minister who translated for her since she did not speak English, a Korean-speaking neighbor, and a petition signed by many of the building's tenants saying that they wanted her to remain and would look after her She looked as if she were about 70 and quite capable of looking after herself. The evidence at the hearing was that she was well regarded by the neighbors and was an active volunteer in her church, who was there almost every day and could greet each of the five hundred or so church members by name. While the project manager made a convincing case that the building was constructed so that a fire would be especially dangerous, Mrs Park's advocates showed that, with the exception of one occasion when the hot pot was apparently dropped, scorching part of a rug, no damage had been done by the several incidents. Except for these incidents, the project manager agreed, Mrs Park was a good tenant and a pleasant person. The Korean-speaking neighbor who lived across the hall was a friend who said that she would look in on Mrs Park daily and boil beans for her once a month, the schedule Mrs Park had followed.

Perhaps the key to the hearing was that the Authority's prosecutor did not think that Mrs Park should be evicted, nor did he think that the board would be willing to evict her. Thus he shaped the discussion so that it focused on steps that could be taken to ensure that Mrs Park would not pose a fire hazard if she stayed. Mrs Park's lawyer had the same agenda, hence the offer by the neighbor to look in on her. There was also some discussion about whether Mrs Park would be willing to give up her stove and cook with a microwave instead.

The prosecutor had perhaps misjudged the board. At the start of its deliberations one member, a real-estate manager who had just joined the board, moved to evict. Eventually the motion was defeated, and a conditional eviction—a form of probation—was voted. The conditions were that the Authority remove Mrs Park's stove within a week, that Mrs Park secure a microwave to replace it, and that there be no further incidents for three years. It is impossible to say whether this decision, as opposed to an outright eviction, would have been reached had the prosecutor not obviously favored a compromise of this sort.

The member who moved for eviction was intelligent and articulate and he might have persuaded a majority of the board to go along with him had the Authority's representative been pressing for the same action.

The board in this example is exercising three kinds of discretion. First the board has discretion to determine whether there is a lease violation. The determination is discretionary in the sense that the judgment is entrusted to the board and the board must pick out those facts that bear on its decision-making task (Barak 1989: 13). If burning beans does not violate any of the cited lease provisions, not only will the woman avoid eviction, but she may go on burning beans to her heart's content. The second, which is dependent on finding a lease violation, involves deciding whether to allow Mrs Park to remain in housing despite the lease violation.[21]

The third locus for discretion, which is dependent on both finding a lease violation and determining that alternatives to eviction should be explored, is in deciding the conditions under which the woman will be allowed to remain. This discretion too is not clearly confided by the statute authorizing the eviction board, but is firmly rooted in the board's 'common law' and would be regarded by both the board members and the Authority as a necessary concomitant of the board's power to withhold eviction when the Authority has presented a legally sufficient case.

The existence of analytically distinct forms of discretion does not, however, mean that all forms will be equally salient to those involved in the decision-making process. Ordinarily only two discretionary decisions are salient, but they are not the same for tenants and project managers on the one hand and the board members on the other.[22] For

---

[21] From the face of the statute, particularly after it was amended in 1980, it is not clear that the board is authorized to exercise such discretion but the board's statute has always been interpreted by it and the Authority to confide such discretion in it. The existence of this discretion was acknowledged in a 1982 memorandum describing the powers of the eviction board that the Deputy Attorney General who ran the Authority's eviction process wrote to the acting SPHM: 'The Hawaii Housing Authority's hearing boards perform three basic functions: determining whether tenants violated provisions of the rental agreement with the Authority; determining whether the rental agreement should be terminated as a result of the violation; and determining whether tenants should be evicted for the aforementioned violations.' According to a 'script' in the Authority's files, a similar description of the board's powers, with explicit mention of the power to set conditions, was given to the board members at a training session held for them in 1982.

[22] All these stages appear salient to the DAG, at least in some cases. He recognizes that he must show a lease violation, and, while he argued in 1987 that it was

the parties, the first two types of discretion—determining whether there is a legal cause for eviction and if so whether eviction should follow—are lumped together and important while the third is distinct and subsidiary. Thus both the tenant and the project managers are interested in whether the tenant will be evicted immediately or allowed to stay. It does not matter whether the tenant is allowed to stay because no lease violation has been found, or whether, despite a lease violation, the tenant is not expelled. When the tenant avoids immediate eviction, the tenant regards the decision as a victory, and the manager regards it as a loss, regardless of the conditions that are set and the implications that these conditions have for the tenant's prospects of avoiding eviction in the long run. The tenant's attitude is like that of the criminals described in a number of plea-bargaining studies who focus on the sentence which might be received and are relatively indifferent to whether the sentence is a result of charge or sentence bargaining, even though the charge pleaded to will become a matter of record that may have substantial future implications.

From the board's standpoint it is the first type of discretion on the one hand and the second and third types on the other which are distinct. The board must decide whether there has been a lease violation and, if so, how to dispose of the case. The former determination seldom poses any difficulties. But in dealing with the latter issues, the decisions on whether to allow the tenant to stay and on the conditions to be imposed if the tenant does stay are inseparable. Assuming a lease violation has been proven, the more likely it is that the tenant can cure that violation and not violate again, and the more likely it is that the tenant will be given another chance conditional on the cure and subsequent good behavior. Conversely, even a sympathetic tenant may face eviction if it appears unlikely that future violations can be prevented. Thus, had there been no way to meet the Authority's concerns regarding the fire hazard Mrs Park posed, she would not have been allowed to stay. Indeed, at one point it appeared that the board's decision might become unraveled because it was unclear that federal regulations allowed the removal or disconnection of a tenant's

---

inappropriate for the board to refuse evictions when it found that a tenant had not fully met his or her rent payment obligations, he never argued that it was beyond the board's power to do so. Thus he was aware of the board's discretion to refuse eviction notwithstanding a lease violation and if so, he recognized, as in Mrs Park's case, that the conditions set by the board were important.

stove even when all parties desired it.[23] Similarly the board has evicted families for damages caused by their children when it appeared that the families, despite their best efforts, could not control their children's actions.

From an analytic perspective the board's discretion to determine the conditions under which Mrs Park could stay seems stronger, in the sense of being less law bound, than its discretion to determine whether she should be allowed to stay subject to conditions (cf. Dworkin 1977*b*). The law provided no guidance to the board members as they creatively sought to determine arrangements that would prevent Mrs Park from posing a fire hazard, but, in deciding whether Mrs Park should be allowed to stay despite her actions, the board was constrained by its need to respect the goals of the lease clauses Mrs Park was shown to have violated.

This analytic distinction, however, makes no sense from a behavioral perspective. The two determinations cannot be separated, for it is the board's creativity in establishing conditions that determines whether it can allow a tenant to stay, while still respecting the goals of the lease provisions that it is called on to enforce. Discretion is often intertwined in this way, and efforts to limit or extend discretion of one analytically distinct sort may affect how discretion of another analytically distinct sort is exercised. Thus Heumann and Loftin found that the Michigan legislature's effort to prevent judges from sentencing gun-carrying criminals to less than two years in prison affected the charging discretion of prosecutors and the discretion that judges had to accept or reject plea bargains (Loftin, Heumann, and McDowall 1983). It is for similar reasons that Abel (1982*a*, 1982*b*) and others argue that institutions of informal justice may extend state control. When police or prosecutors have the discretion to refer disputes to institutions of informal justice, they may pursue matters that they would have dropped had pursuing the matter necessarily placed it in formal court. Focusing on the discretion that inheres in particular rules may miss important ways that discretion constrains and frees choices. Individual rules must be examined as parts of applied rule systems.

---

[23] I was told in a letter by one board member that, several months after the case I observed, Mrs Park again let her beans burn, was brought before the board, and was this time evicted. The incident may have happened because the stove had not been removed or disconnected, or because Mrs Park had impermissibly reconnected her stove, or because Mrs Park found a way to burn her beans in a microwave. My correspondent did not tell me.

The board's other discretionary decision, the decision about whether there has been a lease violation in the first instance, is, of the decisions entrusted to the board, the one most closely confined by law. In reaching this decision, the board members are to examine the facts and determine whether they make out a lease violation. From a legal–analytic perspective this narrow task may none the less involve substantial judgmental discretion, since the factual determination may be quite difficult, and lease provisions may require interpretation.

From a behavioral standpoint, however, the situation is different. The fact of the lease violation in Mrs Park's case appeared so unproblematic that the board in its discussion did not even address the issue. Rather the members turned immediately to the question of whether there were any conditions under which the woman could be allowed to remain without posing a threat to her neighbors. In the eviction setting this is almost always the case. Lease violations are ordinarily clear,[24] and the board has no discretion, except in the sense that, as in the Teofilo case, they may ignore the law, to find otherwise. Thus, what is conceptually a major locus for the exercise of board discretion is behaviorally almost never the occasion for discretionary decision-making. The question whether there has been a lease violation seldom merits discussion.

The case of Mrs Park reveals one other way in which the board's discretion is affected and, in effect, limited. In this case, the DAG, despite the manager's position to the contrary, did not seek eviction. Rather he participated with the board members and Mrs Park's lawyer in a discussion of arrangements that would remove the threat of a fire yet still allow Mrs Park to cook her beans, and he concluded the Authority's case by stating: 'If the board feels that there has been sufficient corrective actions . . . then I would see no problem with some kind of conditional deferment that there be no further forgetfulness of boiling beans down or whatever. Some type of condition; that is what I would recommend. Let her stay on probation.' This prosecutorial concession further limited the board's discretion. While the board might have decided to let Mrs Park stay, even if the prosecutor had sought her eviction, when the prosecutor is willing to accept a conditional deferment, the board as a behavioral matter is

---

[24] The major exception is in the occasional case involving troublesome behavior where different witnesses present different stories about an event (e.g. who started a fight) or the Authority has difficulty finding credible witnesses to testify to the defendant tenant's misdeeds.

unlikely to offer less. The point applies generally. In an adversary system, whatever the discretion of the decision-maker, a party is unlikely to do worse than the opposing party requests.[25] Thus, the board did not seriously consider the motion of one member to evict Mrs Park. Had the prosecutor's concession not been made, the motion certainly would have divided the board and might well have carried.

The cases of the tenants who owed rent (I)

Mrs A, a woman of about 35, owes $300.00, or a little more than two months back rent. She appears before the eviction board with three children, all under 6 years of age, in tow. After the board chair introduces himself and the board members, Mrs A is told the cause of action and asked whether she is willing to proceed without counsel (which she agrees to do). She and the project manager, who will report on her payment history, are placed under oath.[26]

The Authority's prosecutor, in this case, the SPHM, lets the project manager present the details of the Authority's case. He reports that Mrs A has often been late with her rent and that about three months before the hearing she stopped paying entirely. Three notices to speak with him were ignored, and he did not find her at home on two occasions when he went to her house. Two weeks before the hearing, shortly after she was subpoenaed to appear, Mrs A came to the project office and paid $120.00, but $300.00 on a monthly rent of $140.00 is still outstanding.

At this point Mrs A is asked if she wishes to make a statement. She explains that she got behind in her rent when she fell on some stairs and injured her back. To get treatment she had to spend her rent

---

[25] There are exceptions such as juries that give a plaintiff greater damages than his lawyer sought or a judge who imposes a stiffer sentence than a prosecutor requested. However, these exceptions are empirically rare occurrences. The plea-bargaining system, for example, could not work if judges insisted on more severe sentences than those agreed to by prosecutors, and rejections of civil settlements are almost unheard of, even in class actions where judges have a special obligation to consider the interests of the plaintiff class as a whole.

[26] The cases discussed in the previous sections are based on actual transcripts of cases I observed. The cases in this section are composites and so are described in the present tense as they might appear to an observer attending the hearing. No one case exactly fits the descriptions which follow, but these cases are as typical as any I might offer of the kinds of cases involving non-payment of rent that the eviction board hears. The quotations I use are not composites; they are taken from transcripts, although some extraneous material has been eliminated and portions have been rendered more grammatical than their spoken form.

money on doctors' bills. She also says that she lost time from her work in a candy factory, and that she had to spend the first paycheck that she received when she got back on food. The manager interrupts to say that two years before, when Mrs A fell behind on her rent, she also said that she had injured her back, and he reminds the board that, during the period when Mrs A was supposedly home from work with her back injury, he went to her unit twice to talk to her but she was not in. The board does not know whether to believe Mrs A's story or not.

The board chair then takes control of the discussion. He asks Mrs A where Mr A is. She explains that she was divorced more than two years ago. He then asks whether Mr A pays child support. She replies that he left the island after the divorce and that she cannot locate him. At this point the chair asks her whether she wants to stay in public housing. Mrs A replies that she does because she does not know where else she and her children can live. Another member asks whether she has considered welfare? She replies that she gets food stamps, but that with her job her income is above the AFDC (Aid to Families with Dependent Children) cut-off. The chair asks her whether, if she is allowed to stay in housing, she could manage to pay her current rent as it accrues and pay an extra $50.00 a month on her debt. She replies that she could. The chair then reminds her that next to food for her children, rent must be her highest priority. Mrs A nods her agreement. She is then excused, and the board retires to deliberate.

After a quick and almost perfunctory deliberation, spiced only by some discussion of whether Mrs A really did injure her back, the board returns, and the chair tells Mrs A that they have voted to evict her (Mrs A looks crestfallen) but that they have deferred the execution of the order and that Mrs A can stay in housing if she keeps her rent current and pays an extra $50.00 a month until her back charges are paid off. (Mrs A looks relieved and happy.) The chair further explains that, should she not stick to this payment schedule, the manager will report back to the board and that they will order her evicted immediately without another chance to be heard. He concludes by wishing her good luck, and she thanks the board members for giving her a second chance. The manager looks disgruntled but unsurprised as he leaves. The next day the project manager complains to another manager that, although he could not prove it, he thinks that Mrs A was vacationing on another island with a male friend during the two weeks she claimed to be away from work with her injury. At least this is what a neighbor told him she was doing on one of the occasions when he called on Mrs A and found that she was not at home. He did not mention this to the board, he tells his friend, because his evidence was only hearsay and he did not think the board would buy it. His fellow manager sympathizes and they both agree that cases like Mrs A's cost the Authority oodles of money.[27]

Mrs B's case was exactly like Mrs A's case except that she went to the project office and paid the $300.00 she owed five days before the hearing. The case was cancelled. If Mrs B fell behind on her rent sometime during the next six months, she would again be summoned to appear before the board and she, no doubt, would be allowed to pay off her rent debt over time. If Mrs A should miss a rent payment or an instalment payment during the next six months, she would, if the manager brought the default to the board's attention, find that the board voted to execute the deferred order, and she would be evicted.

The board is clearly not exercising discretion in the case of Mrs B, for it did not hear her case. However, as we shall see when we look at the case of Mrs Y in the next section, the Authority need not have cancelled Mrs B's hearing. There is an important point here which, perhaps because it is so obvious, is often missed in studies of adjudicative discretion. This is that the discretion of an adjudicator is typically constrained by the discretion exercised by others, which in turn shapes the observer's perceptions of how discretion is exercised.

Mrs B's case is extreme. Because the Authority chose to drop the case once the lease violation was cured, the board had no occasion to decide whether a cured lease violation might merit a probationary sentence or some other sanction. Other instances are less extreme in that the adjudicator reaches a decision, but possible decisions are foreclosed by the discretionary determinations of others. Thus, when the project manager did not mention the information he received from Mrs A's neighbor, the board could not base a decision on this information, even if they would have believed the hearsay and been prepared to evict for such irresponsible behavior.[28] More generally,

[27] My research reveals that the managers are wrong if by this they mean that the Authority's losses when conditionally deferred tenants fall deeper in debt exceed its gains when such tenants pay off all or part of what they owe (Lempert 1972). The Authority reached conclusions similar to mine when, in 1979, it examined the effect of eviction-board deferrals on subsequent rent collections. I cannot, however, say whether the managers are wrong if they mean to make the general deterrence argument that knowledge of board leniency means that some tenants who would otherwise pay their rent on time do not do so.

[28] In one case a woman told the board that she had taken several months' rent money (which I expect was from welfare) and gone to the outer islands on vacation. She

as I have already pointed out, it is usually the case that in an adversary system the adjudicator is constrained to be no more severe on a party than the party's opponent demands.

Mrs A's case, unlike Mrs B's, appears to involve discretion of a far-ranging sort. Mrs A violated her lease agreement and could legally have been evicted for that violation. The law, however, does not demand this result but leaves it to the board's discretion. Moreover, nothing about the law suggests that, if Mrs A is to be allowed to stay, it should be on the condition that she repay her rent at the rate of $50.00 per month. Yet, despite this rule-granted discretion, if we look at the way the board actually makes decisions, we find that the board does not see itself as having much choice.

Indeed, the decision to allow Mrs A to stay on the condition that she repay her rent hardly involved a choice at all, for, at the time of Mrs A's case (which is based on observations I made in 1969), the board virtually never evicted a tenant who owed rent and claimed to be able to clear that debt. Instead eviction was voted but, as with Mrs A, the execution of the order was stayed on the condition that the tenant keep current and pay off the accrued debt. By 1969 this practice had been routine for nearly a decade.

During the period when this practice of always deferring was being established, which is to say at the outset of the independent board's existence, the board may well have regarded each case as an occasion for the exercise of discretion in that it may seriously have considered the facts of each non-payment case and may have decided each action without feeling that its decision was preordained. Yet the decisions were invariably the same: the tenant was put on conditions and allowed, at least for the moment, to stay. But any sense of discretion receded over time as precedent developed, so that an immediate eviction in circumstances like Mrs A's was almost unthinkable. I found evidence for the development of precedent in the transcripts that were available for fifty-six non-payment cases heard during the board's first two years of existence. The correlation between case order and transcript length as measured in lines is $-.538$, meaning that the more non-payment cases the board had heard, the less time,

said that she had been too poor ever to leave Oahu, that she was happy that she had chosen to spend her rent money in this way, and that she was prepared to live with the consequences. The board evicted her, but the members who had voted to evict remembered the woman with fondness. They admired both her integrity in admitting what she had done and the spirit which led her to want to see something more of the world.

on the average, it took to dispose of new ones. Such a negative correlation is to be expected if what were once discretionary decisions, which required an in-depth investigation of circumstance, became routine, meaning that there was less to talk about.[29]

Students of discretion often argue that officials with discretion, particularly low-level decision-makers like police, prosecutors, and trial judges, generally seek to maximize their discretion. The argument may be correct but only in one sense of the word 'discretion'; that is, the 'authority' or 'finality' sense (Dworkin, 1977*b*). This we have seen may involve 'legal' or authorized discretion, but it may also be a situational discretion, such as that enjoyed by the cop on the beat, to ignore the law. Observing the eviction board suggests that the opposite phenomenon also occurs. Where a decision-making body has legal discretion, it may act to minimize its discretion, that is, to limit the discretion that it must, and, eventually, can, exercise.[30] Familiarity, as Professor Sanders and I argue elsewhere, breeds precedent (Lempert and Sanders, 1986; cf. Schauer, 1987), and a precedent for interpreting facts may be every bit as powerful as precedential pronouncements of law.[31] Thus, there were cases I observed in which board members were suspicious of a tenant's story or felt that the tenant's prospects of repaying his or her rent debt were poor, yet none the less voted to defer eviction because that was the way non-payment cases were handled. Assuming the situation of the HHA's eviction board is not unique, we may expect to find that decision-makers with discretion routinely act so as to limit their discretion as a behavioral matter. Those that do not, such as the United States Supreme Court or the eviction board when it is considering a family

[29] The negative correlation does not appear to be due to a generalized experiential effect. For fifteen income-violation cases that the board heard over the same time period, the correlation between transcript length and case order is an insignificant .031 which differs from the similar correlation for non-payment cases at the .05 level. Income-violation cases often involved disputed allegations about whether tenants had properly reported their entire family earnings and, if not, whether they had innocently misunderstood their responsibility. Of course, had the board confronted as many income violations as it did non-payment cases, the board might have developed discretion-limiting precedent in such cases as well.

[30] Individual decision-makers, no doubt, do the same, but the mechanism involves not the establishment of subjectively binding norms but rather the establishment of protocols or routines such that alternatives to the routine precedential disposition are not consciously considered (Emerson 1983).

[31] Ultimately a precedent for interpreting facts is hard to distinguish from a rule of law, for the factual interpretation matters because it entails specific invariant legal consequences.

accused of fighting, do not hear large numbers of factually similar cases.[32] I shall expand on these points later.

In non-payment cases the eviction board exercises greater discretion in deciding the conditions under which a deferment should be given than in deciding whether to give a deferment. This is not surprising, since cases differ substantially in the size of accrued debts, the reasons for them, and the ability of tenants to repay what they owe over time. Indeed, in the 1960s much of the hearing time was devoted to determining the resources available to the tenant and the conditions under which the tenant's accrued rent debts could be paid. Again, however, the image of an adjudicator exercising authorized discretion by using its judgment to reach a wise decision is misleading. What we have instead is what might be called 'co-operative discretion'. Although Mrs A as a legal matter had no say over the conditions that were set for her continued occupancy, as a practical matter she considerably influenced the board's decision because the board realized that there was no point in setting conditions that Mrs A could not meet. Thus the board negotiated with her over the terms to be set, and used its discretion to confirm the results of the negotiation.

People with discretionary authority can be expected to negotiate with and be influenced by those over whom they are supposed to exercise discretion. Moreover, the eviction-board example suggests that this does not just occur in situations such as the typical plea bargain where the object of discretion has something to offer the adjudicator, like a speedier disposition of the case. Rather it depends on the goals the decision-maker seeks to achieve. Since the eviction-board that heard Mrs A's case wanted it to end with Mrs A remaining in housing and the Authority paid in full, they wanted a solution which she thought would make this feasible. Regulatory officials, like water-pollution inspectors, for example, engage in similar negotiations with those who are subject to their discretion (Hawkins 1984), and some students of regulation have argued that such negotiations are not only common (Winter 1985) but desirable (Scholz 1984).

---

[32] What is factually similar depends, of course, on how closely one looks at different cases (Lempert and Sanders 1986). The Supreme Court chooses to look quite closely at those cases it accords full hearings. Where it examines such large numbers of cases that it cannot look closely at them, as at the *certiorari* stage, rules of thumb develop which systematically and predictably cut down on the scope of exercised discretion, even though the Court has the authority to hear what cases it will. The primary rules seem to be a strong presumption against granting *certiorari* unless one of a small number of conditions are met (Tannenhaus *et al.* 1963).

The cases of the tenants who owed rent (II)

Mrs X's case is like that of Mrs A. She is charged with the same offense, she owes the same amount of money, and she offers the same reasons for falling behind on her rent. She fell down the stairs, hurt her back, had medical bills, and lost time from work. However, at her hearing the Authority's prosecutor is not the SPHM, but a lawyer who devotes almost all his time to the eviction process, and this lawyer, not the board chair, dominates the proceedings. Mrs X's story does differ from Mrs A's in a few particulars. The $120.00 paid before the hearing was paid not at the project office but at a bank, and Mrs X has a bank receipt which she brings to the hearing. No board member asks about Mr X, for they presume there is no Mr X, nor is Mrs X asked whether she can manage time payments. Both the prosecutor and the board question her. She is asked about whether she receives aid from welfare and about whether she has any sources from which she can borrow money to pay off the debt. She tells about her food stamps and says that maybe she can get some money from her mother but that her mother is not too well off either.

After Mrs X has told her story and answered some questions, the prosecutor summarizes the situation:

OK let me explain. What happens here is usually everybody is treated pretty much the same before the board. Usually when somebody comes in here and they owe rent, we ask for an eviction from the board, and if you can get the money together and take care of everything then you can file an appeal. If by the time you put in the appeal you have everything paid off—zero balance— nothing owed—then usually the Commission that runs the housing authority will look at that and in general they will let you stay. So if you can borrow, like you said you could from your mother, and pay off the debt, it usually works out.[33]

'Rosemary,' the prosecutor then says turning to the project manager, 'do you have any other recommendations than that?'.

No [says the manager], eviction without conditions. I talked to her several times and told her that her best chance would be to get a zero balance by the time she came here. She had some time to get the money together but except

---

[33] These comments and those that follow are taken from hearings that I observed and tape recorded. Some grammatical corrections have been made and all names have been changed.

for that $120.00 there has been no payment, so eviction without conditions is what I'm asking for.

The prosecutor then asks the board whether they have any questions. One member asks Mrs X whether the candy factory where she works has a credit union she might borrow from, and she answers that she already owes it $800.00. Another member lectures her for not going to the manager when she hurt herself and explaining her problem.

The board then retires to deliberate. The discussion is even quicker and more perfunctory than in the case of Mrs A. Indeed, the members soon turn to small talk about their private activities because they do not want to give Mrs X the impression that they have not genuinely considered her case. After about eight minutes, they send for the parties.

The chair explains to Mrs X that, because of her rent debt, the board has voted to evict her. The chair adds, however, that it will take several weeks to get the eviction papers in order, and that, if during that period she can come up with the money to pay everything she owes, she will have the 'new facts and evidence' needed to appeal to the HHA's Board of Commissioners. In these circumstances, he says, the Commissioners are 'more than likely' to allow you to stay. If she has any questions about how to appeal, she is told to bring the eviction papers to the project manager along with a bank receipt showing that she has paid off her debt, and the manager will tell her what needs to be done.

Mrs Y's case is like Mrs X's except that she, like Mrs B, cleared her debt five days before the hearing. However, unlike Mrs B, Mrs Y's hearing is not cancelled.

Mrs Y's case takes less time than Mrs X's. After the 'due process' preliminaries, the prosecutor checks with the project manager to make sure the entire rent debt has been paid and that Mrs Y currently enjoys a zero balance. He briefly ascertains the cause of her rental delinquency and her intention to keep up with her rent in the future. As if to justify bringing Mrs Y before the board, he adds, 'Well, you can't be delinquent because the federal government is really down on us to make sure that we make everybody pay on time. It isn't just the state, it is the federal government too.' He then asks the project manager whether the tenant is otherwise a good tenant and, when she says that there have been no other problems, he recommends that the family be allowed to stay but put on six month's probation through a conditional deferment. The manager expresses her agreement with this disposition, and the prosecutor invites the board to ask questions. They briefly go over the reasons for Mrs Y's delinquency and then retire to deliberate. When they return the board chair says:

Mrs Y, the board has decided on an eviction, but with conditions. In other words, an eviction order is deserved but it is held back, not given to you, but you have to comply with a couple of conditions. One is that, beginning this month, you pay the rent on time, within the first seven days of each month, and you verify the payment with the receipt, go to the office, within the very next day, twenty-four hours.[34] Do both of these for six months and then the eviction order is dissolved and everything is OK. Do you understand?

The prosecutor reiterates the conditions. He emphasizes that, not only must Mrs Y pay her rent on time, but she must bring her payment receipt from the bank to the project office the day after she pays (the 'verification' requirement). The case concludes with a pleasant interchange between the prosecutor and tenant:

MRS Y: Thank you very much.
PROS.: Good luck.
MRS Y: Have a good day.

The cases of A and B differ from those of X and Y in one important particular. The first two cases were heard in 1969 while the latter arose in 1987. In the case of Mrs B, the board had no discretion, for her case was never brought to the board. In the cases of A, Y, and X, however, the board had essentially the same legal authority to choose among various outcomes. The board that heard Mrs A's case could have evicted her and relegated her to a right to appeal. The board that heard Mrs X's case could have allowed her to stay on the condition that she pay off her rental debt in $50.00 monthly instalments. And in the case of Mrs Y, the board might have decided that there was no cause for an eviction order since no money was owing at the time of the hearing.

While the decisions in the cases of X and Y were quite different from the decision in the case of A, the board in these cases was not

---

[34] The official reason for this is so that the manager will learn whether the rent has been paid without waiting for the computer print-out that reports rental payments five days after the due date. Thus, if the rent is not paid when due, eviction proceedings can start immediately. It also is an inconvenience that penalizes the tenant for his or her delinquency and may be a reminder to the tenant that he or she must pay the rent on time.

exercising greater discretion. Indeed, the board's decision-making was so perfunctory that the prosecutor of Mrs X and Mrs Y could tell them during the hearing what the outcome was going to be, just as the prosecutor of Mrs A could have done had he so chosen.[35] Thus the cases of X and Y provide further evidence of self-limiting discretion. The board, which had the legal authority to choose among a wide variety of outcomes, acted as if it had virtually no discretion in the cases that it most commonly faced.

But, as I shall discuss in more detail later, the choice of how to be bound is itself a discretionary act. We see this when we compare the cases of A and X. In 1969 the board, whatever its opinion of Mrs A, felt that it had no 'discretion' to evict her. In 1987, on facts identical in all important respects, the board felt that it had no choice but to evict.

Philosophers, we saw at the outset of this chapter, commonly define discretion in terms of legal authority or, to be more precise, in terms of freedom from the constraints that legal authority imposes. Discretion involves an authorized freedom of choice. From a behavioral perspective this conception translates not into freedom to decide as one will, but into the freedom to be influenced by factors other than the law. The example of the eviction-board suggests that such non-legal influences may be strong enough and pervasive enough that a pattern of legally discretionary decisions may be as predictable and as rigidly tied to a few key facts as the decision patterns generated by adjudicators consciously applying specific and detailed legal commands. Indeed, a body with discretion may not only act as if its hands are tied, but it may come to believe that this is the case.

The Strength of Law

These observations lead to two final questions that should be addressed in an effort to understand discretion from a behavioral perspective. The first is when is a legal mandate strong enough to foreclose adjudicative choice? The second is how do extra-legal factors come to constrain the decisions of adjudicators vested with legal discretion? The questions are obviously related, for the influence of the law will

[35] In the period between 1960 and 1969 only about 5 per cent of non-payment cases resulted in immediate eviction. In 1987 I saw one of perhaps twelve tenants who came before the board owing money put on conditions. Both the prosecutor and board members told me that this was the first time in about a year that any non-payment tenant owing money had been put on conditions.

vary inversely with the influence of extra-legal factors, and vice versa. For this reason a law that will strongly influence the decisions of some legal actors may have little or no influence on the behavior of other such actors. Thus the prohibition against illegal searches and seizures in the US Constitution may lead most judges to discard certain types of evidence, although it might not prevent most police officers from acquiring it.

This case study of an eviction board was not aimed at answering the question what makes a law influential, but it does illustrate some factors that are likely to have this effect. First, the mandate and clarity of the law as understood by the decision-maker seem important. Before 1980 the statute establishing the eviction board did not require the board to evict simply because it found a violation, and the board developed a pattern of not evicting. One of several amendments passed in 1980 could arguably have been interpreted as mandating eviction whenever a lease violation was found, but it does not clearly require this and the Authority has not so interpreted it. Indeed, in training sessions both before and after the passage of the 1980 amendments, board members were told that their discretion extended to withholding eviction even if they found lease violations, and for five years after the passage of the amendments the board sometimes did this.

The board has, however, almost always complied where a legal mandate appeared clear. Thus, the Case of the House that Burnt was a unique act of rebellion against the law. In other cases, the board has regretfully evicted tenants who were over the income ceiling, citing federal law that required such tenants to move within six months of the over-income determination. In similar fashion the board, beginning in the mid-1970s, limited the period over which tenants were allowed to repay their rent to six months, because they were told that that was the limit which federal law provided for the repayment of back charges. Tenants who had no prospects of repaying their rent debts in six months were evicted.[36]

A related factor which affects the binding power of law on an adjudicator is his role conception. An attitude toward the binding

---

[36] It is not clear that the law was correctly interpreted for the board, since the provision in question specifically addressed the time that a tenant whose rent had been inappropriately set would have to repay the difference between the proper rent and the rent actually paid, rather than the time a tenant would have to repay a debt accumulated by defaulting on the proper rent.

nature of statutory language and precedent is usually an important aspect of judicial role conception. The eviction-board members are somewhat similar to a jury in the way they define their role. The members feel that they are to exercise common-sense judgment but that in doing so they are bound by the law. Thus, if board members believe a particular action is legally required, they comply. It follows that one way to affect the board's exercise of discretion is to convince its members that certain actions are or are not legally permissible.

A major difference between the board and a jury is that board members serve sufficiently lengthy terms that some come to feel that they are experts on what the law requires. For example, in one case I observed in 1987 the prosecutor erred slightly in making his customary speech. Rather than telling the tenant that the board's usual procedure in cases like hers was to evict, he suggested that the law gave the board no choice but to evict. The board chair, who had served for about a decade, interrupted the prosecutor to emphasize that the board had discretion to refuse eviction regardless of its usual practice. In a later case this chair's panel granted a tenant a conditional deferment despite an outstanding rent debt, the first time in almost a year that it had been lenient in this fashion. One member commented jokingly that it must have been my influence. He may have been right. In questioning board members about their usual practice and changes in it over time, I reminded them of their discretion to defer evictions despite rent that was outstanding and of the fact that they once exercised it.

The board is like a jury, however, in that the salience of other values affects the law's actual binding authority. The Case of the House that Burnt illustrates this. The Teofilo family's situation induced so much sympathy and respect that the board refused to evict, despite its understanding that this was what the law required. I observed a similar conflict in 1987, except that strongly held sentiments clashed not with the demands of external law but with the requirements of the board's by then well-established precedent. The case in which this occurred was a non-payment action involving a divorced woman, let us call her Mrs Sua, with ten children. Mrs Sua had not cleared her debt by the time of the hearing but said that she expected soon to receive a special welfare grant to pay it. In 1967 or 1977 the board would have deferred eviction on the condition that the debt be paid by a certain date; in 1987 the board regularly evicted on such facts, relegating the tenant to her right to appeal. In Mrs Sua's case the board did neither. Rather it continued the case for two weeks to allow her to secure her grant without the stress of an outstanding eviction order and the need to proceed through an appeal that would have left her vulnerable to an eviction without a hearing for the slightest defalcation over the ensuing twelve months. In the DAG's judgment the woman's large family was the factor that led to this special treatment. Judges are supposed to be better able than lay decision-makers to ignore personal values when these clash with legal interpretations. Perhaps they are, but judges too balance the importance of the values affected by their decisions with their understanding of what law or consistent practice requires.

Canalized Discretion

Since the law as understood by the eviction-board members gave the board considerable leeway in deciding how to dispose of cases, our investigation can address the second question, which asks what shapes the exercise of authorized or rule-given discretion. One important factor is that, when a decision-maker is repeatedly confronted with cases of a particular type, there is a tendency toward what Professor Sanders and I call 'shallow' decision-making (Lempert and Sanders 1986). That is, there is a tendency to eschew a deep probing of circumstances and to rely instead on a few key facts that can be used to fit cases to stereotypes.[37] There are no doubt many reasons for this, including psychological mechanisms[38] and the efficiency that routine-processing allows. This tendency is complemented by a common element of judicial role conceptions, the sense that, regardless of the range of outcomes that discretion allows, cases that are similar in relevant particulars should be decided in the same way. Thus we can expect adjudicators to see cases as similar on the basis of a few particulars and to dispose of cases that are seen as similar in a similar fashion.

As a consequence, adjudicators who have discretion to decide a series of similar cases will generate a pattern of decisions which is

[37] The tendency applies to judges in general, but is not confined to them. Other examples include insurance adjusters (Ross 1970), public defenders (Sudnow 1965), private defense counsel (Skolnick 1967), and prosecutors (Maynard 1984*b*).

[38] See the discussion of the 'representativeness heuristic' in Nisbett and Ross (1980: 24–8; cf. Fromm 1965).

sufficiently regular to call into question the actuality of their discretion.[39] Indeed, it may be, as was apparently the case with the eviction-board, that adjudicators with broad discretion to decide will feel in most cases that their decisions are tightly constrained despite their knowledge of the leeway law gives them. Thus to understand how extralegal factors come to constrain the decisions of those vested with discretion, we must explore those conditions that lead an adjudicator to feel that cases of a certain type should systematically be decided in one way or another.

In the case of the eviction board, the predominant factor leading to the early precedent of never ordering an immediate eviction may have been the values that the original board members brought to their work. The original five-person board included a social worker and a minister among its members and was dominated by a chair who did considerable volunteer work on behalf of the poor. Moreover, in establishing the independent board, the Authority conveyed the impression that special sensitivity to the interests of the poor was appropriate. The choice of members reflected the notion that the impoverished tenants were a constituency with interests that deserved representation.

In addition, the Authority's original prosecutor was untroubled by leniency in cases where it appeared that tenants would be able to repay their rent. The members' natural sympathies coupled with their difficulty in deciding which of the tenants who promised to pay back their rent could be believed fostered the development of a precedent that allowed all tenants who said they would pay back their rent a second chance.[40]

Other factors also contributed to this outcome. One was probably the desire of board members to avoid the responsibility for evicting

---

[39] This is not to call into question the existence of rule-granted discretion, nor is it necessarily to call into question the phenomenological reality of discretion. Rather it is to suggest that for practical purposes the adjudicator appears to be acting without discretion, and one who did not know the rule but only observed behavior might reasonably think that the law did not authorize discretion and that the adjudicator in acting had no sense of exercising any. In fact, I believe that adjudicators who act in the way described in the text often will have the sense that they lack discretion, but a sense of being without discretion is not entailed by behaviorally regular decision-making.

[40] Where the wisdom of a discretionary decision will be validated by another's (or even an object's) hard-to-predict future behavior, discretion is likely to be abdicated in favor of rules of thumb or, as is the case with many college admissions officers and parole boards, in favor of mathematical formulae. I am indebted to my colleague Carl Schneider for calling my attention to the general importance of 'subject unpredictability' in his comments on an earlier version of this chapter.

tenants with innocent young children, even when the parent's failure to pay rent was blameworthy. The strategy of deferring eviction placed the responsibility back on the tenant. For tenants had their eviction deferred only if they promised to repay their rent. If they then failed, they were not only shirking their responsibility, but were also breaking their word, and the subsequent eviction could easily be seen as their own doing rather than as the result of the board members' refusal to accept the sympathy-inducing story they were likely to have heard at the initial hearing. Moreover, the board members would not have to confront the tenant again, but would take the Authority's word that conditions were not being met and would vote to execute the deferred order.[41]

The forces that establish a precedent are not necessarily those that keep it in motion.[42] Members, like a retired project manager, who joined the board with neither an inclination to sympathize with financially troubled tenants nor an optimistic view of their prospects for repaying their debts none the less respected board precedent and voted to defer eviction despite their doubts. Other factors also served to keep the precedent alive. One was the appointment of a 'bleeding heart' (the managers' term) board chair in the mid-1960s who served for sixteen years. As chair he dominated the discussion. Moreover, as the years passed and new board members were appointed, this chair's experience gave him a special claim to expertise about how different types of cases should be decided.

Another factor that may have helped maintain the pattern of lenient decision-making is the feedback that the board members received during the 1960s and much of the 1970s. When the board gave tenants a second chance, they were often warmly thanked by the tenants. Managers did not thank the board in the cases in which the board evicted, and they usually hid the depth of their displeasure when the board failed to evict. The board members also learnt about what happened after they deferred eviction, since they voted to cancel eviction orders when debts were cleared or voted to evict or set new conditions if tenants failed to live up to the conditions of their initial

---

[41] This changed in 1975 with an informal ruling by the Attorney-General's Office that deferred tenants who did not meet their rent-payment conditions were entitled to a hearing before the eviction order could be executed.

[42] Joe Sanders made this observation in a conversation many years ago. I have often been indebted to him for it. One reason for this, as Fred Schauer (1987) notes, is that the values of precedent are logically distinct from the values of a precedent.

deferral. More often then not, tenants cleared their debts, and even those that did not often repaid a portion of their debt before again falling behind. Thus the board members felt that, when they were lenient, they were usually right.[43]

Finally, the attitude of the Authority officials who prosecuted cases was important, for these were the officials who regularly met with the board and presented the Authority's positions. The prosecutors during the 1960s and early 1970s not only respected the board's authority but were also relatively passive in presenting the Authority's case. While in some cases involving behavioral violations, like fighting or harboring unauthorized guests, the SPHM or other prosecutor might press hard for eviction, in non-payment cases they conveyed the impression that it was for the board to decide what was to become of the tenant. Indeed, this was the attitude that the Authority's central office staff conveyed to the project managers when the managers tried to get their superiors to press the board to evict more often. The staff's attitude was that the board was given the power to decide cases as it saw fit, and that the board's pattern of leniency was tolerable. One reason for this attitude was that the Authority's prosecutors during the 1960s, at first the HHA's Assistant Executive Director and later in most cases the SPHM, devoted relatively little of their attention to evictions. Handling evictions was one duty among many, and, given the nature of these officials' other responsibilities, their role in managing evictions could not have seemed particularly consequential.

The transformation of this 'second chance' pattern to a pattern of always evicting is interesting because the transformation required a 180-degree change in precedent. The attempt to turn the board around began in 1979, and it took about seven years before the transformation was complete. It was spurred by the Authority's serious financial troubles,[44] by a sense that the Authority was losing a

---

[43] The board members were correct if the criterion is the Authority's net rent-collection experience in cases where the board deferred eviction. Even allowing for tenants who did not meet the board's conditions and fell deeper in debt before they were evicted, the Authority's losses were less in cases where the board set conditions than they would have been had the board evicted immediately (to cut the possibility of further loss) in each instance. I discovered this in examining data from the 1960s, and an internal authority memorandum tells the same story based on data from the mid- to late 1970s.

[44] At one point the Authority was labeled by the United States Department of Housing and Urban Development (HUD) a 'Financially Troubled Housing Authority'. HUD provided operating subsidies to the HHA and the HHA had to subject itself to HUD audits and comply with certain HUD policies in return.

substantial amount of money in unpaid rent[45] and by the feeling, confirmed by HUD auditors, that the Authority's lenient eviction system was largely responsible for this.[46] It also reflected a different, less welfare-oriented attitude at the highest levels of the HHA toward the task of housing poor tenants.

In 1979 the HHA, in part responding to pressure from HUD and in part as a result of its own increasingly businesslike (as opposed to welfare) orientation, decided to get its 'eviction house' in order. There were two basic elements to its strategy. One was to rationalize the eviction process and make it more efficient. The second was to transform the board so that it was more appreciative of the Authority's concerns and stricter in dealing with non-payment tenants.[47]

---

[45] It was, however, always recognized that this was not the primary source of the Authority's financial troubles. Rather, these troubles were due to the HHA's failure to establish adequate reserves for maintenance and renovation and a federal subsidy which, because of the formula that had been used to calculate it, was inadequate. HUD audits confirmed this diagnosis of the source of the Authority's financial troubles, even while suggesting that there was a great need to tighten the rent-collection process.

[46] It appears that the HUD judgment did not reflect their auditor's independent judgment of the situation, but instead reflected the field staff's acceptance of the managers' explanation for their rent-collection problems. The managers, at least in 1969, believed that board leniency cost the Authority substantial amounts of money, and they shared horror stories about tenants who failed to meet board conditions and eventually left or were evicted owing three or four times what they had owed at the initial hearing. As mentioned in n. 43 above, both my research and an Authority investigation reveal that the managers' views about the costs of board leniency were wrong. Although there were horror stories, the incremental losses in such cases were more than offset by cases in which rent debts were eventually paid in full or where partial repayment occurred before further default, so that the the tenant when evicted owed less than at the initial hearing.

The managers also told a general deterrence story, arguing that knowledge of board leniency was common and that this prospect encouraged tenants to fall behind on their rent in the first instance. Eventually, I hope to analyse some data that may bear on this, but for the moment all I can say is that, although the argument sounds plausible, based on what I know of the eviction process and the few tenants I talked with, I would be surprised if it were true. An argument not made by the managers may, however, hold: namely, had the board been very strict and had this strictness been publicized at the project level, rent-collection patterns that were not altered by unpublicized board leniency might have been improved. Some data I saw are consistent with this hypothesis. In 1986 and 1987 the proportion of tenants behind on their rent was strikingly low at one project. Two of the tenant members of the eviction board resided at this project. They told me that one or the other goes to every tenants' union meeting at their project and reminds tenants that, if they do not pay their rent, they will be 'kicked out'.

[47] The reforms were motivated entirely by a concern with non-payment cases. By 1979 there were no income limits on the federally aided projects, and the board was always more willing to evict in behavior cases than in non-payment cases, so no great

The effort to rationalize the eviction process began in 1979 with the appointment of an administrator whose primary responsibility was to handle eviction actions and the appointment of a secretary to work full time on the paperwork of the eviction process. Prior to these appointments responsibility for evictions at both the secretarial and the administrative levels were part-time duties of staff members who had other tasks that both they and the Authority deemed more important.

One of the first tasks of the new administrator was to study the eviction process in order to respond to HUD's position, which was that the Authority should abolish its eviction board and use the ordinary judicial process when it wished to force tenants out. The administrator found, as I had found a decade before, that the eviction board seemed to save the Authority money by securing time payments from the majority of those tenants whom the managers (and a court) would have immediately evicted. Thus the decision was made to retain the eviction-board but to increase the efficiency of the eviction process. The major changes are mentioned earlier in this chapter, where I note the differences between the eviction process I studied in 1969 and that which I observed in 1987. I will recapitulate briefly.

First the then existing board was split into two seven-member groups which allowed weekly eviction hearings. Secondly, the HHA drafted and the Hawaiian legislature passed amendments to the Act establishing the eviction board that removed a requirement for in-person service of process in eviction cases and limited appeals to the HHA's Commission to cases which alleged that relevant 'new facts and evidence' had become available only following the board hearing. Later the Commission delegated the task of determining whether such new facts existed to the Authority's executive director, who in turn delegated it to the Director of Housing Management (DHM), and it was the DHMs policy never to find new facts and evidence in non-payment cases when rent was outstanding. Thirdly, the HHA reformed its system for recording rent payments and computerized the process of sending delinquency letters to tenants. Coupled with this was close supervision by the SPHM of project delinquencies and instructions to the managers to process tenants more quickly for eviction. Before 1980, by the time the board heard their cases, tenants

problems were seen in this area. After the reforms, non-payment cases, were given a special priority, so the proportion of cases brought for non-payment was somewhat higher in the 1980s than it had been in earlier decades.

were often three months or more behind on their rent. By the mid-1980s it was not uncommon to have a tenant up for eviction six weeks after the initial default.

While the Authority was revamping its administrative structure in these ways, it was also seeking to develop an eviction board that would view cases from the new, stricter perspective it had come to prefer. One step in this direction was to fill the new slots that became available when the board was split in two with people, like private real-estate managers, likely to be sympathetic to the Authority's point of view. Also, board members were given terms, and a few members who were thought to be unduly sympathetic to tenants were not reappointed. The long-time board chair was among the first to go.

A second step the Authority took was to be more specific in its expectations about how the board should behave. A training session was held for all board members at the time the second panel was established, and another one was held several years later. The board members were told of the seriousness of the rental delinquency problem which the Authority faced, and their task was defined in neutral, judicial terms rather than from the welfare-oriented perspective of how best to help tenants. Later the chairs of the board's two panels were sent at the Authority's expense to 'judge's school' in Reno, Nevada, to encourage them further in a legalistic approach.

Complementing these formal actions were attempts at informal influence. The Authority's Executive Director and his assistant occasionally attended board parties[48] or otherwise chatted informally with board members. On these occasions they discussed the Authority's rent-delinquency problems and their expectations about how the board should act, and they complimented board members for acting in accord with their expectations.

Even after these steps had been taken, however, the Authority was not insisting on immediate evictions in all cases in which tenants owed money. Rather, board members were given discretion to allow tenants up to six months of time payments to clear accumulated debts. However, the changes in board composition and in the rigor of prosecution had their effect. The board evicted many people outright, including some who owed no rent when they appeared before the board but had histories of chronic delinquency.[49]

[48] Board members are paid a largely symbolic $10 per meeting attended. Rather than collect the money themselves, they pool it and hold parties twice a year.
[49] Between October 1979 and December 1985 12.7 per cent of those owing nothing

In about 1985, perhaps coincident with the replacement of the Authority's eviction specialist with another attorney, the Authority further toughened its policies. With the concurrence of the Executive Director, the DHM decided that the Authority should seek the immediate eviction of *all* tenants owing rent at the time of the hearing and should place all tenants who cleared their rent debts between the time they received the subpoena and the hearing on probation for six months.[50]

The Authority's Executive Director and its Director of Housing Management may have communicated these new expectations to board members, but it was largely left to the HHA's eviction specialist, whom I call C, to cement a new precedent. C may have been particularly amenable to this since he did not have experience under the former system, and the new system had its own way of allowing tenants to avoid eviction:[51] namely, by payment, after the hearing but before the time for appeal had lapsed, of all the rent that was due.[52] Moreover, since the time for appeal did not start to run until the tenant was officially notified of the board's decision, C, who handled part of the paperwork of notification, had some leeway to delay giving notice where he thought a tenant could secure money if given extra time.[53]

at the time they appeared before the board were evicted, as were 24.6 per cent of those owing one to three months' rent and 56.8 per cent of those owing more than three months' rent. Some of those evicted were allowed to stay by the HHA's Commissioners on appeal. The figures on board evictions suggest that the board may have been exercising genuine discretion in this period. Unfortunately, I was not in Hawaii then. My interviews suggest that board members who served at this time had more of a sense that they had real choices to make than did the board members serving in 1987. Clearly the rent owing influenced these choices and it may be that a tenant's rent-payment history, whether good or bad, did as well. Other factors are harder to identify.

[50] If such tenants did not attend the hearing or had records of chronic delinquency, they might be evicted.

[51] C began practice as a legal-aid attorney and in conversation expressed sympathy for the plight of poor people.

[52] Paying the debt in a lump sum became more feasible as the Authority's eviction process grew more efficient, since tenants often found themselves before the board with less than two months' rent owing. At an earlier time, when eviction actions were not so speedily commenced, many tenants who could have managed time payments to clear rent debts of three months and more would have found it difficult or impossible to come up with a lump sum to repay their debt. Of course, there are still tenants who cannot pay off everything they owe before their time for appeal has lapsed who could have paid their rent debt on an instalment plan.

[53] By 1987, however, C claimed the process was so efficient and the backlog of cases so small that much of the leeway he once enjoyed was gone. C was also continually pressed to speed up his end of the process. The DHM took what he called a 'business-

C recalls the process of persuading the board to change its decision-making standards as a lengthy and difficult one. It took about a year of continually pressing the board to decide cases as he wanted—which is to say always to evict when rent was owing—to persuade them that this was the right thing to do. C's strategy was to persuade the board to take a legalistic approach and to convince the board members that their vote to evict immediately did not make them responsible for a tenant's eviction. C recalls:

My argument was that the board had to make findings of fact and if the findings of act were that the person was delinquent then they had to—they could give some kind of conditional deferment—however that was more the prerogative of the Commission than of the board members. Once they saw that these tenants were not going to get evicted for sure just because they said, 'Well you're behind and we order an eviction' . . . the board felt more comfortable in saying, 'OK we will send it on up to the Commission . . .' I remember going in there and standing up and addressing the board with what their functions were . . . the selling point was that this board wasn't going to be responsible for the people getting thrown out on the street, that there was still a safety net . . . [Once they saw this] that was probably the major reason for the change.

In addition, C tried to justify stringency by noting that the welfare of all tenants depended on the rents collected and by pointing out that evicted tenants were replaced by equally needy and presumptively more responsible tenants from the Authority's waiting list. Themes like this, along with the 'safety-net' and 'legal-duty' points, recurred in C's presentations to the board for as long as held his office.[54]

In making his arguments and persuading the board to exercise its discretion to change the way in which it routinely decided cases, C benefited from more than the logical force of what he said. First, on each of the boards' panels several members, as I have pointed out, had been chosen because they were likely to be sympathetic to the

like attitude', which some might see as a hard line towards non-payment tenants. For example, in 1985 the DHM was apparently instrumental in getting the Authority to adopt a rule that, if a tenant was evicted for non-payment of rent, he or she would never again be admitted to an HHA project. Unless this rule has an unlikely general deterrent effect, it can only cost the Authority money, for evicted tenants seldom repay what they owe unless they seek readmission to an HHA project and are told—as they once were told—that they are ineligible until their old debts are cleared.

[54]   C left for another position in September 1987, shortly after I completed my second stint of fieldwork.

Authority's position.[55] In part for this reason, the board had since 1980 moved a substantial distance in the direction C wanted it to go.[56] Secondly, C was a lawyer officially attached to the Hawaii Attorney-General's Office and not the Housing Authority. Thus he spoke not fully as a partisan and with considerable legitimate authority. Thirdly, he was a repeat player before the board. Every week he addressed the board, and he could stress his themes without counter-argument. Tenants usually appeared before the board only once, and defense counsel, including legal-aid paralegals, were seldom present in non-payment case hearings. Thus there was no adversary knowledgeable enough to question C's characterization of the board's duties or of the tenant's situation, and no one, other than the more experienced board members, to point to the board's historic ability to set conditions. Few tenants even knew enough to plead that, while they could make time payments, they were unable to pay off their debt in one lump sum. Instead, the natural reaction of tenants was to emphasize their ability to pay, in the belief that if they could convince the board they could clear their rent debt they would stave off eviction. Thus, 'Most people', according to C 'would tell the board straight out that they are going to get the money together and would pay it.' For C, such promises made it easier to secure outright evictions, for, if such tenants did as they promised, they would be allowed to stay by the Commission. Thus the tenants' promises to pay distanced the board from responsibility for the consequences of its eviction decisions.

In sum, what we see behind the transformation I have discussed is an adjudicative body responding to various pressures to change the way in which it exercised the discretion the law accorded it. Behaviorally and phenomenologically, however, the new standard the board developed was no more discretionary than the one that existed in 1969. Whereas tenants once had to be given a chance to repay their debts over time even if they were poor risks, by 1987 tenants had to be evicted if they owed money, even if they were unlikely to meet a lump-sum demand but were a good bet to clear their debt on an instalment plan. In 1969 members who predicted tenants would never pay

---

[55] Two members of each panel were tenants who were chosen in consultation with the HHA's island-wide tenant association. For reasons that need not be explored here, tenant board members were usually disposed to deal severely with tenants brought before them.

[56] The other major factor was that C's two immediate predecessors had pushed the board for a much harder line toward non-payment tenants, although they had not suggested that the board always evict those behind in their rent.

nevertheless voted to defer their eviction. In 1987 members whose sympathies were aroused by tenants voted to evict them.[57] The board, in short, possessed throughout the period legal discretion to change its standards and it did so, but it never developed a standard that allowed much room for the play of discretion.

I expect that the discretion of trial judges and other 'first-instance' adjudicators is often of this sort.[58] Its operational locus is not where we usually imagine it—in deciding particular cases; rather it is in deciding on a rule to apply in categorizing cases and in deciding how categories of cases should be treated (cf. Tweedie 1989). In so doing, trial judges who have discretion to evaluate facts and reach wise judgments may often be exercising a discretion more akin to that of appellate judges. They are, as a matter of practice rather than pronouncement, making law for the range of cases that come before them, and they are then acting as if they are without discretion; that is, as if they are bound by the law they have made. To understand adjudicative discretion one must understand the rules that judges make for themselves. To appreciate how discretion is, as a behavioral matter, constrained, one must understand the forces that lead judges to make particular rules. These forces may not be the same for all courts, and this study of the HHA's eviction board may provide no more than a few general clues. However, any court is likely to exist in a context of forces which systematically constrain its so-called discretionary decisions in a particular direction.

Conclusion

I said at the outset of this chapter that discretion can be a property of rules, a property of behavior, or a sense that people have of their freedom to act. Legal philosophers tell us that, when rules authorize discretion, it means that decision-makers are free to choose from a range of legally permissible options. Yet, if we look at how adjudicative discretion is actually exercised—that is, at the pattern of decisions generated—little advantage may be taken of this supposed freedom.

---

[57] I witnessed several occasions on which one member, who had just voted to evict a tenant, spoke privately to her, after she had been informed of the board's decision, about ways she might acquire money to pay her debt. He even directed some tenants who were not Catholics to his Catholic church for help.

[58] The discretion of law-making appellate courts obviously includes the discretion to change received standards and create precedent that is presumptively binding even on itself.

Although the law leaves open a range of decisions, adjudicators may adopt routine ways of disposing of cases that admit of only a few outcomes within that range. Following routines, however, may be more than a matter of convenience, for routine ways of disposing of cases are easily transformed into subjectively binding precedent. The result is that a decision-maker with legally authorized discretion may lose the awareness of discretion and come to feel that in a particular situation a particular decision is required.

Thus where rules accord a range of discretion to a decision-maker, the decision-maker may be both less and more bound than he appears. The decision-maker is less bound because there is always discretion to ignore the limitations of the discretion given. Whether this occurs will depend both on the decision-maker's conception of his role and on the kinds of incentives that shape decisions to comply with any rule. For example, a police officer who is bound by law to ticket a speeding motorist may, if no one is watching, pocket a twenty-dollar bill and let the motorist go.

The decision-maker with discretion may be more bound than he appears because he may feel that he is bound. Thus a police officer authorized by law to stop any motorist going faster than sixty-five miles per hour may never stop any motorist travelling less than seventy miles per hour, and he may come to feel that he has no authority to do so, perhaps believing that motorists are entitled to a range of grace or that radar guns have a five-mile-per-hour margin of error. His beliefs, however, may have been shaped by motorists who responded with particular hostility when they were stopped for barely exceeding the speed limits, by courts that chose to believe motorists' speed estimates in close-to-the-limit cases, or by fellow officers who mocked him for 'chicken-shit' arrests.

What the law gives in discretion—that is the authorization to reach one of a number of possible decisions and the awareness of this freedom—social forces may take away. This is not surprising, for what legal discretion necessarily accords is the freedom to be influenced by factors other than the law. When the law leaves open a range of choices, unless the choice is made randomly, it must be influenced by something other than and in addition to the law. Not only is the exercise of discretion influenced by the social and psychological circumstances in which a decision-maker finds himself, but the existence of discretion invites others to try to influence its exercise. Moreover, the very act of choosing in one case affects the choice made in the next, and the experience of making a number of similar choices often leaves a decision-maker feeling that no choice exists at all.

This sense of constraint is not necessarily a bad thing, for the consistent exercise of discretion is ordinarily something to be aimed at. Problems arise, however, because the tendency to use shallow case logics in repetitive decision-making make it likely that not all the factors that might shape the wise case-by-case exercise of discretion are considered. Thus the 1987 eviction board, in routinely evicting non-payment tenants who owed rent, ignored the reasons why the family was in debt, the family's need for public housing, and the likelihood that a family that could not make a lump-sum payment was nevertheless a good prospect to repay its rent debt over time. The 1969 board behaved similarly. In regularly giving second chances, it ignored the Authority's valid interest in immediately evicting tenants who, with no prospects of meeting the terms of a conditional deferment, could only increase their debt. At both times it might be said that the board abused its discretion by not using it, for the reason the legislature granted the board discretion was, at least arguably, so that it could consider each case on its peculiar facts and reach an appropriate decision. Had the legislature wanted non-payment tenants behind on their rent to be always evicted or always given a second chance, it could have written this standard into law.[59]

Behavioral regularities do not, of course, necessarily reflect the subjective mental processes that underlie them. It is conceivable that actors conscious of their own discretion and scrupulously attending to the variety of factors they are authorized to consider might none the less generate a pattern of decisions that an observer could easily categorize knowing only a few particulars. In the case of the eviction board, however, phenotypes do not obscure genotypes. Board deliberations indicate that board members feel bound by the same factors that one with access only to decisions would identify as crucial. Yet, there are one or two cases (e.g. the case of Mrs Sua) that do not fit the mould. These exceptions suggest that board members retain some sense of having discretion, but that it takes a truly striking situation to awaken this sense. Moreover, even exceptional decisions are constrained by the usual way of dealing with cases 'of this type', with type being defined not by the family's extraordinary situation, but by the factor

---

[59] It is conceivable, although I do not think it is the case here, that a legislature that wanted always to give tenants a second chance nevertheless wanted that chance to appear to be a fortuitous act of grace rather than a legal entitlement.

or factors that are ordinarily sufficient to determine outcomes. Thus the 'breaks' that the 1987 board gave a few tenants in circumstances that made an extraordinary case for leniency would have been regarded as particularly hard-hearted and narrow by the board that sat in 1969.

I expect the same is true of other decision-makers with discretion. When decisions can be consistently predicted by a case feature or two that stand out, it is likely that the decision-maker, like the observer, senses that little is left to discretion.[60] In these circumstances it takes extraordinary circumstances to awaken in the decision-maker a sense that a range of choices is open to him, and even then the range is unlikely to be co-extensive with the decision-maker's legal authority but is instead likely to be constrained by the decision-maker's sense of what is usually allowed.[61]

These conclusions are based on a study of one institution, a public housing eviction board. Thus they must be regarded as hypotheses to be tested rather than as *a priori* predictions confirmed by investigation. Nevertheless, I believe that the eviction board does not differ greatly from many other decision-makers in the way it exercises the discretion that law accords it, and I have cited studies of other decision-makers that support this claim. Notably absent from these citations have been studies of the law-making activities of appellate courts,[62] the discretionary decisions that have received the most attention from philosophers and legal scholars. This is not an accident. Although a number of my conclusions may apply to discretionary law-making at the appellate level, there are two important reasons to expect that not all my conclusions will hold. First, the ability of most higher courts to control their dockets[63] means that such courts are less likely than lower courts to be confronted with the steady stream of similar cases

---

[60] By contrast, the ability to predict decisions on the basis of decision-maker characteristics like those one finds in some studies of judicial behavior (Ulmer 1973; Goldman 1973) is likely to tell us little about the decision-maker's sense of acting with discretion.

[61] This may reflect a psychological phenomenon called 'anchoring and adjustment'. this phenomenon suggests that, when a right answer is *suggested* but is *known* to be wrong, final decisions are distorted in the direction of the answer originally suggested. See, e.g., Tversky and Kahneman 1974.

[62] I have cited some research on appellate courts to support other points and I have suggested that an appellate court's exercise of discretion to hear cases conforms to what one would expect based on principles derived from this study of the eviction board.

[63] The dockets of appellate courts are also shaped and limited by sociological factors such as the costs of appeals.

that is conducive to shallow case logics and a retreat from discretion.[64] Secondly, the law-making discretion that is accorded appellate courts contemplates that they will establish rules that are not only binding on others but will also bind their own future behavior except in exceptional circumstances. Thus the substitution of rules for discretion, which can betray the authority given by law in the cases of trial courts, hearing boards, and street-level bureaucrats, may embody that authority in the case of appellate courts, particularly 'highest' ones. One reason why legal philosophers have focused as much as they do on discretion as a quality of rules may be that for the courts that most attract their attention—supreme courts—there is less of a disjunction between discretion as a quality of rules and discretion as a quality of behavior than there is when legal discretion is exercised at other levels of the system. I hope, however, to have shown in this chapter that, if we are to understand discretion in all its aspects, we must not only look at the stars—we must cast our eyes down as well.

[64] Where there are streams of cases that can be easily seen to be of the same type, one should expect to see appellate court decision-making that resembles the decision-making of the eviction board. Thus intermediate appellate courts seem to deal with the stream of criminal appeals they confront by broad rules of thumb (Davis 1969), and I would argue that the recent decisions of the United States Supreme Court on the administration of the death penalty has, as a result of the many such cases they confront, resulted in decisions that try to deny the relevance of distinctive facts and in this sense constitute a retreat from discretion. See, e.g., *Lockhart* v. *McCree* 476 US 162 (1986)—holding that, even if data show that death-qualified juries are more conviction prone than juries that are not death qualified, a defendant has no cause of action—and *McCleskey* v. *Kemp* 481 US 279 (1987)—holding that, even if data show that death sentences in the aggregate appear to turn in part on racial considerations, an individual defendant has no cause of action. Recently a Committee of the Judicial conference of the United States, appointed by Chief Justice Rehnquist, recommended that the number of appeals allowed defendants sentenced to death be drastically limited, thus removing occasions on which courts could exercise discretion. When the full Judicial Conference and the Congress refused to act on this recommendation, the court managed to implement the rule by judicial decision. See *McCleskey* v. *Zant* 111 S. Ct. 1454 (1991).

7. Organizational Horizons and Complaint-Filing

ROBERT M. EMERSON AND BLAIR PALEY

MANY socio-legal analyses conceptualize *discretion* as decisions made relatively unfettered by rules, and advocate 'confining, structuring and checking' decision-making as an antidote to the resulting 'problems and abuses'. For example, in his classic analysis of discretion, Davis argues that a 'public officer has discretion whenever the effective limits on his power leave him free to make a choice among possible courses of action or inaction' (1969: 4). In this view discretion involves decisions that are unconstrained by rules, whether because rules do not apply, are vague, or multiple. Nondiscretionary decisions, in contrast, are those that accord with (and presumably are determined and constrained by) rules. Such an approach therefore dichotomizes 'rules' and 'discretion': the more of the former the less of the latter, and vice versa.[1]

It is now well established that a sharp rules–discretion dichotomy presumes and perpetuates overly narrow and mechanistic treatments of discretionary decision-making. This dichotomy obscures the contingent and variable processes of rule interpretation inevitably unspecified by the rules themselves. It specifically neglects the use of discretion to determine the relevant 'facts' or 'situation' to which specific rules apply, since, in the words of H. L. A. Hart, no rule can 'itself step forward to claim its own instances' (1961: 123). (See also Heritage 1984: 120–9).

Furthermore, dichotomous rules–discretion models strip decisions of their relevant contexts. As Baldwin and Hawkins have argued, this approach tends 'to see a "decision" at a particular point in the legal process as an isolated matter, as something logically separable from what surrounds it in the processing of cases' (1984: 582). In contrast, contextually sensitive approaches which view decision-making as

The authors wish to thank Keith Hawkins, James A. Holstein, Jack Katz, Melvin Pollner, and Carol A. B. Warren for their helpful comments on earlier drafts of this chapter.

[1] Davis, for example, characterizes administrative decision-making as an area 'where decisions necessarily depend more upon discretion than upon rules and principles' (1969: 216).

'complex, subtle and woven into a broader process' (ibid.: 581) allow for fuller appreciation of the intricate and pervasive character of discretion.

Yet context has often been conceptualized in ways that inhibit such broader analyses of discretionary decision-making. Viewing context as objective, fixed variables standing outside of and influencing or determining particular decision outcomes has just this effect. Many researchers adopt such an approach by equating context with 'factors' that correlate with decision outcomes but that do not refer to acts or conditions providing the legitimate focus of decision-making. In criminal justice decision-making, for example, many 'extra-legal variables' (contrasted with such core 'legal variables' as seriousness of offense or strength of evidence) are termed contextual.[2]

More subtle analyses of discretion are encouraged by approaches which view context as an interactionally and situationally emergent phenomenon. Here context refers not to variables defined by particular traits but to the *processes* whereby particular traits are invoked or made relevant to specific decisions.[3] Thus context is not pre-given but is created by 'filling in' relevant informational background and decision concerns in order to reach and justify particular decisions at specific times and places. Maynard has elaborated this approach in analysing the use of 'defendant attributes' in criminal justice decision negotiations:

there is no abstract set of factors or descriptive variables, the values of which are determined for each defendant when that person's case is discussed. . . . On the contrary, defendants' attributes are systematically made visible in relation to arguments for and against various dispositions, as justifications for the positions taken up by prosecution and defense.(1984: 138)

Other forms of context as well will vary in relevance for decision-makers not only across decisions but also over time within any particular decision.

---

[2] One recent study of the processing of rape complaints, for example, identified as 'interpersonal context' such variables as the victim–suspect relationship and the location of the incident in or outside the home (LaFree 1989: 97–8).

[3] These processes characterize the understanding of context not simply in decision-making situations, but in interactional exchanges more broadly. As Schlegloff has argued with regard to the latter: 'It is not . . . that some context independently selected as relevant affects the interaction in some way. Rather, in an interaction's moment-to-moment development, the parties, singly and together, select and display in their conduct which of the indefinitely many aspects of context they are making relevant, or are invoking, for the immediate moment' (1987: 219).

The phenomenological concept of the *horizon*[4] systematizes and extends the radical situationalism at the core of this approach. Decision horizons refer to 'context' as known and understood by decision-makers as they confront and grapple with some current decision task. Decision-making is horizontal in this sense in that relevant context for *decision-makers* emerges and shifts in salience in and over the course of weighing and evaluating particular decision possibilities. Given decisions already made, researchers (and the decision-makers themselves) can specify a set of pertinent contextual factors; but such specification inevitably occurs after the fact, and rigidifies and distorts the more open spectrum of choices, possibilities, and alternatives that decision-makers experience in confronting decisions yet to be made.

Bittner (1967*b*) provided the seminal treatment of decision horizons in analysing decision-making in police patrol work on skid row. Yet the import of Bittner's analysis is restricted by its focus on a distinctive kind of informal police decision-making. Keying on the patrol officer directly encountering a disoriented, mentally ill person on skid row, Bittner emphasized police preference to respond informally, avoiding arrest or referral to psychiatric institutions in favor of immediate, street- or community-based remedial action. These decisions were informed and shaped by horizons of the following sorts:

the *scenic* horizon, consisting of all the more or less stable features of the background that can be brought into play as employable resources to handle the problem . . . the *temporal* horizon, including both the changing nature of the problem as it is being attended to and what can be known or surmised about its past and future. . . . [and] the *manipulative* horizon, which consists of considerations of practicality from the standpoint of the police officer. (ibid.: 283)

These horizons reflect the distinctively street-centered and informal character of this form of police decision-making.[5]

---

[4] The concept of 'horizon' has a long history in phenomenology of perception, particularly in the work of Husserl. Gurwitsch (1965) provides a concise, critical treatment of some of these issues in 'The Phenomenology of Perception: Perceptual Implications', although he rejects Husserl's term 'inner horizons' in favor of the concepts of 'perceptual adumbration' and 'perceptual implications' to emphasize the processes whereby 'noematic components not given in genuine sense-experience are effective in shaping and molding the perceptual noema' (p. 25). Our approach to decision horizons draws heavily upon Bittner's (1967*b*) use of the concept to analyse police decision-making toward the mentally ill encountered in the course of patrol on skid row (see below).

[5] Bittner's grounds for distinguishing between these three forms of horizons are open to question: to the extent that 'scenic' and 'temporal' horizons facilitate and reflect

We can extend the concept of decision horizons by noting that, under other conditions, horizons become relevant that involve distinctively institutional or organizational (as opposed to street or communal) realities and courses of action. When they do turn from informal to formal responses to the mentally ill, for example, the police come to evaluate and weigh mentally ill persons' likely treatment or fates in institutional settings such as jails, courts, and/or psychiatric hospitals; thus, decisions are now contexted within these institutional realities. Similarly, when we turn our attention from the police, who possess original jurisdiction in many decision situations, to decision-makers at secondary and tertiary processing stages, a variety of other institutional courses of action become increasingly central to decision-making. In particular, the interests, concerns, and circumstances of institutional agents who have initiated some present case increasingly come to define what that case is 'really all about', and have to be taken into account in disposing of it (Emerson 1991). Similarly, the foreseeable interests and reactions of institutional agents at future processing points become increasingly salient concerns in making some present decision about a case.

Indeed, the relevant horizons for most social control decision-makers will draw significantly upon knowledge of the practices and processes of various institutions and their agents. To the extent this occurs, cases come to be processed within distinctively *organizational horizons*.[6] This concept directs attention to decision-makers' use of background knowledge of the institutional sources, meanings, and parameters of the cases that now require decision. Decision-makers, then, do not see and treat cases as self-contained, isolated entities, but rather as practical decision tasks embedded in known and foreseeable courses of institutional action.

concerns with practical manipulation, they would appear to be two subsets of the third horizon rather than separate types. In any case, it is this core project of practical manipulation as the patrol officer actually confronts it, i.e. within the constraints and possibilities available 'here and now', at this time and place, that reflects the fundamentally street-focused character of these horizons.

   [6] We would suggest that decision horizons shift from street- or encounter-focused to organizational-focused under the following conditions: (1) the preference for informal response is superceded or weakens, such that alternative formal courses of action, typically linked to institutions and institutional agents, come to be considered; (2) decision-makers anticipate being held accountable for decisions by some agency outside the immediate situation; (3) issues of immediate, physical and/or interactional control decline in salience; and (4) decision-makers confront cases that are referrals, i.e. the products of prior decisions by other institutional actors.

In what follows we will examine the nature and uses of organizational horizons in one distinctive situation—complaint filing in a district attorney's office. The junior author observed the operations of the Los Angeles County District Attorney's office for a period of approximately six months, focusing much of her attention on the decision about whether or not to file complaints in cases brought by the police to a Central Filing department. This department was staffed by senior Deputy District Attorneys (DDAs) who reviewed requests by police officers to file formal complaints. These filing deputies relied primarily upon written arrest reports, supplemented by verbal reports from the police, in coming to a decision to file and what specific charges to file, to refer the case to the City Attorney's office for filing as a misdemeanor, or to dismiss all counts.[7]

The announced standard for filing in this office was to prosecute 'good' cases, and to dismiss or refer 'bad' cases.[8] But DDAs identified as 'good cases' those in which the evidence was strong enough to make it likely that a conviction could be obtained, and where the offense and the accused's prior record made it likely that a state prison sentence would be imposed. In this way, 'good cases' combined the elements of 'strength' and 'seriousness' that Mather had analysed as separate concerns in an earlier study of the same setting: 'The seriousness of a case refers to a prediction by attorneys of the severity of sentence to be imposed upon conviction. A "serious" case is one with a high chance of state prison sentence. A "light" case is one with no real likelihood of state prison and a good chance of a sentence of probation' (1979: 27).

In examining the nature and role of organizational horizons in the complaint-filing process, we will distinguish between the retrospective and the prospective horizons of cases. The former involves local organiz-

---

[7] In most cases, the observer was present during complaint filing sessions as an instructed novice: here the DDA used the filing as an occasion to inform her as to how filings were done. Thus it was common for DDAs to address observations and even evaluative commentary to the observer in the presence of the police detective seeking the complaint, as will be apparent in many of the field notes that follow. The filing deputies were, for the most part, remarkably amenable to observation of their work. Frequently they would interrupt their discussions with the detectives whose cases they were reviewing to invite questions or to explain any issues they thought might be unclear.

[8] Decision-making processes in complaint-filing and the relevance of the distinction between 'good' or 'strong' cases on the one hand, and 'bad' or 'weak' cases on the other, have been examined by Carter 1974; Neubauer 1974; Mather 1979; Stanko 1981; Ericson 1982; A. Sanders 1987.

ational knowledge about where, why, and how a case has now come to its present point. In this sense cases acquire *organizational histories*, that is, knowledge of the judgments and practices that have led others to send cases forward and that must be considered in deciding how now to dispose of cases. The latter involves knowledge of what is likely or will happen to a case 'of this kind' if it were to be filed or otherwise disposed of. These *organizational futures* specify known or likely institutional outcomes and consequences, and hence inform decision choices between future alternative courses of action. Both these sorts of organizational horizons provided key resources in the decision-making process.

Retrospective Horizons: Implications Drawn From the Sources of a Case

The police initiate almost all requests to file complaints. But to filing deputies the police are not an anonymous agency, but familiar local entities staffed by known actors pursuing known organizational and individual goals. Exactly *who* brings a complaint for filing, *how* they bring it, and *why* they have brought it, constitute one sort of organizational horizon of cases and can shape filing deputies' understanding and handling of specific complaints.

In the first place, the individual identity of the police officer bringing the complaint may hold important implications for the filing deputy; an officer known to be lackadaisical or careless in the preparation of cases, for example, could expect rigorous review and substantial changes from his or her initial requests, whereas an officer known to be conscientious could expect to have most of his or her complaints quickly filed. In the following forgery case, for example, the filing deputy praises the detective's preparation of a confession: 'DDA comments that he can see in the report how good this detective is and that he knows what he is doing. The confession is signed in five different places, so the woman [the accused] cannot claim that she never made some part of it. "A lot of other guys don't know to do that. Let's file." '[9]

In processing cases prosecutors also draw upon a second sort of local knowledge, knowledge of the specific police *units* which regularly bring cases to be filed. As one DDA noted: 'It's a quasi-judicial

[9] In the field data reported in this study, direct quotations are used to indicate comments either tape recorded or written down as nearly verbatim as possible during complaint filing sessions.

function. We're rubber stamps for the police. But we're getting filings from ten different stations. There's a different range of competencies. So it's difficult sometimes. We're semi-judges here.' At one extreme of police competence, filing deputies anticipated certain features in any complaint brought by detectives working in a special fraud or 'bunco' unit: 'As a detective walked in to file a bunco case, the filing deputy remarked: "These guys are the best and the brightest. These guys know we're going to file before they come in here 'cause they're so good."' Note that 'bunco cases' are identified not simply by where they come from (i.e., by organizational source), but more fundamentally by a series of organizationally based actions and decisions inferentially linked to this source. For bunco cases are assumed to be 'good' because those in this unit are known to prepare their complaints in legally sophisticated, systematic ways.

Thirdly, exactly how a police officer presents a complaint for filing can signal to a knowing filing deputy something about the police view of its seriousness and/or of the likelihood of getting it filed. For example, filing deputies know that the police will often bring forward cases that they expect to be rejected or even want to have rejected. They do so for a variety of reasons—to 'cool out' complainants who are seen as 'inappropriately' insisting on prosecution, to 'cover' themselves by putting the formal onus on the District Attorney for rejecting potentially controversial cases, and so on. In this particular jurisdiction DDAs came to assume that, when police officers *telephoned in* a request to file a case, as opposed to bringing it in person, they were expecting or desiring a 'reject'. As one DDA commented: 'We just had a three day weekend, and a lot of guys [police officers] will call so they don't come in with stuff they're [filing deputies] not going to file. The best don't call 'cause they already know; the next best call first; and the last best bring in stuff they're not going to file anyway.' Telephone calls to request filings, then, were assumed to involve such 'rejects', and were anticipated to be 'bad cases' that did not merit close review. Coming in person to present a case, on the other hand, increased the likelihood that the case was one that the officer wanted filed.

Finally, the actual presence of a particular kind of case in the filing office may allow inferences about prior organizational actions and decisions that can effect initial judgments about the strength or weakness of that complaint. Specifically, DDAs working at the main complaint office ('Central') are very aware that police officers generally prefer to take appropriate cases to specialized units in the District Attorney's office, units which conduct their own independent complaint screenings.[10] Hence, when the police bring a case that clearly falls within the scope of such a specialized unit to the main complaint desk, the filing deputy at the main desk tends to assume that this current complaint was judged not strong enough to have been filed by the unit in question. Consider these comments about 'gang cases' which get to Central Filing made by a filing deputy to a police officer working with CRASH (Community Resources Against Street Hoodlums), a special gang program, in the presence of the observer: 'If it's good stuff does it come to Central? If it's the best, it goes to Gangs. [the Gangs unit of the District Attorney's office].' Thus, merely presenting a 'gang case' to Central Filing suggests to the filing deputy that that case is likely to be 'weak' or hard to win. One filing deputy characterized this sort of 'gang case' in the following terms: 'CRASH cases are usually crap cases. You usually don't have any witnesses. They could be a robbery, a homicide, or usually assault with a deadly weapon. . . . This detective is probably very gung ho and wants to do a good job. There's usually a clash between the filing deputy and the officer.' Similar inferences are typically drawn from sex-offense cases brought to Central Filing: 'They have a specialized Sexual Crimes unit. They get the best rapes. The hard rapes come to us. Their better gang cases go to Gangs.' Thus, the presence of a gang or sex-offense case in Central Filing usually leads the filing deputy to assume that some prior criminal justice actor has seen that case as 'bad'. It may be that the police themselves view the case in this way and so have decided not to take it to the appropriate special unit; or that the present complaint had previously been brought to and rejected by that special unit.

In various ways, then, cases may 'acquire' distinctive retrospective organizational horizons, horizons which can inform and frame current filing decisions. In so arguing, we are not asserting that these sorts of horizonal inferences act as prejudgments which rigidly and automatically determine subsequent filing-decision outcomes. Rather, such inferences provide a first, tentative frame for attending to and beginning to process any particular case. A 'gang case' or a 'rape case' coming to Central is anticipated to be 'crap' or 'hard'—until the detective says

---

[10] The District Attorney's office had separate units to handle child abuse, sex crimes, gang-related crimes, major fraud, major narcotics, white collar crime, and career criminal cases.

something to the contrary or until the arrest report is read to indicate otherwise. Horizonal inferences hold only 'until further notice' (Garfinkel 1967), that is, until the filing deputy comes on information that contradicts or elaborates in different directions this initial inference. A competent detective may have brought in a weak case, a gang case coming to Central may turn out to be strong and to merit filing. Or, more commonly, in the course of the case being handled, factors may emerge as relevant that can lead to decisions to file even cases that are 'bad' and unlikely to lead to convictions. In the CRASH case discussed above, for example, the deputy ultimately agreed to file the case, but in doing so pointed toward factors other than its strength as justification for this outcome: 'We'll file this one. It's gonna get lost. And not because he [CRASH detective] yelled, but it'll keep the guy off the street.'

Prospective Horizons: Anticipating 'Downstream Consequences'

Filing deputies routinely elaborate the foreseeable institutional future of any particular case, as well as its institutional past, in order to make sense of what has been done and what now can be done. Specifically, in evaluating whether or not to file a particular complaint, filing deputies may give close attention to the *organizational consequences* of any current decision. Identifying and assessing such consequences build on intimate knowledge of what is likely to happen at future institutional decision points if 'a case of this sort' were to move forward. To draw upon the metaphor offered by a filing deputy reflecting on the temptation to file a 'bad case' when the accused was a particularly dangerous or heinous offender: 'A good filing deputy is aware of the downstream consequences. It's frustrating to see a really bad guy in a shakey case, 'cause you know he's dangerous, you know he did it, you know he's gonna go out and do it again! But if you ain't got it, you ain't got it.' Such anticipatable 'downstream' outcomes provide prospective organizational horizons commonly used to context and make meaningful current options about how to handle a case.

Filing deputies routinely invoke a variety of 'known' decision-making tendencies and practices held to characterize different 'downstream' processing points in order to account for and justify some present decision. Consider, for example, the kinds of prospective organizational horizons that can come to be elaborated in dealing with police pressure to file bad cases.

District attorneys insist that filing bad cases will in general clog up the court system and waste time and energy. As one deputy argued to a disappointed detective: 'Your job is not to file. Our job is to file the ones we can win. 'Cause if I throw crap into the system . . . we got to keep the system clean.' But the asserted need to 'keep the system clean' rests upon a series of more specific likely 'downstream' consequences. For example, filing deputies contend that to file a bad case may place the district attorney who subsequently picks up that case in a deep quandary. One experienced filing deputy, for example, sketched the following scenario:

> If it's weak, a record is immaterial. If you don't have a winnable case, it doesn't matter—if the case is a dog. You run into a lot of frustration. You get a really bad guy. But you can't let it influence your filing, if it's a dog. It'll get past the prelim, but you get to trial, you've placed the burden on the trial deputy. You've got a candidate for state prison. He's an experienced criminal litigant. He knows he can beat the case, so he's not interested in a disposition. An experienced hardened criminal, the defense, they won't make a deal. The poor trial deputy, he has to either waste four days or dismiss it. He goes to his boss, asks 'Can we dismiss it?' The boss won't put his name on it, open himself up to criticism. 'Better you go to trial for four days and lose.' Nobody has the guts to dismiss it.

In elaborating this likely 'downstream' outcome, the filing deputy shows that the trial deputy would personally be made to look 'foolish' in having to prosecute a case that could not be convincingly presented let alone won. The deputy also identifies known organizational practices—here, supervisors' reluctance to dismiss cases that have been filed for fear of being identified as 'soft on crime'—that will stymie efforts to avoid this débâcle.

'Good cases' as well as bad cases are identified by invoking prospective organizational horizons. Procedurally, a 'good case' is simply one that would be won with a felony conviction if it went to trial. In identifying 'good cases', district attorneys specifically invoke the way the judge or jury who might hear the case in the future will treat and decide it. To say that 'we only file good cases' is thus to call up these 'known' (i.e. anticipated, inferred) consequences and outcomes. Consider, for example, one filing deputy's comments about bunco cases and their anticipatable outcomes: 'A lot of DA's get scared by these [bunco] cases 'cause there's so much paperwork, but they're the easiest to file, 'cause they're usually already laid out. These cases hardly ever go to trial cause they're usually already laid out.' Here we see a prospective inference that most 'bunco cases' will be settled by some sort of guilty plea, exactly because of the care that has gone into preparing the case.

Filing deputies invoke more specific 'downstream' consequences than simply 'winning' or 'losing' to fill in the context around and hence account for processing decisions in given cases. In the first place, in reviewing arrest reports and making filing decisions deputies anticipate *likely evidentiary problems* and their outcome in the courtroom. For example, a deputy explained a current filing decision to the observer in these terms:

The defendant sneaks into a building, breaks into eight or ten offices. Someone discovers him, they call the police. They bring a dog in, there's a big scuffle. The guy got eaten by the dog. At eight o'clock they interrogate him. He makes a confession.

There's a couple of issues we're concerned about. . . . First, the constitutionality of the confession. The ultimate question is always voluntariness. The guy made the confession right after the dog ate him, and he might say 'cause he was under medication. He ended up in the hospital. There's two questions: One, was he confessing 'cause he thought he might get more of the same treatment? And two, more likely, because he was under medication, it might influence what he said. That's what worries me. He might say he didn't know what he was doing. Except he made a statement about what a fool he was. I could argue that if he could be flippant he must have known what was going on.

Here the filing deputy identifies a likely evidentiary challenge, but also locates an additional 'fact' in the arrest report that can be used to counter this challenge. In this way it becomes 'reasonable' to file the complaint.[11]

The evidentiary strength of many cases depends upon assessing the testimony of victims and witnesses, assessments which in turn rest on assumptions about how such persons will behave and what they will say in subsequent hearings. Note the courses of witness actions

---

[11] Note that the filing deputy here is identifying only a viable courtroom strategy (i.e. an argument that can 'reasonably' be put to the judge), and has taken no stance on whether the judge is likely to accept or reject the argument in this specific case. Preliminary observations suggest that DDAs tend to use this 'it's reasonable to proceed' rhetoric in instances where they intended to file the complaint, using the 'known downstream outcome' rhetoric in refusing to file.

anticipated by this filing deputy on learning that the attempted murder of a gang member is 'dope related':

A CRASH detective is trying to get a charge of attempted murder filed against a gang member. After laying out the details of the offense, the detective mentions that the case might be dope related. Filing deputy: 'Oh now he tells me.' He then tells the observer that the detective probably knows that this arrest report isn't all true, that with gangs they're all lying. . . . Later the deputy explains to the observer: 'This isn't your typical gang case. It's probably related to drugs. They usually lie. So and so did it. They may get back at each other. So I've got to weed through it. When we get to court, we can't get our witnesses. Even guys that are shot, they'll take care of it on their own.'

Invoking this horizon fills in the prospective organizational context which makes it unreasonable to file this case.

Identifying evidentiary problems may also involve anticipating the specific strategies and tactics defense attorneys are likely to employ. Filing deputies review the materials contained in the police report with an eye for how they could be challenged by a defense attorney before a judge and/or jury, linking filing decisions to having some response to these anticipated courtroom moves. In the following excerpt, for example, the filing deputy elaborates the ways in which witness identifications can be attacked by a defense attorney during trial:

Like I.D.'s. You show the victim a mug board. The pictures are all supposed to look pretty much alike. The victim says he thinks it's number 6, but he's not sure. Then you show him a line up. Now he's sure it's number 6. A photograph doesn't have height, weight; there's mannerisms. Something happens when you get two people in the same space. And the fact that three weeks ago he was only 70 per cent sure, you have to live with that.

You get to the prelim and the defense attorney says, 'Mr. Liquor Store Clerk, didn't you identify my client only because you've seen his picture before, not because you saw him at the robbery? And when you saw all six pictures didn't they all look alike? So isn't it possible it could be number two or number three? Or isn't it possible his picture isn't even there?' By now the jury's so confused. And all you need is one for a hung jury. And when you get to trial, the defense says, 'Are you identifying my client 'cause you saw him at the prelim? I mean you saw him for thirty minutes. And didn't you identify him then because he was the only black man in the courtroom and he was in a jail uniform?'. You have a couple of black jurors.

Or if a suspect is caught twenty minutes later or four blocks away, you do a field show-up. The defense can say, 'Didn't you identify him because he was in handcuffs or he was in the back of the police car?' There's a strong element of suggestibility here. In the process of being fair, there are lots of points of attackability.

Finally, filing deputies often insisted on filing not simply cases where they would get a felony conviction, but rather those where the felony conviction would lead to a state prison rather than a jail sentence. That is, even if a felony conviction were likely, a case might not be filed as a felony if the chances of the defendant receiving a state-prison sentence were considered to be remote. Prospective horizons linked to judges' known sentencing proclivities are thus critical here, as illustrated in the following:

A police detective brings in a case in which a man walking down the street is accosted by four young men. They attempt to steal his radio, but are interrupted by the police. Two escape in a car, while the other two are arrested. The filing deputy asks if they have records. The detective says they do not. The filing deputy says the question is, will he send it to the City Attorney for prosecution as a misdemeanor. Did they actually get the radio? No. 'Then it's only an attempt.'

The deputy then offers this commentary: 'Now this is important. If it's a robbery, then it's a felony. If it's a grand theft person, then it's a felony or a misdemeanor. What's the most expedient thing to do, save the taxpayers' money? This is a 20-year-old El Salvadorean. He's not going to state prison. I'll read the report and see how bad it is. . . . OK, it's a legal robbery, but I'm going to send it to the City Attorney. But I don't like it. But there's no reasonable anticipation of a state prison sentence.'

Later the deputy remarked to the observer: 'He's a 20-year-old stealing a ghetto blaster. Do you think he should go to prison? Guys with guns should go to prison.'

Here the deputy invokes knowledge of the kinds of sentences certain kinds of defendants will (and should!) receive for offenses assessed as having particular degrees of seriousness. Most judges will not give state-prison sentences to young defendants without a prior record convicted for 'stealing a ghetto blaster' without using a gun. He uses this organizational knowledge to justify referring the case to the City Attorney for prosecution as a misdemeanor.

To this point we have focused on complaint filing in routine cases, cases in which a filing deputy is and remains committed to the practice of 'only filing good cases'. In such 'normal complaint filing' the relation between a desired outcome and the likely outcome remains a key determination; if the former does not match the latter, do not file that case. There are, of course, recognized 'exceptions' to this practice; e.g. 'file a bad case if it will keep a bad guy in jail for a while'. Here the anticipated outcome is offset by other, more compelling factors. In other instances, however, the likely outcome becomes less salient, as 'downstream' consequences become barriers to be overcome rather than obdurate realities that have to be faced. In this vein, while discussing the dangers and frustrations of not filing weak cases against bad guys, the deputy who initially spoke of the 'downstream' consequences of filing outlined the following alternative approach:

Another analysis is you might file it hoping something magical will happen at the prelim. The detective just walks over the paperwork. The police report is only a summary, just their interpretation of the people they talked to. It's only as good as the people writing it. You'll ask, 'Did you talk to the victim?'. 'No.' Sometimes the victim can give you a lot. I'll have the investigator go out and talk to the victim. The prelim is two weeks away.

This approach involves 'risk' and uncertainty; the victim having nothing more to say, the police report may contain the strongest possible case. The decision to file is thus 'magical'—reflecting a *hope* that 'something good' will come out at the preliminary hearing. But this very 'magical' characterization rests on and plays off the normal, organizationally routine practice of making 'reasonable' filings by patterning a current decision on how such matters usually turn out.

In some instances, the question of whether decisions should be made 'reasonably' on the basis of the likely outcome, or in a risk-taking, 'magical' mode on the basis of the best-possible outcome, can become a matter of explicit organizational policy and conflict. Consider, for example, the twists and turns of the following complaint involving a student demonstrator in a Kent State-precipitated 'riot' (from a branch office of the same district attorney in an earlier era):

When disturbances broke out at a local university campus (in reaction to the killings at Kent State), an experienced trial deputy was assigned the specific task of securing a felony conviction against at least one student dissident.

A number of cases stemming from those disturbances were deliberately 'overfiled'. One of them involved a black student who, according to police accounts, had threatened an officer with a broken coke bottle while the officer was attempting to control a disturbance in the men's gym. The experienced deputy purposefully 'overfiled' the case, charging the demonstrator with attempt to commit violent injury on a police officer and assault with a deadly weapon [ADW] upon a police officer, despite the fact that ADW with a broken coke bottle was not generally regarded as a 'good' felony filing, particularly in the absence of serious injury. This case involved no physical injuries at all. . . . Ironically, at one point . . . another deputy who was unaware of the 'special' circumstances surrounding the case . . . read the complaint forms before they were actually typed and filed; he intercepted them and prepared a new filing more in line with the standards and methodologies applicable to 'routine' cases. . . . The filing, as prepared by him, eliminated the count of ADW on a police officer and reduced the second count from attempt to commit violent injury on a police officer to a lower grade felony—i.e. attempt to commit violent injury. His actions, premised on his belief that an inexperienced deputy had 'overfiled' the case initially, resulted in a sharp reprimand when the original trial deputy discovered what had happened to his 'special' case. The original charges, following some sharp exchanges between the deputies, were retyped and filed.(Krueger 1978: 173)

Here, the second deputy insisted on normal complaint-filing procedures by invoking a standard organizational horizon—juries will not return convictions for assault with a deadly weapon where the alleged weapon was a coke bottle (see Krueger 1978). The deputy who filed the initial charges insisted that this normal horizonal inference did not hold in this instance, since the case was 'special'— i.e. subject to specific administrative command and attention.

Conclusion

If we view discretion simply as decisions that are unguided by rules, we dichotomize decision outcomes into those that are in accord with the relevant rules and those that are not. We often invoke the notion of 'context' to explain instances of the latter category, holding that rules recede in salience when decisions are fitted to the contextual circumstances of given cases.

Such an approach precludes full analysis and appreciation of the relations between discretionary decisions and context, particularly as understood and experienced by actual decision-makers. For this notion views context as static variables standing outside of and influencing decision outcomes. As a result it analytically distorts and rigidifies decision-making processes as understood from within, as they are occurring. From the point of view of a decision-maker, relevant 'context' does not stand outside a decision, but is emergent with the shifting, contingent processes of interpretation and judgment that arise in coming to that decision. Thus, decision-makers do not first determine the 'facts of the case' and then look for 'relevant contextual factors'. Rather 'context' presents itself to decision-makers as horizons of possibilities: as one comes to confront 'a matter needing decision' (itself an evaluative, interpretive, i.e. discretionary process) and begins to weigh alternative ways of proceeding/deciding, one sees at a glance or upon reflection relevant connections, dimensions, implications. We have used the term 'decision horizons' to highlight and capture these processes.

Decision-making understood in these terms can give rise to a variety of different horizons. In examining the work of prosecutors screening criminal complaints, we emphasized the special significance of organizational horizons for their decision-making. The concept of organizational horizons points to the deeply ingrained institutional character of these decision-making processes. In determining what any given case is 'really all about' in order to decide how to handle it, prosecutors 'fill in' knowledge about where and how that case has come to them and what is likely to happen to it at future processing points. For a filing deputy, then, a case is not simply a complaint alleging that an offender committed a particular offense. Rather, a case is an institutional phenomenon wherein decision possibilities for an offender are linked to known courses of organizational activity, both past (e.g. what happened previously so that the case has now arrived at this point) and projected (e.g. the likely 'downstream' organizational implications of any current decision).

To this point we have been looking at organizational horizons as understood and experienced by prosecutorial decision-makers themselves. But we have done so by specifically examining prosecutors' *talk about* the horizons of specific cases. This feature suggests that decision horizons are not simply experienced, but are specifically invoked by decision-makers to present and establish the orderly, practically rational character of their decisions.[12] That is, in specifying organizational horizons decision-makers make relevant particular organizational concerns as grounds or reasons for their decisions; these horizons establish (or more accurately, assert) a rational, 'necessary' character for a decision. In invoking prospective horizons in refusing to file a complaint (e.g. 'no jury will believe the victim's story'), for example, filing deputies assert not only that this case

---

[12] By 'practically rational', we refer to decisions produced and framed as 'necessary', 'appropriate', 'reasonable', not for all cases but *for decisions reached in these particular circumstances*. See Garfinkel 1967: 272–83; Emerson 1981.

cannot be won, but that this very 'outcome' has to be taken into account in making 'reasonable decisions' in this setting. Similarly, contemplated decisions that ignore 'known' downstream consequences can thereby be characterized and dismissed as 'impractical', 'going by the book', or self-defeating wastes of time and energy. In this respect, organizational horizons as asserted and established by legal and other institutional agents lie at the core of the use of discretion in organizationally appropriate, practically rational ways.

8. 'Big-Bang' Decisions: Notes on a Naturalistic Approach

PETER K. MANNING

THE assumptions that underlie the use of the concept of discretion in reference to legal decisions require careful examination. Discretion in legal terms is said to occur when a decision once made comes under review using legal standards (rules) set by someone with authority (Dworkin 1977*b*). The implication of such a definition is that, prior to the review, regularly unreviewed choices were made (Reiss 1974*a*). It also implies that an individual case is decided on its merits in the absence of explicit consideration of socio-legal factors other than those stated in the opinion; that is, the reference is to judicial decision-making. The idea that discretion is fettered, and that guidance for examining cases derives from precedent and to a lesser extent, doctrine, explicitly denies the political–economic surround or broad social context in which decisions are made, the organizational context of decisions, and the cognitive framing of the elements, other than the facts of the case, that govern decisions. These matters may be seen as a set of implicit or background features to be put aside in explaining or accounting for any given decision outcome. The idea of the isolated case being adjudicated by a decision-maker thoughtfully weighing up the issues is a useful legal fiction, but perhaps too narrow for socio-legal analysis.[1]

I am grateful to Keith Hawkins, Lee Clarke, Kathleen Daly, and Betsy Cullum-Swan for perceptive comments on previous unwieldy drafts. Portions of the following argument were rehearsed at the Society for the Study of Social Problems in 1990, and at the American Society of Criminology in 1990.

[1] The case-focused view is limited in part because it contains a conception of holding and examining relevant facts that is unmanageable (people are often overloaded with information and make compromises or 'satisfice' rather than maximize). It also omits the process of sense-making and interpretation that lies behind a decision. It omits the cognitive and institutional structure within which law operates (Feldman, this volume, Chapter 5). The case-focused view excludes the role of non-legal rules, structures, and relationships (e.g. influences of the economy or of political trends on legal decisions) as well as the organizational context within which (legal) decisions are taken. The questions of shifting goals and objectives, unclear or conflicting ends, the prior problem of deciding as defining a problem, rather than taking a decision, and the role of inconsistent and situational preferences, decision rules, and knowledge of consequences, are elided (cf. March 1981; Feldman 1989). The case-focused view is a stark and impoverished depiction of deciding and those who decide.

Much socio-legal research or organizational decision-making addresses a very limited set of questions (see Hawkins and Manning, forthcoming). In part this is a question of method and focus, but it is also a problem of data. Not all legal decisions are recorded, adjudicated, evaluated as a part of a legal record, or become the basis for case law, yet they are a part of the family of relevant legal decisions. Many kinds of decisions are made by authoritative actors within the legal system, only some of which are reviewed, focused, rule guided, and precedent bound. Legal decisions are made with authority by social workers, police, governmental clerks, prison administrators, customs officials, and others who exert governmental social control (D. Black 1976). They are made at many points in the legal system, and only some are reviewed or audited. Some are made by groups and some by individuals. By focusing on a single moment of decision, or single type of decision, one omits at the very least the field in which the decision is viewed, and its organizational context (including time-bound effects of cumulative decisions in which, for example, previous decisions constrain present ones, or where the anticipation of a future decision shapes the present instant case (see Emerson and Paley, Chapter 7)).

Since the socio-political events accompanying the decisions may shape them, a broad conception of decision-making is needed to fill in the current rather patchy picture of even the most-studied systems such as the criminal justice system, governmental regulation, or other aspects of administrative law. There is a need to see decision-making in organizational context and to spread the notion of legal decision-making to cover decisions taken authoritatively in the name of the state. A socio-legal analysis should direct attention to matters that provide a context for given decisions, and serve to distinguish the effect of differing sociological conditions on decision-making.

The Scope and Content of the Chapter

This chapter intends to 'provide a plausible interpretation of [decision-making], or to see how organizational events fit together' (March 1981). It uses organizational analysis and the conventions of case-based socio-legal research as background rather than as a foreground. It does not entail an analysis of legal cases, even those considered 'easy cases' in the sense that they establish, in retrospect, the limits of a legal paradigm or the extension or contraction of a legal doctrine (cf. Schauer 1985). That line of reasoning would lead in the direction of assessment of legal mechanisms designed to maintain the integrity of law as a system of rules and would also entail a consideration of patterns of precedent-setting case decisions. These matters, amongst others, concern law as an 'autopoietic', or self-sustaining, closed communicational system in which 'decisions' are seen as messages to society (see Luhmann 1985; Teubner 1988). An analysis of this kind would extend beyond the scope of this chapter. Nor does the chapter explicitly outline a theory of organizational decision-making, although that is implicit in the formulations. Finally, the chapter concerns the *form* of deciding more than the content or consequences of decisions.

The central concern here is organizationally based decision-making. Since organizations are based on routines and contain stabilizing mechanisms to absorb the shock of potential changes, such as slack resources or screening devices to reduce demand, analysis of organizations in crisis reveals ways in which they cope. Revealed are both the centrality of routines and assumptions about why and how one acts as well as the particular consequences of alterations in conceptions of 'business as usual'. Examples used in this chapter are drawn from organizational responses to untoward events, disasters, catastrophes, and scandals—crises that engender extraordinary or what I shall call 'big-bang' decisions.

The primary question here is how changes in patterns of organizational decision-making are shaped by disruptive, large-scale events, and how whatever is defined as discretion might be patterned as a result. The chapter first characterizes decisions and organizational influences on them, then outlines an alternative, naturalistic view of studying decision-making. The penultimate section discusses aspects of 'big-bang' decisions. The chapter concludes with a consideration of changes in discretion in situations of crisis, and of the implications of these findings for naturalistic or ethnographic studies of legal decision-making. In perhaps the classic brief article on the subject, E. C. Hughes (1971) argues that the moral division of labour divides societies' tasks and provides protection and respect for work's obligations. A corollary of this is the epithet, 'one person's emergency is another's routine'. The point here is that, within an organization, routines are the mode of dealing with others' emergencies but also with internally generated crises. A clue to decision-making is routines, and the ways in which routines function in crisis should inform us in a significant fashion about discretion. This suggests that all such analysis should be comparative, should look at routines, legal decisions, and discretion in more than one organizational setting and derive from that comparison more general inferences about discretion.

Decisions

In some respects legal decisions resemble other decisions and insights can be gathered from studies of organizational decision-making that describe the context of decision-making (Emerson 1969; Manning 1980; Feldman 1988*b*). Legal decisions differ primarily in that they have authoritative consequences and can be enforced with the violence of the state. *A legal decision is a verbal or written justification or account (a message) for a known, public outcome of deciding (weighing, reflecting, arguing about), ascribed to legal actors* (Mills 1940; Scott and Lyman 1968). Accounts are 'situated', that is, are reflective of the status and power of those who render them and to whom. They are 'standardized within cultures so that certain accounts are stabilized and routinely expected when activity falls outside the domain of expectations' (Scott and Lyman 1968: 46). Weick writes of this process as pinning down or stabilizing meaning within an organization (1979: 58 ff.). Verbal or written justifications or accounts are offered for problematic acts of deciding, and it is these that are the traces of the behavioral events to which the law refers. In that sense these verbal justifications or texts are *indexes* of decision-processes; when written, they are now representations of events in a stylized fashion. Legal decisions are often equated, incorrectly to be sure, with identified decision-points made by visible individuals (e.g. police officers, judges, or social workers), or groups (e.g. parole boards, juries, and tribunals). These decisions are actually summations of many decisions that are, in effect, glossed with a name or label such as a 'parole decision', a 'sentencing decision', or a 'judgment'. Legal decisions stand apart from the process of reflection and action in everyday life, and are dependent on a proper institutional legal context.[2] Finally, legal

---

[2] From a semiotic point of view, legal acts can be classified into commands or decisions which are implicitly responses to requests, questions, claims, or complaints (Kevelson 1989: 29, summarizing Friedman 1975). Semiotically, a decision arises from a question (the linguistic index) put in an institutional context. The answer to a legal question is thus a conflated sign or 'conventionalized sign structure', the result of a connection between a set of expressions with content(s) encoded by legal rules and seen as reflecting legal facts (ideas or images based in experience: cf. Peirce 1931–). The legal system itself is constituted formally or symbolically as a system of signs that are conventionalized and stabilized to yield predictable outcomes. Ironically, this does not

decisions have other special features. They are embedded, on the one hand, in the legal culture, or modes of thinking and reasoning that are implicit and tacit as well as deductive and inductive, and, on the other, in the common-sense world that assumes the relevance of legal outcomes to everyday decisions. They usually include or involve socially constituted facts framed phenomenologically within associational contexts or paradigms. A legal decision may be appealed or questioned, raising issues about the rule applied and the command that is implicit in the existence of the rule. In order to understand these processes, some of the organizational influences on deciding should be reviewed.

Organizational Influences on Decision-Making

Two sorts of work on organizational influences on decision-making exist. The first is work on collective factors in decision-making and the second is a growing literature on organizational responses to recent disasters (i.e. those which have occurred since 1984: see, e.g., Cherniack 1986; Shrivastava 1987; Clarke 1988; Kreps 1989; Kroll-Smith and Couch 1989; Weick 1989; see also Levine 1983 and Perrow 1984). Let us review first some of the collective factors in decision-making that ethnographic work has revealed.

Studies of organizational aspects of decision-making show that perceptions of risk and trust are collective and embedded in assumptions about the organization, its institutional bias and mandate, the sanctioning strategies it employs, and the organizationally narrowed semantic field within which the concept of risk is defined (Short 1984; Douglas 1985; Jasanoff 1986; Manning 1987; Shapiro 1987). Organizational context (or the taken-for-granted background factors embedded in language, metaphor, and ideology that organizational members take into account) has been shown to be an important concept that influences routine decision-making (Janis and Mann 1977; Janis 1985; May and Neustadt 1986). The assumptions held by members of organizations produce systematic blindness.[3] The organizational

mean that legal discourse is closed, or logically tight; it is more often inferential, and lacking precise connections and constructions (Kevelson 1989). It features styles of argumentation that are often open-ended syllogisms.

[3] For example, Robert McNamara (lecture on WUOM radio, Ann Arbor, Mich., Nov. 1989) noted that some ten key assumptions made at the time of the Cuban missile crisis about the nature of the Soviet commitment to Cuba (including the size of the

context is not fully taken into account in psychological or individual models of risk (Heimer 1988).

Considerable research on organizational responses to disasters and decision-making in such public events suggests that cover-ups, lies, misdirection, dissimulation, disingenuousness, and attempts at the manipulation of public opinion are standard practices engaged in by both public agencies and private corporations (Katz 1977). Maintaining the public appearance of legality is an important fiction in such exercises. As a result, attempts to define the social reality of the event as being consistent with the law and legal obligations confounds any *ex post facto* analysis of decision-making at the time or immediately after the accident. As Clarke notes, discussing decision-making after a large office building was contaminated and several organizations attempted to decide what to do, public claims by the organizations notwithstanding, 'actions were taken and then justifications later sought for them' (1988: 30). Maintaining the appearance of rule-following behavior during and immediately after a crisis shapes present and future decisions in important ways.

Information is only one feature of decisions. As Feldman and March have pointed out, there is an organizational tendency to gather and store far more information than can be used; doing so takes on symbolic properties: 'The gathering of information provides a ritualistic assurance that appropriate attitudes about decision-making exist' (1981: 177). The presence of abundant information may well obscure or blur decision-making. It may also, for those deciding, or those trying to understand how the decision was made, increasingly force what might be called 'retrospective information assessment' or post-decision rationalization of decisions (Reiss, personal communication, Nov. 1989). It would appear, further, that many decisions are enactments (that is, expressions of beliefs and values) of previous presumptions and beliefs rather than responses to isolated, independent, cognitively-discrete events (see Weick 1979). In other words, both problems and solutions have organizational histories and are part of the organization's 'decision-making equipment'.

Inter-organizational relationships shape organizational decisions.

Soviet and Cuban forces in Cuba, the number of missiles involved, the Soviet willingness to send missiles, and their fear of US first strike action) were false. Yet they were the basis on which decisions were made. These false assumptions were based upon a mixture of inaccurate and absent intelligence as well as values and beliefs brought to decision-making by the key players.

These influences may appear at any point in a sequence of decisions (Vaughan 1983; 1990). As Vaughan has shown, these decisions might be located in a semi-closed, self-governing system (such as a criminal justice system), or in a network of regulatory agencies, each of which have their own autonomous drives for maintaining their own mandates, discretion, and boundaries. Clarke's work (1989) on the Binghampton office-building disaster suggests in addition that organizations construct pictures of their actions that mimic rational decision-making but that are in fact influenced by external political decisions. Clarke describes an organizational disaster in 1981 in Binghampton, New York, which resulted when an electrical fire in the basement of a building released PCBs (polychlorinated biphenyls) and dioxins (chemicals very toxic to humans; the PCBs were used as coolants for electric transformers). The chemicals were vaporized quickly in the heat and spread throughout the eighteen-storey office block. The actual chemical leaked was not known until after initial clean-up efforts began, and janitorial workers were exposed. The clean-up involved many agenices and was focused on a contamination problem that had not been faced before and for which science had few clear answers. Neither the solutions nor the process of reaching them was well understood. The eventual configuration of organizations responsible for decontamination of the building was a result of political bargaining and produced new definitions of the problem and a new set of solutions.

The context of transactions between organizations produces organizational interdependence and power-based hierarchies based on information exchange costs and trust (Heimer 1985b; Shapiro 1987) that shift costs to the less powerful deciders in the network. These network relations are especially evident and relevant in the case of disasters and untoward events that alter organizational routines (Feldman 1988b). Decisions may also be shaped by other matters, such as historical developments (see, on liability decisions for example, Friedman 1985; Cherniack 1986). Decisions also reflect changes in political parties and ideologies. Responses by politicians to previous events, and previous decisions by those deciding, contribute to decisions taken subsequently. Immediate, recent events serve to make people aware of the consequences of legal decisions. The 'shadow' of the incidents at Three Mile Island and Chernobyl attends any reported nuclear incident, just as the Challenger accident haunts all subsequent space shots.

Intragovernmental relations also affect patterns of decision-making.

These very complex symbolic transactions (imagery of other agencies guides actions toward them (Vaughan 1983)) seem governed more by tacit conventions and practices than by written law (Heimer 1985*a*; Shapiro 1987). Governmental agencies differ from private organizations in their lesser vulnerability to legal regulation and control. In industries deemed essential to the national defense, for example, secrecy surrounds, clouds, and alters the public and the private record of decisions, and affects the nature of admissible evidence in trials (e.g. the trials of Colonel Oliver North in the United States, and of Clive Ponting in England (Ponting 1986)). In the British case, strong unwritten conventions govern ministerial decisions and isolate ministerial sovereignty. In the past, these conventions were seldom subject to judicial review (Griffiths 1990).

Internal organizational processes further shape decisions. Fieldwork within organizations suggests that individual decisions are affected both by sequence effects on them (these arise from the order in which a case is decided) as well as by holistic effects (arising from the set within which a case is decided: see, generally, Emerson 1983). Both cumulative decision effects and contingencies resulting from face-to-face encounters result when groups of decision-makers (rather than isolated individuals), acting either in parallel or in sequence, are involved in a decision process. Other research has documented the influence of 'pressures to produce' (Blumberg 1967; Manning 1980); organizational rewards for consistency in decisions (Emerson 1983); social typifications of sets or groups of cases (Sudnow 1965; Cicourel 1968; Waegel 1981); and moral typifications of organizations by decision-makers that guide their actions toward such decisions (Hawkins 1984). As is discussed below, routines play an important role in sequencing, stabilizing, and reproducing organizational decisions (see Feldman 1988*b*, this volume, Chapter 5). One way of reproducing them is to employ the rule 'ration the service given'. Lipsky (1980) has shown, for example, how public organizations work to 'ration' their services in spite of their being collective goods. This means that there is a strong pressure to withhold or retract services, leading to what is seen as 'red tape', 'delays', and 'bureaucratic runarounds'. Such effects describe features of organizational processing that interact with the features of a given case.

Some generalizations can be made about organizational effects on deciding. Organizational processes and language, such as the nature of their classification system for communications, the metaphors used to assess events, and the ideology or mandate that unifies their actions, provide social bases for justifying decisions. Organizations with specific legal constraints operate with a mandate of public trust that serves as a tacit ground or set of rationalizations for their decisions. Delegation of responsibility does not obviate the problem of trust and the 'agency problem' (Shapiro 1987). Regardless of legal constraints, internal features of organizations shape and locate decision processes. Such issues as the complexity of rule systems, the shape of the hierarchy, and the number of ranks between the top and the bottom of an organization pattern decisions (Manning and Hawkins 1989). As noted above, organizations are embedded in a complex network of inter-organizational relations that constrain individual options and discretion, and reflect the political processes at work in these negotiations (Clarke 1989). The decision made in 'risky' situations is an example of the limiting case (it is rare). The norm for making organizational decisions is deciding according to conventions and within routine background assumptions, not as 'rare' cases (Heimer 1988).

Taken together, these organizational factors suggest that the dominant yet highly restrictive individualistic concept of decision-making should be modified to include relevant organizational and inter-organizational factors. Given these generalizations, the study of legal decision-making in organizational context would seem to require field-work combined with a naturalistic perspective. This strategy incorporates direct observation of the phenomenon in addition to analysis based on official versions of decisions and events (Emerson 1986).[4]

Perspective

Naturalistic research seeks to remain true to the nature of the social world studied. A naturalistic approach to decision processes will allow

---

[4] I argue here for a naturalistic sociological analysis. A number of scholars have advocated similar non-individualistic models of decision-making (e.g. March and Simon 1958; Hirschman 1970; Allison 1971; H. A. Simon 1974; Janis and Mann 1977; May and Neustadt 1986; Feldman 1989) that illuminate the question of discretion. Some important legal theorists have also cast doubt on the case-based perspective (see Dworkin 1977b, 1986; Jackson 1986), and the fields of administrative and criminal law have spawned a number of interesting case-studies that suggest the power of organizational paradigms or models of decision-making (Packer 1968; Asquith 1983; Mashaw 1983).

the tracking of decisions and reveal their organizational patterning. It will illuminate the experiential basis of the social organization of legal life fundamental to naturalistic studies of decision-making. Such studies permit one to link the social world of meaning with the formal legal world. Qualitative and descriptive studies of decisions made *in situ*, naturalistic social science studies of socio-legal structures and processes, should be comparative. Cross-sectional studies describing a sequence of relevant decisions in a given setting (such as the courts, the police, or probation officers) are incomplete in so far as they omit comparative analysis (see Sudnow 1965; Cicourel 1968; Emerson 1969; Ross 1970; Needham 1981; Waegel 1981).

In order to understand legal decisions naturalistically, decision-making must be located in a field of social forces, an organizational context, and within an identifiable sequence of decisions or a decision process. Such a study must be based on close field observation in more than one setting; it should be systematic as well as comparative. As March states, 'If there are insights found in modern perspectives on organizational choice, they are borrowed from the fine detail of good field observations' (1981: 206). Since there are many kinds of legal decisions, analysis must consider not only features of what is brought to the decision, but tacit as well as recognized constraints on decision-makers. The variety of outcomes possible also should be studied and situated. 'Situated' in this context means located with respect to the social forces that are at play in the decision process. Such an approach does not eliminate nor deny the perverse and dubious rationality of decision-makers, and should integrate the strong points of the case-based paradigm with those of the sociological perspective of organizations. It should be noted that the merits of the case method are unquestioned. Its strengths, however, make it ill suited for organizational analysis. The case method, well understood in jurisprudential circles, focuses on the individual case, including a known set of established facts, sees it in the context of a series of prior legal decisions taken by rational individuals, is decided on its merits as a result of due deliberation, and is disposed of in line with procedural standards and rules (that is, a decision is produced). Discretion is understood and delimited and varies for given agents making decisions. Its strengths are that it enables communication about legal decisions to be made on the assumption that that which is brought to law implies compliance with the outcome, procedures that are known and repeated, and a format for deciding that simplifies and reproduces decisions.

Naturalistic Concepts

Five major concepts, some of which are rehearsed above, organize this analysis. Naturalistic studies of organizational decision-making should address the relevance of the following concepts for explaining the process

Framing

A frame, according to Goffman (1974: ch. 2), provides the rules and principles which guide an understanding of the meaning of experienced events. Framing, in other words, sets the primary experiential orientation of actors. Examples of frames might be 'game', 'war', 'courtship', and 'conversation'. The frame links or stands between the everyday world and the internal cognitive world of the organization (how the world is divided logically). The individualistic research perspective on legal decision-making (e.g. Gottfredson and Gottfredson 1980) focuses almost entirely on the immediate cognitive focus or frame (Goffman 1974: ch. 2). Framing is cognitive isolation of an event. It names the process by which the rules or principles governing 'what is going on here' may be brought to the surface. Frames are keyed, or indicated, by cues or signs which stand in a part–whole relationship to the matter(s) framed. For example, a gesture, such as raising a hand, may indicate a 'threat', or a 'wave', or a 'caution', depending on the frame. A key is 'a set of conventions by which a given activity, already meaningful in terms of some primary framework, is transformed into something patterned on this activity but seen by the participants to be something quite else' (ibid.: 43–4). By means of a change in key, then, a conversation can be converted into a courtship; a marriage into a separation; a separation into a divorce; a family argument into a domestic assault; a reportable incident in a nuclear installation into an 'accident'. Producing these transformations by means of routine procedures and ways of thinking is the work of organizations.

An organizational frame is a structure of knowledge, experience, values, and meanings that organizationally located decision-makers bring to a decision. Framing in organizations patterns but does not determine what information is sought, or seen as relevant and significant, and what such information conveys for organizational actions. A frame in use in an organization, such as 'burglary' in a police agency or a 'pollution violation' in a pollution control organization, indicates that organizational actors have assembled and stabilized the distinctive cues that key that frame. (It is clear also that 'burglary' may not have the same function or power in another organization such as a victimized shipping company.) The existence of a frame, however, does not, in itself, isolate the particular relevant facts needed to take a decision. A frame must be applied to an event; 'facts' must be selectively organized by the application of the frame. Further actions are needed to define the implications of the use of this frame and to apply it to an event; these actions are guided by organizational routines and practices. The primary framework in organizations is 'business as usual'. This means that the usual sets of conventions serve to frame and sustain such normality. Routine grounds in organizations are keyed by shared stimuli as a result of standardized work performances and sequences.

In practical terms, frames organize and reduce unique human experience and vicissitudes to routine, and from mere routine to organizational routines (Feldman 1988*b*), shared and collectively defined. A master organizational frame is that which defines a matter as relevant to this organization and its activities in the first instance and serves as a basis for screening facts. Organizations maintain large numbers of personnel at their boundaries such as operators, inspectors, or receptionists, who screen and filter data and who use organizational frames to manage potential overload. The master frames used by the police, for example, are quite broad and encompassing, but those used by the telephone company or the fire department are much narrower in scope. While the police are obliged either to receive or to refer matters, they rarely officially refuse to consider or process a request. The telephone company, on the other hand, will refuse to come to investigate an electrical failure in the house, or to put out a fire, or will routinely refer matters elsewhere.

In an important sense, legal frames that define facts as legal and have potential for authoritative consequences overlap with organizational frames. There is often a tension in legally established agencies, such as the police, regulatory agencies, or social service departments, between organizational practices and legal frames and the 'shadow' of the anticipated legal frame. Organizational frames may be shaped by legal moves anticipated by organizational decision-makers, just as legal frames are shaped by organizationally dominant frames. For example, physicians in hospitals base their decisions about withholding a respirator for near-terminal patients on their knowledge of State and US Supreme Court decisions, and legal decisions on such matters are based, at least in part, on expert testimony about acceptable patterns of practice in given localities.[5] The influence of the 'external' world is never fully excluded in decisions, for personal values, ideologies, and beliefs are the 'background' against which people are able to order the 'foreground' of salient facts in the decision field.[6]

Decision fields

A frame, although a sharply drawn boundary around a messy and unfolding process, exists within a field of activities. Cognitive frames are contained within decision fields which are subject to or shaped by social pressures and developments. A decision field is the social basis for labeling a situation of deciding: the seen-as-relevant-at-the-moment assemblage of facts and meanings within which a decision is located. Fields constitute both the 'background' and 'foreground' for decision-making activity. Foreground matters are seen against an often unrecognized background of assumptions. The boundaries of the field tacitly, if not explicitly, exclude material that is recognized but not explicitly included in the frame. For example, the police have a conception of 'events' that helps them to translate calls made to them: events are seen as volatile, changing, problematic, or constructed in their own self-interest by callers, and likely to deteriorate if not controlled in some fashion (Manning 1988d: 21–2). This set of ideas about social life constitutes the 'normal' field in which officers decide. If a nuclear safety inspector takes a decision about asking a manager of an installation to secure a door in a part of the plant, he or she is locating that decision in a field that includes taken-for-granted authority to make this request, as well as the background possibility that objections may be raised, that the costs may be negotiated, and that major policy changes about the safety of this type of reactor (e.g. a decision to decommission it) are not in the field at the time of the decision. The excluded or 'out-of-field' material may sometimes be recognized,

---

[5] This is based on a personal communication (Jan. 1991) from Dr Howard Brody, an MD with a Ph.D. in philosophy, who has written on medical ethics.

[6] One source of such organizational changes are tensions between expectations set by individual experiences and the institutional frame. Distinctions should be made between the socially organized and sanctioned frames used within institutions and those employed by individuals. Individual, organizational, and institutional frames may be shared, but the degree of consensus is a matter for empirical investigation within any legal setting. Change emerges from this tension. Having said that, however, it is not clear exactly how a frame is transformed or re-keyed, or what the organizational implications of such a development might be. Some of these changes will be explored here.

such as the tacitly known potential for a major shift in policy about decommissioning, or it may be outside recognition. In both cases, such material is termed the surround (see below). A frame sits inside a field and is bounded by a surround. They are nested or embedded in each other and are in mutual interaction.

Organizational context

Organizational context includes the assumptions, values, ideologies, and social norms brought to the deciding process by the decision-maker(s). It serves to constrain and shape decisions. Once decisions are given a name (e.g. 'an arrest', 'a sentence', 'a pardon'), or accounted for in some fashion publicly, they are sorted out using organizational standards. Decisions do not stand alone, for they are units or tokens that fit within a set of types of organizational decisions. Types of decisions can be associated by their connotative meanings into paradigms or clusters. In nuclear safety regulation, for instance, there are inspectorial decisions, policy decisions, ministerial decisions (and those made by the government of the day), decisions about design, and emergency planning decisions about the site, each of which is framed and set within a field of decision-making. These named types reduce variety into workable limits. Types of decisions (for example, those within the paradigm called 'design decisions') can be further broken into domains or subtypes that cluster together. Within a set of decisions about design, further divisions, such as those about reactor design, turbines and generators, building structure, and plant security, are possible. These groupings are decision domains or divisions within a given type of decision or paradigm. Although all organizations have paradigms (associational contexts) and denotative domains, organizations differ in the complexity, number, and content of paradigms and domains (Barley 1983). For example, while a police organization may have as few as a handful of associational domains used to classify actions (crime/non-crime; to be done/in progress/ finished; rush/as soon as possible/maybe; trustworthy call/terminate), a university bureaucracy dealing with admissions may have fifteen or twenty domains. Any organization may have overlaps of cases in more than one domain (anomalous cases), an index of complexity of processing routines, and can accommodate, at a given time, a variable number of cases in process (think, for example, of the difference in current workload for an urban magistrates' court, an urban police department, a fire department, and a car insurance agency).

The social surround

The social surround contains organizations and associated decision fields and frames. The surround, the broad political and economic currents and developments within which decisions are cast, embeds any frame set within a decision field. Events in the surround are metaphorically 'over the known horizon' during the normal course of events. However, the social construction of the event changes. Consider two recent examples where the surround changed. The racial incidents—'riots'—in Britain in Bristol and Brixton in the early 1980s suddenly forced British police officials to recognize that the external world was shaping the organization in new ways and that the organizational context of British policing had been altered. New paradigms, such as 'community consultation', and 'community policing', and new domains such as 'racial incidents', became part of the decision-making context. These changes, in turn, created new fields (and frames) for the decisions of officers on the ground. When the explosion at the nuclear reactor at Three Mile Island occurred, the potential for such events altered the horizon of the US Nuclear Regulatory Commission, leading to changes in training and administration of licensing procedures, and led to international meetings at which new standards and practices were set. Special attention was given to additional training of control-room operators, especially in the response to serious events. The altered social surround of political and economic forces in both cases became a part of the organizational context and the decision fields of the British police and nuclear regulators and utilities managers respectively, and it remains so.

Codes

The idea that messages are encoded, or organized into very broad principles that grant them meaning, is exemplified in such ideas as morse code, the code of etiquette, the highway code, or a legal code. Codes have four interrelated aspects. They contain a structure for organizing difference or 'inner combinatory laws', a syntactical aspect (Eco 1976: 36). Codes also include a semantic aspect, referring to the meanings attributed to contents of messages. Codes may be relatively open or closed in the rules used for classifying messages, and may organize the messages by differing principles (Guiraud 1972). Finally, codes include a set of behavioral responses. In operational terms, a code will be used to include the above aspects when it operates to couple some items from each aspect to organizational decisions (Eco 1976: 37). In the following section, the claim is that messages are encoded in two basic or primordial codes in organizations: routine and emergency. The usual operational status is routine coding and unexamined use of frames, paradigms, and domains to carry out organizational work. The surround remains stable. However, when a crisis is defined, the encoding and decoding of messages change and a kind of metacoding (recoding of events and the coding of events) takes place. As a result, certain messages are encoded as emergent, while others, the routine business of the organization, must also be coded, and worked on. Coding, in many respects, is tacit work, even though the surface features of the activity (e.g. classificatory schema) may be known. The scheme may remain, but the code changes. Observations of actual practice and modifications thereof are necessary to establish the claim that messages are coded as about 'crises' or 'emergencies'.

These concepts constitute the rudiments of a naturalistic perspective on decision processes. Let us consider two examples of crisis coding, one from the police and one from nuclear power regulation.

The Police.   A primary frame in policing is 'routine patrol' and this is keyed by cues that set the frame as normal, such as levels of traffic for the time period, consistent pedestrian activity, sporadic radio calls at the expected level for the time and day of the week, and the usual or 'regular' workload. The decision field includes the officer and partner in a car responding to calls for service as usual on the radio, and the content of radio calls (messages) is set into domains and paradigms. The paradigms used are classification of events (in fact, the calls the officer hears on the radio are partial pictures of the events being reported to him or her: 'crime/non-crime', 'rush/non-rush', 'information only' calls). The domains into which the calls are sorted (category-specific jobs such as 'crime in progress', a report of a burglary, or 'man down', as described by the dispatchers) are seen as either in the domain of action required or non-action related. This sorting-out of messages draws on symbolic resources that are found in the occupational culture. In this case, the occupational culture provides themes of uncertainty combined with authority, a penchant for action, and clinical definitions of police work. The police conception of events orders and creates an attitude of anticipation of action. The broad surround embedding events, such as the current 'crack epidemic' and youth violence, lingers, but does not directly shape decisions taken by the officers unless a 'crackdown' on drug-dealing is decided by policy-makers. The workload (accepting about three to four calls an hour) remains, and the routine by which decisions are ordered is stable. Discretion in these circumstances is unaltered by external forces, and is fettered in the usual fashion. Whatever decisions are taken are taken within this analytic framework. If an event touches off actions that are not dealt with within the organization by its routines, such as an overload of calls as a result of massive accident, bad weather, or a hostage crisis, a new coding of messages emerges: that of 'emergency'. The organization must routinely process messages as well as respond to some as crisis-related. As it does so, the organization is facing a self-defined crisis. A change in coding is a change in organizational self-definition; its representation of itself to itself.

Nuclear safety regulation.   In the case of nuclear safety regulation, one organization is auditing the performance of another, so the interaction between the two is the basis for 'crisis coding'. A primary frame in inspectorial work is a monthly 'inspection' in which the inspector tours the plant, holds meetings with management, or selectively visits and interviews plant personnel. In this case the field includes the assumptions that the nuclear plant that produces electricity is operating safely, that the plant is well managed, that various forms of inspection ensure compliance, and that design and construction ensure the basic character of operations (Manning 1987). A 'reportable incident', say a change in the operating pressure in the reactor, is a routine event, and is framed as such. The broad surround (the price of oil, the current energy policy of the government, the policies and legal requirements of operation in US Federal law) is unchanged, however, and stabilizes operations. If the reportable incident remains unsolved, and continues for longer than a stipulated period (usually less than twenty-four hours), and organizational routines are varied, a new coding of messages takes place. A crisis emerges. For example, a crisis emerged in the autumn of 1990 at the Detroit Edison Fermi 2 plant in Monroe, Michigan, when a shaking turbine could not be stilled. The Nuclear Regulatory Commission was notified, and the entire plant was closed until the problem was identified and solved.

Some Aspects of Big-Bang Decisions

From the organizational perspective, big-bang decisions result from an alteration in the nature of the coding of decisions. The event itself may vary in scope, in intensity, in the numbers of persons involved, in the organizational network in which it becomes entangled, and the time (Kreps 1989). A crisis seen from the perspective of the organization(s) is the result of responding to an event recoded as an emergency. *Big-bang decisions are those taken within an organization in response to organizational definitions (codings and recodings) or enactments of the raw materials that erupt as a result of a known, public event that disrupts organizational routines.* The defining feature of these decisions is that they are encoded as emergency decisions.

It seems likely that decision-making after or in the course of an organizationally defined disaster, an unexpected code-altering event, differs from routine decision-making. Other decisions, taken at the same time and place, remain coded as routine decisions. These two types of decisions interact, under some conditions, to produce an emergent organizational crisis.[7] If the coding of decisions changes, then it would appear that the nature of discretion, *ipso facto*, is altered.

The following section discusses distinctions between types of events, their relationship to routine organizational decision-making, and how routines and codes are altered. Recoding or 'business as usual' does take place. The four matters discussed constitute a natural history of changes in the nature of organizational decision-making.

Events and decisions

Legally mandated bodies respond or react indirectly or in an interpreted (Weick 1979), loosely coupled, lagged, hesitant, indirect fashion to events in which a known delict or crime is alleged, and where a decision is rendered and/or requested. They respond to an enacted or socially constructed environment. When changes in the perceived or enacted surround occur, shifts in routines result. These modifications in thinking and acting, in turn, are reflected in patterned alterations in attention, affect, and the locus and quality of interpersonal and inter-organizational trust (Shapiro 1987). The series of changes outlined

---

[7] Crisis-generated justifications (explanations that accept that an event has occurred, but without accepting responsibility) play with the questions of moral responsibility, blame, and luck (see Manning 1988*c*; Scheppele 1989). On the other hand, some decisions are excused as not being the fault of the organization.

serve to pattern discretion; changes in the coding of decisions have a ripple effect.

Some events precipitate an organizational crisis (an alteration in the decision code or mode seen as resulting from a change in the workload internally and changes in the external environment of events) and organizational response. A full analysis of crisis decision-making would examine a typology of decisions and specify the kinds of effects on discretion that result.[8]

One can imagine a number of examples in which the surround changes as a result of catastrophic events. Socio-legal work has so far dealt primarily with organizational response to bounded and temporally restricted events or crises, while less research has been done on unfolding scandals or chronic disasters (see, however, Kroll-Smith and Couch 1989). Furthermore, most socio-legal work analyses the nature of the response or reaction of agencies to an external event such as a natural disaster, earthquake, fire, flood, or a socio-technical or socially precipitated disaster or scandal, rather than to internal scandals and corruption of legal agencies.

The different response to crisis is in part due to the role of state regulation and control of the functions at issue. To put the case clearly at the outset, important differences result when the events are seen as 'natural' as opposed to 'man-made', since social causation comes into play in the latter (who is to blame, and why, are the salient questions), whether they are acute or chronic, and the extent to which, at the time of the analysis, they are ongoing, moribund, or essentially resolved. Most importantly, when the state is the primary responsible agent as well as the cause of the problem, as in errors made by the army that cost lives, nuclear weapons testing, radiation leaks and accidents, an issue of the extent to which the state can regulate itself is raised (Manning 1987).

Finally, there may be need to develop a typology of decision-making events. There are indications that decision-making, and associated discretion, changes in its nature and quality when crisis-like events alter the surround and hence, through organizational response, the coding. Table 8.1 shows the distinctions between acute and chronic disasters, whether or not they are continuing, and natural or social in origin. The relationship of the focal organization

[8] Some examples of the analysis of these events and their consequences have been published (Cherniack 1986; Clarke 1989; Manning and Hawkins 1990; Vaughan 1990).

TABLE 8.1   *The nature of the event called a disaster, and the time period in which it takes place*

EVENT	TIME			
	Active		Resolved	
	Natural	Social	Natural	Social
Acute	earthquake	scandalous event	earthquake	Chernobyl Three Mile Island Bhopal
Chronic	coal fires* deforestation desertification greenhouse effect	corruption sequence	many floods	corruption sequence

* Long-burning underground fires in old coal shafts.

to the state, and whether the focus is internal or external to the organization, are also important considerations.

Note that the event may be defined as acute or chronic, depending on the time at which the investigator examines the event. The distinction between events that are active or resolved also contains an implicit diachronic dimension, since the decision about when a scandal or natural disaster is resolved is a value-laden social decision. The natural or social aspect of the event or process may also be difficult to disentangle since some things seen as 'natural' are indirectly a consequence of social decisions—e.g. the greenhouse effect, the erosion of the Sahara, or the slow destruction of the Amazonian rain forest. An analysis of decision-making is likely to be internally focused on changes in patterns of decision-making resulting from the event and the crisis. One could look externally, as has Diane Vaughan (1983) in her analysis of relationships between organizations engaged in formal organizational control of organizational deviance, to examine the source of the enacted crisis.

Where the state defines the nature of the event, it is clear that the socially ascribed risks that result from the cells in the table are quite different. Although 'natural' events are morally neutral with respect to causation and blame, in the case of governmentally produced risks, or governmental responses to disasters, the nature of governmental liability and the ability and propensity of the state to control itself changes definition of the external (enacted) environment. One might imagine a second table set beside the first in which the governmental organizations were studied to examine the role of the state's self-interest in patterns of decisions and the nature of permitted discretion.

Frame, field, and routine

The decision field remains relatively stable in organizations, anchored by the relevant technology, the fixed and legitimated roles and tasks sanctioned by authoritative social control, and the codes employed for interpretative activity (see Manning 1988*d*). Weber (1958) has argued that people seldom wish to give up the right to control the nature and speed of their work, and has shown further that industrialization merely modifies the modes of control from traditional to rational. Even the work of making sense of calls, interpretative work in organizations that enables facts to be set within formats and records and to be filed and disposed of, is very resistant to change (see Manning 1988*d*: ch. 7). Police officers, for example, still loath 'paperwork' even when it is merely filling a format on a laptop computer. Even the introduction of computer-assisted dispatching in policing has not changed the framing of the officers' decisions, only introduced the additional constraint of technology on dispatchers and operators. Technological noise and technological facilitation of decisions, once made, modifies officers' work, but the framing and the field are fairly stable, and the routine of call and response and radio-driven patrol time remain, whether the department is organized by computer technology, or merely uses basic two-way radio and patrol. Once the field for decisions is set in place, inertia maintains its grip.

Routines order the sequence of deciding. Stable routines, or shared patterns used to shape and control the flow of work (seen broadly as a stimulus (Feldman 1988*a*)), are embedded in beliefs or ideologies growing from the mandate of the organization, and represented publicly in organizational discourse (Manning 1987). Examples of organizational routines are ways of shifting cases through the detective division of a police department (Waegel 1981), ways of processing policy data and papers through federal bureaucracies (Feldman 1988*b*), set (and frequently violated) procedures for processing information, files, evidence, and money through specialized vice units of police departments (Manning 1980), and workers' modes of coping with uneven workflow (D. L. Roy 1955). Routines govern work flow and these means of control are reflective of themes found in the occupational or organizational culture, such as 'don't stick your neck out', or 'don't rock the boat'.

Routines also serve a variety of other functions. They provide a subtle and powerful stabilizing force (Feldman 1988a; 1988b). They serve to control individual actions, because they provide expectations of, and are part of the setting of, accountability; they function as a kind of resident organizational memory; and they are embedded in the flow of collective organizational action that serves to stabilize the organization, keep it 'conservative', and resist change. Routines may lie just beyond direct acknowledgment, or be the tacit basis for working, something people simply take for granted as part of the 'grounds' of organizational life (Garfinkel 1967). Actors may be unaware of the various consequences of the routines to which they respond. For example, the police decision-making field is set for patrol officers by the routine activities of patrol, driving around aimlessly in no set order or place, in the interests of being visible, available, and a deterrent to wrongdoing. The radio calls are sequenced and responses set by routines. Yet officers believe they act as their own bosses, that 'no one tells me what to do', and that they control their own workload. Academic routines are set by the timing of classes, the ebb and flow of terms, the academic year, and the oscillation between reading, research, writing, and teaching, yet academics deny that they are merely another set of smart bureaucrats whose movements and actions are responses to externally set routines.

Yet routines can also facilitate social change (Feldman 1989). Actors may not share an awareness of their routines and their functions in the work setting. Awareness of routines is the first step to change, and participants act on their awareness of the need for change. Organizations adjust to their ambiguous goals, their changing environments, and the ambiguous and unfolding nature of others' decisions by means of routines. Routines therefore are the patterned source of emergencies and emergency decision-making.

Routines order bureaucratic rhetoric and enhance the fiction of stable bureaucratic control. They do so because they are set cognitively, and, because they are visible and collective, they enhance mutual trust. They provide a gloss on the rules used strategically to maintain power and position of groups within the organization. As a shared, focal, response to a joint or shared stimulus, routines set up or stimulate procedural or rule-based activities (Feldman 1989). They contain a tacit or assumed feature, joint action in pursuit of goals or objectives, that reflects social relationships and reinforces mutual trust. Thus, although a routine, such as inspection, or the dispensation of monies within a police department, is rule-guided and governed by overt written guidelines, forms, and deadlines, it also reflects the cognitively salient foreground for actions and choices, and signals mutual dependence of officers on each other for resources. In this sense, routines are highly consequential and a source of consensus, agreement, and administrative control. Thus, it is not surprising that 'red tape', the negative face of routines, is a metonymic representation of bureaucracies, one of its figurative guises, as well as a distinctive focal characteristic of such organizations.

Routine and emergency

Recall that 'business as usual' is the code for processing work in a organization. When a routine coding is broken by the inability of the organization to cope routinely with events, the current routine and the need to respond to the overload (as well as the event) produce an interaction effect. The ways in which encoding of messages is altered from routine to emergency may not be understood either, since the members of the organization conflate 'events' and the environment with its own 'cognitive equipment' (frames, fields, routines, organizational context [paradigms and domains], and the relatively stable surround). Alteration in internal routines may take place as a result of the resultant shifts in perception. Frames remain in place, but the field and organizational context are affected because work takes place in an emergency. The epistemic break occurs when routine coding is no longer adequate to cope with the change in the workload and event-processing. The resultant recoding, it must be emphasized, does not alter the number and kinds of initial frames used to frame messages. Events may be re-keyed, or a new frame applied, but they are still framed.[9]

---

[9] Re-keying, discussed elsewhere (Manning and Hawkins 1990), should be distinguished from breaking a once-established frame. In re-keying 'normal' heuristics are used to sort out the nature of the uncertainties and options associated with the possible outcomes. A broken frame remains at the interpersonal or 'organizational boundary', but does not mean that routines are disrupted.

When recoding takes place because the organization defines itself as being in a new operating mode (whether the proximal stimulus is an accident, catastrophe, or disaster), it appears that new ordering heuristics are required. These heuristics are the procedures by which problem-solving takes place.

When organizations exceed some level of capacity to cope with the message load, when their routine segments enstructured for coping with such heterogeneous events are overloaded, then the potential exists for recoding, and for redefining the grounds for organizational action. The interaction of event and response may lead to a questioning of basic organizational premises. It usually does not. Thus, the transition from routine to emergency coding should be seen as a short-lagged response, and not an epistemic break that signals possible societal change. Societal reaction following an organizational response to an event may indicate a rupture of past patterns for coping with an event (Foucault 1970). Organizational emergencies may signal major reorganization of cognition and affect, and they may indicate new modes of decision-making that emerge as a result of ruptured routines. Not all big-bang events, or obvious societal disasters, produce this basic kind of questioning. If they do, however, change in decision-making and discretion may take place. The nature of the decision-making process itself will be altered by the conversion to viewing events within an emergency code, and this is the immediate organizational result that patterns discretion.

The focus analytically here is on how changes in coding and routines alter discretion, not simply on describing changes. Given the organization as characterized by the five concepts, what can one expect to change if an outside event intrudes into organizational action, shifting it into an emergency status? Here are some thoughts about how decision-making is modified and how that shapes discretion.

Return to normal

It would appear that striving urgently to recover the appearance of 'normality' or 'business-as-usual' functioning is a basic organizational rule. Hence, the importance placed within the organization upon carrying out routine functions, even though the organization may be in some disarray as a result of a current 'crisis'. The salient features of maintaining this 'appearance of the normality' of organizational operations vary widely by organizational type, field, and surround, and by the degree to which organizational life, shifts in workload, and demand in routine time frames, cycles and rhythms, are affected by the crisis. But it should be emphasized that this is not a direct function of the scale of the external disaster.

As a result of a *code-shift*, in the first instance, no major questions about the response of the organization to the external environment may be raised. Assumptions about the nature of the environment, operations in respect of it, and extant routines may not be questioned. The problem lies in the extraordinary events, their serendipity, rarity, and odd properties. After the fact, in the aftermath of a crisis, the luxury of an overview may be permitted (or required by law, Commission, or regulatory body). Questions at that time will be asked such as: What is the nature, quality, and duration of this external event? In what ways does it resemble (and not resemble) previously framed events? What remedies are to be entertained for internal and external procedures? To what degree will society or the legal system consider a variety of modes of response, including criminal prosecutions, political actions, firing relevant persons, civil suits for damages, and/ or international court cases? Will the grounds for deciding used by organization members shift fundamentally as a result of this response to these events? Do they see it as 'fundamental', or merely a new routine? The focus here is upon the relationship between the defined and represented events and their organizational consequences. Our focus now shifts to decisions and discretion.

Example: Sellafield, winter 1986. The organizational response of HM Nuclear Installations Inspectorate (NII) to events at the chemical nuclear fuel-reprocessing plant at Sellafield[10] is illustrative of big-bang decision-making. The plant, a huge nuclear-fuel waste-reprocessing operation spanning many square miles in Cumbria on the far north-west coast of England, a product of the uneven development of Britain's nuclear power and weapons programmes since the Second World War, has been a constant source of concern since it opened. Decisions taken as a result of a series of leaks there were the basis for an alteration in the shape of discretion.

In early winter of 1986 the semi-private governmental corporation, British Nuclear Fuels Ltd. (BNFL), the licensed quasi-governmental

---

[10] Once called Windscale, the village was the scene of one of the most serious radioactive release accidents in British history in 1957 and a massive fire in 1979. The nearby village and plant were renamed in a rather pathetic attempt to obscure public knowledge of its dubious past (see Patterson 1983).

operator of Sellafield, announced that the plant had sprung a leak, releasing into the air a cloud of steamy radioactive gas. Little was made in the Press or in Parliament of this event. The surround produced a set of contingent events for organizational processing, in this case for the regulatory body (NII), to which our attention now turns.

Then other leaks were reported. The boundaries of the decision-making field for NII were altered because the series of leaks, although they were all contained for the most part within the relevant safety structures and the releases did not produce known damage, suggested underlying problems that might cast doubt on the continued safe operations of the plant. Immediate actions by the licensee had not prevented further leaks.

When another leak took place, and yet another, the safety of the plant and its workers was questioned in the Press. The plant's operation became subject to public scrutiny and reassessment. The media became involved further when former employees wrote to and gave anonymous interviews to the élite and liberal British Press (the *Observer* and the *Guardian*) stating that previous incidents had not been reported. (This was a reframing of past events, since the fact that there was no requirement that they be reported at the time, or that national security interests were different, was not mentioned in the articles.) Fanned by the media, public outcry raised questions about the safety and security of the plant and about the nature and risks of fuel-reprocessing generally. These arguments had raged previously in Britain in the late 1970s (Patterson 1983), when it was claimed that Britain would become a 'nuclear waste bin', and in late 1985, when a fast breeder reactor and fuel-reprocessing plant was mooted for Scotland.

Other political developments made this event part of a broader politico-economic mosaic. The claimed safety of nuclear-fuel-reprocessing, one aspect of the chain of production and waste extrusion, was an essential in past Conservative energy policy and was in fact a fundamental facet of the Thatcher government's policy. Past safe performance of fuel-reprocessing was one basis for arguing for a renewed nuclear power programme. The Conservative Government's programme was at that time under consideration by Frank Layfield QC, who was in the process of writing the report on the hearings held over the previous two years at Sizewell on the Central Electricity Generating Board's proposal to build a pressurized water nuclear reactor

(PWR). There were no pressurized water reactors in Britain at the time (one is now being built at Sizewell in Suffolk), and the shadow of Three Mile Island, which involved a PWR, loomed constantly over the hearings (see Layfield, 1987). The absence of large-scale reactor accidents, other than the 1979 Windscale fire, gave credence to the claim that the present ageing reactors were safe, albeit near decommissioning. The anticipated positive response was a report by the Inspector that would permit the site to be used, and ultimately to facilitate licensing of the reactor. This was the necessary step prior to building the proposed plant, Sizewell B. Licensing by NII, designing and building a PWR at Sizewell B, were seen as stimuli to industry confidence, increased demand for electricity, and requests to build additional reactors. But the leaks appeared to threaten the programme. This threat was great if the leaks continued and/or if further evidence of risks were to be revealed by the Press. It was feared that disgruntled present or former workers at the plant might give to the media evidence of past events or accidents that had not been previously published. The general well-being of the workers in the plant was raised by the media and linked to health and safety broadly. The risks to employees were in fact high at the ageing plant, and this (probably) had long been well known to members of the government of the day, the nuclear industry, and civil servants (see the review in Patterson 1983; Bertell 1985).

The NII, a regulatory agency within the Health and Safety Commission which is headed by the Health and Safety Executive (HSE), was brought directly into the problem. The NII has active inspectorial responsibility for assuring that the licensee meets agreed-upon principles and standards, national and international, for continued operation and licensing, responsibilities for emergency planning and the well-being of residents around power stations, and obligations to Parliament for the enforcement of the relevant Acts of Parliament.

A series of decisions suggest that the coding of processed and framed events changed from routine to the non-routine in the NII. New resources were marshalled, and new organizational innovations resulted. The following series of decisions and activities constituted the official response to the leaks and public response.

The first position was that everything was well in hand, and that established routines would continue. This first position included routine inspectorial functions and the continuance of routine inspection while higher authorities were taking charge during the period of crisis. The public position was that this series of leaks suggested that intervention in the form of 'tinkering' and fine tuning to improve routine enforcement of procedures and inspection was required. The second, emergent position, when recoding occurred, was that some extraordinary measures were to be taken. Leadership, a co-production of government and industry, came to the fore. Publicly staged and filmed visits were made to the plant by the Chief Inspector of NII, the Director General of the HSE, the Secretary of State for the Environment, and representatives of BNFL. These visitors were shown on a grand tour of the plant wearing white coats as a safety precaution, and were filmed listening attentively to the plant manager describe changes in safety procedures. Special intraorganizational links were forged. The Director General of the HSE announced he was carrying out an investigation in co-operation with the newly appointed Chief Inspector of NII. Special meetings were called: meetings were held between heads of industry, the HSE, and the Department of the Environment. Extraordinary information on past inspections and leaks was sought. Reports on the leaks were requested from Branch Three of NII (the branch which works in Bootle, near Liverpool, and has responsibility for fuel-reprocessing) and were collected and assembled at HSE headquarters in London.

During the first and second phase of the crisis, assurances were given that business as usual, only safer, was taking place currently at NII and Sellafield. It should be noted also that the basic position was that the safety of the Sellafield operation, or of fuel-reprocessing as an activity, was not questioned by members of the government, the NII, or representatives of the industry. Their position was, and is, that the plant is fundamentally safe, although in need of work. The enacted environment (Weick 1979), or the political and economic matters that constitute the surround, as defined by the organization's members, was itself unchallenged.

As a result of this series of radioactive leaks at Sellafield and the nature of the organizational response, policy-driven questions were raised within the NII about the procedures and practices of Branch Three of NII, those responsible for inspection of the Sellafield site. New efforts had to be seen to be made. In due course, the situation became an extraordinary one, loaded with the implications bearing on emergent national economic policies. Questions were raised in the media concerning the adequacy of the current practices—would they guarantee safety? This questioning was the result of the appearance of a low-probability or 'unlikely' event (a series of leaks). Such events remain potentially very damaging and worrying to the public at large.

As Perrow (1984) has suggested, policies are developed to deal with the routine, the usual, and the probable, while the rare event can only be vaguely (and never fully) anticipated. Some accidents are 'normal' in the sense that combinations of two or more events can never be fully anticipated in complex, tightly-linked systems. In spite of the presumption of rationality in the regulation of highly dangerous substances and technologies, much is left to the workings of chance. Since the likelihood of a full melt-down of a reactor is calculated as 1^{-16}, chance alone means this has only a remote chance of being a threat to current operations. On the other hand, the consequences of such a rare event could be widespread and very costly in human lives and productivity. Thus, in many respects, the management of public fear and the reassurance required to maintain the mandate of the Inspectorate, for example, may take precedence in such situations over changes in technology or in inspectorial operations. Of course, this is not meant to suggest that forms of prudent policy intended to anticipate and reduce the consequences of rare events are not possible.

From the media reports it is not possible to discern how production or operations within the plant were altered, if at all, by the crisis. There were no more reported leaks that winter at Sellafield, but it is possible that little was actually done within the plant, while public accounts were being provided and the emergency coding was admitted to the public. The appearance of business not as usual may have been contradicted by the workings of the vast plant. The Layfield Report on the licensing issue, published late in 1986, did not find that it was unacceptable in principle to license such a station, and the reactor is currently under construction.

Decision-Making and Discretion

The naturalistic perspective on decision-making should identify points requiring further research on discretion. The following set of issues is placed within a natural history framework. Let us start with the event.

It should be clear that the matters about which decisions are taken are socially defined and organizationally defined. The previous material focuses attention on the internal processes of deciding. Legal decisions are made about events, and events, or the social world of activities, are represented by the organization to itself. The organization reflects on its own actions. This 'reflection' takes the following form: events are converted into messages, seen as sets of signs (something that refers to something else that is interpreted in some fashion), and transformed and kept in files, cases, texts, or other forms of record. This process of 'conversion' translates events from the everyday world to organizational and legal worlds. This transformation is done by organizations using framing processes, and yet another transformation takes place when organizational decisions are reviewed externally as legal decisions. How then does the apparatus by which an organization 'sees' the environment and its events arise?

The first and fundamental questions in this regard are those about the industrial or socio-technical system itself and its links to the political and economic order (e.g. the legally required safety systems in place at Bhopal when compared to the similar plant in Institute, West Virginia). A parallel question is how multinationals exploit the differential capacity of developing countries to tax, regulate, and sanction them for delicts. In the Sellafield case, the HSE had to liaise with BNFL, the Department of the Environment, the local county council, the media, and members of Parliament. These activities, carried on by the executive administrators at the top of the hierarchy, increased the symbolic importance of the executives. These considerations reduce the salience of one of the ironies of compliance, the fact that the government complies with the industry's rules and preferences (Manning 1987), and elevates the symbolic role of governmental leaders in a crisis (Edelman 1964).

Organizations are creative actors in a political environment. Once in place, organizations create bounded concerns within their mandates. Events called accidents are initially in the surround and are responded to by routines. A routine is embedded in the history and development of an organization, and is thus a feature of a larger organizational narrative. Routines shape responses to crises and subsequent decision-making. Recall, as a simple rule of thumb, that extant organizational routines underlie the sorts of emergencies an organization will encounter and process. Therefore, *ipso facto*, routines will pattern the nature and quality of the organizational response to the emergency or crisis encountered. The organization's structure, history, and mandate are constraints as well.

The nature and definition of accidents, especially socio-technical accidents like the Sellafield leaks, is a good case in point (see Manning

1988*a*; 1988*c*). Accidents of this kind are problematic. Generally, they are private matters contained within the private sphere of negotiations between the production organization and regulatory agencies. Such events rarely become widely known to the public (Katz 1977). However, it is difficult to contain information in a media-driven society, and accidents are 'news'.

Accidents unfold in time and possess a history. The history of accidents suggests that, if they can be dealt with routinely as 'reportable' events, bureaucratic procedures bury them in bureaucratic bowels. If and when they emerge, they might be called, for want of a better term, 'inter-organizational objects', because they are negotiated between organizations and their publics. An accident involving radioactive materials or any major ecological disaster is typically first denied by the industry, subsequently admitted, and then justified as having done little damage (Austin 1970: 173 ff.). After the event, redefinition unfolds, usually in the context of media and public discussion, often leading to the claim that the accident was not routine or 'normal', it was a rare event or aberration caused by or exacerbated by 'operator error'. The definition of 'accident' itself is shaped by the routine operations and structure of the industry and the regulators, the shared understandings between them forming a 'regulatory culture' (Meidinger 1987). An accident is an event that has come to public attention, a function of inter-organizational and negotiated definitions, and is confirmed by the authoritative capacity to label an event an accident. Understanding inter-organizational negotiations is of primary importance in the process of attributing blame and responsibility for industrial accidents (Clarke 1989).

Bearing in mind that the concept is really a family of related ideas, a core meaning of accident would appear to be: an untoward and heretofore private event that has become a matter of public knowledge and is labelled as an accident by those in authority (see Manning 1988*c*). Often, organizational decision-makers may not consider a crisis is unfolding, or that an 'accident' has occurred, until it becomes public.

An event is the necessary but not sufficient stimulus to modification of a pattern of decision-making. Decisions are accounts ascribed by and to legal actors, and are 'echoes', metaphorically speaking, of actual events, cases, or crises. It has been suggested that active and resolved crises differentially affect decisions, perhaps because *it is only after the fact that one can make systematic sense of the decisions made.*

Events do make a difference. The primary difference between natural and social events is fairly clear morally, since one ascribes blame to those involved in socio-technical and social events, even given a degree of uncertainty (Manning 1988*a*; 1988*c*). Natural disasters, the response apart, are seen as lacking the essential features of blameworthiness: responsibility, malfeasance, an untoward event, and public attention and knowledge. It is the issue of blameworthiness, especially as it is found in the law, that animates public accounts of decisions in crises.

In the case of the NII's response to Sellafield, several features of the structure, operation, and history of NII acted to pattern the choices of HSE executives. These were: the decentralized decision-making of the inspectorate, its eschewal of general policies and enforceable principles constraining operations and inspections, the self-regulation or compliance model used to enforce safety, and the inspectorial model of monitoring events. All were necessary conditions for producing the kind of crises and responses noted above (Manning 1987). The history of the NII is also revealing. The NII was established as an inspectorate and uses inspection as a routine source of information. The structure of licensing and inspection, along with the belief in the absolute safety of nuclear reactors, selectively obviates certain basic questions about risk and safety and the nature of any impending or emergent crisis. The co-operative model of self-regulation used in the United Kingdom and in the United States (with the exception of OSHA under President Carter, 1976–80) for governmental monitoring of its own operations assumes that the status quo entails the maintenance of essentially safe operations. Like the compliance model, the co-operative model is predicated on mutual trust and the integrity of the licensees' reporting practices to provide the information enabling the inspectorate to identify actual or potential changes in the status quo. A contrast to this licensing and inspection routine is the random inspection model of sanction-based enforcement and reporting adopted by the US Occupational Safety and Health Administration in the late 1970s (Bardach and Kagan 1982; Calavita 1983), or, indeed, the use of the civil and/or criminal law to regulate nuclear power production and fuel-reprocessing.

Events and organizational structure or agency are also inextricably linked. It is implicit that an emergency in the everyday/anyday world—the event—stands analytically separate from the organizational response to that event. The event takes its meaning from the enactment process (Weick 1979) by which the organization responds to the interpreted environment. The basis of organizational response to an event will be current routines as they merge with and are elided by emergent routines. An organizational crisis is several-sided: it begins with the response of the organization to the event as processed; a failure in organizational routines; and the organizational response to its own response to the emergent or apparent failure of its routines.[11]

What happens, one might ask, to decision-making given these outward changes that are represented internally? It would appear that centralization of decision-making may take place 'naturally', even in relatively decentralized organizations (as are inspectorates and police organizations), and that generalizations based on routine decision-making patterns of a centralized or decentralized type may not hold in crisis. This suggests further that two competing and overlapping patterns, a routine and an extra-routine mode of decision-making, occur simultaneously. These two modes may compete for the attention, resources, and time of the responsible decision-making agents.

Social time, or sense of time, is affected by emergencies. The time perspective for the deciders shifts toward emergency actions, and actions (of the most diverse sort) are valued above a 'wait-and-see or business-as-usual' attitude (see Janis and Mann 1977; Janis 1985; May and Neustadt 1986). Karl Weick (1989), on the basis of an analysis of the collision of two airliners at Tenerife airport, has argued that, when interruptions of important routines amongst interdependent systems take place, interdependencies are increased, heightened arousal occurs, and cognitive efficiency and communicative accuracy are reduced. The cognitive, information-processing, functions of actors are shaped and the focus alters the process of chunking and coding of information. In general, there is an increase in *stereotypic thinking* (thinking using categories and types, rather than particular facts). There is also an increase in *chunking* (organizing data into blocks of similar kinds of information or employing metaphor or metonomy, such as 'drawing a line in the sand', or 'Saddam Hussein must get out of Kuwait'), *reducing variety* (using fewer metaphors or paradigms to order data), and *coding* (classification into a few denotative categories

---

[11] The role of decisions in unfolding legal discourse and in the open-ended arguments of the law, and the centrality of legal decisions for producing the necessary fictions that close legal anomalies and facilitate adaptation to external changes, are addressed in Fuller (1964) and Scheppele (1988a).

or domain) of incoming information. One might assume that, in crisis, information should be processed in a more refined fashion, but it is more likely that decisions are not taken more reflectively.

The nature of the decisions that result from a regulatory response are negotiated and shaped by the regulatory culture in which regulators and regulated (as well as the audiences to which they play routinely) participate (Meidinger 1987). Decisions are symbolized within the shared discourse, sign systems, and moral worlds of both. The potential for organizational paradox arises repeatedly, since the basic assumptions of the shared culture are that the regulated processes or technologies are 'safe' unless and until credible evidence is produced that they are not.

Conclusion

Since unreviewed decisions are rarely known to the public, and instead are concealed behind organizational records, it is difficult to know precisely how 'big bangs' affect legal decisions.[12] The naturalistic mandate suggests that there is an urgent need to gather materials on organizational decisions and to examine how they are shaped by recoding.

The naturalistic perspective advanced here draws on socio-linguistic and semiotic analyses and seeks to understand decisions and the process of decision-making retrospectively, rather than to predict decision outcomes. The aim here is to increase understanding of the relative importance of what might be called 'organizational discourse', or the way the organization communicates to itself about its decisions. In this view, 'raw events' or mere data from the senses shape, and are interpreted in line with, the justifications that are called 'decisions'. This directs attention to the importance of describing changes in decision-coding rather than deciding, and the importance of the character or texture of the process of deciding, rather than outcomes of decisions. Legal decisions reviewing organizational decisions are important phenomena which feed back into organizations and affect their future or anticipated response to events.

Organizations are embedded in many networks of relationships which change as a result of emerging intraorganizational exchanges. Inter-organizational relationships are made more salient. Decision-

---

[12] I thank Betsy Cullum-Swan for pointing this out.

making becomes, in short, more constrained in complex ways by other organizations' decisions (Vaughan 1983, 1990; Clarke 1989). It would appear that decision-making becomes more focused at the top of the hierarchy and that centralization of decisions increases. As a result, the symbolic importance of leadership increases (Pfeffer 1981a).

In part because of the added workload and the sense of rationing of resources that organizations entertain, the time frame of leading decision-makers shifts from attention to business as usual to a foreshortened frame in which 'time is of the essence'. The decisions made and legitimated publicly have mutually contradictory potential because communication does not always move from the margins to the center, and the location of the decision affects the pattern of decisions. Internally, organizations are composed of many overlapping fields, segments, and subcultures. Decision-making takes place in several settings within the organization, and is loosely coupled to procedures, outcomes, and objectives (Weick 1979).

Information is one of the several factors in decision-making, and the level and kind of information input at the boundaries of organizations increases dramatically in times of crisis. Movement upward and downward of messages is facilitated and associated with more socially defined noise (that is, unwanted data at the time of decision). Thus, as more information is circulated, it becomes less possible to comprehend it and more necessary to simplify information-processing.

Having said this, it should be emphasized that the basic assumptions about the composition of the enacted environment (Weick 1979)—i.e. the assumed-to-be-stable surround—are unlikely to be questioned. The organization's work is to continue to encode the environment in a manageable fashion. The set of frames used to define the range of responses does not change, while the number of work tasks and the workload may change. Furthermore, daily routines remain to carry out the day-to-day workload, while specially developed action (crisis) sequences overlie the in-place routines. Both must be carried out.

Resources are seen as both inadequate to the task *and* extraordinarily available. The reallocation of resources takes place without regard to long-term plans and budgets. As Jackall (1988) suggests, maintaining the infrastructure of organizations is not in the best interests of ambitious managers in any case. Jackall shows in his study of the management of a large chemical company that managers preferred 'production' and output (meeting quotas) more than maintaining and painting plants, or adding additional machinery, because these represented costs assigned to them. They aimed to keep production up, hide the problems, and pass them on to the next manager. A crisis defined as outside the control of the manager can provide an occasion for reallocation. The sense of crisis legitimates reallocative decisions.

Discretion is exercised in both emergency and routine conditions. Freedom to act without review by courts or internal review is permitted to higher administrators, while lower level functionaries are likely to be scapegoated as a result of their discretionary acts. The point of this is that one cannot tell an 'emergency decision' from another on the basis of the justifications offered alone. Decision-making during a crisis is not a change in form or even in content: it is a matter of recoding routine practices. Some decisions made in a crisis are, of course, routine and the discretion involved does not differ from other decisions. The need for expediency and rapid action will always be claimed, and only occasionally denied as prudent in *ex post facto* review boards or courts. It is only by close examination of the organizational context at the time of the crisis that one can identify and distinguish crisis decisions from routine decisions. The disruption of routines keys the recoding activity.

The increase in information adds to the tendency to chunk and code data while reducing the capacity to focus attention sharply; hence the need for ramifying figurative language, metaphor, and irony. This sense of crisis also predisposes decision-makers to the use of facile, immediate, and simple analogies. The background environment is seen as frozen, while the foreground is very salient indeed. Extraordinary resources, once freed from normal constraints, assist administrators. They have new freedom as a result. Daily and normal routines are made secondary to the ongoing crisis decision-making and in fact will command less attention. Routine evaluation and measures of performance will fall off drastically. The rhetoric of emergency grants greater power to senior managers to define the parameters of discourse. Thus, as the surround becomes volatile, the decision field increases in the number of relevant features taken into account, and is more permeable. The organizational context, as has been argued, remains relatively stable and the organization switches its coding practices.

Finally, discretion in internal 'emergency', a crisis that arises *within the organization*, disrupts routines and response to disrupted routines, produces recoding of actions, and differs from the externally generated 'big bangs' described here. Comparison with the Sellafield crisis of organizational responses to the beating of a motorist by officers of the Los Angeles Police Department in March 1991 and resultant calls for the resignation of the Chief of Police, and the scandal in Detroit concerning the mismanagement of $2.8 million in funds from the secret police fund, would suggest dimensions along which to compare changes in discretion. The hypothesis would be that internal crises are less likely to produce affirmed discretion than responses to external ones. The dynamics discussed in this conclusion are mooted and modified to expand the discretion of those at the top and elevate their importance (and vulnerability to scapegoating), and increase and accelerate the 'return-to-normal' stage.

PART III

Thinking About the Uses of Discretion

IN what directions can thinking about the nature and implications of legal discretion be advanced? This question is pursued in Part III in three distinctive but related ways. In the first chapter Roy Sainsbury pursues procedural aspects of discretion and develops ideas of administrative justice. The second chapter, by Joel Handler, analyses some of the broad social policy implications arising from the exercise of discretionary power. Finally, Nicola Lacey suggests ways in which lawyers and others need to recast their view of legal discretion. A powerful critical theme joins these latter two chapters in the form of a questioning of liberal legal theory which accords primacy to the ideal of the rule of law.

Guiding and controlling discretion by the use of rules and other devices of a procedural kind is a preoccupation of lawyers. Sainsbury analyses empirically the exercise of discretion in one of those parts of the legal system in which benefits are dispensed to needy or deserving people (in this case the officials of the Department of Social Security (DSS) dealing with the administration of industrial disablement benefit). This focus contrasts with most social science studies of discretion, which have emphasized questions of social control by examining the work of criminal justice or regulatory agencies. Sainsbury argues that the conception of discretion in British social security research has been excessively narrow, being confined to those areas not covered in legislative rules, and those designed to address the exceptional needs or circumstances of claimants. His concern is to show that discretion exists in many areas of the social security system, and he seeks also to propose the concept of administrative justice as a means of analysing all such decision-making activity. Sainsbury, like other contributors, adopts a holistic view of the legal process. This he relates to the idea of choice, which he sees as pervasive, with each supporting decision made in the course of producing a result potentially of crucial significance for the ultimate outcome.

The chapter introduces the issue of normative theory about the use of discretion, drawing on the work of Jerry Mashaw (1983). Adopting Mashaw's definition of administrative justice ('those qualities of a decision process that provide arguments for the acceptability of its decisions' (1983: 24–5)), Sainsbury seeks to identify what those qualities might be in social security administration. He argues for two major characteristics: accuracy (which speaks to outcome) and fairness (which speaks to procedure and consists of promptness, impartiality, participation, and accountability).

Sainsbury shows that it is important to distinguish between the procedures involved in reaching a discretionary decision and the substance of discretion. To do one well does not necessarily mean that the other will be done well. Procedures are important since they are the means of attaining and realizing outcomes, though Sainsbury observes that enhanced procedural rights may merely symbolically confer the appearance of greater fairness and justice to the substantive outcomes. The effect is to question those who may assume that good procedure will tend to lead to good outcomes, and that poor decision-making procedure will lead to poor outcomes.

The interaction of procedural and substantive aspects of discretion is important to understand since they may work against each other. Though procedural controls on discretion may in principle be attractive to lawyers as an ostensible means of improving the quality of substantive discretion, they may lead to unintended or counter-productive effects on it, arising from the application of particular procedures. The requirement to give reasons for decisions may, for example, lead to an increased likelihood that substantively less desirable decisions may be reached, for fear of prompting an appeal or review which might well be regarded as organizationally undesirable. Openness of decision-making routines may similarly lead in some circumstances to the subverting of the decision-making system (for an example, see Hawkins 1971: 108).

Handler's chapter is advocacy of a powerful kind for a fair and benevolent system of discretion. He starts from the position that discretion is inevitable and all-pervasive in the modern welfare state and goes on to consider how discretionary systems may be employed in the furtherance of social justice. His concern is with bureaucracies created to serve and regulate the disadvantaged, with the dependent people who have to deal with them, and with the problems created by the unfair application of power in the use of discretion. The imbalance of power arises, Handler argues, because officials have choice: discretion 'contemplates a conversation within a normative framework'. Dependent people, however, lack information and the various social skills needed to make an effective case for their interests, putting them at a disadvantage. To increase client participation at field level Handler proposes a new conception of implementation centred upon the creative use of discretion, one requiring fundamental changes in the structure and ideology of public programmes. It needs the creation of space for choice through decentralization, an emphasis on informality rather than on rules, and professional autonomy. Adequate resources are also needed to foreclose the tendency for discretionary decisions to become routine and mechanical.

Since discretion has a capacity to manipulate or to coerce, Handler wants to change the conditions under which it operates. He takes the view that ideas about the rule of law, in which efforts are made to circumscribe and control discretion through the application of legal rules, are of limited use, given that disadvantaged people have restricted access to legal remedies. He wants instead to seize the opportunities granted by discretion to ensure that it is employed in a positive way and to empower people who are the subjects of discretionary decisions. In his 'human service agency' there is a high level of discretion which operates with serious inequalities of power between the parties involved. Drawing from a rich array of writing and empirical research, Handler proposes structural mechanisms intended to equalize power and maximize the participation of dependent people confronting bureaucracy in an effort to transform dependent people from being objects of discretion to participating subjects. Handler argues that this can come about by establishing relationships based on reciprocal trust, in which the balance of power has been altered. In the agency (one concerned with the education of handicapped children) power relationships were altered as a result of the active involvement of parents; sanctions were not employed, but 'instead there was conversation and persuasion', leading to 'active, understanding participation' and a change in self-conception.

People, as a result, became partners in the exercise of discretion. What this means is that the dependent person has to have discretion, the ability to consider alternatives. In effect, authority to make decisions is shared more equally because the self-conceptions and the personal ideologies of the empowered people have changed. Handler argues that such changes need to be actively cultivated and pursued if they are to continue to work effectively. This is because relationships may be transient and partial and, as other chapters in this book show, there are familiar tendencies where discretionary behaviour is concerned which will reassert themselves: bureaucratic routine, on the one hand, and quiescence, on the other.

Handler contrasts adjudicative discretion with the flexibility and informality of the discretion used in alternative dispute resolution or negotiation, suggesting that there are implications of more choice as to procedure and substance in the latter. Since discretion is inevitable, he argues that it should be used positively and effectively, and in ways which prevent the exploitation of power advantages, with both parties being able to participate in decisions being made. Many commentators have opposed discretion, noting that, where legal outcomes are reached by bargaining, rather than by adjudication, power relationships are rarely equal. Discretionary determinations arrived at by negotiation, it is said, may permit legal standards to be bargained away; the compromise involved in bargaining means that concessions have to be made in the interests of securing an agreement; while the lack of procedural protections may put the less powerful at a disadvantage.

Conceptions of power are connected by Handler with the notion of quiescence, a characteristic of the dependent people with whom he is concerned. In a setting like social work practice, considerable power is vested in social workers by virtue of their various social competencies and resources, and the services controlled by their agencies. If clients want these resources, they must 'yield at least some control over their fate'. The relationship between client and agency has to be seen as one of exchange in which social workers and clients exercise variable amounts of power. For the most part, however, agencies and their workers, Handler argues, possess greater power than their clients because, while agencies do not depend on their clients for resources, most are monopoly suppliers of resources to clients, and thus at an advantage.

To power and quiescence Handler adds trust. Trust is important because it has the potential to alter power relationships and because people have an incentive to co-operate in their relationships, therefore to trust one another. In settings like Handler's social work practice, where decisions are arrived at by negotiation, trust is the key to the nature of the relationship between the worker and the client. Trust is bound up with goodwill and with discretion: we trust people to use their discretion wisely, competently, and fairly. Consequently the subject about whom discretion may be exercised becomes vulnerable; people are prepared to be vulnerable owing to the symbiotic nature of social relationships and the mutual interdependence they imply. Trust therefore has a moral component.

Handler is critical of the tenets of political liberalism and the ideal of the rule of law. This view is shared by Nicola Lacey, and with her chapter we return to issues which introduced the book. Where Handler presents an analysis of how discretionary authority can be harnessed to advance social policy by serving the needs of powerless social groups, Lacey is concerned with the question of the extent to which discretion is relevant to the concerns of lawyers, legal theorists, and social scientists, and what each group may learn from the others.

The rule of law ideal is central to political liberalism. The legal paradigm ('the typically legal and jurisprudential way or ways of looking at the world, constructing disputes, identifying "problems" and framing solutions') embodies a conception of rules which are clear, public, and general, and operate prospectively, consistently, and rationally. It emphasizes the procedures by which decisions are made by legal actors, the protection of individual rights, and the values of predictability, openness, and consistency in the application of rules by impartial third parties. Problems which arise are typically those of lack of clarity or lack of coverage, creating ambiguity or gaps in the rules. Conflicts are to be resolved according to the tenets of procedural due process. But if it is the case that legal methods are not the most suitable form of regulation in certain areas of social life, the relevance of legal analysis conducted within a framework of liberalism will be significantly limited.

In Lacey's view political liberalism informs (often tacitly) the thinking of many commentators on discretion and her critique of the ideology can be read as a plea for lawyers to display greater humility and intellectual openness in addressing the problem of discretion and its control. In short, she questions the relevance of the legal paradigm. The burden of her argument is that much of jurisprudence is unable to stand outside the legal paradigm, since it is shaped by wholly legal ways of framing and thinking about issues, which in turn mould legal theorists' prevalent conceptions of discretion. The often unstated assumptions of those who work within this legal paradigm lead, she says, to emphasis upon characteristically legal views of problems and their solutions. Thus there tends to be a preoccupation with discretion in adjudicative rather than negotiated settings, a tendency to regard legal rather than administrative solutions as more appropriate, and a belief in the importance of courts and adjudicative procedures associated with the model of the adversary trial when thinking about the problem of discretion. Remedies typically tend to be framed in terms of rules and standards, and emphasis is given to the importance of legal review. One implication of this line of argument is that too ready an emphasis upon procedural justice can damage the interests of substantive justice: injustice can occur despite procedural controls. Lacey shows by reference to developments in English administrative law that, while judges have changed their views of the natural justice of discretionary behaviour, leading to a greater flexibility in the concept, fundamental views about the character of natural justice remain firmly legal. Liberal legal theorists also tend to treat the exercise of discretionary power as a public rather than a private matter. Lacey is critical of the validity of this dichotomy, and suggests that it again constrains the thinking of its adherents who, for instance, raise questions about the essential legitimacy of discretion and about the accountability of those who exercise it. This stems from the usual view that public power is regarded as a threat to private interests.

Lacey prefers a view of discretion as a political matter whose legitimacy is crucial, a matter best understood through the contributions of a number of disciplinary perspectives. She critically explores the appropriateness of lawyers' and legal theorists' approaches to analysing discretion, arguing that jurisprudence currently reproduces the inherent limitations of legal scholarship when confronted with such a complex phenomenon as discretion. By recognizing discretion, she argues, lawyers are compelled also to reflect on the relevance of legal method and whether law's typical methods of control are always effective. For instance, she takes Davis (1969) to task for his proposal that legal methods of controlling discretion exist and can be employed for the purpose. Instead Lacey believes that once lawyers extend their horizons they must be concerned to learn about the limitations of traditional legal method, some of whose frailties have already been exposed by social scientists.

For legal theorists like Dworkin, discretion tends to be treated as a matter to be defined in the tradition of analytical jurisprudence. Lacey is again critical of this approach for its tendency to reinterpret the nature of the world by essentially imposing legal or quasi-legal categories of thought. Juris-prudential analysis of discretion is also bound up with normative concerns, however, ranging from debates about the political legitimacy of discretionary power, to questioning about the accountability of administrative decision-makers. The broad set of assumptions informing these arguments also rests, Lacey points out, upon a foundation of political liberalism in which the exercise of discretion poses particular problems owing to its potentially malignant effects upon individual rights. Similarly, remedies are aimed at protecting individuals from state or bureaucratic abuse by extending the legal methods of procedural due process, or confining or structuring discretion in various ways.

The methodology associated with the legal paradigm also invites criticism. Lacey takes issue with the approach of legal theorists who adopt broad generalizations and categories, often relying on simple dichotomies, which are then employed as the basis for normative argument. This style of enquiry is often associated with limited empirical observation which provides the basis for assertions about the nature and functions of discretion. The result is often to do violence to the subtleties and nuances of the real world in which discretionary decisions are made. The analytical language of contrast charac-teristic of legal method creates an over-simplified view and at the same time marginalizes alternative views of reality.

Lacey concludes that any dichotomy between legal and social science approaches to discretion should be rejected. She wants jurisprudential and legal approaches to discretion to be modified to accommodate the contributions of the social sciences. She makes a plea for a pluralistic approach to the issues raised by discretionary power in legal contexts, an approach in which conventional disciplinary barriers, with their preformed styles of thinking, are broken down. In particular she argues that, for those concerned with normative political issues, the insights of the social sciences should be taken by jurisprudence scholars as a starting-point for the study of discretionary power because they embody, for those who would change things, greater appreciation of the complexities of legal discretion. Lacey thus prefers to see discretion in the context of the continuity of legal, political, and social power, and not simply as a legal matter.

As other chapters in this book have shown, emphasis upon the courts and adjudication amounts only to a partial view of the legal process. Lacey's view is that jurisprudential and social science approaches to understanding the uses of legal discretion should be seen as essentially interdependent. That idea was the basic premiss on which this book was prepared.

9. Administrative Justice: Discretion and Procedure in Social Security Decision-Making

ROY SAINSBURY

STUDIES of the delivery of social security in Britain and the United States have been dominated over the past twenty-five years by two related concerns: the operation of discretion and the structure of the appeals system. However, despite its prominence, the way in which discretion has been treated in social security research has been limited. In essence the elements of British social security that have been described as discretionary are those (1) not covered in legislative rules (either primary or secondary legislation), and (2) those designed to address the exceptional needs or circumstances of claimants. In 1990 this means essentially that discretion is only discussed in the context of the Social Fund,[1] introduced in 1988 as a system of loans and grants to cover claimants' exceptional needs. This is a very narrow conception of discretion, since most a priori definitions make no reference either to statutory regulations or to exceptional needs. It also implies a clear distinction between rules and discretion. In contrast, definitions of discretion in the academic literature recognize its relationship to rules and its relevance for all types of decision-making and all the stages in a decision-making process (Davis 1969; Hawkins 1986).

Though discretion has a wide applicability, this narrow conception still has a powerful influence over British social security policy. By describing a particular part of social security as 'discretionary' policy-makers have sought to justify the adoption of certain administrative procedures which would not be acceptable for a non-discretionary scheme. For example, the lack of independent appeal rights against Social Fund decisions is justified partly on the grounds that they are inappropriate for a discretionary rather than a rules-based scheme. Discretion is also a very seductive topic. If some legislative provisions are described as discretionary, then they are virtually guaranteed to attract academic interest and political debate. Unfortunately this has been the indirect effect of shielding supposedly non-discretionary

[1] Social Security Act 1986, Part III.

elements of social security from the kind of scrutiny that discretion attracts. The contention seems to be that, if it is not discretionary, then it must be rule-bound, so there is little to argue about. I wish to disagree.

In this chapter I will present the case that discretion is a far broader concept than the one usually applied to the British social security system, and that, in contrast, it is endemic to social security decision-making. The argument follows that analyses of discretion and other variants of decision-making are essentially embarking on the same task and that therefore a single analytical framework can be applied to both. The framework which I adopt, that of 'administrative justice', is developed in the first section of the chapter. It is then put to the test in the second section, in an analysis of what is often thought of as a non-discretionary part of British social security, industrial disablement benefit. In doing this I will draw on empirical research that I have carried out on the administration of industrial disablement benefit by officials of the Department of Social Security (DSS).[2] The research was carried out in thirteen DSS local offices, three Regional Offices, and five medical boarding centres in three DSS regions in Great Britain and used the techniques of semi-structured interviews, casepaper analysis, and documentary analysis of DSS records, instructions, and guidance. In this chapter I will use extracts from interviews held with officials, and from claimants' casepapers. For the sake of anonymity, quotes and case studies will be referenced according to the relevant local office (e.g. Office A, Office B etc.) or the relevant DSS Region (e.g. Region X).

I will conclude that administrative justice is robust as a normative theory of the relationship between individual citizens and the administrative agencies of the state and is potentially a useful framework for analysing administrative decision-making.

Discretion and Administrative Justice

Within the literature of administrative law and social policy there are numerous analyses of the concept and practice of discretion.[3] It is an

---

[2] This formed part of a wider study which also embraced the administration of mobility allowance. See Sainsbury 1988.

[3] See, e.g., Hill 1969; Titmuss 1971; Jowell 1973; Lister 1974; Adler and Bradley 1976; Donnison 1977; Bull 1980; Adler and Asquith 1981*a*; Ham and Hill 1984; Goodin 1986; Galligan 1986*b*.

important, though seemingly elusive, concept and central to a consideration of administrative decision-making. I do not propose to analyse discretion in any great detail here, since this is more than adequately covered elsewhere in this volume. All I wish to demonstrate, in an admittedly abbreviated way, is that discretion is not limited to certain parts of the social security system but is present throughout. However, I do not want to avoid completely the interesting and tricky theoretical ground, since in discussing discretion we first need a definition. At a high level of generality, the definition formulated by K. C. Davis has been influential and has formed the starting-point for many examinations of discretion;[4] it is enduring in its clarity and comprehensiveness: 'A public official has discretion whenever the effective limits of his power leave him free to make a choice among possible courses of action or inaction' (1969: 4). Whilst this sentence forms the core of Davis's definition of discretion (and is usually cited in isolation) there is an equally cogent observation which follows: 'Discretion is not limited to substantive choices but extends to procedures, methods, forms, timing, degrees of emphasis, and many other subsidiary factors' (ibid.: 4). Davis's definition clearly emphasizes that a central characteristic of discretion is choice. But what has failed to satisfy later analysts is that a definition which is so broad encompasses virtually all decision-making, since it is rare that making a decision does not involve some element of choice. However, the generality of the definition should not be seen as a weakness but an initial strength, since it allows the possibility of exploring the complexities of different forms of discretion.

A second point to emphasize is the inevitable link between rules and discretion. After several decades of discretion literature one might think that this would be unnecessary, but, as I have noted above, the rules/discretion dichotomy is still mobilized by British policy-makers to justify certain substantive and procedural legislative provisions. The link between rules and discretion is neatly captured by Dworkin in his graphic metaphor of the 'hole in the doughnut': 'Discretion, like the hole in the doughnut, does not exist except as an area left open by a surrounding area of restriction' (1977b: 31). That discretion is a relative concept is an important observation which serves to refute any supposed dichotomy between rules and discretion. In Dworkin's view, in order to describe what discretion officials have

---

[4] Though influential, Davis's was by no means the first treatment of discretion; see Bradley 1974: 37–8.

it is necessary to refer to the rules which define their latitude for choice. Others have characterized the relationship as a continuum or scale, with total discretion at one end and absolute rules at the other (Davis, 1969). Decision-making can be located at some point on the continuum and can move between the two end points.[5]

Davis's definition of discretion and a refutation of the supposed dichotomy between rules and discretion are sufficient to conclude that discretion is endemic in social security decision-making. Harlow and Rawlings, in their analysis of the transition from discretion to rules in the 1980 Social Security Act, introduce the notion of 'embedded discretion' to describe the choices in the substantive decisions which are not usually thought of as discretionary.

Much officer discretion is still embedded in the rules. We find constant allusion to standards: 'necessary', 'essential', 'exceptional', or 'reasonable'. The familiar discretionary formula 'in the opinion of the benefit officer' also recurs throughout the rules. So benefit officers possess significant freedom of manœuvre. (1984: 617)

Harlow and Rawlings emphasize the important point that much 'embedded discretion' remained in what was ostensibly a scheme based on entitlements and rights, and part of whose rationale was the elimination of discretion.[6] They are able to pursue this argument because they equate discretionary behaviour with 'significant freedom of manœuvre'. However, where they draw the line between 'significant' and other, presumably smaller, degrees of freedom of manœuvre is not made clear, or even how such a distinction is to be made.

Remembering Davis's argument that discretion applies to procedures as well as to substantive choices, we can extend Harlow's and Rawlings's analysis to argue that the possibility exists that discretion is embedded in the procedural rules that officials are meant to follow (whether or not these rules carry legislative force or are contained in, for example, procedure manuals).

[5] The move from rules to discretion, or vice versa, is a familiar way of explaining changes in decision-making behaviour in the literature of discretion (see, e.g., Bradshaw 1981).

[6] Harlow and Rawlings cite as an example regulation 19 of the Single Payment Regulations 1980, which permitted a single payment 'in respect of expenses essential for internal redecoration to a claimant's home'. The guidance manual for social security officials elaborated further: the decoration must be necessary to prevent insanitary conditions or deterioration of the internal structure . . .' (So, the benefit officer has guidance to help him interpret 'essential' in terms of 'necessary'. Not much of a clarification.)

In British social security policy-making the debate about discretion reached its peak in the 1970s when the negative aspects of discretion formed the basis of a campaign for a more rights-based scheme.[7] By emphasizing its negative connotations, discretion was presented as a 'problem' about which something needed to be done. In some ways this is not a helpful background to contemporary studies of discretion. If, as I argue above and I hope to demonstrate in the pages that follow, discretion is endemic in the substance and the procedures of social security and that therefore all decision-making contains some 'freedom of manœuvre', then a more useful pursuit would be to seek measures that promote the highest quality of decision-making. As a means of identifying what these might be I wish to pose a broader question about what should be expected of administrative agencies in the performance of their functions. If this question can be answered then we have a framework for assessing that performance.

The administrative justice perspective

As mentioned in the introduction, the study in Britain of social security administration in the past twenty-five years has concentrated on the operation of discretion and the structure of the appeals system.[8] The two debates are closely linked at a practical level but have lacked a common conceptual and theoretical framework. An important contribution towards filling this gap is Mashaw's *Bureaucratic Justice* (1983), in which he examines the concept of administrative justice and questions its meaning for an administrative agency responsible for implementing a welfare programme. His task as he saw it was to reorient debate away from a preoccupation with appeals mechanisms (which he called 'external' administrative law) towards the administrative agencies themselves, and to ask questions about the operation of an 'internal' administrative law which guides their

---

[7] The negative aspects of discretion were cited extensively in the debates preceding the reform of Supplementary Benefit in 1980 (see, e.g., Donnison 1982; Walker 1983; Harlow and Rawlings 1984). The debate was not totally one-sided, however (see, e.g., Titmuss 1971). Partington (1980), quoted in Harlow and Rawlings (1984: 588) summarizes the anti-discretion arguments in the 1970s as follows: (1) discretion leads to inconsistent decision-making on the part of officials and appeal tribunals, (2) it leads to arbitrary decision-making, (3) it leads to undesirable social control by officials, (4) it diverts attention away from more fundamental issues such as the adequacy of benefits, (5) it encourages feelings of stigma in claimants, (6) it prevents claimants understanding how the scheme works, and (7) it leads to feelings of jealousy between claimants.

[8] This section presents a summary of the more detailed development of the concept of administrative justice to be found in Sainsbury (1988).

routine activities. If such an internal administrative law could be identified, then it could be utilized as a set of normative standards to promote the fair and equitable treatment of individuals in their dealings with state welfare agencies.[9]

Mashaw begins his enquiry by offering a definition of administrative justice which is succinct and persuasive; for Mashaw the 'justice' of an administrative system means: 'those qualities of a decision process that provide arguments for the acceptability of its decisions' (1983: 24–5). The apparent simplicity of this definition, however, conceals a depth of complexity which can be explored by considering a number of questions raised by the wording of the definition itself. The first of these concerns Mashaw's emphasiz on the *process* of decision-making rather than the substance. At this stage one objection must be met, i.e. that of the irrelevance of a concept which is concerned primarily with procedures and not substance, a criticism succinctly captured in Zucker's challenge 'what happens when the decision process is just but the outcome is not?' (1985). The warning implicit in the question is that satisfaction with sound and fair procedures should not be confused with approval of the outcomes of those procedures. A further criticism arises not from conflating outcome and substance with process but from keeping them separate. It has been argued that the substantive rights of individuals are not always enhanced by increasing their procedural safeguards (Handler 1966; Prosser 1977), i.e. what a welfare applicant receives at the culmination of the process will not necessarily be affected by the process itself. Furthermore, as Prosser (1977) has argued, enhanced procedural rights ensuring greater fairness and equity may also grant, by association, the symbolic appearance of fairness and equity to the substantive outcomes themselves, thus deflecting critical appraisal of those outcomes. The reason that criticisms arise from opposite viewpoints is that in practice procedure and substance are closely linked; as Galligan writes: 'the object of procedures is to realise a given object, and so in this sense procedures are instrumental to outcomes' (1986*b*: 138). So,

---

[9] Space does not permit a wider discussion of Mashaw's thesis here. As might be expected from a rejection of what Mashaw calls 'external law' in favour of the quest for the internal law of administration, his position is controversial. For example, critics have questioned the consensual view of justice presented in *Bureaucratic Justice* arguing that the radical left or the right holds antagonistic and irreconcilable views on justice. Mashaw has also been criticized for his emphasis on technocratic solutions to problems that are imbued with value choices, and for rejecting the contribution that external controls can make to the pursuit of justice. See, e.g., Boyer 1984 and Maranville 1984.

whilst it may be true that increasing procedural rights does not necessarily improve substantive outcomes, it is equally true that it may do so where this enables welfare recipients to obtain their full entitlements. Some welfare benefits and services may not be considered generous, but, if the intended recipients cannot exercise their rights to them, then they are doubly disadvantaged. If greater procedural rights can ensure that welfare recipients get all they are entitled to, then their welfare is enhanced even if their substantive entitlements are not.

The second question concerns the 'acceptability' of decisions. If acceptability is a yardstick of administrative justice, then the question of 'acceptable to whom?' is raised—the recipients of decisions? the decision-makers? the wider society? If the answer is 'the individual citizen', then the qualities required of the decision process (using Mashaw's definition of administrative justice) will be different from those had the answer been government ministers, administrative officials, or the general public.

For individuals, having their needs or entitlements fully met will be their main demand from an administrative agency distributing welfare, but for the relevant agency or the government this will represent only part of their concerns. The position adopted in this analysis is that the issues raised by the concept of administrative justice will be addressed from the perspective of the individual citizen; this follows the approach of, *inter alia*, Davis (1969) and Mashaw (1974 1983). However, this approach can be criticized for ignoring the processes of policy-making which provide the substantive rules which are intended to delimit the decision-making behaviour of front-line officials (see, e.g., Baldwin and Hawkins 1984). The answer to this line of criticism is to recall the process-versus-substance discussion above and argue that administrative justice, analysed from the perspective of the individual citizen, does not preclude or attempt to reduce the importance of decisions about the substantive content of welfare policies. Rather it focuses on an area of public administration which does not usually receive as much attention as policy analyses but which, for the individual, may be far more relevant in securing or improving his or her substantive welfare (at least in the short term).

Having tackled these questions we can address the question which is the crux of the definition of administrative justice: can we identify the 'qualities' that an administrative agency should embody in order for its decisions to be considered acceptable?

For individual citizens, probably the most important aspect of their dealings with an administrative agency is the substantive decisions that they receive. Hence I will argue that the primary demand of administrative justice is that decision-making produces *accurate* decisions. I consider accuracy to be the primary demand of administrative justice because, no matter what other desirable attributes a decision-making process might embody, its decisions are unlikely to be acceptable if they are wrong.[10] The second demand will be that individuals must be satisfied that they are treated with *fairness* at all stages of the process.[11] It is only in this way that a decision not in a person's favour might become 'acceptable' in their eyes. Accuracy refers to the substantive outcome of a decision-making process, whilst fairness refers to the process itself. As demands of administrative justice, they should be relevant to all tiers of decision-making within an administrative hierarchy. Though I contend that analytically they can be treated separately, the two demands of accuracy and fairness are closely linked since, although fair treatment is a demand in its own right, it can also be seen as a means of promoting and demonstrating accuracy. I will now discuss in more detail what is meant by accuracy and fairness.

Accuracy

Mashaw provides a useful definition of accuracy in relation to social security when he describes it as: 'the correspondence of the substantive outcome of an adjudication with the true facts of the claimant's situation and with an appropriate application of the relevant legal rules to those facts' (1974: 774).

This definition illustrates well how an 'accurate' decision relies on

---

[10] Of course, inaccurate decisions may be acceptable to a person if they benefit him or her in some way. But such a conclusion would be a response to the question '*was* the decision acceptable?' and not the normative question 'should the decision be accurate or inaccurate?'

[11] In distinguishing between accuracy and fairness as elements of administrative justice I am assuming that 'fairness' can be treated as independent of, but nevertheless contributing to, the concept of justice. As Dworkin expains: 'Most political philosophers . . . take the intermediate view that fairness and justice are to some degree independent of one another, so that sometimes fair institutions produce unjust decisions and unfair institutions just ones' (1986: 177). Why 'justice' is linked to decisions and 'fairness' to institutions and not vice versa is not clear—it could be argued that the two terms are interchangeable. Nevertheless, inasmuch as 'justice' is frequently used in connection with substantive outcomes and 'fairness' with procedures, I will also follow this convention, whilst emphasizing that one of the attractions of the concept of administrative justice is its potential of subsuming both substantive and procedural elements.

the separate tasks of collecting information and of applying the relevant decision-making criteria (which in Mashaw's example are legal rules). With the necessary changes of context it would apply equally well to other types of decision-making, such as those based on administrative rules or a body of professional knowledge rather than legal rules. For example, in the provision of medical treatment, an 'accurate' decision would mean the response most appropriate to a patient's condition in the light of his or her symptoms and the current state of medical knowledge.

Fairness

'Fairness' is something of a vague notion but, as I will argue below, can be considered to comprise four elements: *promptness*, in reaching a decision, *impartiality* in decision-making, *participation* of the individual in the decision-making process, and *accountability* for the decision to the individual. These elements of fairness encompass the familiar attributes of natural justice. They are common in judicial and other forms of legal decision-making but have rarely been applied to the first tier of a decision-making hierarchy.

Promptness. The question of the time taken to produce a decision is fraught with difficulties and probably incapable of satisfactory resolution. As a starting-point, the maxim quoted by Nonet has a simple and persuasive force: 'Justice delayed is justice denied' (1969: 211). A possible interpretation of this maxim is that a decision should be made as soon as possible and without delay, where 'delay' implies an interval of time where the case is receiving no positive attention either within the administrative agency or outside. Again, though, avoiding delay applies to both the collection of information and the application of the decision-making criteria, and it is frequently in the former activity that most delay, as defined above, actually occurs. Waiting for a reply to an enquiry sent to an employer, for example, cannot necessarily be considered a delay on the part of the decision-maker; having the case lying idly on a desk without making the necessary enquiries, or after the required information has been received, does, however, constitute an unproductive period and thus can be considered delay.

Impartiality. The essence of the demand that the decision-making process is conducted impartially is that all sentiments of bias or prejudice on the part of the decision-maker must have no bearing on the decision arrived at (Robson 1928: 214; Franks 1957: para. 24). And, since bias and prejudice are manifestations of an individual's personal values, we can say that it is the exclusion of these values that is required. The difficulty in this has been recognized by Robson: 'Continuous mental effort to suppress or exclude rigidly all subjective considerations of an emotional kind tends . . . to create methods of reasoning that are "artificial" in the sense that they demand an unnatural objectivity and the suppression of a large number of important instincts' (ibid.: 214). Bias and prejudice can intrude at all stages of the decision-making process; for example, in the collection of information, in the sifting of the evidence, in the application of the decision-making criteria, or in the personal treatment of the individual.

Participation.   Participation in the decision-making process is a demand of administrative justice, *per se*, but is also desirable as a means of promoting accuracy. If we consider Mashaw's definition of accuracy, we can see that eliciting the 'true facts' of a case is a prerequisite for accurate decision-making. So, the difficulties encountered in the decision-making process over the evidence, such as incomplete, unclear, or contradictory evidence, can be overcome in part through the active involvement of individual claimants in the information-collection stage, since they are likely to be the principal source of that information. Individuals will often be in a vulnerable position since they may not understand fully the requirements of the decision-maker or the significance of certain pieces of evidence, and hence may unintentionally give unhelpful or misleading answers to enquiries about their claims. Participation in the process therefore can enhance the quality of evidence and also serve to convince individuals that a decision is accurate in their particular circumstances (i.e. increase the 'acceptability of the decision process').

The individual need not take part personally or directly in decision-making but may do so through an intermediary, such as an advice agency worker. The important point is that procedures should provide opportunities, or even facilitate participation, and not discourage it or present obstructions.

Ganz admirably sums up the importance of participation in her conclusions to an analysis of planning mechanisms, but they are equally applicable to welfare decision-making systems:

It is necessary to involve people more directly in decision-making if their active co-operation rather than passive resistance is to be enlisted. There is more scope for this in the process leading up to a decision than at the level of decision-making itself. Open consultation enables the individual to have his point of view considered and weighed against other considerations. (1974: 112)

Accountability.   Like participation, accountability, as a demand of administrative justice, serves a dual purpose. First, it is desirable, *per se*, that individuals understand why certain decisions have been taken about them in order that they can be convinced of their acceptability. They should therefore receive comprehensive and comprehensible explanations of decisions that affect them and the reasons behind those decisions. Secondly, if decision-makers know that they must account for their decisions, then they will be encouraged to be diligent and assiduous in the task. Robson has admirably captured the importance of accountability:

The obligation to give reasons for the conclusion may have an important influence, not only in persuading those who are affected by the decision that it is a just and reasonable one, but also in developing the mental capacity and sense of fairness of the adjudicator.

There is a lack of conviction, an apparent arbitrariness, about a decision which is unsupported by an account of the reasoning process on which it was based . . . (1928: 208–10)

Nonet also argues strongly for the need for accountability where a decision is not self-evident but must rely on choices made by the decision-maker (i.e. where discretion must be exercised): 'Accountability to rules does not necessarily reduce discretion; rather it disciplines its exercise by imposing on the decider a duty to establish a reasoned relation between his judgment and recognized authoritative standards' (1969: 236).

Accountability should be satisfied not only for the final decision but also at the information-collection stage of the process; i.e. individuals should receive explanations why certain information is required (or is to be considered irrelevant) and what use will be made of it.

To summarize: if we return to the question of what qualities an administrative system ought to display, a clear proposition emerges, which can be summarized in the normative statement: the qualities that a decision process ought to exhibit, which provide arguments for the acceptability of its decisions, are the ability to provide accurate decisions and the ability to produce them in a manner which is fair, by being prompt, impartial, and allowing claimants to participate and receive accountable decisions. An administrative agency should hold the promise of administrative justice in its structures and procedures, and be able to demonstrate the achievement of administrative justice in its practices.

Discretion, Administrative Justice and Industrial Disablement Benefit

In the second section of this chapter I wish to apply the administrative justice framework to the administration of one British social security benefit, industrial disablement benefit. This benefit is intended to compensate workers who are injured or become ill through their work; it is non-contributory and non-means-tested.[12] By choosing industrial disablement benefit it is intended to show how, in what has often been considered to be a part of the social security system untouched by discretion, there are numerous holes in doughnuts, or opportunities for freedom of manœuvre in legislative provisions which satisfy all a priori definitions of discretion but have not been subject to the sort of scrutiny that the traditional areas of discretionary activity have been in the past.[13]

The discussion below is based on a study of the decision-making behaviour of DSS officials who administer industrial disablement benefit in local social security offices and medical boarding centres. Before we can begin, however, it is necessary to describe briefly the essential characteristics of decision-making arrangements within the British social security system.

The social security decision-making system

In the British social security system the majority of decisions on claims emerge from the formal 'adjudication system', which comprises three separate tiers known as the 'independent statutory authorities'.

---

[12] The origins of industrial disablement benefit lie in the Workmen's Compensation Act 1897 but the main elements of the current structure of industrial injury benefits were introduced in 1948 (see Brown 1984: ch. 4; Lewis 1987; Ogus and Barendt 1988 ch. 7).

[13] This exercise could be repeated for other social security benefits, whether means-tested or insurance-based, contributory or non-contributory, dependent on lay or medical eligibility criteria (or both).

At the first tier, decisions are made by one of two groups of officials.[14] First, officials appointed as adjudication officers by the Secretary of State will consider the majority of questions in social security legislation (which we may define as *lay* questions). Secondly, medical practitioners appointed as adjudicating medical practitioners will make certain decisions defined in the legislation as *medical* questions (Social Security Act 1975 and Social Security (Adjudication) Regulations, SI 1984/51, as amended). (On some medical questions it is actually the lay officials who make decisions, although this is invariably on the basis of a medical report of some kind.) Appeals against the decisions of adjudication officers or adjudicating medical practitioners will be heard by social security appeal tribunals on lay questions or medical appeal tribunals on medical questions acting as the second-tier independent statutory authority. At the third tier the two systems merge: the Social Security Commissioners decide certain cases within their jurisdiction (i.e. on a point of law only) on appeal from either of the tribunals.[15]

Since all adjudication officers are independent statutory authorities, the function of monitoring the standards of their work and of advising them in their interpretation of social security legislation is carried out by an independent body, the Office of the Chief Adjudication Officer.[16] The Chief Adjudication Officer has a statutory responsibility to report annually to the Secretary of State on standards of adjudication of adjudication officers (not adjudicating medical practitioners, however, for whom no comparable organization exists). This is fulfilled by the operation of a monitoring system in which the performances of forty-two DSS local offices (and the central offices where some benefits are processed) are scrutinized each year. In addition every DSS local office will receive a visit every two years from a DSS monitoring team working to the same terms of reference as the Chief Adjudication Officer teams. The Chief Adjudication Officer discharges his advice function in two ways: first, by the publication of the multi-volume Adjudication Officer's

---

[14] There are some (comparatively few though increasing) questions which the Secretary of State must address, although in practice this is carried out by adjudication officers acting in a separate capacity. The questions are few and there seems little rationale for them remaining under the Secretary of State's jurisdiction (see Ogus and Barendt 1988: 569; Partington 1989).

[15] For a full discussion of the evolution of the adjudication system, see Bradley 1985.

[16] For an evaluation of the work of the Chief Adjudication Officer, see Sainsbury 1989.

Guide, and, secondly, by responding to requests from local offices for assistance with individual cases.

An analysis of industrial disablement benefit decision-making

The final outcome of a claim for industrial disablement benefit, whether due to an industrial accident or prescribed disease, is the result of a series of lay and medical adjudication decisions. In practice the lay conditions must be satisfied first before the medical criteria are considered. This is an administrative arrangement designed to avoid the possibly unnecessary cost of requesting medical reports; the legislation does not prescribe the order in which lay and medical decisions are considered.

Section 50(1) of the 1975 Act lays down the basic test to be satisfied for industrial accidents: 'where an employed earner suffers personal injury caused after 4th July 1948 by accident arising out of and in the course of his employment, being employed earner's employment, there shall be payable to . . . him the industrial injuries benefits specified . . .' This section of the legislation requires adjudication officers to look for three conditions to be satisfied: i.e. that the claimant has (1) suffered personal injury, caused (2) by an accident, which (3) arose 'out of and in the course of his employment'. In other words, they will be looking for evidence that some sort of incident (or series of incidents) has taken place which caused an injury to the claimant (however minor), and that such an incident occurred during working hours in a normal place of work whilst doing something connected with the work. The freedom of manoeuvre for adjudication officers begins when they receive the initial claim form. The question that the claimant is asked on the form which is intended to enable adjudication officers to decide whether the three conditions have been satisfied is 'what were you doing at the time [of the accident] and how did the accident happen?' In practice, the quality of the initial evidence from the claimant can sometimes be poor and this will frequently necessitate further enquiries. And in all cases confirmation of an accident is always requested from the claimant's employer. Even at this early stage there is a large freedom of manoeuvre afforded the official which can have a crucial bearing on the outcome of the claim and yet is a long way from the point at which a decision on that outcome has to be made. The following two case studies illustrate the importance of this stage in the decision-making process.

An oil-rig worker claimed an industrial accident had taken place when he struck his shovel against a grating and strained his abdominal muscles. The claimant's application was received in April 1985, although the incident, which he stated had been reported to his employer, was alleged to have taken place over six months earlier in September 1984. The routine response to an accident claim is to ask the employer for confirmation of the claimant's version of events. However, in this case the enquiry form was returned by the employers stating that they had no knowledge of such an incident and that it had not been reported. This apparent conflict of evidence required a decision from the official as to how to proceed. Because employers often fail in their duty to record accidents or occasionally deny they have taken place in order to pre-empt the possibility of a claim for damages in the courts, the adjudication officer decided to give the claimant a further opportunity to substantiate his story. The claimant was informed of his employer's reply and asked to supply the names of any witnesses who could support his account. At this stage the claimant requested an interview at the local office at which he said that he had been told by his employer that a record had been made of the incident although he admitted that he had not seen it himself; he also gave the name of a witness (who was subsequently asked to supply his version of events). The recollection of the official who conducted the interview was that the claimant appeared to him untrustworthy in some way. When pressed to explain why he had this impression, the official could only refer to a 'gut feeling' based on the claimant's numerous complaints about his (by now ex-) employer. The official decided to make further enquiries to the employers noting the claimant's response. The reply came that, as far as they were concerned, the incident had not taken place; furthermore they noted that the day before the alleged incident they had a staff record that the claimant had complained of abdominal and chest pains. The putative witness replied that he had no recollection of the incident. At this point the official was again faced with a number of courses of action to choose between. He could have written to the claimant, asking him to respond further to the replies from the employers and the (failed) witness, or invited him in for a further interview; he could have asked for documentary evidence of the staff report from the employer; or he could have decided the case on the evidence before him. Since all the external evidence collected so far was against the claimant, the official took the latter course and disallowed the claim (Office H).

The number of choices facing the adjudication officer in the course of processing this claim illustrates the considerable embedded discretion in the procedures. When the officer made his final decision he also had a number of other options but his choice was guided primarily by his subjective assessment of the reliability of the claimant. Even though the officer could offer a justification for the decision, other outcomes were possible. When it was suggested that the claimant may have confused the date of the accident (six months having elapsed before the claim was made), and that, had he reported that it had taken place a day earlier, the staff report could have been considered as corroboration of his story, the officer admitted that this possibility had not occurred to him. Had the official reported the employer's second reply to the claimant, instead of choosing to conclude his enquiries, this possible confusion could have been resolved, and the final decision been the reverse. There appears to have been a reluctance to allow the claimant to participate beyond the routine requests for information on standard forms, and a lack of accountability in that the claimant was not apprised of all of his employer's nor his witness's replies. The accuracy of the decision is questionable, since the information collected may have fallen short of the 'true facts of the case'.

As in the case above, the second example also reflects the influence of the adjudication officer, but this time with the opposite outcome.

A lorry driver was sleeping overnight in his cab away from home. During the night he was attacked and sustained serious head injuries. The brain damage which he suffered prevented him from supplying any evidence directly. The appalling personal tragedy suffered by the lorry driver and his family evoked great sympathy within the social security office. The adjudication officer recounted that he decided at an early stage that the claim would succeed despite the problems with it. The first difficulty was the lack of any evidence at all (apart from the man's injuries), the only witnesses being the assailants themselves, who had been quickly apprehended after the incident. At their subsequent trial they claimed in their defence that they had been provoked and attacked initially by the claimant. If this had been the case, it would have been difficult to sustain the argument that the lorry driver was doing anything connected with his job (that is, acting 'out of and in the course of his employment'). The adjudication officer decided to reject their evidence as being of doubtful reliability. The second, similar difficulty was that it was not clear to the adjudication officer that sleeping in the cab of a lorry was likewise 'out of and in the course of employment', since the driver was officially off duty at the time and not being paid. Discussing the case with colleagues in the office it was decided that, if it was normal practice for drivers to sleep with their vehicles, for example, so that they could provide at least some protection for the lorry's load, then this would be strong evidence that were they acting in the interests of the employer and hence that they were acting 'out of and in the course of employment'. This suggestion was put to the employer (deliberately not in writing but in a telephone conversation), who cautiously admitted that the practice of sleeping in cabs was informally condoned though not officially acknowledged, since it was mutually advantageous to the driver and the firm: the firm got a night-watchman and the driver kept his overnight allowance. After receiving this confirmation, the adjudication officer promptly allowed the claim (Office E).

In this case the adjudication officer did not reach his decision by establishing the facts from the evidence and then applying the appropriate law. Instead he based his decision on what were extraneous decision-making criteria (his sympathy for the claimant), and then worked backwards trying to find reasons to justify his decision. Had he carried out the proper adjudicatory procedure, the decision may have been the same (although whether or not the incident took place 'out of and in the course of his employment' would have been difficult to assess). What is clear is that in this case there was sufficient embedded discretion within the substantive and procedural rules to allow the adjudication officer to make the decision that he wanted.

The alternative route to eligibility for the range of industrial injuries benefits is for a worker to establish that he is suffering from a prescribed disease or injury caused by a prescribed occupation (Social Security Act 1975, section 76(1)). The arrangements for deciding claims to disablement benefit as a result of a prescribed disease are slightly different, though there are again both lay and medical criteria to be satisfied. The lay questions are collectively called the 'prescription test' and are considered by an adjudication officer who must decide whether the claimant's employment matches the specification of the relevant prescribed occupation (Social Security (Industrial Injuries) (Prescribed Diseases) Regulations 1985). If the prescription test is satisfied, the adjudicating medical authorities (in practice a medical board in the first instance) will consider the 'diagnostic test' of whether the claimant is actually suffering from the prescribed disease or injury as he claims. This invariably requires a report from an expert in the field (usually a hospital consultant) which can be considered by the adjudication officer; alternatively, the decision can be referred to a medical board. If the diagnostic test is satisfied, then the board will consider the extent of disablement.[17]

There are fifty-four prescribed diseases and industrial injuries listed in the Social Security (Industrial Injuries) (Prescribed Diseases) Regulations 1985, each accompanied by a description of the relevant prescribed occupation (a few of which are associated with more than one disease). For adjudication officers, however, the bulk of their work in this area is dominated by a small number of prescribed diseases, namely dermatitis, tenosynovitis, and occupational deafness, which between them account for 90 per cent of awards.[18] Occupational deafness in particular was considered by almost all adjudication officers to present them with the greatest problems, most of which result from the 'holes in the doughnut' left by complex legislative rules.

The eligibility criteria for occupational deafness are arguably the most complex of all the prescribed diseases. The reasons for this lie in the intention behind the regulations. Damage to hearing caused by exposure to noise at work has long been recognized as a risk in some industries, but a deterioration in a person's hearing is also a normal consequence of ageing for most of the population (Industrial Injuries Advisory Council, 1973). The prescription test is designed to identify only industrially caused deafness. The regulations therefore specify a range of frequencies over which hearing loss must have occurred,[19] and a comprehensive list of machinery and the circumstances in which it must have been used. There is also the requirement that exposure must have lasted for at least ten years,[20] the last exposure being not more than five years before a claim is submitted. The

---

[17] Social Security Act 1975, section 108(1)(b). In cases involving pneumoconiosis, byssinosis, or asbestosis, the diagnostic test and disablement assessment are initiated immediately a claim is received because of the poor prognosis for claimants suffering from these usually fatal conditions.

[18] These figures are from the statistical year 1981/2 quoted by Wikeley (1988). They are from Health and Safety Statistics 1981/82, Health and Safety Executive, 1985, HMSO (the latest figures available at the time of writing).

[19] Normal degenerative changes within the ear reduce the ability to hear certain frequencies of sound. The damage caused by loud noise often encountered in industry affects a different range of frequencies, thus allowing audiometric tests to indicate the underlying cause of a person's hearing loss.

[20] Regulation 2, Social Security (Industrial Injuries) (Prescribed Diseases) Regulations 1985 (SI 1985/967). The original prescription test required that exposure to noisy equipment lasted for at least twenty years, but this was relaxed in 1983 (SI 1983/1094).

adjudication officer, therefore, needs information on the claimant's work, the machinery used, the physical characteristics of the workplace, the type of exposure endured, and, in order to satisfy the five- and ten-year tests, the claimant's employment record. This is formidable in itself, but one must also remember that some of this information will relate to periods many years beforehand (and, because of the ten-year test, some of it will necessarily be at least ten years old). The most common problem for adjudication officers is incomplete information. For example, in some skilled occupations it is quite common for workers to be employed on temporary contracts interspersed with short periods of unemployment, as the following case illustrates.

A joiner made his living by working in the shipyards of north-east England. The nature of shipbuilding is such that joiners and carpenters are only employed during specific phases (such as fitting-out) and not throughout the whole of the construction of the ship. Workers therefore tend to move from yard to yard as work becomes available. Joinery is not a particularly noisy activity but whilst working the claimant was exposed to the usual, high-level noise of the shipyard, which would bring him within the scope of the regulations. The claimant had worked for forty years since 1944 and listed 120 spells of employment in that time with a large number of employers (though not all in the yards). So, the task of collecting enough information to satisfy the ten-year test was hampered, first, by the need to aggregate a large number of short periods of employment, secondly, by the long period which had elapsed since some of them (which meant that employers did not have the records of his time with them), and, thirdly, by the closure of many of the firms that the claimant had worked for (as the shipbuilding industry has declined since the war). After four months of enquiry the adjudication officer had confirmation of only five years' relevant employment and was forced to reject the claim (Office I).

As in the case above, to satisfy part of the prescription test it is not necessary for the claimant to have worked with the relevant machinery or equipment himself but merely to have been 'wholly or mainly in the vicinity of' the prescribed machinery. Before the adjudication officer grapples with the legal complexities inherent in this phrase he must gather evidence concerning how far the claimant worked away from the machinery and whether there were any intervening obstructions which may have afforded him some protection. (This is a good example of the entirely specific nature of the problems which rules of general application must address.) For work carried out many years previously, this can prove extremely difficult and often impossible to obtain. Recourse frequently has to be made to colleagues of the claimant to supply their personal recollections of working conditions. Prescription is also partly based on the type of equipment or machinery that caused the relevant noise. Hence the adjudication officer needs to know what tools the claimant worked with (or near), which again can be extremely difficult to identify; the claimant may not know exactly what machinery he or she was using or how to describe it, or alternatively it may have become obsolete.

Even when evidence is supplied by the claimant, there is often doubt over its validity which affords the adjudication officer some freedom of manœuvre in deciding whether or not to make further enquiries of, for example, a claimant's employer or workmates, and in deciding how to treat any new information. Some fresh evidence was not also considered reliable. There might be a number of innocent reasons for what appeared inconsistent information (for example, ignorance, or confusion caused by official forms), but adjudication officers more often suspected ulterior motives (for example, collusion between work colleagues, or fear of civil action against the employer): 'Using witnesses is difficult because they may be in cahoots; we would prefer to go to managers or foremen because they are more trustworthy' (ex-Adjudication Officer, Office A). The preceding discussion has cited a number of examples of embedded discretion in the substantive and procedural rules that officials must apply when dealing with industrial disablement benefit claims. In addition, embedded discretion is also present in the consideration of the medical criteria which claimants must satisfy.

Medical questions. If it is established that a claimant has suffered an industrial accident or has satisfied the prescription test for a prescribed disease, then a claim for industrial disablement benefit can be made. The next set of criteria which must be satisfied, therefore, is medical in nature and defined as comprising 'disablement questions' (Social Security Act 1975, section 108(1)). In short, the claimant must show that he or she has sustained a 'loss of faculty' due to the accident or disease which has resulted in a 'disablement' being suffered.

The responsibility for deciding the disablement questions lies with the adjudicating medical authorities (Social Security Act 1975, section 108(2)), in practice either a single doctor acting in the capacity of an adjudicating medical practitioner, or two such doctors acting as a medical board (or, on appeal, a Medical Appeal Tribunal). They will assess the extent of the disablement, which is expressed in terms of a percentage figure. The 1975 Social Security Act 1975 requires that: 'the extent of the disablement should be assessed, by reference to the disabilities incurred by the claimant as a result of the relevant loss of faculty . . .' (Social Security Act 1975, schedule 8, para. 1). A close reading of this sentence reveals that there are at least three elements (or four in the case of accidents), forming a logical progression, to making a percentage assessment of disablement. There must be a relevant loss of faculty (and for accidents an identifiable injury to cause it) which must cause a disability or disabilities, which in turn results in a disablement. A DSS training hand-out explains the distinction between these terms as follows:

Loss of faculty—this is something which the Act envisages as resulting from the injury and from which, in turn, there results some disability. It may perhaps be best described as a loss of power or function of an organ of the body. Loss of faculty includes disfigurement. It is not in itself a disability but it is a cause, actual or potential, of one or more disabilities . . .

Relevant loss of faculty—this means the loss of faculty resulting from the relevant injury.

Disability—this means the inability, total or partial, to perform a normal bodily or mental process equally well as a person of the same age and sex whose physical condition is normal . . . The availability of artificial aids should be taken into account in considering whether and for how long the loss of faculty would result in disability.

Disablement—this is the overall effect of the relevant disabilities, i.e. the overall inability to perform the normal activities of life—the loss of health, strength and power to enjoy a normal life.[21]

As often seems to be the case in social security decision-making, the more attempts that are made to clarify legislative rules, the greater the freedom of manœuvre created. For example, 'loss of faculty', as expanded above, could be considered as embracing virtually any

---

[21] The following two examples are also taken from internal DSS training material used by the Regional Medical Officer and his staff:
  1. Injury—fracture of left femur; relevant loss of faculty—reduced movements of the left hip; disability—impaired locomotion; disablement—claimant can walk only ¼ mile or so.
  2. Injury—musculo-skeletal injury to lumbar spine; relevant loss of faculty—reduced and painful movement of lumbar spine; disability—impaired spinal function; disablement—unable to lift more than 20 lbs. without pain.

injury. As one DSS medical officer remarked: 'Whether there has been any "loss of faculty" means nothing in medical terms; it is a legal term, and doctors do not very often think legally' (Medical Officer, Region Y). The actual level of assessment is either dictated by or guided by statutory regulations.[22] For some fifty-five disablements there is a prescribed percentage assessment; for example, the loss of a thumb is rated at 30 per cent, loss of an index finger at 14 per cent, loss of two phalanges of the index finger at 11 per cent. For some the description is extremely precise; for example, amputation below the knee with stump of between 9 and 13 centimetres is assessed at 50 per cent disablement, whilst for other conditions the medical authorities must make their assessment by comparing the relevant disablement with the scheduled assessments and coming to a reasonable figure.

The disablement figure arrived at by an adjudicating medical practitioner dictates the amount of industrial disablement benefit awarded (if any). Prior to April 1988, a lump-sum gratuity was awarded for disablements assessed at between 1 and 19 per cent inclusive. For assessments of 20 per cent and above a weekly pension was paid. However, the Social Security Act 1986 amended the 1975 Act such that no award is made on assessments of 13 per cent and less, whilst for those of 14 per cent and above a pension is paid. The gratuity has been abolished. Apart from those assessments which are prescribed there is considerable freedom of manœuvre for the adjudicating medical practitioner in deciding the level of assessment. For the most part, making a percentage assessment is considered to be fairly straightforward. 'After thirty years you have a pretty good built-in computer telling you what assessments should be. Occasionally, though, you get the one where it does not seem to fit immediately into your previous pattern of assessments' (Adjudicating Medical Practitioner, Region Y). This quotation shows how medical practitioners, in practice, impose constraints upon their freedom of manœuvre in order to facilitate their decision-making. These constraints act as a further set of 'rules' within the framework of the legislation. Such rules are part of the practitioner's 'built-in computer' and therefore beyond external scrutiny and effectively secret. There is little doubt that the practitioner is obliged to resort to what are additional decision-making criteria but for the claimant the outcome is usually a

---

[22] Schedule 2 to the Social Security (General Benefit) Regulations 1982 (SI 1982/1408).

reduced understanding of the reasoning that lies behind an individual decision.

Some conditions occurred frequently and yet regularly caused difficulties. These included back injuries, and the types of head injury that resulted in psychological damage to the claimant.

The most difficult to assess are low back pain, but this applies equally to the out-patient clinic as the medical boarding centre, i.e. having to decide how much is true pathology and how much is overreaction by the claimant. Also head injuries, complaining of post-concussion syndrome, headaches, forgetfulness, that sort of thing; you cannot put your finger on anything. (Adjudicating Medical Practitioner, Region Y)

The most difficult to assess, even after years of experience, are head injuries, by which I mean the resulting psychological effects. In fact any injury affecting the nervous system can be hard. (Adjudicating Medical Practitioner, Region Z)

Where there are large areas of freedom of manœuvre in relation to the lay requirements of industrial disablement benefit, there are also mechanisms for guiding and checking how that freedom is used (i.e. the advice and monitoring arrangements). However, in contrast there is little to promote accurate or fair decision-making in relation to the arguably larger areas of discretion inherent in the medical criteria.

To summarize: the analysis of industrial disablement benefit decision-making has shown that, in a supposedly discretion-free area of social security, discretion is endemic. There is freedom of manœuvre in the legislative provisions and in the procedures which lay and medical staff operate. This is not to argue that embedded discretion should be eliminated. An alternative approach would be to ask whether the exercise of discretion satisfies the demands of administrative justice. The following section addresses this question.

An administrative justice analysis of industrial disablement benefit decision-making

Accuracy and the lay decision-makers.   The first task for the adjudication officer is to establish, in Mashaw's words, 'the true facts of the claimant's situation'. For a decision to be considered accurate, the true facts must be established and then the law must be applied correctly. In many industrial disablement benefit cases problems do not occur, but when they do there is a burden on adjudication officers to be as rigorous in their pursuit of the 'true facts' as possible, since their decisions will either commit what are often very large sums of public money, or alternatively deny claimants compensation for an injury or illness which may make a considerable difference to their standards of living, possibly for life.

Of course, it is often not possible to establish exactly what the facts of a case are. In some instances (as in the first case cited earlier) there is a conflict of evidence and in other instances (as in the second case) the information is incomplete. In such cases it is quite possible that one adjudication officer will decide a case one way, in accordance with his or her assessment of the evidence, whilst another adjudication officer will decide the case differently.

Despite the difficulties of defining accuracy, elements of the system promote it either directly or indirectly, for example, through training, the advice network, the monitoring arrangements, and the procedures of the tribunal system.

The function of the advice structure is to resolve difficult individual cases and, by ensuring accurate decisions, to promote consistent decision-making across cases by different decision-makers and over time by individual decision-makers. The Adjudication Officer's Guide is intended to do both, although a direct approach to the Office of the Chief Adjudication Officer can also be made if necessary. In practice the status accorded the Guide by adjudication officers varies. For some it is treated almost as a code of instructions to be obeyed: 'For me it is very powerful; I wouldn't ordinarily, or even ever, go against the advice in the Guide' (Adjudication Officer, Office L). Others appear to have a somewhat cavalier approach to the Guide and feel able to select when, and if, they take note of its contents: 'As one of our Senior Medical Officers once said "If you can't live with the answer don't ask the question." I suppose I must have conveniently "forgotten" the advice in the Guide on some occasions' (Adjudication Officer, Office D).

Overall the influence of the monitoring system operated by the Chief Adjudication Officer does not appear to be very great. This is principally due to the long periods between visits (two years) combined with the administrative practice of moving staff around the office for the purpose of career development. One adjudication officer summed up the problem thus:

Suppose you have a new adjudication officer on disablement benefit, by the time they see any of his work he may well have got into bad habits or misunderstood something important, so that for the first however many months he may be doing something daft. And with the number of decisions that are made in two years combined with the small percentage that the monitoring teams check I really don't see how they can expect to get any realistic idea of how good, bad or indifferent you are. (Adjudication Officer, Office E)

One way in which a monitoring system might be expected to promote accurate decision-making is by providing an incentive to individuals to maintain high standards, and a disincentive to poor decision-making. However, since only about one hundred cases are scrutinized during each two-yearly visit, adjudication officers know that there is little chance of any one decision being selected for scrutiny. Any potential incentive or disincentive effect of monitoring therefore virtually disappears. The limitations of the present monitoring arrangements were clearly recognized at Regional level also: 'I would have to say that overall I don't think we are making much of a contribution to improving standards' (Monitoring team member, Region Z). The monitoring system at present does not fulfil its intended role of helping to maintain and improve standards of adjudication. Furthermore, its function of providing an assessment of adjudication standards is satisfied only in the sense of providing 'snapshot' assessments; if a monitoring team had visited a local office six months earlier or later it could well have recorded a different picture, since standards inevitably tend to follow a cyclical pattern of improvement and decline as adjudication officers gain in expertise only to be replaced by inexperienced officers.

The contribution of the social security appeal structure to the achievement of accuracy is twofold. First, there is the direct effect of the tribunal altering a decision that it finds to be incorrect in some way. Secondly, there is an indirect effect on first-tier administration which pulls in two directions. It encourages adjudication officers to scrutinize their own decisions more closely (especially on borderline cases) and to seek further evidence, or refer for advice in order that the decision is more firmly grounded and not dependent on subjective judgments. However, it also encourages taking the easy option in hard cases by allowing a claim where perhaps it is not justified. This prevents appeals, since claimants awarded a benefit generally do not complain, and, even if the decision is not justified, there is only a slim possibility that the case will be scrutinized as part of a monitoring check. Such practices are not officially sanctioned but are attractive to busy adjudication officers. It is ironic that those who adopt the more rigorous approach (being the one which promotes accuracy) may cause themselves more work, have more of their decisions challenged (since they are likely to make more negative assessments), and therefore have more of their decisions overturned by tribunals, thereby attracting the criticism of their superiors for 'losing' cases.

Fairness and the lay decision-makers.   Of all the thirty plus social security benefits, industrial disablement benefit is probably the most vulnerable to delays caused by factors outside the control of the DSS. On every claim there will be at least one enquiry to an existing or previous employer, and, in the case of some prescribed diseases (for example, occupational deafness), the total can easily run into double figures. In addition, it will frequently be necessary to contact witnesses on industrial accident cases. Furthermore, once the accident decision has been made or the prescription test satisfied for a prescribed disease, then a medical report from an adjudicating medical practitioner or medical board will be required. It may also be necessary to seek additional information from hospital records or consultants. Much time in the decision-making process is therefore spent waiting for replies to enquiries, or for routine medical reports to appear; the whole procedure usually takes months.

No official measure of promptness (for example, 'clearance times') is made by the DSS and it is clear then that any meaningful form of 'performance indicator' based on the time taken to clear a case would be virtually impossible to construct. Nevertheless, there seems little reason to believe that cases are delayed deliberately; it would certainly not be in the interest of adjudication officers, nor the local office, to delay matters. Backlogs of work and the potential for complaints from claimants (and the time required investigating and replying to them) are sufficient disincentives to adjudication officers and managers to ensure that as much time as is considered necessary for a satisfactory conclusion to a case is actually expended. If dangers exist in the lack of formal measures of promptness, they lie in the tendency to cut short investigations in order to clear a case.

Disablement benefit decision-making relies heavily on the quality of the evidence upon which the adjudication officer has to base a decision. In the two distinct phases of, first, the collection of information and, secondly, deciding the facts from the evidence, there is scope for bias and prejudice to intrude. The official response to this possibility is that adjudication officers are independent statutory authorities (and hence insulated from Departmental influence) and are advised in the Adjudication Officer's Guide to refrain from personal contact with the claimant and make decisions only 'on the papers'. This advice was received differently by adjudication officers:

. . . if you haven't seen the claimant then you cannot be adversely affected by him, or vice versa. I think it is better for there to be a degree of separation so that you are only dealing with the facts of the case and not the personalities involved. (Adjudication Officer, Office D)

However, some adjudication officers thought the advice more a hindrance than a help:

. . . there may be something that comes out in a conversation that could be very relevant, but the claimants do not know the rules and regulations and so don't know what is relevant to us and what isn't. I've always thought that more contact with the public would give us more of an opportunity to explain what it is we want from them and what it is we are trying to achieve. (Adjudication Officer, Office M)

If the official advice is followed, then claimants are denied the opportunity to participate in decision-making. In addition, the opportunity is lost for officials to demonstrate accountability by explaining how and why decisions are made.

The first case cited earlier illustrated how personal contact with the claimant led the official to form an adverse opinion of the claimant, which affected his handling of the case. It is clear that the adjudication officers' desire for good quality evidence has to be balanced against the need to detach themselves from claimants and any personal impressions that may have been formed about them from whatever source. However, because industrial disablement benefit relies so heavily upon the quality of the evidence, it would seem that the former should take preference, since, the clearer and fuller the evidence, the less the scope for bias and prejudice to intrude.

There is little to indicate, however, that participation is treated as an inherently desirable feature of the decision-making process. Rather, the involvement of the claimant serves two purposes; first, as mentioned above, to collect information, and, secondly, to take the opportunity of telling claimants about their claims, particularly when a disallowance looks likely. Whilst claimants can always request an interview, nearly all are instigated by the adjudication officer, who will in effect retain control over the encounter, the claimant having to respond to a series of questions whose relevance or importance he or she may not grasp. The interview takes place primarily for the benefit of the adjudication officer, who is concerned with gathering information on which to adjudicate. This will occasionally involve weighing incomplete or contradictory evidence, but it is rare that the claimant will be aware of this, and so will not be in a position to respond to the evidence of others which is prejudicial to the claim. For some social security benefits, satisfying the eligibility criteria entitles the claimant to a fixed amount of benefit (for example, mobility allowance, attendance allowance, invalid care allowance). For such claimants, there is probably little of interest in a formal notification letter from the DSS without the good news that the benefit will be paid. However, where the amount of the award is not fixed but dependent on means-testing (such as income support or family credit) or on an assessment of disability (such as industrial disablement benefit or severe disablement allowance), and, possibly more importantly, where a claim is disallowed, knowing the reasons why a particular decision has been made is essential for the 'acceptability of the decision', or for an effective appeal to be made. Many adjudication officers felt that the standard decision letters issued by the DSS are too legalistic, steeped in jargon, and lacking any real explanation of decisions, even though improvements have been evident in recent years.

The claimants are generally unaware of what factors have been considered in reaching a decision, even appeal decisions. (Adjudication Officer, Office D)

If every time you asked for a piece of information you've got to tell them what it is in connection with exactly, and every time you make a decision you've got to explain the reasons behind it, it would be totally time-consuming and impossible. (ex-Adjudication Officer, Office J)

As with participation, the attention paid to accountability in disablement benefit decision-making results primarily from other motives, in particular gathering more information. There is also a concern to minimize the number of appeals since they are a source of extra work. Claimants therefore may receive a detailed letter of explanation in response to an appeal request which adjudication officers hope will lead to appeal being dropped. In this way some claimants may receive more explanation than they otherwise would have done. But there are also dangers inherent in this approach. Claimants are in a particularly weak position, lacking knowledge of the law and of decision-making procedures, and vulnerable to a seemingly authoritative refutation of their case which may dissuade them from continuing an appeal which may nevertheless have been successful.

Accuracy and the medical decision-makers. The Chief Adjudication Officer, under whose aegis lay decisions are monitored, has no jurisdiction over medical adjudication. Furthermore, there is no comparable monitoring system by which standards can be measured. However, DSS medical officers operate a percentage check on cases both before and after they have been seen by an adjudicating medical practitioner. Harking back to an earlier time when medical boards comprising two doctors assessed all cases, these checks are called the pre-board and the post-board scrutiny.

The 'pre-board scrutiny' is restricted to a narrow range of cases where hospital records or consultants' reports are almost invariably necessary. This typically occurs when the adjudicating medical practitioner cannot be expected to have the requisite specialist knowledge to decide a claim, for example, on eye or ear injuries, or neurological damage caused by head injuries. The purpose of the scrutiny is to allow a DSS medical officer to assess whether or not additional information should be sought before the claimant is seen. Anticipating the information requirements of the adjudicating medical practitioner is intended to avoid a possible delay later were the case to be adjourned. It also contributes to accuracy by ensuring that the adjudicating medical practitioner has as many of the 'true facts' as possible before making a decision.

The 'post-board scrutiny' is a 10 per cent check[23] on the decisions of adjudicating medical practitioners to ensure that they are reasonably based on the evidence and to identify any simple errors that might have been made. The Adjudication Regulations 1984 allow the decision of an adjudicating medical practitioner to be referred back when there has been an obvious clerical or technical error (such as quoting a wrong date, or transcribing left leg as right leg), but do not sanction any disagreement with the percentage assessment being raised.[24]

---

[23] Until the mid-1980s a 100 per cent check was carried out, but this was reduced to 10 per cent on cost grounds.

[24] However, the official can refer the case to a Medical Appeal Tribunal (the Social Security (Adjudication) Regulations 1984 (SI 1984/451), regulations 9 and 10 (now

Training for adjudicating medical practitioners tends to be tailored to what the Regional Senior Medical Officer perceives as necessary for each individual. The new recruit usually joins an experienced adjudicating medical practitioner as the second member of a two-doctor medical board until considered competent to act alone. There are no official training courses comparable to those for adjudication officers.

Without a medical equivalent of the Chief Adjudication Officer, the arrangements for advice giving to adjudicating medical practitioners are poorly developed. The adjudicating medical practitioner's equivalent of the Adjudication Officer's Guide is the Industrial Injuries Handbook (DHSS 1986). However, in practice it is rarely used. Past experience, or occasionally the help of other adjudicating medical practitioners, is relied upon to resolve difficult cases. Although it was the practice until the mid-1980s for DSS medical officers to advise adjudicating medical practitioners, this practice has now been proscribed in order to maintain the status of adjudicating medical practitioners as 'independent statutory authorities'.

I've opened the II Handbook only on rare occasions—five times in 40 years. There were no problems getting help when there was a Medical Officer on site, but now if I'm stuck I'll ring the Regional Office, or I'll pop in and ask—we're not supposed to do this, by the way. But we must not talk specifically about individual cases, only in general or hypothetical terms. It's a damned nonsense; two heads are always better than one. (Adjudicating Medical Practitioner, Region Z)

Whereas the spectre of a Social Security Appeal Tribunal hearing often prompts the lay adjudication officer to take a more rigorous approach to decision-making on individual cases, there was little evidence of an equivalent effect on medical practitioners. The difference may be partly explained by the almost non-existent contact between them and Medical Appeal Tribunals. Doctors are not required to prepare appeal documents nor appear at a hearing. In most Regions they may not even know that one of their decisions has been challenged until they eventually receive a copy of the tribunal's decision. As a result, adjudicating medical practitioners were little, if at all, affected by the anticipated response of a Medical Appeal Tribunal to their assessments, nor (and here they resembled adjudication officers) were they much influenced by decisions that had been overturned.

regulations 10 and 11 of the Social Security (Adjudication) Regulations 1986 (SI 1986/2218) with one minor amendment)).

Whilst less rigidly specified, there are structural features of medical adjudication which can promote accuracy. The structure of training is designed to ensure that adjudicating medical practitioners reach an adequate level of competence before commencing their solo careers, even if some seem to lack a full appreciation and understanding of the legal nature of much adjudication. The advice system has been severely weakened, however, without any compensatory developments. Monitoring, despite its recent retrenchment, can at least identify weak adjudicating medical practitioners whose decisions appear inconsistent or poorly based on the evidence, and can prompt remedial, educative action. The appeals structure, however, appears largely irrelevant to routine medical decision-making.

Fairness and the medical decision-makers. Like elements of the lay decision-making process, medical adjudication relies on evidence from outside sources (mostly hospital notes and consultants' reports) which makes promptness a difficult concept to put into practice. The adjudicating medical practitioners themselves have no control whatsoever over the process.

Bias and prejudice can find expression in the assessments of adjudicating medical practitioners, since, apart from some prescribed percentage assessments, there is usually an element of choice in what percentage figure to award. Whilst adjudication officers can remain separate from claimants, there is no question of adjudicating medical practitioners similarly keeping their distance, since they must carry out a physical examination. There is always the potential, therefore, that this interaction between practitioner and claimant may colour the adjudicating medical practitioner's judgments.

There is little meaningful participation by claimants in the medical decision-making process. In practice, claimants are subject to a series of questions from which the adjudicating medical practitioner will complete the 'claimant's statement' on the medical report form, but, apart from that and the medical examination, the adjudicating medical practitioner will proceed with little or no further contribution from the claimant. No indication of the adjudicating medical practitioner's assessment is given until the claimant receives the official notification of the decision later. One doctor saw this as inadequate:

I go to some lengths to explain the implications of the examination, although I never mention percentage assessments. For example, on a second board after a provisional award I would explain that the examination might lead to an increase or a fall in benefit. Claimants should know what is happening to avoid the possibility that they may feel they were 'being done' by the system. (Adjudicating Medical Practitioner, Region X)

The medical assessment is recorded on a standard form which, compared with adjudication officer decision letters, is relatively informative, giving the adjudicating medical practitioner's assessment of the claimant's condition and any other conditions which affect the percentage figure awarded. Nevertheless there is doubt about whether this is adequate.

It would be very difficult to explain to a lay person why they were assessed, say, at 5 per cent for a lower back injury. It might be easier to put it in words on a form; for example, '5 per cent is awarded on the basis that he was only off work for three weeks after the accident, there are no neurological signs, and physical examination shows only minimal limitations of movement', something like that. I think that would be entirely reasonable, and far more useful from the claimant's point of view than worrying about the relevant loss of faculty. I do not see why you cannot give these people a simple, straightforward explanation in non-legalistic terms, they pay into a scheme to cover them against injury at work and so should be entitled to know why they have been awarded so much money. (Medical Officer, Region Y)

The difficulty of giving a meaningful explanation of an assessment mentioned above results from the artificiality of a scale of percentage points assigned to various disabilities. To say that a person who has lost a thumb is 30 per cent disabled, or a person having had both legs amputated is 100 per cent disabled, is meaningless in any medical sense; the quantification of disablement is only a convenient legal construct. The prescribed assessments[25] at least provide a comprehensible explanation of a particular assessment where relevant (i.e. 'you have lost a thumb, therefore you are assessed at 30 per cent because that is the law'), but for other disabilities (for example, those resulting from back injuries) such an easy explanation is not available. Nevertheless, this should not prevent a greater level of explanation, such as that suggested by the Medical Officer quoted above, being possible. At present, however, accountability to the claimant is as poorly served on the medical questions as it is on the lay questions.

---

[25] In Schedule 2 to the Social Security (General Benefit) Regulations 1982 (SI 1982/1408).

Conclusions

In this chapter I have tried to do several related things. First, I have provided an analysis of a little-researched area of the British social security system which I hope will appeal to audiences on both sides of the Atlantic. In so doing I have presented evidence for the argument that discretion is present in both the substance of industrial disablement benefit law and in the procedures that lay and medical officials operate in processing claims. In particular I have tried to show the importance of procedural discretion for the final outcome of a claim. It is an aspect of discretion which rarely attracts attention (and which I believe to be seriously under-researched), although this might not be the case if more attention was paid to Davis's important observation (quoted above) that discretion extends, *inter alia*, to procedures and methods. My second aim was to offer a framework around the concept of administrative justice which could be used in analyses of decision-making, regardless of whether it is concerned with substantive or procedural issues or whether it is described as 'discretionary'.

The elements of administrative justice were arrived at by posing the question of what should be required of administrative agencies in the performance of their functions. In responding to the question we have necessarily become involved in normative theorizing about the relationship between individual citizens and the administrative agencies of the state. Normative theory can only be based on necessarily subjective foundations, not fixed, provable propositions. There is, therefore, no fundamental theory of justice that awaits discovery and hence no definitive conception of administrative justice; each must be based ultimately on moral beliefs or principles which cannot be, as MacCormick points out, 'the result of a chain of logical reasoning' (1978: 5). If we are to accept the development of an argument that is based on a normative theory, then that theory and its ultimate principles must be laid bare and found to be convincing. Kamenka sets out how a normative set of ideas must be judged: 'It is to be judged by its internal coherence and logical consistency, by the truth of its associated empirical claims and its relation to relevant empirical material that it may or may not take up and, in the last resort, by its relation and that of its consequences and implications to our own beliefs' (1978: 12).

My efforts at normative theorizing (in the first section of this chapter) have led to an elaboration of the concept of administrative justice around the elements of accuracy and fairness. Administrative justice, it has been argued, is only fully satisfied if several conditions are met. In the context of social security, claimants must receive an accurate, prompt, and impartial decision on their claim. They must have been able to participate fully in the process by providing information and being able to comment upon other information affecting their claim. They must have had the process explained as the claim has progressed, and received an adequate and comprehensible account of the reasons for the final decision. We now need to consider how robust the framework of administrative justice is as a practical tool for analysis.

The framework can be used in two alternative ways. First, the various elements of the DSS decision-making machinery (its structures, personnel, and practices) can be evaluated against the criteria of accuracy and fairness. Alternatively, we can take the elements of administrative justice and ask how each is promoted (or undermined) in practice. By either route, problems and weaknesses of the existing arrangements can be identified and remedial action proposed, and new ways of enhancing administrative justice can be suggested. Applying the analytical framework to industrial disablement benefit decision-making has revealed a picture of a system beset with anomalies and deficiencies. Such a conclusion arises not only from an analysis of available documentary data but also, and perhaps more tellingly, from the experiences of those who have responsibility for operating the system.

Administrative justice also provides a framework for the examination of discretion, which, I have argued, is endemic within the rule-bound social security system in Britain rather than restricted to areas where there is an absence of rules. Where discretion is exercised, therefore, or where choices have been made, administrative justice requires that it has been made clear to the individual why those choices have been made, and what evidence and decision criteria they were based upon. Treating discretion in this way, it is argued, is to acknowledge the inevitability of discretion in decision-making whilst trying to ensure that extraneous criteria do not intrude into the valid and legitimate decision-making process. Devising an analytical framework based on administrative justice will not prevent discretion being used to justify diverse decision-making structures in future. However, it may help to ensure that comparable standards of decision-making are applied regardless of how the process is described.

Against Kamenka's test for an adequate normative set of ideas I am encouraged that administrative justice has the necessary internal coherence, logical consistency, and relevance to empirical material to succeed as normative theory. It fails only if it does not accord with our ultimately subjective feelings and beliefs about justice. Administrative justice is not limited to the external scrutiny of administrative practices. It also presents a series of challenges for administrative agencies themselves—a challenge to articulate what the concept (in its elements of accuracy and fairness) means in their particular setting, and a challenge to demonstrate how their internal operations meet these demands. The challenge is not only relevant to current administrative arrangements; prospective changes in administration should also be able to meet the requirements of administrative justice. Proposed legislative amendments or new provisions could be scrutinized in two ways: first, to identify where problems with evidence or with the interpretation of the law are likely to occur, and, secondly, to identify what response would be necessary in institutional terms to ensure that accuracy and fairness are not undermined. Furthermore, any administrative rules that act as additional substantive decision criteria should be subject to the same administrative justice requirements as legislative provisions. Reconciling 'administration' and 'justice' may be, in Mashaw's words, 'a subtle enterprise' (1983: 17), but in the modern administrative state such an enterprise is surely necessary.

10. Discretion: Power, Quiescence, and Trust

JOEL F. HANDLER

DISCRETION has emerged from the shadows. Always known, grudgingly tolerated, it is now celebrated. Command-and-control regulation is challenged by decentralization, bargaining, and flexibility. Alternative-dispute resolution—various alternatives to formal adjudication—is now an industry: there are numerous and multiple forms of 'informal-justice' structures, a large scholarly literature, and public and foundation support. Even the very essence of legal practice is questioned; lawyers, we are being told, may well serve their clients better by replacing an adversary approach with bargaining or co-operative styles of negotiation. Trends in practice are reflected in jurisprudence and critical theory. A common theme in Critical Legal Studies, feminist jurisprudence, and continental reflexive law is that space has to be created within structural frameworks to allow for the flexible, creative resolution of conflicts. Modern and postmodern philosophers argue for conversation, for dialogue, and for community, rather than governing relationships through rules.[1]

Discretion is ubiquitous, hence difficult to define.[2] Basically, it involves the existence of choice, as contrasted with decisions purportedly being dictated by rules. A common, and useful, example involves enforcement. The police officer, in assessing an event, exercises choice as to whether to invoke authority and how much authority; the prosecutor, after weighing the evidence, decides whether to prosecute or not. Similar kinds of choices are available to many regulatory agencies—whether to cite violations or to institute other kinds of actions. The opposite would be situations where the officer feels that there is no choice, that the rules dictate a particular decision. This is a

---

[1] There is by now a considerable literature on all of these topics. Some representative examples include: regulation: Bardach and Kagan 1982; alternative dispute resolution: Abel 1982a, 1982b; Menkel-Meadow 1984 (also on the practice of law); critical legal studies: Kelman 1987; Tushnet 1986; Peller 1987; feminist jurisprudence: Olsen 1984; Sunstein 1988; West 1988; Continental reflexive law: Habermas 1986b; Luhmann 1986; modern/postmodern philosophy: Bernstein 1985; Cornell 1985. The relationship between these various developments and discretion is more fully discussed in Handler 1988.

[2] For recent discussions of discretion, see Brodkin 1987; Adler and Asquith 1981a.

theoretical distinction, and it should not be exaggerated. While it is probably true that, in a great many situations, officers do feel that they are bound by rules, many important decisions are made by low-level eligibility workers, tax auditors, licensing officials, and other kinds of bureaucrats (R. A. Kagan 1984*a*). Discretion is everywhere in the bureaucracy (G. Smith 1981; Winkler 1981). Choice has been exercised in the framing of the rules, and quite often, more often than we would like to acknowledge, officials conceal their choices behind the excuse of a rule (Lipsky 1980). In any event, in the relationships that I will be discussing in this chapter—those involving human service agencies—the distinction is not important; the officials—doctors, social workers, teachers, mental health workers—have lots of choice.

Discretion has somewhat different characteristics when one compares formal adjudication with alternative dispute resolution. The essence of adjudication is the existence of an authoritative third party (i.e. the judge) who is empowered to make a binding decision on the competing parties. The judge, of course, usually has a great deal of discretion. The process, though, is formally structured; the decision-making body 'finds' the facts—what happened—and then applies the law. Alternative dispute resolution, in its many forms, stresses informality and flexibility, and, instead of fixing liability on the basis of past events, tries to look to the future in resolving disputes. A similar approach is argued for in bargaining. Instead of bargaining 'in the shadow of the law'—that is, arguing over past events and anticipating what a court would do—the parties are to explore needs and focus on the future (Menkel-Meadow 1984). Informal justice, alternative dispute resolution, and bargaining imply more choice as to both procedure and substance than does adjudication.[3]

---

[3] Compare Keith Hawkins's definition of negotiation:

In contrast with adjudicated decisions, negotiations is a means of solving problems arrived at in the absence of an authoritative, imposed outcome. It is a flexible system of decision-making relying on bargaining, and to that extent the agreed outcome is tolerable to both sides. Negotiation works in the absence of an authoritative decision-maker because there is at least a measure of consensus and commitment to the outcome of the decision-making process felt by both parties. They must be 'in agreement with it . . . and must accept it as the best that can be obtained in the circumstances. Acceptance is by compulsion, of course, but it is the compulsion exercised by the other party and not by overriding external authority.' It is decision-making by compromise rather than by the imposition of one verdict or another. There is no fully authoritative party (though of course bargaining strengths may well differ between the parties), thus the complete acquiescence of one side of the other in an all-or-nothing outcome is unusual. To the extent that each side enjoys at least

Discretion, especially in its contemporary manifestations, has been attacked on both substantive and procedural grounds. As compared to the idealized version of the rule of law, where parties have equal access and the court applies neutral rules evenhandedly, it is argued that discretion allows for the bargaining away of publicly defined normative standards and may further disadvantage the weak and the powerless. With regulation, for example, negotiated resolutions will fall short of substantive goals; without procedural protections and the applicability of substantive rights, the poor and weak will be even more victimized by employers, landlords, merchants, and bureaucrats. Bargaining takes place within a normative framework. How are the rules of the game to be maintained? If one party can exploit the rules, there will be an unfair advantage.[4]

The contemporary literature extolling discretion generally ignores distribution issues. Whether arguing for flexibility in regulation, informal justice, or even communitarianism or philosophical dialogism, with few exceptions it is more-or-less assumed that the parties are relatively equal; the issue is how can the parties better relate to each other. There has been little systematic consideration of how discretion would work when there are serious inequalities. This chapter focuses on the unequal relationship. Specifically, I am concerned with discretion when a dependent person is dealing with a large-scale public bureaucracy. Discretion gives the official choice. Choice, at least normatively, should be based on a careful weighing of the interests and needs of the client in relation to public considerations. Should this child be placed in this particular special education program? Does this particular applicant qualify for social benefits, and, if so, under what conditions? Discretion contemplates a conversation within a normative framework, but dependent people—the poor, minorities, the uneducated, and unsophisticated—are often at a serious disadvantage. They lack the information, the skills, and the power to persuade. The official has the unfair advantage.

---

some measure of bargaining strength, the negotiated decision is mutually arrived at, not imposed, giving negotiation the character of a search for a solution to a problem (where the character of adjudication tends to be that of finding an answer to a question). This search takes place in informal settings which are unencumbered with a structure of formal rules and procedures, in contract with adjudication, for there is no authority to decide which norms apply. (1986: 1161, 1169).

[4] There is also a considerable literature attacking discretion in informal justice. See, e.g., Abel 1985; Delgado 1985.

It is for these reasons that the advocates for the poor and the weak have been so opposed to discretion. My argument is different. Discretion is inevitable, especially in a great many human service agencies. It ought to be approached positively and creatively; but ways have to be sought to ensure that power advantages are not exploited, that effective bargaining does in fact take place, and that both parties meaningfully participate in the choices that are to be made. However, before getting to solutions, the issues have to be examined more closely. How is power exercised in the bureaucratic setting? And what do we mean by participation? Power and participation will be examined sociologically. Then we will consider structural mechanisms designed to equalize power and maximize the participation of dependent people dealing with bureaucracy.

The Manifestations of Power

The standard definition of power is: A has power over B to the extent that he can get B to do something that B would not otherwise do.[5] At first blush, the definition seems unproblematic, especially in the context of the dependent bureaucratic client. The client, as the price of receiving something that is needed, has to do something that the official insists upon—participate in a work program, reveal a matter of privacy, or engage in other kinds of behaviors. The model assumes an objective conflict of interests; there is a direct exercise of power and a knowing albeit unwilling submission. The legal rights regime has a response to this situation. If the official acted *ultra vires*, then the

---

[5] While this may be a common, and for our purposes useful, definition of power, there is, in fact, no agreement on the various meanings of power. According to Talcott Parsons,

> Power is one of the key concepts in the great Western tradition about political phenomena. it is at the same time a concept on which, in spite of its long history, there is, on analytical levels, a notable lack of agreement both about its specific definition, and about many features of the conceptual context in which it should be placed. There is, however, a core complex of its meaning having to do with the capacity of persons or collectivities 'to get things done' effectively, in particular when their goals are obstructed by some kind of human resistance or opposition. (1986: 94)

Lukes's volume (1986) contains a series of essays on various approaches to power. At the end of the introduction, Lukes says: 'in our ordinary unreflective judgments and comparisons of power, we normally know what we mean and have little difficulty in understanding one another, yet every attempt at a single general answer to the question has failed and seems likely to fail' (ibid.: 17).

dependent person has a right to challenge the exercise of power and a neutral third party will order a remedy.

Suppose, however, that the client willingly submits? Has there been an exercise of power if B *appears* to do what A wants? Now the situation becomes more problematic. What does consent mean in a hierarchical relationship? Can we take the client's position at face value? What other choice do we have? Steven Lukes (1974) addresses the problem of power and quiescence. He argues that there are three dimensions of power. The one-dimensional approach is the example given above, where A gets B to do something he otherwise would not have done. In the power debate, it is the view associated with the pluralists, principally Robert Dahl (1986; see also Gaventa 1980: 4). This dimension focuses on observable behavior: 'who participates, who gains and loses, and who prevails in decision-making' (Gamson 1968: 3; see also Polsby 1963: 55). As such, it assumes that grievances and conflicts are recognized and acted upon, that participation occurs within decision-making arenas which are assumed to be more-or-less open, at least to organized groups, and that leaders, or decision-makers, can be studied as representatives of these groups. Non-participation, or in-action, then, is not a political problem: 'the empirical relationship of low socio-economic status to low participation gets explained away as the apathy, political inefficacy, cynicism or alienation of the impoverished' (Gaventa 1980: 7). As Gamson puts it, inactivity can be seen as confidence (consent), alienation, or irrelevance (1968: 46). Quiescence lies in the characteristics of the victims; it is not constrained by power.

The two-dimensional view of power seeks to meet this last point. Bachrach and Baratz argue that power has a 'second face' by which it is not only exercised upon the participants within the decision-making arenas but also operates to exclude participants and issues altogether; that is, power not only involves who gets what, when, and how, but also who gets left out and how (1962, 1970; see also Gaventa 1980: 9). Some issues never get on the political agenda—for example, the issue of pollution in a company-dominated town, or the failure of southern Blacks to register and vote prior to the 1965 Voting Rights Act. Apparent inaction is not related to the lack of grievances. Bachrach and Baratz argue that the study of power has to also include the barriers even to expressing grievances (Gaventa 1980: 10).

Lukes argues that the two-dimensional view, while a considerable advance, does not go far enough; it fails to account for how power may effect even the *conception* of grievances. The absence of grievances may be due to a manipulated consensus. Furthermore, the dominant group may be so secure that they are oblivious to anyone challenging their position—'the most effective and insidious use of power is to prevent . . . conflict from arising in the first place' (Lukes 1974: 23). This is the third dimension of power. A exercises power over B by getting him to do what he does not want to do, but 'he also exercises power over him by influencing, shaping or determining his very wants' (ibid.: 23). Lukes argues that this may happen in the absence of observable conflict, even though there is a latent conflict, between the interests of A and the 'real interests' of excluded B.

An important characteristic of the third-dimensional view is that it is not confined to looking at the exercise of power in an individualistic, behavioral framework; rather, it focuses on the various ways, whether individual or institutional, by which potential conflicts are excluded. It is much more sociological than either the one- or perhaps the two-dimensional views. Under the third dimension, two theoretical approaches are combined—the hegemonic social and historical patterns identified by Gramsci (1971) and the subjective effects of power identified by Edelman.[6]

The two- and three-dimensional approaches promise to be particularly relevant when considering dependent or relatively powerless people: 'In the two-dimensional approach is the suggestion of barriers that prevent issues from emerging into political arenas—i.e., that constrain conflict. In the three-dimensional approach is the suggestion of the use of power to pre-empt manifest conflict at all, through the shaping of patterns or conceptions of non-conflict' (Gaventa 1980: 13).

What are the mechanisms of power in the three dimensions? In the first dimension are the conventional political resources used by political actors—votes, influence, jobs. The second dimension adds what Bachrach and Baratz call the 'mobilization of bias'. These are the rules of the game—values, beliefs, rituals, as well as institutional procedures—which systematically benefit certain groups at the expense of others. The mobilization of bias operates not only in the decision-making arenas but also, in fact primarily, through 'non-decisions' whereby demands are 'suffocated before they are voiced, or kept covert; or killed before they gain access to the relevant decision-

---

[6] 'Political actions chiefly arouse or satisfy people not by granting or withholding their stable, substantive demands but rather by changing their demands and expectations' (Edelman 1971: 8; see also Gaventa, 1980: 13).

making arena; or failing all of these things, maimed or destroyed in the decision-implementing stage of the policy process' (Bachrach and Baratz 1970: 43). Quiescence can be the product of force or its threat, co-optation, symbolic manipulation, or the silent effects of incremental decisions or institutional inaction (Gaventa 1980: 15).

The mechanisms of power in the third dimension are the least understood. Here is where

> power influences, shapes or determines conceptions of the necessities, possibilities, and strategies of challenge in situations of latent conflict. This may include the study of social myths, language, and symbols, and how they are shaped or manipulated in power processes. It may involve the study of communication of information—both of what is communicated and how it is done. It may involve a focus upon the means by which social legitimations are developed around the dominant, and instilled as beliefs or roles in the dominated. It may involve, in short, locating the power processes behind the social construction of meanings and patterns that serve to get B to act and believe in a manner in which B otherwise might not, to A's benefit and B's detriment. (Gaventa 1980: 15–16)

Third-dimensional mechanisms of power include not only the control of information and socialization processes, but also fatalism, self-deprecation, apathy, and the internalization of dominant values and beliefs—the psychological adaptations of the oppressed to escape the subjective sense of powerlessness. Voices become echoes rather than grievances and demands. Behaviors and beliefs intertwine. Political consciousness and participation are reciprocal and reinforcing; those who are denied participation will not develop political consciousness. In Paulo Freire's words, because dependent societies are prevented from either participation or reflection, they are denied the very experience necessary for the development of a critical consciousness; instead, they develop a 'culture of silence'. Moreover, it is the culture of silence which may lend legitimation to the dominant order. Finally, if their voices do emerge, they are especially vulnerable to manipulation by the powerful (Gaventa 1980: 15–16; Freire 1985).

Gaventa argues that the various mechanisms of power as well as the attributes of powerlessness, in all three dimensions, are interrelated and cumulative; they serve to reinforce each other. Repeated defeats lead to quiescence which give the dominant group more opportunity to create barriers of exclusion. The maintenance of power becomes 'self-propelled'; thus, 'power relationships can be understood only

with reference to their prior development and their impact compre-
hended only in light of their own momentum' (Gaventa 1980: 23).

The challenge to power has to operate through the three dimensions.
In order genuinely to participate in the first dimension, B must
develop a consciousness of needs and strategies; then he must overcome the mobilization of bias through his own resources. Gaventa
believes that, just as the dimensions of power are cumulative, so too
are the challenges: 'Once patterns of quiescence are broken upon one
set of grievances, the accumulating resources of challenge—e.g.,
organization, momentum, consciousness—may become transferable
to other issues and other targets' (ibid.: 25).

While the three-dimensional view of power may have a theoretical
plausibility, it does pose significant methodological problems. A
major challenge raised to the two-dimensional view was the empirical
difficulty of observing a 'non-event'. With the third-dimension, 'how
can one study what does not happen?' (ibid.: 25). How can one tell
whether B would have *thought* and *acted* differently? There is a real
issue of imputing interests and values to the voiceless.

In real life, however, the methodological issues may not, in fact, be
that severe in many situations. If there are major inequalities in social
relations, at least as a first step, one should not assume that quiescence is
natural but seek other explanations. In less obvious situations, Gaventa
suggests a number of steps to try to explain the inaction. He would
look to the historical development of the apparent consensus to see
how the situation was arrived at and how the consensus has been
maintained. He would look at the processes of communication and
socialization and the relationship between the ideologies and beliefs.
There may be comparative examples with different power relationships.
However, 'if . . . no mechanisms of power can be identified and no
relevant counterfactuals can be found, then the researcher must
conclude that the quiescence of a given deprived group is, in fact,
based upon consensus of that group to their condition, owing for
instance, to differing values from those initially posited by the observer'
(ibid.: 25).

Power in Human Services Agencies

Hasenfeld (1987) describes the exercise of power from a political
economy perspective. The traditional view of social work practice
theory is that the client–caseworker relationship is voluntary, mutual,

reciprocal, and trusting; traditional theory tends to underestimate unequal power relationships by assuming that, in most relationships, natural power advantages will be neutralized through the voluntary mutuality of interests. Hasenfeld challenges this view. The principal source of social worker power derives from the resources and services controlled by the agency. Workers are members of organizations, and it is the organizations that determine how their resources are to be allocated. If the clients want these resources, then they must yield at least some control over their fate. In addition, workers have other sources of power: expertise, persuasion, and legitimacy. They have specialized knowledge and interpersonal skills.

A great deal of the organizational power is exercised through its standard operative procedures—the type of information that is processed, the range of available alternatives, the decision rules. The agency is concerned with maintaining and strengthening its core activity—the delivery of services. The environment matters; goals represent the interests of those who control the key resources of the agency, which may or may not incorporate professional norms and/or the interests of the client. In public agencies, which chronically lack the resources to meet demand, social workers are relatively powerless to change the situation; thus, they develop various personal coping mechanisms, such as withdrawal and client victimization.

Hasenfeld rejects the concept of mutuality of interests—that agencies and clients share the common goal of helping the client—in favor of a transactional approach. The interests of the client and the agency are determined by their respective systems. Each wants to maximize its own resources while minimizing costs. A person becomes a client to obtain needed resources but tries to do so with a minimum of costs; the social worker needs the resources controlled by the client while minimizing his and the agency's costs. The relationship is governed, then, by the power that each person has over his or her own interests. Thus, the amount of power that A has over B is a direct function of the resources that A controls and B needs and the inverse function of the ability of B to obtain those resources elsewhere. In short, '*influence is synonymous with resources*' (Gamson 1968: 93, emphasis in original). Agencies which have a monopoly of services exercise considerable power over clients. On the other hand, clients can exercise considerable power if they possess desirable characteristics. Thus, the exchange relationship between the client and the agency can be voluntary or involuntary depending on the degree of choice that each possesses.

Furthermore, even in situations where social workers possess considerable power, that power may not necessarily be used. There are rules and regulations, and workers, in varying degrees, are influenced by professional norms and values. But, in any event, the traditional social work practice theory assumption of client self-determination is largely untrue for vulnerable groups. There, relationships tend to be involuntary. The asymmetrical power relationship between the agency and the client, and hence between the worker and the client, is maintained throughout the structure of social services. The agency is not dependent on the client for its resources. Demand exceeds resources, and most agencies are in monopoly positions. Social workers increase the power advantage through their monopoly of expertise, limiting client access to other workers, making the offer of services conditional on compliance, and limiting options for alternatives.

Agency processes, the structures of discretion, reflect the evaluative criteria of the external funding and legitimating sources. The more powerful the agency, the more it will use its advantages to maintain its position; it will maintain a superior practice and select the more desirable clients. Within the agency, the more powerful workers are better able to control the conditions of their work. In this way, the dynamics of power perpetuate the unequal distribution of quality practice. Poor clients tend to receive poor services. This results not only in an inequality of practice, but, Hasenfeld argues, the practice of inequality.

The distinguishing characteristic of a human service agency is its technology (Hasenfeld 1983: ch. 5). These agencies are designed to change people; thus, the technology requires knowledge of the complexities of human behavior, but is also a *moral* system. As Hasenfeld points out, clients are invested with moral and cultural values that define their status. The processes of the organization—intake, intervention, and termination—are crucially shaped by the workers' moral evaluation of the client. Moreover, as clients progress within the system, moral and social attributes change. The technology is based on a conception of human nature, and this conception is reinforced through the selection, processing, and evaluation of the clients.

Because of the inherent uncertainties of the technologies and the demands placed on the workers to respond to demands, the workers develop what Hasenfeld calls 'practice ideologies'—sets of ideas or ideologies which seek confirmation in self-fulfilling prophecies by screening incompatible information and resisting change or reappraisal. The workers select and deal with those clients that will serve their interests—either to confirm their ideologies or to comport with the demands of their working conditions, or both. Since technologies and resources are limited, the attributes of the clients who *enter* are important to organizational success. Thus, organizations seek to attract desirable clients and to screen out the undesirable. Although public agencies are often limited in their ability to pick and choose, they employ other mechanisms for acceptance and rejection.

Hasenfeld describes the selection and processing of clients as 'typification', which is a pervasive feature in the exercise of field-level discretion. The organization identifies client characteristics in terms of diagnostic labels which then determine the service response. Agency perceptions of the client's moral character are often determinative. Is the client responsible for his or her condition and is the client amenable to change? Is the client morally capable of making decisions? Is the client a subject or an object? The answers to these questions, in turn, determine the workers' moral responsibility to the client. The social construction of the client's moral character will have a decisive impact on the treatment that the client receives; thus, the constructed moral character becomes reinforcing.

The mechanism through which the agency delivers the services and gains control over the client is the relationship between the client and the worker. The core of this relationship, according to Hasenfeld, is the nature of the *trust* between the client and the worker. The client has to believe in the desirability of the services and the skill of the worker; the worker has to believe that the client will not abuse the relationship. The worker has to trust the client in order to make the necessary moral commitments. Successful agency intervention depends upon client trust. However, in order for there to be trust, goals and interests have to coincide. There are many barriers to developing a compatibility of interests, but a crucial one, according to Hasenfeld, is the social construction of the client's moral character; in a word, is the client a subject or an object?

We will return to the issue of trust shortly, after we consider the application of the three dimensions of power to the political-economy perspective of social worker–client relations. The first dimension is the paradigm of liberal, legal adversarial relations. A dependent person applies for welfare; a condition of aid is a behavioral change— for example, a work assignment—which the person would prefer not to do, but feels that she has to as the price of receiving assistance. Assume that the agency is acting illegally—the woman may be legally exempt from the work requirements, the agency failed to follow required procedures (e.g. evaluation, offers of training, etc.), or adequate day care was not available. The client knows of the illegality but needs the aid, has no other adequate alternative, but lacks the resources to challenge the agency. Or, the client has available competent legal services and does challenge the agency. This is the first dimension of power: there is an objective event—individualized conflict and empirical evidence as to who won what under what circumstances. Power can be defined and measured.

Suppose, however, that the client acquiesces in the condition. Why is there quiescence? Assume that the client is of the same frame of mind—that is, she would prefer not to work. It may be that the agency is acting legally; in this case, the decision has been made legislatively and the agency is not exercising its discretion but is following a rule. The client is now precluded from voicing her grievance, certainly in this forum, but probably not in any other arena as well. This would be a case of the second dimension. There is a grievance—the woman feels that she unjustly has to pay a price for the aid—but she has been effectively precluded from contesting the decision. There are other ways in which the second dimension of power can also operate. The agency may be operating illegally; the woman feels her grievance, but lacks the resources with which to pursue her remedy or for some other reason feels that it would be either useless or even counter-productive to pursue her remedy. She may, for example, fear retaliation.[7] These are examples of the second dimension of power because, even though there is no objectively observed conflict, there is a grievance. Moreover, one could empirically verify, not only the grievance, but also the reasons for quiescence. Different client behaviors could be empirically established.

There are also several variations on the third dimension of power— where the absence of conflict is due to a manipulation of consensus, where A shapes and determines the very wants of B. The very idea of welfare as an *entitlement* is of recent vintage. Prior to the legal rights revolution of the 1960s, welfare was considered a gratuity, something that was offered on the terms and conditions of the grantor, much as private charity is given today. Given the extremely low level of legal

---

[7] For a discussion of the barriers to exercising rights to administrative fair hearings, see Handler 1986: ch. 2.

challenges in social welfare programs, one questions even now how far the concept of entitlement has penetrated the consciousness of the disadvantaged (Handler 1986: ch. 2). In what sense does one accept or think about challenging participation in salvation as the price of receiving aid from a religious organization? The work requirement is deeply ingrained in American public values—witness the astonishing consensus on work-for-relief today; many think it perfectly normal and appropriate that an applicant for public assistance should work at a public job as the price of the grant; there is very little support for the idea that one is *entitled* to a minimum level of support without any corresponding obligations.[8] To the extent that the applicant for assistance has internalized these values—the obligations of work, responsibility, and welfare—then the dominant group has prevented even the conception of the grievance. As Gaventa points out, this view of power is not individualistic; it is much more institutional, more in the nature of the hegemonic social and historical patterns identified by Gramsci and the subjective effects of power discussed by Edelman; power prevents the manifestation of conflict at all. The poor have been socialized into believing that there is no entitlement to a minimum standard of living without a corresponding obligation to work.

The social and historical patterns and the subjective effects identified by Gramsci and Edelman are, of course, much more deep rooted, much more pervasive, than even the complex example of the work obligation. They are manifest in many of the relationships between the dependent citizen seeking services or trying to avoid sanctions and the officer who controls the resources. Both the powerful and the powerless carry into the relationship their respective characters and self-conceptions, their root values, nurtured through immediate as well as past social relationships. Who they are and where they come from—class, race, childhood, education, employment, relations with others, the everyday structures of their lives, their very different social locations—crucially affect their languages, social myths, beliefs, and symbols—how they view themselves, their world, and others—which produce vastly different meanings and patterns in their encounters. How does the staff-professional view herself in this context, and the person sitting across the desk? How does the client view herself in her context, and the person sitting across from her? It is no surprise that

---

[8] See, e.g., Hartmann 1987: 33, 58; see also Mead 1986. For a discussion of the current consensus on work and welfare reform, see Handler (1987–8).

in social welfare clients fail either to pursue their grievances or even to conceptualize a grievance. The structures of their social life shape their identities and direct their behavior (Binder (n.d.); Molotch and Boden 1985).[9]

The difficult problem comes in empirically verifying the third dimension. When there is quiescence, how do we know whether the consent is genuine or manipulated? How does the researcher (the dominant group) avoid imputing her values, the social construction of meaning, to the quiescent?

An approach that I will use will be to analyse the issue of trust. Recall that Hasenfeld argues that the core of the worker–client relationship in human service organizations is trust—treating clients as subjects rather than objects. What I will argue is that, if there is trust, then we can be more confident that the consent is genuine. If there is quiescence without trust, then I will argue that the consent is problematic.

Dependency and Trust

Trust is as ubiquitous as discretion. As a form of social organization, it is used whenever there are principals and agents, whenever we invest resources, responsibility, or authority in others—for example, family members, stockbrokers, secretaries, clerks, truck drivers, doctors, baby-sitters, and so on (Barber 1983; Shapiro 1987). We trust strangers as well an intimates; trust, it is said, is necessary to reduce the complexities of life (Luhmann 1980: 4). Annette Baier (1986) draws a distinction between merely relying on the dependable habits of others and trusting; the latter relies on *goodwill*. When one relies on another's goodwill, one becomes vulnerable; but, while there is the opportunity to do harm, one does not expect this to happen. We place ourselves in this vulnerable position because we need the help of agents to achieve or maintain things that we value—our lives, our health, our children, our property. Trust also involves discretion; we trust our agents to use their competence in our best interests, which also means that they have the ability to conceal their mistakes or their ill-will under the pretense of honest judgment. Trust can be unconscious or cultivated.

---

[9] There is a vast theoretical and empirical literature dealing with the problems of lack of rights consciousness. See, e.g., Felstiner, Abel, and Sarat 1980–1; Handler 1986: ch. 2; Bumiller 1988.

Baier distinguishes trust from contract. Making contracts and promises includes trust, but Baier argues that contract does not capture the full variety and moral dimensions of trust. Contracts are mainly used by adults who are more-or-less equal in power; Baier is interested in trust relations with dependent people—children, servants, wives, and slaves.

Baier argues that trusting relationships are not necessarily morally decent; they can also be morally rotten. How can one tell the difference? Baier proposes a moral test in terms of *expressibility*—can the trust relationship survive the knowledge the parties are relying on to continue the relationship? The example she uses is an old-fashioned husband and wife where the wife is entrusted to care for the child. As long as there are not radical disagreements as to child-rearing practices, the husband can trust the wife to use her discretion. The trust, however, would be undermined if there were serious conflicts in values and the husband knew that the wife was willing to sacrifice his interests for hers. Trusting is rational. If the husband knew that the wife was only conforming to avoid sanctions, then he would rely on threats rather than trust. Similarly, the wife would only conform as long as she thought that keeping the trust would produce more of the benefits that she and the child were interested in than breaking the trust. In other words, rational trust can exist in a variety of situations where the parties are, in fact, quite suspicious of each other; threats and concealments would keep the trust going. This would be a 'morally rotten' trust. Under the expressibility test, knowledge of what the other is relying on weakens the relationship. Conversely, with a moral trust, knowledge would strengthen the relationship— 'the other's love, or concern for some common good or professional pride in competent discharge of responsibility' (Baier 1986: 256).[10]

Trust, under Baier's more expansive concept, alters power relationships. The most basic, elemental trust is between the infant and the parent; it is trust that does not have to be won, but can be destroyed. Even though this is an example of extreme dependency and unequal

---

[10] Baier's definition of trust is as follows:

trust is morally decent only if, in addition to whatever else is entrusted, knowledge of each party's reasons for confident reliance on the other to continue the relationship could in principle also be entrusted—since mutual knowledge would be itself a good, not a threat to the other goods. To the extent that mutual reliance can be accomplished by mutual knowledge of the conditions of that reliance, trust is above suspicion, and trustworthiness a nonsuspect virtue. (1986: 259–60) vulnerability, Baier argues that it is still to some extent mutual; the parent is 'vulnerable to the child's at first insignificant but ever-increasing power, including power as one trusted by the parent' (ibid.: 242).[11] The goods that the parent supplies are nutrition, shelter, clothing, health, and love. Why should the child expect the parent to keep supplying these goods? Because the goods that the parent supplies are also goods to the parents—they are *common goods*. Harm to these goods would be self-harm. Trust and vulnerabilities between the parent and child become more mutual over time, and, eventually, adult children may become responsible for their parents; but this latter relationship, however contractual or not it may be, does not transform the initial trust into a contractual exchange. The childhood relation may be a moral reason, says Baier, for taking care of one's parents, but it is not consideration. Trust, then, between unequal participation does not necessarily have equality as its goal; what it does have, under the expressibility test, is equal moral agency.[12]

Baier's expressibility test connects Hasenfeld's definition of the client–worker relationship in human service organizations with the empirical problems of the third dimension of power. The core of the relationship, argues Hasenfeld, is trust whereby the worker treats the client as a subject, not an object. The empirical problem of the third dimension of power involves the issue of what appears to be manipulated consent that suffocates even the conception of a grievance. There are situations, I argue, where expressibility meets both objections; if the true reasons for the relationship are disclosed and the relationship is thereby strengthened, then the client is closer to a subject, and consent seems more genuine and less manipulated. This point can be illustrated by the use of some empirical examples.

---

[11] This conception of reciprocal power relations within an example of extreme dependency seems to fit Foucault's conception of the nature of power:

> Power must be analysed as something which circulates, or rather as something which only functions in the form of a chain. It is never localized here or there, never in anybody's hands, never appropriated as a commodity or piece of wealth. Power is employed and exercised through a net-like organization. And not only do individuals circulate between its threads; they are always in the position of simultaneously undergoing and exercising this power. They are not only its inert or consenting target; they are always also the elements of its articulation. In other words, individuals are the vehicles of power, not its points of application. (1986: 234)

[12] Baier's view of trust seems very close to Hannah Arendt's conception of power, which is the ability to agree upon a common course of action in unconstrained communication; see Arendt 1986: 59–74; Habermas 1986a: 75–93.

Some Empirical Examples

I will use two examples—one from special education and the other from water-pollution-control regulation in England.[13] The special-education example will demonstrate how trust alters power relationships and the expressibility test illuminates the problem of quiescence. The water-pollution-control regulation will illustrate the limits of the analysis.

The Education for All Handicapped Children Act, enacted in 1972, was part of the legal rights revolution in the United States establishing rights for minorities, the poor, women, the elderly, the mentally ill, and the handicapped. It was claimed that many handicapped children were either excluded from schools, or were improperly classified and segregated, and that their lives were wasted. The Act granted all handicapped children the right to an 'appropriate' public education but left it to the local participants to decide what the content of that education was to be. Schools would decide on the specific programs but parents were given the right to participate. Specifically, parents were to be notified and had to give written consent before a child was to be selected for diagnosis, evaluation, and placement in a special education program. Evaluation and the placement decision had to take place in a conference which the parents had the right to attend and participate in. If the parent disagreed with any decision, there were two administrative appeals (the district and the state) with the right of judicial review.

In most jurisdictions, the procedural innovations do not work. The law requires extensive paperwork, conferences are costly in terms of scarce professional time, and there are strong incentives to routinize the process, place a child in available slots, and keep the child there. Reimbursement is usually based on filled slots. At the same time, most parents, especially those from lower socio-economic classes, lack the ability to participate. In addition to psychological burdens, the parents lack the necessary information and resources. The result is that, in most jurisdictions, participation in the meetings and the written consent are formalities only. School officials decide cases beforehand, parents are presented with the staff recommendations, the consent forms are ritualistically signed. The parents confront a group of professionals who have worked together and struck a bargain;

---

[13] These examples are fully discussed in Handler 1988.

the discussion is in technical jargon, often with the subtle implication that the child or the parent is at fault. In large districts, the average time for the conference is about two and a half minutes. While there is variation, somewhat by social class, participation is ritualistic. What we have is the classic case of either the second or third dimension of power; parents who have grievances are overpowered; many have no idea that there are alternatives—they are so grateful that the district is taking their child each day. And for many, as subordinate individuals and parents, doubts as to the wisdom of the powerful are not even raised; these parents are in a culture of silence (Heller, Holtzman, and Messick 1982; Handler 1986: ch. 3).

The Madison (Wisconsin) School District has a vastly different relationship with the parents—one that is based on trust (in Baier's sense), that treats parents as subjects, where power relations are altered, and where consent appears to be genuine.[14] For historical reasons, prior to and without regard to the Handicapped Children Act, the district made three conceptual moves that serve as the foundation for their approach. First, the district decided that parents had to be part of the *solution* to the task of educating handicapped students; if students were to be successful in school *and* in life outside and after school, then the parents had to be *active* participants; the school could not do it alone. Secondly, at least with the classification of mildly mentally retarded, the technology was uncertain; therefore, diagnosis and treatment had to be flexible and experimental. By taking uncertainty seriously, the district lowered the level of potential conflict; participants could feel comfortable in agreeing to a course of action knowing that it would be open to renegotiation. Thirdly, although parents are given the opportunity to participate, they lack the resources. So the third move was to supply parent advocates—lay people who were experienced in the process (usually they were parents of handicapped children)—to help the parents. The parent advocates were to advise the parents as to the range of alternative services and programs, so that the parents could get independent evaluations; they would counsel them, accompany them to the meetings, and help them in the negotiations with the school people. The parent advocates were deliberately to introduce conflict, in the words of school psychologists and teachers; they would ask questions that parents were afraid to ask or did not know how to ask.

[14] The Madison example is discussed in detail in Handler 1986: ch. 4.

The deliberate introduction of conflict as necessary for communication demonstrates the commitment of the school district to genuine shared decision-making. A genuine dialogue involves questioning, listening, and openness. The parents not only had to feel comfortable with the decisions; they also had to be *active* participants in the plan. Quiescence, the standard practice in other school districts, was not enough. There were other things necessary to make the Madison approach work. There was social movement activity: parent groups, training sessions, and outings, all designed to decrease alienation and share information. The parents had access to independent experts who were welcome in the conferences.

This was the theory of the Madison approach to parental participation. If the participation operated as planned—and shortly I will discuss some of its failings—then we would see a system whereby the parents were considered subjects, not objects, where the foundation of the relationship was reciprocal trust, where power relationships had been altered, and where consent appeared to be genuine. The school had to get the parents involved; it would not do this unless it had confidence in the parents—that the parents understood what was expected, were capable, and would be active. The parents would not agree to this *and* perform in the manner that the school system considered necessary unless they understood and trusted the school people. Sanctions were not involved; instead there was conversation and persuasion.

Moreover, since the plans were tentative and experimental, always subject to renegotiation, the conversations had to continue. The teachers needed the active, understanding participation of the parents through the school life of the child.[15]

The parents were still parents and the teachers were still teachers; there were no redistributions of income and changes in social class. In real life, there were still great imbalances of power. Each brought with them their vast cultural differences. Yet, in this relationship, the parents approached equal moral agency. Trust based on goodwill, where Baier's test of expressibility would strengthen the trust relationship, altered power relations. The parents were given information

---

[15] Consider the following quote from a lower-class parent: 'Our family has never been criticized, they've never said, "you're failing him". They've encouraged us to allow him to do more and try more, and not to be afraid. They've convinced us he can do more than we think he can do' (Handler 1986: 79).

and responsibility; they were empowered. Jurgen Habermas describes this conversation as follows: 'In communication, individuals appear actively as unique beings and reveal themselves in their subjectivity. At the same time they must recognize one another as equally respons-ible beings, that is, as beings capable of intersubjective agreement— the rationality claim immanent in speech grounds a radical equality' (1986*b*: 217).

The parents were not only changed *vis-à-vis* the teacher; they themselves were also changed. Changes in practices necessarily mean a change in ideologies. The ability to take more control over their life and the fate of their child meant that there was a change in their self-conception, in their views about themselves. Ideology is integral to social practices; it defines experiences and constructs reality. Events only become socially meaningful when they are interpreted. 'There is no social world except as it is lived and experienced, and events become socially meaningful only when they are interpreted . . . [Thus] ideology is constitutive, in that ideas about an event or relationship define that activity, much as the rules about a game define a move or a victory in that game' (Merry 1986: 254). In other words, the empowerment of the parents, in this transaction, was both transformative and constitutive.

Was consent genuine? If there was knowledge about alternatives, if there were genuine listening and mutual respect, then the answer would be yes.

Did the Madison system work? There is considerable evidence that, in many situations, practice did approach theory. On the other hand, there was also evidence that the system was falling short of expectations. The reasons, however, for its developing weaknesses illustrate its theoretical coherence. The Madison system is interna-tionally famous—not because of parental participation, but because of its substantive program. As a result, a creeping system-wide co-optation is taking hold. More and more parents begin to think that, if they are dissatisfied, they must be wrong—the insidious psychological adaptations of self-deprecation and the internalization of dominant beliefs, always a danger, stir and begin to take root. Teachers complain that parents are becoming passive; there is too much quiescence; the use of parent advocates seems to be declining. Teachers go to considerable efforts to encourage participation, but they, too, worry about how much they are listening to parents and independent experts. Social movement activity has also declined. As the system improved substantively and became increasingly responsive to parents, the fires of protest banked.

What appears to be happening in Madison is a failure to realize that empowered participation is not a stable relationship; rather, it requires constant attention and renewal. The participatory relationship is only one part of the lives of participants who are otherwise enveloped in alien contexts. Even under benign circumstances, the bureaucracy will slip into its dominating practices; after all, teachers, psychologists, and administrators are busy. Parents, too, have other demands on their time. Empowerment is draining as well as exhilarating; subordinate roles are familiar and quiet. The system should not have let the social movement groups, the training sessions, and the use of the parent advocates decline.

In other areas that I have been working, I have found similar kinds of discretionary decisions where powerful officials enter into conversations with dependent people, where information and decision-making authority are shared. The dependent people become partners, in effect, in the exercise of discretion. There is an alteration in power relations. One area is in medicine, and the other is community-based care for the frail, elderly poor.[16]

Most of the time, informed consent in health care operates as most decisions in special education: informed consent is a legal, bureaucratic hurdle that the physician has to negotiate; there is no real communication; the task of the physician is to get the patient to sign the form to protect the physician from malpractice liability. Power has not changed. The paradigmatic example is the surgeon presenting the form the night before surgery. Informed consent works differently with the chronically ill. There, the task of the physician is to get the patient to come to accept the chronic condition *and* to participate in the therapy (President's Commission, 1983; Katz 1984). A prominent example are renal-dialysis patients. Here, patients become extremely knowledgeable; they become very active in their treatment; they often speak in jargon and diagnose their own problems; and doctors listen. Patients are encouraged to learn about alternatives and are given real choice (Lidz and Meisel 1983).

Community-based care programs for the frail, elderly poor are demonstration projects designed to provide cheaper, more effective

---

[16] These examples are more fully discussed in Handler 1988.

care to people who are at risk of becoming nursing-home residents. The clients are typically very old, single, usually women, who either have no family or are cared for by an adult daughter, who may very well be in her sixties, and not all that well herself. The clients need help in a variety of activities of daily life—transportation, chore services, nutrition, bathing, toileting, and health needs. For most of the elderly in this situation, home care is provided by spouses or other family, but for those without such supports, or where the support is having great difficulty in helping, then unless this care is provided, there will be rapid deterioration and the client will have to be institutionalized.

I have been researching three voluntary agencies in the Los Angeles area that are operating community-based care programs. While the programs vary somewhat, basically the agencies recruit clients, provide case management, and contract for services according to need. Most of the services are for the routine, mundane tasks of daily living—the most popular service is home help. If possible, the agencies work with the family. For a variety of reasons, the agencies have to enlist the active co-operation of the clients. Those who are familiar with the elderly know that it is no small matter to get the elderly to participate in service programs; not infrequently, they are fearful, confused, or have a determined, if not counter-productive, sense of independence. These agencies, however, have to do more than get the clients merely to accept the services that are offered. The clients have to be engaged—for example, they have to interview the home-help aides, supervise their work, and report to the agencies on the quality of the performance. The agencies assist in various ways, but they simply do not have the resources to provide this kind of close supervision. They rely on the clients, and, where available, family members, to provide the necessary information. As a result, instead of being passive recipients of services, the clients become active participants in the selection and supervision of a variety of services. They become part of the solution. This is often a difficult transition. It is accomplished through careful, patient conversations; clients and family are slowly brought along; confidences are established; gradually, agency staff and clients and family begin to rely on each other. There is co-operation based on understanding and trust.

These are three examples where consent or quiescence appears to meet the objections raised in the third dimension of power. In order for the dominant person—teacher, physician, social worker—to perform the professional task, the dependent person has to be an active, understanding participant. I stress the word understanding because the dominant person relies on the dependent person for accurate information and judgment. In order to have this kind of participation, the dependent person has to have discretion, the ability to consider alternatives. At least in some respects, this satisfies the empirical concerns about the third dimension of power—how do we know that there is genuine consent. Here, potential conflicts (alternatives) are considered. We also have the kind of trust that Baier is talking about—where, under the expressibility test, if the reasons for the relationship are disclosed, the relationship would be strengthened. Power has been altered in two senses. It has been altered instrumentally but it has also been altered constitutively. The self-conceptions, the ideologies, of the empowered persons have been changed.

How much change, and how significant? As the Madison special-education example shows, the kind of transformative empowerment that occurred is both partial and transitory. It is partial in the sense that it may only apply to the particular transactions between the parents and the teachers over the specific programs for the students. Further, it may not apply to the full range of alternatives; the parents (as well as the teachers) may be constrained within an unduly limited set of alternatives. The teachers are still middle-class professionals employed by a bureaucracy; the parents are still dependent people— in my example, of lower socio-economic status. Even though the frail, elderly poor did remarkably well in their associations with the agencies, they are very dependent people—very old, quite infirm, alone, and poor. One would hope that the moral values developed in these relationships would have effects in other arenas—that teachers, doctors, and social workers would be more responsive to dependent people who come their way, and, similarly, that dependent people would use their enhanced self-conception in their other relationships. Gaventa thinks that power and consciousness are self-propelling and that dependent people will use their new-found consciousness and empowerment in additional situations; he reports on examples of small West Virginia communities oppressed by coal-mine operators (1980: Part IV). As expected, there is contrary evidence. So we are talking about meeting the objections of the third dimension of power in an important, but nevertheless selected, area; in other areas, in other relationships between agencies and clients, and in other relations with these very same people, power may still be exercised in the conventional manner. The participatory examples are enclaves, alternative practices, within larger, hierarchical structures.

Moreover, the relationships may also be transitory. We saw that, in the Madison example, insufficient attention was being paid to renewal, and there was evidence that old patterns were reasserting themselves. In the medical area, it has been verified that, when the renal-dialysis patients become acute-care patients, they and their physicians revert to the traditional role. With the frail, elderly poor, the case managers have constantly to work with the clients to maintain their active, understanding participation.

These limitations should not be surprising. Lawyers especially put too much faith in the relevance and durability of process, but process is always molded by substantive events. Partial relationships may be necessary for autonomy; even communitarian philosophers worry about the social distance (Unger 1975: 279; MacIntyre 1984: 142–3). The task is to discover the conditions which will facilitate the creation and nurturing of empowerment in discretionary dependent relationships, not to search for some magical procedural formula.

To illustrate more sharply the issues that are raised with dependent people, I will use an example from Keith Hawkins—water-pollution-control in England—where power relations are more-or-less equal (Hawkins 1984). Hawkins studied field-level decisions in two very large areas. Instead of 'going-by-the-book' regulation, the enforcement agents initially relied on negotiation. Prosecution was always in the background, but resort to the legal machinery was regarded as a failure by the agency. The normative framework for the agency–industry interaction was the social and moral ambivalence of water-pollution-control regulation—there were always competing economic demands—as well as the ambiguous nature of much of the conduct; while sometimes clearly blameworthy, this was more often than not the result of accident. Judgments of blameworthiness mediated the strict enforcement of the law; sanctions were imposed if violations were deliberate, or, if negligent, accompanied by unco-operativeness. When conduct was judged accidental and the industry was co-operative, then agents would give warnings, advice, information, and consultation. They would concentrate on the major problems, insisting on only a few 'consent' conditions; the emphasis was on surveillance and prevention, preserving relations and building new ones. Co-operative relations relieved the industry from the burdens of prosecution; in return, the agency had easy access to property, information, and the ability to raise sensitive topics. Hawkins observed that it was not unusual for the industry to self-report its breaches of the law.

As with the previous examples, there are large elements of trust in the water-pollution-control example; the actors trusted each other to abide by the rules. Nevertheless, it was a different form of trust. What would the test of expressibility show? It would show that this use of discretion in a co-operative style of regulation works because of the avoidance of the costs of strict enforcement. Both the agency and the industry will have lower costs if they co-operate rather than fight. This is not a 'morally rotten' kind of trust where exposure of motives destabilizes the relationship; in fact, clarity would strengthen the relationship. But knowledge of the respective costs of enforcement are not *common goods*, such as mutual respect, love, goodwill, and professional pride. Co-operation is not the common good; it is only instrumental to reducing individual costs; if the costs of one of the parties begins to exceed benefits, then co-operation ceases. Co-operation, then, in the regulatory example, can be based on trust or on suspicion or fear—as long as there is clear information. Niklas Luhmann makes the point that 'distrust is not just the *opposite* of trust; it is also a *functional equivalent* for trust' (1980: 71). In the water-pollution-control example, distrust would work as long as the parties had good information as to their relative costs. Luhmann goes on to point out that the strategies of distrust are usually more difficult and burdensome, and require more energy; hence, 'relatively, trust is the easier option, and for this reason there is a strong incentive to begin a relationship with trust' (ibid.: 1980: 72; see also Barber 1983: 21).

In the water-pollution example, there has not been an altering of power relations; what is usually presumed is that two relatively equal parties are dealing with each other. While they both will be better off, and thus there is change, power has not been changed. In the Madison special-education example, while there was no change in economic and social positions, power was altered; the parents moved from dependent persons to equal moral agents.[17] The change on the part of the parents was constitutive in the sense that their ideologies changed—their conception of themselves and their relationship with the teachers. Constitutive and transformative empowerment is not

[17] Lukes (1986: 4) says that, while affecting behaviour is certainly a centrally important form of power, co-operative and communicative aspects of empowerment are also aspects of power.

necessarily implied in instrumental co-operation. In the Madison example, the relationship thrived on goodwill, mutual respect, and altruism, qualities which were not necessarily excluded but also not necessarily included in the water-pollution-control example.

With instrumental regulation, we are in the first dimension of power. Conflicts, or potential conflicts, are readily observable; each party brings what resources it has to the decision-making arena; and the outcome can be observed. This, of course, is quite clear with command-and-control regulation. Co-operative relations, as in Hawkins's example, are not as readily transparent, but still not that conceptually nor empirically difficult. The exchanges are usually observable, especially if the relationship extends over time. When power becomes more unequal, however, then quiescence becomes more problematic; we are in the second and third dimensions. This would be how special-education decisions are normally decided—in most jurisdictions there is consent, and one does not know whether there are no grievances, or grievances are not pressed, or grievances never become conscious. This is also how most decisions are made in health care and care for the frail and elderly. Quiescence becomes less problematic when the expressibility test is satisfied.

Structuring Empowerment

If discretion is not be used to manipulate or coerce the dependent client, then how are clients to be empowered? In many of Baier's (1986) examples, dependent people become equal moral agents solely through values such as love, mutual respect, altruism, and professional pride. Many have argued for such values in client–bureaucracy relations, such as informed consent in health care (Katz 1984) and social work (W. Simon 1986). In the principal example that I used—the special-education program in Madison, Wisconsin—plus the two other illustrations (renal dialysis and community-based care for the frail and elderly poor), there were the humanistic values of mutual respect, altruism, and professional pride, but there was also something more, what I call *reciprocal concrete incentives*. That is, the bureaucrat or agent (teacher, physician, case manager) could not perform his or her professional task unless the parent, patient, or client participated as an equal moral agent, that is, *actively* co-operated on the basis of understanding and trust. In other words, although I distinguished these examples from Hawkins's water-pollution-control example by pointing out that, in the latter, co-operation was based only on instrumentalism, the other examples also had strong instrumental elements. They were more than instrumentalist, but I want to emphasize that instrumentalism was at the base. To state the matter most directly: the power relationships are so unequal when dependent people are dealing with large-scale public agencies that, unless there are strong, reciprocal, concrete incentives, I do not believe that the humanistic values of mutual respect, love, altruism, and professional pride are enough to sustain equal moral agency, at least in the long run. In the examples that I use, active, understanding participation was necessary if the teacher, physician, or case manager was to perform satisfactorily his or her professional task. More than reciprocal, concrete incentives are required; they are a necessary but not sufficient condition; but they are required. Power must serve the interests of the powerful; that is not disputed (Lukes 1986: 5). But, in these examples, the interests are even better served by empowering the client.

How, then, do dependent clients acquire these valuable resources? Hasenfeld, it will be recalled, argues that social work practice is the exchange of resources; therefore, the way to alter power relations is to increase client resources. Clients have to have sufficient resources to be able to make choices and exercise more control over their environment; this is the theory of empowerment—the capacity to control one's environment. Social work practice has to shift from an individual-oriented practice, where there is the tendency to blame the victim, to a more structural orientation—to 'help people to connect with needed resources, negotiate problematic situations, and change existing social structures . . .' (Hasenfeld 1987: 478).

If clients have valued resources, such as money, particular characteristics, or collective support, then they can negotiate favorable outcomes with the worker. According to Hasenfeld, the greatest resource is the ability to choose alternatives. He argues that there are four ways in which clients can gain power in the social service environment: reducing the need for services; increasing the range of alternatives; increasing their value to those whose services and resources they need; and reducing the alternatives available to those whose resources and services they need. Empowerment must occur at all levels in the organization—between the worker and the client, at the organizational level, and at the policy level. Strategies at the worker level include increasing information and knowledge, assertive training and improving personal skills, increasing collective strength, and improving links to alternatives. At the organizational level, clients have to become a more important interest group. Workers can help by adopting empowerment-based practice technologies and press for the adoption of different kinds of accountability measures—ones that emphasize empowerment rather than social control—for example, the degree of fairness and equity, client freedom of choice, the mobilization of resources, client feedback and evaluation, and so forth. At the policy level, there has to be an increase in client control over resources—for example, vouchers—and the availability of alternative services.

In short, Hasenfeld calls on social workers to engage in a wide range of political activities that 'transcend the boundaries of their own agencies and professional specializations' (1987: 479). He relies heavily on the workers to change the definitions of their professional tasks. Client empowerment would come about through a redefinition of professional norms.

The idea of reciprocal, concrete incentives incorporates this redefinition, but it is also something more—the incentives increase the client's value to the worker and thereby encourage change in the power relationship. With reciprocal incentives, if the client fails, the worker fails; thus, the worker has a professional stake in empowerment. This is not inconsistent with changes in professional norms and ideologies; but, since professional norms and ideologies are often used to manipulate or suffocate grievances, the presence of reciprocal concrete incentives gives one more confidence about the meaning of consent.

While Hasenfeld casts his analysis in terms of political economy, it is evident that the structural changes that he calls for will also affect the cultural contexts of the participants. To the extent that the organization and the relative positions of the actors are destabilized through shifts in power relationships, then ideologies and beliefs change; through changes in structure and roles, the agency and the worker–client relationship will take on different meanings.

Incorporating client participation into field-level decision-making requires basic changes in the ideology and structure of public programs. There has to be decentralization and a conscious effort to create and structure arenas of discretion; there has to be informalism within parameters rather than rigid rules; and there has to be professional autonomy. This involves a rethinking of law, administration, bureaucracy, and the role of social movement organizations.[18] The top-down ideological framework is not only inaccurate descriptively, but also harmful to client participation. Structures have to allow sufficient space to allow for flexibility and choice; in Hawkins's (1986) terms, there has to be a framework for discretion that encourages participation.

Creating frameworks by itself, however, will be insufficient; after all, that is what the procedural requirements of the Education for All Handicapped Children Act tried to do and the law of informed consent in medicine requires. In addition, steps have to be taken so that the incentives for bureaucratic domination do not become manifest. This requires a new kind of professionalism that Hasenfeld and others have called for and that we saw in the Madison school system (Hasenfeld 1983; W. Simon 1986). It also means that important funding formulas have to restructured. In special education, for example, most formulas reward speedy, not thoughtful, participatory decisions, and permanent rather than experimental decisions. In medicine, physicians are paid for medical services, not conversations. On the other hand, the reimbursement formula encouraged participation with the community-based care for the frail and elderly poor. Similarly, accountability procedures have to be rethought. Program integrity is important, but there is often great pressure to standardize operations into objectively verifiable units, and the effects of this quantitative monitoring often produce profound distortions. Activities are shaped to produce desirable statistical quotas. These internal control measures have to be changed to encourage the goals of participation. The frail and elderly poor example provides one approach: there, client information not only contributed to empowerment (clients possessed an important resource) but also provided valuable regulatory data on quality. Client evaluative feedback can be encouraged in other areas; for example, hearings and other kinds of dispute resolution procedures should be viewed as a window on administration.[19]

The field-level environment has to be changed to encourage the new professional. If there are inadequate resources, if workers are overwhelmed, then routinization supplants discretion. Conversely, to

---

[18] See Handler and Zatz 1982 for a description and application of the above theory of implementation in the context of deinstitutionalization programmes for juvenile status offenders.

[19] In the 1960s, prior to *Goldberg* v. *Kelly* 397 US 254 (1970), the Supreme Court case that established the right to an administrative hearing in statutory entitlement cases, the Wisconsin District Director system used county-generated fair hearings as a method of learning about weaknesses in county administration (Handler 1969).

the extent that workers control resources, they will be able to encourage and reward client participation. The staff not only needs a commitment to client empowerment; it also has to have the resources.

Dependent clients, too, need resources; merely providing the opportunities to participate will not be sufficient. Psychological burdens, of course, will vary; some clients will be able to take advantage of the opportunities being offered, but others will not. Here, it would seem that social-movement groups are crucial. Groups provide solidarity, encouragement, and information. They show the clients that they are not alone, that others share their burdens; they can collectivize grievances. Groups can provide training and experts. Clients need groups in order to be able to participate—recall one of the reasons for the co-optation that seems to be going in Madison is probably the decline of the parent groups. This means that the bureaucracy also needs the groups if it is to get the kind of client participation that it wants. In other words, autonomous client groups have to be part of the implementation framework. The professional task is reconceptualized so that clients are part of the solution, but, in order for clients to participate, client groups have to be part of the solution as well.

The fact of discretion is inevitable in the modern social welfare state, and, as long as government and large-scale agencies are serving and regulating the disadvantaged, then the problems of unfair power in the exercise of discretion must be addressed. The solutions of the legal-rights revolution—the reduction of discretion through the application of tightly drawn legal rules, and the enforcement of those rules through procedural due process, that is, the assertion of the rule of law—has limited application, especially since procedural due process protections are such a problematic remedy for the vast majority of dependent people. Instead, discretion must be addressed more positively, more creatively; ways have to be explored that will restructure relationships to empower dependent clients. This requires changes in professional ideologies, redesigning reciprocal incentives, and providing resources to clients so that they can participate. Still, one must proceed cautiously. The examples that I have outlined are special and fragile. While they may indicate beginnings, it must not be forgotten that they exist in small corners of large-scale, hierarchical structures.

11. The Jurisprudence of Discretion: Escaping the Legal Paradigm

NICOLA LACEY

> Jurisprudence misses many realities about justice because it is much too concerned with judges and legislators and not enough with administrators, executives, police and prosecutors. Furthermore, jurisprudence acknowledges the law–discretion dichotomy and then spends itself almost entirely on the law half . . .
>
> We need a new jurisprudence that will encompass all of justice, not just the easy half of it.
>
> Davis 1969: pp. vi, 233

IN the twenty years since Davis expressed these ideas, much has changed. Lawyers and legal theorists have increasingly come to recognize the insights of Davis's work, and no longer ignore the existence of the areas of discretionary justice which he was concerned to bring to the light of day (Bell 1983; Craig 1983; Harlow and Rawlings 1984; Baldwin 1985). There can be little doubt that the intellectual movement spawned by his work has had important and positive effects in terms of broadening our conception of the legally relevant and forging some links between legal and other social science approaches to the understanding of discretion in legal contexts (Adler and Asquith 1981*a*; Hawkins 1984).

However, Davis's fundamental insight—that lawyers should be concerned with the existence and control of discretionary power—has raised as many intellectual and political problems as it has solved. For the persistent difficulty, exemplified in the work of Davis himself, is that, when lawyers open their minds to new areas of study, they do not necessarily also open their minds to the appropriateness (or lack of it) of applying conventional legal analysis and solutions to the newly discovered areas. The project which I shall embark upon in this chapter is that of identifying and subjecting to critical examination the world-view and concerns with which lawyers and legal theorists typically approach the question of discretion.

Some clear examples of the kind of problem which I shall try to address arise in the work of Davis himself. For instance, Davis speaks uncritically of the 'law–discretion dichotomy', and advocates the extension of typically legal methods of confining, structuring, and controlling discretion—the imposition of law-like standards and generalizations: 'The courts could have been enlisted to help determine what discretionary power is necessary and what is unnecessary; if that had been their assignment, I think a good deal of today's excessive discretionary power could have been avoided' (Davis 1969: 50–1). The assumption not only that distinctively legal methods and techniques exist, but also that their application to areas of discretionary power is unproblematic, underlies the whole argument. Davis is not troubled by the further insight that once we, as lawyers, extend our horizons, we must be ready to learn about the limitations of traditional legal method from these new areas, rather than simply applying those methods unadapted with boundless enthusiasm. Indeed, the limitations of legal methods have been widely recognized by social scientists: 'the attempt to control regulatory enforcement primarily by external legal requirements is deeply troublesome insofar as it induces in both inspectors and the regulated an attitude of legal defensiveness; a concern for adequate documentation rather than substantive achievement, and a degree of rule-bound rigidity' (Kagan 1984*b*: 58). So the 'discovery' of 'discretion' should make us not only question the way in which we define 'law', 'legal contexts' and 'legally relevant' issues, but also reflect on the general appropriateness of legal method and on whether 'legal' controls are always effective in 'legally relevant' areas (including those where they have traditionally been applied).

The question, then, has to do with the extent of relevance of what I shall call 'the legal paradigm'—that is, the typically legal and jurisprudential way or ways of looking at the world, constructing disputes, identifying 'problems', and framing solutions. I shall start out from a basic characterization of legal method as it has developed in many modern Western systems such as those of Britain and the United States, as the subjection of areas of human conduct and practice to regulation according to clear, prospective, publicly announced general rules or rule-like standards. Problems are typically seen as arising from ambiguities or 'gaps' in the rules, calling for clearer interpretations or further legislative or quasi-legislative action. Disputes are seen as calling for resolution on the basis of the given rules and according to standards of due process. This approach is closely associated with the ideal of the 'rule of law' and hence with liberalism as a doctrine of political morality.

The problem raised by the status of this approach as the 'legal paradigm' is a particularly intractable one. This is because the project of persuading lawyers that they should interest themselves in discretion seems to proceed on the assumption that lawyers do have some special insights to bring and contributions to make to these areas, as well as things to learn from them. Yet there is a possibility that a thorough critique of the 'legal paradigm' might collapse into either a general scepticism about the need for lawyers to take a broader approach at all, or the view that lawyers must simply become, or defer to, other types of social scientist. In pursuing the project I have set out, I shall explore the relevance of the issue of discretion for lawyers, legal theorists, and social scientists, and try to make some progress with the general issue of how our concerns and methods relate to each other and what, if anything, we may learn from each other. I shall begin with a brief review of social science concerns in the study of discretion, followed by a discussion of typical legal and jurisprudential approaches to discretion. This will lead to a critique of the failure of lawyers and legal theorists adequately to address the dilemma of the legal paradigm, which threatens to turn a potentially broadening and enlightening development into a piece of intellectual and practical imperialism in which lawyers merely incorporate ever more inappropriate areas of activity into their own analytic and political framework. Ultimately, it will be suggested that the real insights provided by the intellectual movement which we are considering should lead us to reject any dichotomy between legal and social science approaches. Rather, we should recognize the importance of a pluralistic approach to the issues raised by the existence of discretionary power in legal contexts, seen as a pervasive form of social and political power.

The Importance of Discretion as a Social Science and Jurisprudential Issue

It can no longer be doubted that both social scientists and legal theorists recognize the importance of discretion as a focus for research. However, the central concerns of the legal and social science approaches tend to differ. Social scientists (who of course themselves exemplify a variety of perspectives and concerns), and in particular sociologists, stress the prevalence of discretion at every stage of administration—in policy-creation, policy-implementation, problem-identification, and indeed the very definition of issues—in a wide variety of institutional, practical, and political contexts. They typically understand discretion broadly, without becoming too concerned with the analytical issue of its definition which tends to preoccupy legal theorists. The idea that discretion exists whenever the effective limits on power leave an official free to make a choice among possible courses of action (Davis 1969: 4) suffices for the moment to characterize the approach—although we should note that important questions have been raised about whether it is possible or useful to distinguish discretion from decision-making power in general (G. Smith 1981). Sociologists have also drawn our attention to the diversity of functions which discretion can serve, for example in allowing ideological gaps between the rhetoric and substance of the law to be managed (McBarnet 1981); obscuring lack of consensus or unpopular or ambiguous aspects of policy (Prosser 1981); pre-empting the use of formal legal controls (Hawkins 1984), as well as straightforwardly conferring political and administrative power.

Sociologists' recognition of discretion as a crucially important and pervasive source of executive power has also led to an emphasis on the importance of context in understanding the nature of discretion. This acknowledgement of context-relativity has generated not only detailed empirical investigations of the exercise of discretion in particular areas (Hawkins 1984; Baldwin 1985) but also an increasing concern to gather an appreciation of agents' own understandings of their discretionary actions. Thus the meaning and significance of those decisions and actions to the agents undertaking them, the basis on which they act or make decisions, and their understanding of the significance of discretion in making those decisions and undertaking those actions have become an important focus. This interpretive, 'phenomenological', agent-centred approach has in turn generated insights relating to the existence among those who exercise discretion of 'operational ideologies', 'frames of relevance', or 'assumptive worlds'—systems of values and beliefs which allow agents to make sense of, to impose explanations on, and to order events in the world in which they are operating (Emerson 1969; Young 1981; Asquith 1983). Such studies have shown the importance of discretion in disguising and mediating conflicts between these operational ideologies and between different appreciations of institutional objectives which exist both at various stages of administrative processes and even within the viewpoints of particular actors in those processes. A good example of the illuminating nature of this approach lies in the work of Stuart Asquith (1983). His study of juvenile justice in Scotland and in England and Wales describes how, in the context of wide discretionary power, competing ideologies of welfare and punishment turn out not to be in the kind of direct conflict which might be assumed by legal theory. These ideologies relate to the broader professional ideologies of the many groups involved and, in particular, to lay, 'common-sense' understandings of the causes and nature of juvenile delinquency which underpin the operational ideologies of magistrates and lay members of children's panels. Asquith shows how these ideologies and frames of relevance interact with each other to produce a situation in which articulated institutional (i.e. legal) goals are generally subverted or at least distorted.

Thus modern social science has gradually developed empirical and analytical approaches to discretion which generate a complex and sophisticated picture of its existence, who exercises it, and on what basis. Social sciences approaches have also recognized the importance of studying structural and organizational factors (in Asquith's case, the form of the hearing and the nature of the groups involved), and of taking into account the political climate in which areas of discretionary power operate (Prosser 1977; Baldwin 1985). It is worth emphasizing (because it explodes a myth believed in by some lawyers) that it would be a gross distortion to see social science as purely empirical in the crude sense of being interested in quantitative assessments of the operation of particular areas of discretion. Nor indeed would it be apt to see social science as confined to qualitative but 'external' observations of practices in the relevant areas. Inevitably, an empirically based social science approach dictates a certain wariness towards the generalizations of 'grand theory', with a corresponding attention to the complexities of the operation of discretion in particular contexts. But its focus on detail and on agents' own understandings is itself theoretically informed in a fundamental and sophisticated way, not so much by normative political theory but rather by the insights of social theory concerning human behaviour, motivation, and organization. Quite clearly, the insights of social science in this area have important implications for the legal and political project of structuring or controlling discretionary power.

The subtlety of the best social science approaches is not always matched in jurisprudential studies of discretion. However, like social scientists, jurists adopt a number of different approaches, which need to be distinguished for the purposes of exposition, despite their interdependence and frequent coexistence in particular jurisprudential studies. Perhaps most obviously, jurists have been concerned to define discretion in the tradition of analytical jurisprudence. Thus many discussions proceed from Dworkin's famous distinction between two different kinds of discretion (1977*b*): 'weak' discretion, which consists in either having to exercise powers of judgment, or being the final arbiter; and 'strong' discretion, which means not being bound by standards set by any authority. The adequacy of Dworkin's conceptualization (which, it is important to note, was formulated in the context of a discussion of adjudication) has, of course, been called into question. Galligan, for example (1986*a*), points out that discretion may more naturally be regarded as a question of degree: there is no absolute distinction between weak and strong discretion, for in most areas the context in which a decision is made will furnish some standards or at least exclude some criteria as irrelevant, just as in most areas the existing standards are not decisive in constraining a particular decision. Galligan, too, however, employs the analytical method, albeit in a way which is more sensitive to the importance of context than is Dworkin's approach. Identifying discretion as the existence of 'a sphere of autonomy within which one's decisions are in some degree a matter of personal judgment and assessment' (ibid.: 8), Galligan distinguishes between discretion at the policy-making stage, at the stage of determining the facts, and at the stage of applying policy or rules to the facts.

I shall return below to the adequacy of this kind of analytical approach. It is interesting to note at this point, however, the way in which Dworkin's analysis of judicial discretion (and concern to marginalize it and even to deny its existence) leads him to develop an extended conception of law, encompassing 'principles' as well as rules. This illustrates not only the contribution which reflection on discretionary areas can make to jurisprudential analysis, but also, and even more significantly, the way in which traditional legal theory responds to the challenge of discretion by reinterpreting the world so as to accommodate it within legal or quasi-legal categories. This is, of course, a method which expresses in a pure form the legal paradigm referred to above. The same point may be made in relation to Nonet's and Selznick's (1978) conception of 'responsive law', which, like Dworkin's *Taking Rights Seriously*, extends our conception of law in a way which recognizes the importance of substantive values (purposes, in the case of Nonet and Selznick) rather than merely formal procedures or pedigree tests in identifying law. In reflecting on discretion, the further question arises as to whether jurisprudence can match these extended conceptions of law with a more thoroughgoing revision of legal ideology and methodology.

Neither Galligan nor Dworkin, of course, is solely concerned with analysing the concept of discretion; this is rather a preliminary to a discussion of a variety of normative questions which form the other main kind of jurisprudential project in this area. Thus Dworkin is concerned to deny, primarily on political grounds, the existence of strong judicial discretion; and Galligan is concerned with the legitimacy and efficacy of discretionary power in a number of legal contexts. At the most general level, this kind of concern is represented in arguments of constitutional theory about the political legitimacy of discretionary power (Dworkin 1977*b*). Moving to more concrete levels, good examples would be discussions of accountability of holders of discretionary power in the administrative process (McAuslan and McEldowney 1985; Harden and Lewis 1986). This kind of normative jurisprudential concern has gradually generated a wide interest in questions about what kinds of (usually public) officials should have discretionary power, when, under what circumstances, and for what purposes. The general normative theory in this area has typically proceeded from a set of (often unarticulated) liberal political presuppositions according to which discretion raises the most important problems of control and justification when its exercise can affect individual rights (indeed Davis regarded only such cases as involving questions of discretionary 'justice'). Accordingly, the issue of control is often represented in terms of the protection of the individual from state or bureaucratic abuse (Davis 1969; Handler 1979). Thus the results of jurisprudential reflection have often consisted in prescriptions for an extension of legal methods of legitimation and control, confining and structuring discretion by means of rules and guidelines along the lines originally suggested by Davis in a wide variety of areas (Galligan 1976; Von Hirsch 1976; Gottfredson, Wilkins, and Hoffman 1978).

Finally, jurisprudential approaches to discretion sometimes proceed by way of empirical–analytical study of the sources of discretionary power; and here, perhaps, the insights of the social sciences have been adopted most fully. One example would be lawyers' increasing willingness to recognize that discretion does not have to be explicitly or even implicitly accorded by law, but can inhere in particular situations, as in the judicial discretion inherent in the power to direct the course of the trial, question witnesses, and so on, or the jury power to acquit without giving reasons (Kadish and Kadish 1973; Pattenden 1982). The influence of social science research can also be traced in the recognition that administrative processes which are designed to operate in either a rule-based or discretionary way sometimes do not operate as such in practice (Bradshaw 1981; Noble 1981)—for example, because decision-makers find latitude for discretionary interpretation in the rules, or exercise their discretion inflexibly on the basis of rules of thumb. Research in this area has also generated reflection on the significance of discretion in understanding official roles and points of view—such as those of judges, trial lawyers, police officers, and juries—about which legal theory has traditionally exhibited a puzzling lack of curiosity.

The Legal Paradigm, Jurisprudential Methodology and the Study of Discretion

What are the important features of the 'legal paradigm' which I have claimed to have potentially adverse effects on lawyers' approaches to discretion, and how do these relate to the methods and projects of legal theorists? After all, the legal theorist is not (or at least not always) speaking within legal discourse but rather purports to speak about it, to comment on it. Should jurisprudence itself not actually generate a conception and critique of the legal paradigm? This is certainly true of the work of some legal theorists (Unger 1976), but a substantial amount of conventional legal theory in fact proceeds on much the same assumptions about the appropriate ways of framing issues, about the salience of legal rather than administrative solutions, and with the same focus on adjudication as a decision-making method, as do lawyers. And this is, of course, not surprising, given that most legal theorists have been trained as lawyers and often teach or research on (and indeed practise) substantive law as well as legal theory. It is thus important to construct in more detail the substantive features of the legal paradigm, understood broadly as encompassing the world-view of both lawyers and legal theorists, and to relate this to certain prevalent characteristics of jurisprudential method which are influential in shaping its approach to discretion.

First and foremost, we need to consider the connection of the legal paradigm with the liberal legal ideology of the rule of law. As Fuller

(1969) argued, the idea of law can be characterized as the enterprise of subjecting human conduct to the governance of rules. This project distinguishes itself from managerial discretion, which, significantly, forms a major focus of critique for classic exponents of the doctrine of the rule of law such as Dicey (1915, 1959), who sought to insulate the legal sphere from that of discretion. Managerial discretion fails to live up to the rule-of-law ideal in that only the legal method aspires to operate by way of clear, promulgated, prospective, stable, general rules which are consistently applied and possible to comply with. Managerial discretion, by contrast, is seen as unconstrained by any such norms, and tends to be associated with the arbitrary and even capricious exercise of power. The question of whether the rule-of-law ideal in fact generates any substantive values is one which has been a focus of lively debate in legal theory (Unger 1976; Raz 1979; Finnis 1980; see also below) and on which there is still no consensus. Yet the central place which the rule of law occupies in liberal legal ideology and method is clear, for the ideal of subjecting areas of legally relevant activity to general standards, whether substantive or procedural, lies at the heart of the legal paradigm. Thus, in so far as this method of control is inappropriate in certain areas, the relevance of legal analysis and method will be severely limited if it is genuinely the case that the boundaries of liberal legal ideology cannot be widened or, perhaps, transcended.

Furthermore, continuing espousal of the rule-of-law ideal leads many legal theorists to hold on to the law–discretion dichotomy, even whilst acknowledging the relevance and indeed pervasiveness of discretionary action in legal spheres. Thus, theorists who are willing to recognize the political and creative aspects of adjudication (Mac-Cormick 1978; Bell 1983) nevertheless tend to maintain an essentially liberal framework which insists on the special suitability of certain kinds of questions (typically those involving individual rights) for judicial resolution. This kind of jurisprudential approach to judicial discretion flows in part from the centrality of courts in jurists' conception and in part from association of the rule-of-law ideal with the value of formal justice (treat like cases alike) and with the protection of individual rights. The emphasis laid on formal justice relates to the importance of the notion of rationality in the liberal world-view: faith in the idea that openness, rationality, consistency, generality, and predictability (values centrally located in the rule-of-law ideal) will conduce to fairness—exemplified in Galligan's 'public-law model'

(1986*a*: 86 ff.). This conception of fairness is irreducibly process-oriented—reflecting the traditional insistence of legal ideology on a clear distinction between review of process and appeal on the merits.

Further, its roots in liberal legal ideology have meant that the juristic approach has tended, in line with the starting-point of traditional, Diceyan constitutional theory, to focus on discretionary power of a public rather than a private nature. This flows from the fact that the focus of traditional liberal political theory is exclusively the legitimation of public power. On this view, discretion in the public sphere automatically raises the issue of justification and legitimation, is always seen as a potential threat to individual rights, and hence calls for control or checking through the articulation of law-like standards, whereas private power raises no such difficulty. Thus, despite a growing theoretical recognition of the 'compenetration' of public and private spheres, and the ultimate impossibility of distinguishing between public and private power, early studies of discretion have tended to focus on, for example, sentencing by judges and magistrates or the decisions of regulatory agencies set up by government. Only relatively recently has attention begun to be focused on areas such as the (self-)regulation of companies, the adequacy of economic control by the market in the context of privatization, and the contractual activities of public bodies (Baldwin and McCrudden 1987). And even lawyers who do criticize and reject any dichotomy between public and private tend to stop short (with some notable exceptions (Frug 1984)) of the admission that the implication of the critique is that *all* power must be encompassed within our reflections on the legitimacy and effective use of discretion.

Another important aspect of the legal paradigm consists in the fact that legal methodology, and hence many jurisprudential approaches, operate typically by way of generalization. This is true both in terms of the way in which legal discourse uses relatively fixed conceptual categories and in terms of jurisprudential approaches to the empirical plane. Beginning with the conceptual level, legal theorists tend to proceed by way of characterizations of phenomena which then form the basis for normative argument. For example, in discussing controls on discretionary power, legal theorists would typically classify them in terms such as political, legal, or executive; organizational and structural or external and responsive; remedial or preventive; reactive or proactive; retrospective or prospective; review based or appeal based; systematic or *ad hoc*. Similarly, lawyers tend to construct the world in terms of dichotomized categories such as public and private spheres; substantive or procedural issues; bipolar or polycentric issues. This kind of argument tends to picture the world as 'pigeonholed' in a number of rather rigid categories, which often do not correspond to the understandings of the agents involved in the processes in question or to common-sense understandings. It also tends to set up oppositions or dichotomies which constantly ask us to make 'either/or' decisions, suggesting that reality comes with particular labels attached, those labels being radically inconsistent with other labels. Thus, legal discourse presents a monolithic, black-and-white view of the world, and sets this view up, moreover, as 'objective reality' or 'truth'. This is reflected, as Dworkin has observed, in the assumption underlying judicial reasoning that there is a 'right answer' to disputed cases—an assumption which represents the debate between trial lawyers as an argument about 'legal truth' or 'the facts of the matter' (1977*b*). Thus, the marginalization of alternative views of reality and understandings of the world is actually built in to legal reasoning and method.

The conceptual approach which I have outlined combines in jurisprudence with a somewhat cavalier approach to empirical questions. This takes the form of limited empirical observation followed by generalization using fixed legal concepts. Discussions of discretion often set out from a list of hypotheses, presented as facts, about the relative advantages and disadvantages of 'rules versus discretion'—a misleading legal dichotomy if ever there was one (American Friends Service Committee 1971: 124–44; Harlow and Rawlings 1984; Cane 1986: 64–5; Galligan 1986*a*: 169–83). For example, it is often stated that discretion tends to encourage efficiency, professional motivation, the individualization of decisions, speed, and flexibility. On the other hand, it can also engender inefficiency by encouraging the unnecessary consideration of each decision afresh, unfairness through individualization on the basis of suspect criteria, disparity, secrecy, lack of accountability, abuse of power, and uncertainty. This kind of assertion may be perfectly sensible at a very general level, but, when it is approached in discussions of discretion in particular areas as though it had the status of unproblematic truth, it is unjustified. For it cannot replace the social science project of detailed examination of discretion in particular contexts informed by an appreciation of the agents' own understandings and the experiences of clients and other participants. The methodology of conceptualization and generalization generates jurisprudential assertion and conclusion which goes way beyond the competence of the distinctive mode of analysis and prescription which it might offer.

Finally, the legal paradigm is exemplified by a belief in the importance of the law and of courts and court-like procedures in dealing with the existence of discretion. This is evidenced, as I shall try to show, by a tendency to emphasize the need to bring such discretion as is reluctantly determined to be necessary within the 'legal umbrella' by regulating it by means of general rules and standards and by subjecting its exercise to legal scrutiny, for example, by way of allowing challenge by way of appeal to tribunals or judicial review. Moreover, the insistence that discretion be exercised in accordance with fair procedures, which we have seen to be central to liberal legal ideology, is informed by a peculiarly legal conception of fair process—indeed a conception which, in its paradigm expression as natural justice, uses the adversarial trial process as its model. Lawyers have been relatively slow to develop an interest in a wider range (for example, primarily organizational or political) approaches to the legitimation of discretionary power.

Legal Approaches to Discretion

Having made some very general comments about the legal and social science approaches to discretion and the nature of the legal paradigm, I shall now consider some examples of actual legal and jurisprudential studies and the extent to which they exemplify the features I have discussed. I have already noted the growing interest of lawyers in discretionary areas and the accompanying recognition of a blurring of the boundaries between public and private power with the growth of state involvement in a variety of administrative processes and collective provision. In the legal field, one early sign of these developments was an increased interest in administrative law at an academic level and a rejection of the marginalization of public law dictated by Dicey's narrow conception of law. This was matched by a growing willingness on the part of the British courts to contemplate reviewing the actions of administrative bodies and to articulate 'principles' of judicial review (Craig 1983). Thus we have seen the courts reviewing the activities of a wide array of bodies—the BBC, immigration authorities, social security tribunals, ministers, professional bodies, trade unions, local authorities, and so on—on the basis of breaches of natural justice, failure to exercise discretion, or misuse or abuse of discretion.

This represents a significant extension of the role of the courts relative to their previous practice and to the former expectations of the legal profession as a whole. However, legal ideology has maintained the fiction that the courts are involved strictly in review rather than appeal; in other words, that they are concerned only with the legitimacy of the *process* whereby discretionary decisions are made and not with the merits of those decisions. This focus on fair process is a direct reflection of liberal legal ideology both in its implicit faith in the idea that fair process in some sense guarantees substantive fairness and in its contribution to the liberal view of the neutrality of the judiciary, whose constitutional status (most clearly in Britain, but also, arguably, in the United States (Dworkin 1977*b*)) dictates that they do not become involved in political questions. Rather, they should simply exercise a specialized, discrete legal expertise (the muddying of the descriptive and prescriptive waters on this issue is again exemplified in the work of Dworkin (1977*b*)). Yet open-ended standards of review such as the test of 'Wednesbury' unreasonableness used by the British courts (Craig 1983: 353 ff.), which classifies as unreasonable only those actions or decisions which 'no reasonable body could have made' on the basis of relevant evidence and standards, effectively allow the courts to intervene on the merits whilst also facilitating and legitimizing a deferential approach to the administration when that seems appropriate to the judges. The operative criteria of appropriateness are rarely spelt out in the cases, and have to be inferred from patterns of decisions. The insistence that review is concerned with decision-making *procedures* has hampered judicial participation in the development of articulated substantive goals of administration and has left administrative law on judicial review in a chronic state of uncertainty. Of course, the uncertainty can be partially dispelled, given that patterns of decisions in British judicial review cases invite a healthy scepticism about courts' pretensions to political neutrality. But this, in turn, has tempted commentators to an unduly reductivist critique which simply alleges judicial bias and makes little contribution to the important project of carefully building up an understanding of the ways in which and extent to which legal method does constrain the decisions of judges and other legal agents at an ideological as well as at an instrumental level (McAuslan and McEldowney 1986: 1–38).

This is not the place, however, to engage in a detailed discussion of developments in British judicial review. I shall rather select two particular areas where British lawyers have increasingly come to view discretionary decision-making and action as within their purview, so as to illustrate some of the features of legal method which I have identified and to demonstrate the persistence of the legal paradigm. In the first place, I shall consider the extension of the ambit of the 'rules of natural justice'. British administrative law has long recognized the applicability of two principles to judicial decision-making: that the parties should be given a fair hearing, and that the hearing should be before an impartial adjudicator: *audi alteram partem* and *nemo iudex in sua causa*. Indeed, these twin ideas are inextricably bound up with our (stereotypical) conception of adjudication as involving the decision of an impartial tribunal on the basis of pre-existing standards and in a manner which is strongly responsive to the arguments put by the parties (Fuller 1976). However, in the latter part of this century, the British courts have come to recognize the appropriateness of applying these standards of procedural justice outside the narrow confines of what are perceived as 'judicial decisions' concerning individual rights, to cover 'quasi-judicial' and even 'administrative' decisions (Craig 1983: 258–73). Decoding this prime example of legal conceptualization, what this amounts to is that the 'rules of natural justice' have come to be applied by the courts to areas of increasingly wide and visible discretionary power. But, as the ambit of natural justice has increased, so the courts have recognized the need to adapt the content of the rules so as to render them more flexible in applying to a new variety of contexts. Thus a fair hearing, originally interpreted strictly along the lines of the paradigm of a criminal trial, requiring oral hearing, cross-examination, legal representation, and so on, may now be satisfied in some contexts merely by providing an opportunity to make written representations. And the conception of an impartial arbiter has moved away from the judge to encompass the administrator who may well have prior knowledge of and views about a particular issue yet be regarded as a sufficiently unbiased decision-maker in the circumstances. Thus the content of natural justice has been diluted and rendered more flexible as its ambit has increased, incidentally giving rise to a yet wider *judicial* discretion than existed before.

The history of this development illustrates many of the general points I have noted about legal method. First, the applicability of the revised conception of natural justice to exercises of 'private power' is still a vexed issue in British administrative law, one good example being the question of the extent to which natural justice applies to dismissal decisions in the employment sphere, where the introduction of general principles of fair process by unfair dismissal legislation renders quite obscure any line between public and private (ibid.: 280–3). Secondly, the early approach's insistence on distinctions between administrative and judicial decisions (and between rights and privileges), which many commentators allege still to underlie decisions about the stringency of the procedural requirements made by the courts, illustrates the method of conceptualization discussed above. This method 'objectifies' particular categories and suppresses the way in which legal decision-makers *construct* the world in their own particular terms and from a specific perspective. Judges still argue for all the world as if decisions just *were* administrative or judicial, rather than being defined as such by those making or interpreting them. The modern approach to natural justice still assumes a world in which administrative policy-making and policy-application are discrete stages which call for different procedural standards, and in which the former stage is definitely less central to the enterprise of legal supervision and control than is the latter. Legal argument proceeds as if there were some basic truth, for example, to whether parole decisions are administrative or judicial, thus obscuring basic issues about who in practice has the power to make parole decisions, how they go about it, and what *should* be regarded as relevant criteria. This tendency is also reflected in academic commentary: for example, the labels 'bipolar' and 'polycentric' (Chayes 1976) tend to be applied in the context of critical discussions of the adequacy of the judicial process without sufficient recognition of the fact that issues can be moulded and constructed as bipolar or polycentric rather than being 'naturally' so. These assumptions about the discreteness of different categories are quite inconsistent with the findings of detailed research into the operation of complex administrative processes (Baldwin 1985).

Thirdly, although the extension of the ambit of natural justice has resulted in greater flexibility, it has not generated any major revision of the conception. Thus, reflecting the legal paradigm's insistence on the primacy of court-type processes, modern requirements of natural justice, referred to as the 'duty to act fairly', constitute an extension by analogy of standards designed to ensure a fair trial, and apposite to the resolution of certain kinds of questions in a certain kind of way. Having reached the insight that all areas of discretionary power should meet some standards of procedural justice, instead of asking themselves afresh, 'what procedural requirements would conduce to fair and effective decision-making and action in this area?', the courts have simply adapted by analogy the original principles. This has had several unfortunate effects. First of all, an important opportunity for debate about procedural justice—why we value it and how it relates to substantive justice—has been missed. Secondly, there has been a continued reluctance to challenge the liberal-legal tenet (which is built in to the very methodology of judicial review in distinguishing itself from appeal on the merits) that ensuring fair process is and should be the dominant legal goal in ensuring the substantive legitimacy of the administrative process. As we shall see below, the adequacy of this approach is highly questionable. Thirdly, standards of procedure apposite to one very distinctive mode of decision-making and dispute-resolution have been adapted, by use of somewhat murky argument by dubious analogy whose value premises and substantive criteria of likeness are left unexamined, to very different administrative and decision-making contexts. In these extended contexts, their effectiveness in either instrumental terms (improving the quality of decision-making or upholding respect for the system) or in terms of other substantive values (such as treating people involved with dignity and respect) may be doubted. This extension has also, incidentally, created a danger that the stringency with which the rules of natural justice are applied in areas to which they would always have been applied may be weakened. Finally, the shape of this development has meant that areas which simply cannot be fitted (or distorted) into the conceptual straitjacket of trial-type process even by generous analogy continue to be neglected by legal analysis. Thus, for example, issues such as police discretion to arrest or the discretion inherent in plea-bargaining and prosecution processes, where very wide discretion and policy issues are seen as being at stake, are still perceived in Britain as areas in which the issue of fair procedure hardly arises, and continue to be marginalized in much the way Davis criticized twenty years ago. Despite some developments in thinking about the proper requirements for rule-making by public bodies, the persistence of the court-type due process model in significant areas of the modern British judicial approach to procedural fairness in exercising discretionary power constitutes a clear example of the pervasiveness of the legal paradigm.

Another instructive area which has drawn much concern from lawyers and legal theorists in many countries is that of sentencing by the courts in criminal cases. Traditionally, criminal lawyers have shown little interest in this highly discretionary area, but over the last fifteen years, reporting of sentencing cases and renewed academic interest in Britain (to take an example) has revealed the extent of judicial and magisterial discretion and of disparities in its exercise among different judges and magistrates. There has been some recognition of competing and conflicting institutional objectives and the indeterminacy of public policy in this area, but the main focus of debate has been on disparity. This has generated a focus (with one or two partial exceptions (Hogarth 1971)) on statistics concerning what happens rather than why this is the case, and a neglect (both in legal and in positivistic social science research) of the agent-centred approach developed by sociology. On some substantive views of the goals of sentencing, of course, apparent disparities between similar cases may be explained as desirable individualization in terms of the offender's needs or society's goals. However, the growing concern about sentencing discretion has tended to be accompanied by a commitment to the 'just-deserts' view of sentencing: the idea that a person is sentenced by reason of and to the extent of his or her deserts for past voluntary actions and that, with certain limited exceptions, such as the (controversial) relevance of criminal record in determining desert, the sentence should reflect the offender's culpability measured in terms of the seriousness of the harm caused and degree of the offender's responsibility for causing it. This kind of approach obviously favours uniformity and consistency in sentencing, and lends itself to the typical method of legal control by subjecting the enterprise to the governance of general standards. Thus many commentators have advocated the introduction of systems of sentencing guidelines or 'presumptive sentences' which aim to ensure consistency of sentencing practice across the given area.

The arguments put for this kind of sentencing reform, and the practical experience met where they have been put into effect (Galligan 1981; Tonry 1987), echo some of the limitations of legal method which we have already noted. First of all, this kind of reform leads, once again, to an illegitimate assumption that a certain kind of procedural fairness (or at least uniformity) leads automatically to substantive fairness. For, although most advocates of guidelines tend to favour the substantive just-deserts approach, the actual implementation of guidelines often consists in an averaging-out of past sentencing and paroling practice, which can only reflect an incoherent amalgam of all the different approaches being pursued by sentencers at the time (Galligan 1981). Surface-level uniformity comes to stand for substantive justice, diverting attention away (again, with some notable exceptions (Von Hirsch 1985)) from intractable issues of just how to convert theoretical commitment to just deserts into actual sentencing scales. Furthermore, in designing guidelines systems, difficulties inevitably arise in choosing between more rigid systems, which concretize generalized standards into rules and which risk preventing judges from taking account of important and relevant special considerations, and more flexible systems, which accord some measure of sentencing discretion at the cost of risking a gradual subversion of the 'rational' system on the basis of differing judicial preferences.

Secondly, if one is not entirely convinced of the just-deserts approach and sees sentencing as appropriately based on a wider range of policy issues, questions arise about the appropriateness of using the judicial model of procedurally fair decision encapsulated in guideline systems. In other words, a supporter of rehabilitative or educative sentencing would probably not see a detailed guideline system as appropriate, but would also deny that his or her view of sentencing as a policy-based and discretionary decision means that no standards of fair process or substantive justice should apply. And, even for the advocate of just-deserts, it is significant that the focus for academic critique has until quite recently (Von Hirsch, Knapp, and Tonry 1987) tended to be on the sentencing decision and its fairness, rather than on the more difficult question of the setting-up of the guidelines themselves. Since this is still an area in which the existence of discretion and the influence of policy considerations must be admitted, it tends to be one (like police decisions to arrest and plea-bargaining, cited above) which is marginalized due to the reluctance of modern legal approaches to the control of discretion to address directly the issue of policy-creation as opposed to policy-application. Once again, modern developments appear to emphasize procedural at the expense of substantive fairness and to develop the former in terms of the legal paradigm without a sufficient appreciation of possible limitations to its relevance.

The utter inadequacy of an approach which simply grafts on the trimmings of formal justice to a substantively unsatisfactory area of administration or to an area where their application is inappropriate and unlikely to be effective is pinpointed by Asquith in the context of the influence of the 'justice model' in reforming British juvenile justice and sentencing practice: 'To ignore basic social and economic inequality whilst promoting greater procedural equality inhibits the realization of the rights of children and may well achieve a degree of justice within a system of control which has all the hallmarks of material injustice' (1983: 221). On this view, the introduction of legal controls on discretion can actually be counter-productive in obscuring substantive injustice (Jowell 1973; Prosser 1977; Adler and Asquith 1981*b*). It can also have the effect of suppressing debate about the relation between substantive and procedural justice, referring casually to the contribution of procedural fairness to the 'quality' or 'accuracy' of decision-making whilst failing to acknowledge the lack of or disagreement about substantive standards of adequacy or correctness in the areas in question. And, ironically, even attempts to go beyond traditional legal structures and methods, as in the move towards 'informal justice' in resolving family disputes or in juvenile justice, have been criticized as reproducing the legal paradigm by incorporating ever wider areas of conduct within the net of legal control and professional authority, without even providing the minimal formal controls represented by the traditional legal approach (Abel 1982*a*).

But what other kinds of assumptions and judgments about discretionary power and its effective direction and control could and should lawyers and legal theorists have made in widening the ambit of their vision of the legally relevant? Although the subjection of discretionary areas to the governance of general, pre-determined standards is, as I have argued, the paradigm of legal method, alternative methods can hardly be said to be beyond the lawyers' understanding or indeed immune from the utility of lawyers' attention. For example, there seems to be no inherent reason why administrative lawyers and legal theorists should not give more thought to institutions of political accountability (such as through voting and election processes); the structure and organization of areas in which discretionary power is exercised (encompassing questions about personnel, powers, and the relations between them); and substantive questions as to the institutional goals and assumptions of particular areas of administration. Indeed, a broader focus is beginning to be adopted by lawyers (Galligan 1986*a*; Harden and Lewis 1986) who argue for a more pluralistic approach to procedural legitimacy, encompassing values of openness, accountability, participation, and responsiveness, which may be interpreted afresh outside the constraining boundaries of the judicial due process paradigm. There is also an emerging willingness to address substantive constitutional values, or at least to acknowledge the need to address them and to begin to forge an approach to constitutional theory which engages in substantive argument about democratic values and which transcends the traditionally constructed distinction between the legal and the political. In all these areas, legal and jurisprudential study overlaps with and is complemented by social scientific research. What can the two approaches learn from each other, and to what extent are the boundaries between them blurred?

The Interdependence of Jurisprudential and Social Science Approaches

If the dangers of the legal paradigm are to be averted, jurisprudential and legal approaches will clearly have to be modified in the light of the insights of the social sciences. Most lawyers will, however, persist in the belief in the need for some at least provisional conceptualization of discretion as a starting-point for reflection. Obviously, the use of conceptual categories is built in to our very use of language, and, as I mentioned earlier, social scientists themselves often start out from a loose conceptualization of discretion. But it is important to beware of the rigidity which legal categories tend to assume, and to be aware of the assumptions which they tend to make. For example, I have already noted G. Smith's (1981) questioning of whether 'discretion' can usefully be separated from the wider category of 'decision'; it is also important to raise the question of whether 'discretionary power' can usefully be separated from 'power' as a general category. And even Smith's revision builds in the idea, resonant with legal readings of the world, of a discrete event or mental act which can be isolated, whereas 'discretion' might often be thought to inhere in role-related conduct (such as the manner with which an official receives enquiries) and even in processes and situations (such as organizational structure), which cannot be analysed in those terms. Conceptual reflection can be useful in broadening our awareness of different aspects of social phenomena, but it should not be allowed to close off consideration of related phenomena which do not meet rigidly defined conceptual criteria.

Secondly, and related to a flexible approach to conceptualization, jurists must develop their incipient awareness that discretion cannot always be readily identified in terms of explicit or implicit legal grants of discretionary power. Social scientists have noted, for example, that, once a phenomenological and empirical analysis is undertaken, it often emerges that officials who might on the face of it be thought to be accorded wide discretion by the legal and institutional structure (Young 1981) in fact exercise little discretion. This is because they tend to routinize their decisions, adopting rule-like generalizations. Conversely others, such as clerks, who on the face of it have little discretion, in fact exercise considerable discretionary power—for example, in acting as a filter for sending cases and complaints on to the next stage of the process. Lawyers need to be aware, therefore, that discretion is a phenomenon too subtle always to be susceptible of legal identification, and that it may inhere in actors who are not holders of identifiable legal powers or even roles. Furthermore, this kind of assumed or situational discretion seems most unlikely to be capable of being directed or controlled by formal legal means.

Thirdly, the insights provided by the social sciences' approach to discretion suggest that legal theorists should examine carefully the lawyer's typical assumption that discretion is marginal and of dubious legitimacy. A real appreciation of the pervasiveness and subtlety of discretion in administrative processes suggests both that discretion is often inevitable and that in many contexts it is instrumentally and symbolically useful in a variety of ways. For example, nobody would dispute the desirability of the police being accountable for the decisions they make to arrest suspects, on the basis of some substantive set of values about proper police powers and behaviour. However, Davis's (1969) suggestion that such kinds of discretion could usefully be controlled by traditional legal methods seems unrealistic, and his later comparative assessment of the control of discretion in Europe and the United States fails to confront these fundamental problems (Davis 1976). In many areas, prior participation and consultation and/or later political or professional accountability will constitute not only more effective but also more appropriate checks on abuses of power. Thus lawyers need to further their interest in the structures of political and professional decision-making and accountability so as to diversify our appreciation of appropriate mechanisms of direction and control. Moreover, lawyers must be constantly willing to ask themselves to what extent their ready assumption that discretion automatically raises issues of confinement and control, rather than simply the general issue of legitimacy, is a throwback to Diceyan attitudes to the rule of law. For these are attitudes which, if they ever were, are no longer apposite to the British administrative and constitutional process, and which carry with them a heavy ideological baggage which an extended conception of the legally relevant entails we should reject. Legal theorists need to concentrate on ensuring that power rests in the right hands in the first place rather than emphasizing *post hoc* controls. In particular, jurists must learn to accord a central place to discretion at policy-making stages as well as policy-application, recognizing the continuity between the two and the frequent impossibility of distinguishing between them in particular contexts. This would also involve an acknowledgment of the relevance of issues of substantive justice to lawyers and the continuity of legal and political spheres which is systematically obscured by a procedural conception of the rule of law.

Finally, there can be no doubt that lawyers and legal theorists need to keep themselves informed about social science insights into the complexity of decision-making in administrative contexts. This must encompass the existence of competing professional and institutional objectives and ideologies, agents' understandings, and the broader social and political climate in which they operate. Without this, legal interventions are bound to be crude and unsuccessful, pushing discretion around the system from one place to another rather than pursuing the realistic project of trying to ensure its legitimacy and efficiency where it exists. For example, research shows that the outcome of sentencing decisions in British and US juvenile courts and tribunals is determined not only by the existence of discretion in the ultimate sentencer but also by the mediation of conflicting views of the causes of delinquency and the point of the enterprise on the part of a variety of participants (notably social workers and the police as well as sentencers (e.g. Asquith 1983; see, generally, Emerson 1969)). Thus the mere confinement and structuring of the sentencer's discretion may not achieve what it sets out to, because the sentencer's decision is inevitably made on the basis of arguments and information constructed and presented on the basis of the (conflicting) operational ideologies of those other groups, whose discretion may well not be susceptible of legal control. If the phenomenological approach of the social sciences is well directed, as I would argue it is, lawyers must be ready to be more empirically informed, context sensitive, and pluralistic in their approach to discretion in legal contexts, and to bring the issue of operational ideologies and frames of relevance into the open forum of political debate. And this, inevitably, renders problematic the method of generalization used by traditional jurisprudential scholarship. General 'truths' about discretion are either too general to be illuminating or utterly misleading.

Furthermore, jurisprudence must begin to address the crucial and complex problems raised by phenomenological research in terms of what I shall call the question of 'transparency'. For, if competing and overlapping operational ideologies are as pervasive in legal and administrative contexts as research suggests, intractable problems about lawyers' assumptions about the generality and openness of legal discourse and argumentation arise, and with them deep problems about the justice of legal processes. This issue is perhaps raised most acutely in Bennett's and Feldman's (1981) analysis of criminal trials as story-telling, which emphasizes the importance of 'interpretive context' and the existence of different 'social frames of reference' for the different participants in the trial. I have already noted, in discussing the work of Asquith (1983), the importance of popular culture and common sense understandings in constructing the 'problems' or issues with which administrative processes are concerned. What are the implications of this kind of work where the participants in a particular process, be it a trial, a disciplinary hearing, a public inquiry, a piece of explicit policy-making, or whatever, do not share world-views or frames of relevance even to the minimal extent necessary to understand and communicate with each other in a meaningful way? What, for example, does the value of participation really amount to for the inexperienced, inarticulate, and nervous objector at a planning inquiry? In what sense do trial procedures really guarantee fairness for the confused adolescent charged with an offence, notwithstanding his or her right to legal representation (which itself in a sense recognizes the problem of transparency)? How can we have any confidence that the doctors, social workers, statisticians, lawyers, lay people, and others involved in legal and administrative processes are, to put it metaphorically, speaking the same language? If, as Bennett and Feldman suggest, we cannot assume that experience and meaning are universal, what becomes of the legal assumption of legal categories as universal, objective, and transcendent? And how are we to realize the values of the rule of law ideal, aspiring to openness and accountability across operational ideologies and frames of relevance? If, as Young (1981) suggests, the outcome of administrative (encompassing legal) processes is dependent on the extent to which the assumptive worlds of agents involved are *shared*, the focus for jurisprudential thought needs to be somewhat different from, and is much more problematic than, that typically assumed by the rationalistic model of liberal legal theory. Indeed, this kind of agent-centred analysis of discretion in legal contexts raises very serious problems for the project of traditional analytical jurisprudence with its focus on generalization, conceptualization, clarity, and objectivity, and its assumption that a distinctively 'legal point of view' is unproblematically accessible to, and can be imposed on, all participants in the legal process.

The normative enterprises of jurisprudence, however, lend themselves more naturally to context-sensitivity and an appreciation of the empirical aspects of practical moral and political questions, and it is here that I would argue the most useful contribution of legal theory remains to be made. For, without some general normative reflection on the constitutional and political framework in which discretionary power exists, it is impossible adequately to direct our responses to the information and insights provided by the social sciences. Thus jurisprudence, broadly understood, could be expected to provide reflection on the general democratic (substantive as well as procedural) values which found the legitimation of discretionary powers in our society, and explicitly to trace the implications of this theory for, for example, administrative law and the control of discretion. Normative jurisprudential reflection within a general framework needs to be brought to bear on specific contexts and areas: if we do not have some idea of what constitutes acceptable and effective administrative action in particular areas, and views about appropriate official roles and proper institutional goals, a critical and constructive response to the insights of the phenomenological approach cannot be formulated. It seems inadequate, for example, merely to conclude from the social science discovery that competing assumptive worlds, frames of relevance, and institutional objectives exist and interact, that this is inevitable, and that nothing can be done to change the basis on which or direction in which discretionary power is exercised. On the contrary, the insights about the complexity of administrative processes should feed back into social and political reflection on what kinds of administrative processes we want to set up and how to overcome difficulties in realizing the social goals of our administrative institutions. In other words, the insights of the social sciences provide a starting-point as much as a conclusion in the study of discretionary power, and, though social science may teach us the limitations and difficulties of our attempts to change the administrative world, they do not dictate abandonment of the project of change and reform—rather a greater appreciation of the complexity of such a project and the need for subtle and indirect as well as direct means to change.

Let me try to illustrate the implications of this approach by means of an example used by Davis; that of police discretion to arrest. As I have already noted, the project of subjecting this kind of discretion to the confining or structuring by standards which Davis advocated seems both unrealistic and misplaced, and this probably explains why this is an area in which, in Davis's own terms, relatively little progress has been made in the last twenty years. But the inappropriateness of the legalistic approach does not entail that Davis was wrong in finding room for concern and criticism in the present state of practice in this area. It is quite clear, given wide discretion in which policy-formation and application are inextricably intertwined, both that gross abuses of power can and do occur and that important questions of procedural and, especially, substantive justice arise. Recent social science research on the police (Manning 1977; D. Smith and Gray 1986) has furnished important information and insight into the operational ideologies and frames of relevance of police officers making arrests in a wide variety of contexts. It has also increased our understanding of the culture of the police as a professional and political group, and their own appreciation of the political, social, and economic climate in which they operate. We also have important evidence about public and media attitudes to the police and their social role, which in turn generate pressures on the police to behave in certain ways (for example, to be able to produce respectable 'clear-up' rates, or to be confident of the potential success of cases in court before constructing and pursuing them). We understand, too, that the police role is subject to a number of possible institutional objectives which are often in tension with one another.

What is now needed is reflection and public debate on the normative political issues about what the role of the police *should* be in a democratic society, and how the aspects of police culture and practice which are inconsistent with that role (such as police racism, lack of accountability, vulnerability to direct political pressure) can be addressed and changed. Moving from such general normative reflection, we need to address the specific question of how the legitimacy of decisions to arrest can be maximized, both by changing the nature of the police and their goals and motivations and by providing professional and public structures of checking and accountability. Obviously, no system can check on or ensure legitimacy of every arrest; what can be aimed for is to adapt the climate in which arrests are made. This would also lead us to consider broader questions of social justice and the justification for particular criminal laws, again emphasizing the continuity of questions of power in different social spheres. Without the insights of research, the normative approach is of little value, for it is likely to be misdirected. Similarly, were it not for normative direction (and indeed many social scientists do volunteer normative proposals as a result of their research), social science research would illuminate problems but could not point in the direction of change. The two approaches are interdependent to the point that they can hardly be separated: indeed, perhaps one criticism of some social scientific approaches is that they inevitably proceed on normative assumptions which they do not always reveal or articulate.

But if, as I have suggested, the major potential contribution of jurisprudence to the study of discretion in legal contexts is this provision of normative reflection and insight, in what sense is this a distinctive contribution? We have moved a long way, after all, from analytical conceptualization and generalization, and from the 'enterprise of subjecting human conduct to the governance of rules' (Fuller 1969). This kind of normative jurisprudence is rather, as its modern exponents explicitly recognize, a form of social or political philosophy. As such, it is informed by an underlying social theory having to do with the role of legal and political institutions in setting up, maintaining, and consolidating social relations and structures of power and authority. The incorporation of this kind of normative enterprise within the boundaries of jurisprudence is continuous with the critique of liberal legal ideology and the move away from the traditional rule of law ideal in that it may be regarded as weakening those very boundaries by recognizing continuities between the legal, the political, and the social. Thus, far from being concerned strictly to distinguish jurisprudential and social science approaches to discretion, I would prefer to think in terms of working towards a number of complementary, theoretically underpinned, empirically informed approaches to discretion which emphasize particular aspects or perspectives but which cannot be neatly conceptualized as 'legal' or 'sociological', 'political' or 'analytical'—or indeed in terms of any other rigid categories of thought.

This is not to deny that there can exist approaches to social phenomena which are distinctively *legal*; indeed, my characterization and critique of the 'legal paradigm' proceeds on exactly the contrary assumption. But what makes the legal world-view distinctive—its system of conceptualization which insists on closure and its assertion of the relative autonomy of legal reasons and a legal sphere—is exactly what makes it inapposite as a *general* basis for analysis of and reflection on discretionary power. For it can only incorporate in its analysis those forms of discretion which can be likened by analogy to legally recognized forms of power and thus brought within the ambit of the legal world by being regulated in accordance with general standards. As we have seen, this kind of legal perspective is gradually being submitted to ever more extensive critique. Whether this critique will ever issue in a fundamental change in the nature of legal discourse, thought, and practice, and whether such a change would preserve the assertion of a legal sphere and of legal methodology thought of as distinct from the social and political sphere and social science methodologies, remains to be seen. My concern is rather to argue that, whilst conventional legal ideology remains as it currently is, legal approaches to discretion will be inevitably both limited and misleading, in that they purport to give a comprehensive and objective analysis which turns out to be imperialistic and inappropriate. Thus the pressing task for legal theorists, I would argue, is to focus on normative projects which recognize the continuity of legal, political, and social power, which complement the researches and reflections of social and political scientists, and which take a broad approach to methods of addressing the issues raised by discretion.

Conclusion

I have argued that the expansion of our intellectual horizons promised by the work of Davis and others cannot be realized fully unless we are willing to transcend the traditional boundaries set up between complementary academic approaches to discretion. I have suggested that both jurisprudential conceptualization of discretion and the normative positions on discretion which jurisprudence typically generates tend to proceed from an unduly 'legalistic' view of the administrative and political world. In its tendency to produce law-like generalizations about the need for and means of control of discretion, its emphasis on rules, standards, and guidelines, its preoccupation with procedure and formal equality rather than with substance, and its focus on the discretion of 'public' officials, jurisprudence even of a relatively broad-minded type tends unwittingly to reproduce the inherent limitations of more conventional legal scholarship. The sociological research which is now developing a phenomenological, agent-centred approach to understanding discretion in particular contexts suggests that we must rather develop a more context-sensitive and pluralistic approach than that generally offered by jurisprudence.

If we are to escape the dangers and limitations inherent in the 'legal paradigm', we must, I have also suggested, escape the constraints of traditional liberal legal ideology and transcend the category of the 'legal' which conventional liberalism and its commitment to the 'rule of law' set up. The issue of discretionary power poses a challenge which leads us to question the boundaries which have been set up between jurisprudential and social science approaches and which suggests that we must develop an approach which incorporates 'public' and 'private'; policy-formation and application; discretionary and other role-related power. We need to integrate empirical, interpretive, and normative questions in an attempt both to understand discretion and, ultimately, to ensure the legitimacy and effectiveness of the exercise of social power in particular contexts. Discretion must be taken, then, primarily as a *political* question, and one whose centrality in contemporary society calls for the concerted attention of a number of related and interdependent disciplines. Only by pooling our intellectual resources can we work effectively towards the greatest possible legitimacy of political power by meeting the challenge posed by discretion and reaching an understanding of its operation in all its many forms and contexts.

List of Cases

US Cases

Bellotti *v.* Baird 443 US 622 (1979)
Brown *v.* Allen 344 US 443 (1953)
Goldberg *v.* Kelly 397 US 254 (1970)
Kilgrow *v.* Kilgrow 107 So.2d 885 (1958)
Lockhart *v.* McCree 476 US 162, 90 L Ed 137, 106 S Ct 1758 (1986)
McClesky *v.* Kemp 481 US 279, 95 L Ed 2d. 262, 107 S Ct 1756 (1987)
McClesky *v.* Zant 111 S Ct 1757 (1991)
Miranda *v.* Arizona 384 US 436 (1966)
Morgan *v.* Foretich 846 F.2d 941 (1988)
Morgan *v.* Foretich 546 A.2d 407 (DC App.) (1988)
Morgan *v.* Foretich 564 A.2nd 1 (DC App.) (1989)
North Carolina *v.* Rhodes 61 N.C. 445 (1868)
Painter *v.* Bannister 140 NW 2d 152 (Ia. 1966)
Palmore *v.* Sidoti 466 US 429 (1984)
Sparf and Hanson *v.* United States 156 US 51 (1895)

English Cases

Bushell's Case 124 Eng. Rep. 1006 (1670)
R *v.* Environment Secretary, ex parte Nottinghamshire CC [1986]
AC 240

References

Abel, R. (1982*a*) (ed.), *The Politics of Informal Justice*, i. *The American Experience* (New York: Academic Press).

—— (1982*b*) (ed.), *The Politics of Informal Justice*, ii. *Comparative Studies* (New York: Academic Press).

—— (1985), 'Risk as an Arena of Struggle', *Michigan Law Review* 3: 772–812.

Ackerman, B. A. (1980), *Social Justice in the Liberal State* (New Haven, Conn.: Yale University Press).

Adler, M., and Asquith, S. (1981*a*) (eds.), *Discretion and Welfare* (London: Heinemann).

—— —— (1981*b*), 'Discretion and Power', in M. Adler and S. Asquith (eds.), *Discretion and Welfare* (London: Heinemann), 9–32.

—— and Bradley, A. W. (1976) (eds.), *Justice, Discretion and Poverty* (London: Professional Books Limited).

Allars, M. N. (1985), 'Coordination and Administrative Discretion', unpublished D.Phil. thesis, Oxford University.

Allen, F. A. (1959), 'Legal Values and the Rehabilitative Ideal', *Journal of Criminal Law, Criminology and Police Science* 50: 226–32.

Allison, G. T. (1971), *The Essense of Decision: Explaining the Cuban Missile Crisis* (Boston: Little Brown).

Alschuler, A. (1975), 'The Defense Attorney's Role in Plea Bargaining', *Yale Law Journal* 84: 1179–314.

—— (1976), 'Trial Judge's Role in Plea Bargaining', *Columbia Law Review* 76(1): 1059–154.

American Friends Service Committee (1971), *Struggle for Justice* (New York: Hill and Wang).

Arendt, H. (1986), 'Communicative Power', in S. Lukes (ed.), *Power* (New York: New York University Press), 59–74.

Asquith, S. (1983), *Children and Justice: Decision-Making in Children's Hearings and Juvenile Courts* (Edinburgh: Edinburgh University Press).

Atiyah, P. S. (1980), 'From Principles to Pragmatism: Changes in the Function of the Judicial Process and the Law', *Iowa Law Review* 65(5): 1249–72.

Aubert, W. (1984), *In Search of Law* (Oxford: Martin Robertson).

Austin, J. L. (1970), 'A Plea for Excuses', in J. O. Urmson and G. J. Warnock (eds), *Philosophical Papers* (2nd edn.) (Oxford: Clarendon Press), 175–204.

Ayers, E. L. (1984), *Vengeance and Justice: Crime and Punishment in the 19th-Century American South* (New York: Oxford University Press).

Bachrach, P., and Baratz, M. (1962), 'The Two Faces of Power', *American Political Science Review* 56: 947–52.

Baier, A. (1986), 'Trust and Antitrust', *Ethics* 96: 231–60.

Baldwin, R. (1985), *Regulating the Airlines: Administrative Justice and Agency Discretion* (Oxford: Clarendon Press).

—— and Hawkins, K. (1984), 'Discretionary Justice: Davis Reconsidered', *Public Law* (winter): 570–99.

—— and McCrudden, C. (1987) (eds.), *Administrative Law and the Administrative Process* (London: Weidenfeld and Nicolson).

Bankowski, Z., and Nelken, D. (1981), 'Discretion as a Serial Problem', in M. Adler and S. Asquith (eds.), *Discretion and Welfare* (London: Heinemann), 247–68.

Banton, M. (1964), *The Policeman in the Community* (London: Tavistock).

Barber, B. (1983), *The Logic and Limits of Trust* (New Brunswick, NJ: Rutgers University Press).

Barak, A. (1989), *Judicial Discretion* (New Haven, Conn.: Yale University Press).

Bardach, E., and Kagan, R. (1982), *Going by The Book: The Problem of Regulatory Unreasonableness* (Philadelphia: Temple University Press).

Barley, S. R. (1983), 'Semiotics and the Study of Occupational and Organizational Cultures', *Administrative Science Quarterly* 28: 383–413.

Baumgartner, M. P. (1978), 'Law and Social Status in Colonial New Haven, 1639–1665', in R. J. Simon (ed.), *Research in Law and Sociology: An Annual Compilation of Research*, i (Greenwich: JAI Press) 153–74.

—— (1984), 'Social Control from Below', in D. Black (ed.), *Toward a General Theory of Social Control*, 1. *Fundamentals* (Orlando, Fla.: Academic Press), 303–45.

—— (1988), *The Moral Order of a Suburb* (New York: Oxford University Press).

Beattie, J. M. (1986), *Crime and the Courts in England, 1660–1800* (Princeton, NJ: Princeton University Press).

Bell, J. (1983), *Policy Arguments in Judicial Decisions* (Oxford: Clarendon Press).

—— (1987), 'The Judge as Bureaucrat', in J. Eekelaar and J. Bell (eds.), *Oxford Essays in Jurisprudence—Third Series* (Oxford: Clarendon Press), 33–56.

Bennett, W. L., and Feldman, M. S. (1981), *Reconstructing Reality in the Courtroom* (London: Tavistock).

Bernard, J. L. (1979), 'Interaction between the Race of the Defendant and that of Jurors in Determining Verdicts', *Law and Psychology Review* 5: 103–11.

Bernstein, R. (1985), *Beyond Objectivism and Relativism: Science, Hermeneutics, and Praxis* (Philadelphia: University of Pennsylvania Press).

Bertell, R. (1985), *Clear and Present Danger* (London: Merlin).

Betti, E. (1971), *Interpretazione della legge e degli atti giuridici* (2nd edn.) (Milan: Giuffrè).

Binder, G. (n.d.), 'Beyond Criticism', manuscript.

Bittner, E. (1967*a*), 'The Police on Skid Row: A Study of Peace Keeping', *American Sociological Review* 32: 699–715.

—— (1967*b*), 'Police Discretion in Emergency Apprehension of Mentally Ill Persons', *Social Problems* 14: 278–92.

—— (1970), *The Functions of the Police in Modern Society* (Washington, DC: United States Government Printing Office).

Black, D. (1970), 'Production of Crime Rates', *American Sociological Review* 35: 733–48.

—— (1971), 'The Social Organization of Arrest', *Stanford Law Review* 23: 1087–111.

—— (1976), *The Behavior of Law* (New York: Academic Press).

—— (1980), *The Manners and Customs of the Police* (New York: Academic Press).

—— (1989*a*), *Sociological Justice* (New York: Oxford University Press).

—— (1989*b*), 'Taking Sides', unpublished paper, Department of Sociology, University of Virginia, Charlottesville, Virginia.

—— and Baumgartner, M. P. (1983), 'Toward a Theory of the Third Party', in K. O. Boyum and L. Mather (eds.), *Empirical Theories about Courts* (New York: Longman Press), 84–114.

Black, H. C. (1968), *Black's Law Dictionary* (St Paul, Minn.: West Publishing Company).

Blau, P. M., and Scott, W. R. (1962), *Formal Organizations* (San Francisco: Chandler Publishing Co.).

Bloch, P., and Anderson, D. (1974), *Policewomen on Patrol: Final Report* (Washington, DC: Police Foundation).

Blumberg A. (1967), *Criminal Justice* (Chicago: Quadrangle).

Bockel, A. (1978), 'Contribution à l'étude du pouvoir discrétionnaire de l'administration', *Actualité Juridique—Droit Administratif* 355–70.

Boehm, C. (1984), *Blood Revenge: The Enactment and Management of Conflict in Montenegro and Other Tribal Societies* (Philadelphia: University of Pennsylvania Press).

Boris, S. B. (1979), 'Stereotypes and Dispositions for Criminal Homicide', *Criminology* 17: 139–58.

Bowers, W. J., and Pierce, G. J. (1980), 'Arbitrariness and Discrimination under Post-*Furman* Capital Statutes', *Crime and Delinquency* 26: 563–635.

Boyer, B. (1984), 'From Discretionary Justice to Bureaucratic Justice' (book review of Mashaw 1983), *Michigan Law Review* 82: 971–80.

Bradley, A. W. (1974), 'Research and Reform in Administrative Law', *Journal of the Society of Public Teachers of Law* 13: 35–44.

—— (1985), 'Recent Reform of Social Security Adjudication in Great Britain', *Les Cahiers de droit* 26: 403–49.

Bradshaw, J. (1981), 'From Discretion to Rules: The Experience of the

Family Fund', in M. Adler and S. Asquith (eds.), *Discretion and Welfare* (London: Heinemann), 135–47.

Breitel, C. (1960), 'Controls in Criminal Law Enforcement', *University of Chicago Law Review* 27: 427–35.

Brodkin, E. (1987), 'Policy Politics: If We Can't Govern, Can We Manage?', *Political Science Quarterly* 102: 571–87.

Brown, J. (1984), *Disability Income: Part II The Disability Income System* (London: Policy Studies Institute).

Bryner, G. C. (1987), *Bureaucratic Discretion: Law and Policy in Federal Regulatory Agencies* (New York: Pergamon Press).

Bull, D. (1980), 'The Anti-Discretion Movement in Britain: Fact or Phantom', *Journal of Social Welfare Law*, 65–83.

Bullock, H. A. (1961), 'Significance of the Racial Factor in the Length of Prison Sentences', *Journal of Criminal Law, Criminology and Police Science* 52: 411–17.

Bumiller, K. (1988), *The Civil Rights Society: The Social Construction of Victims* (Baltimore: Johns Hopkins University Press).

Burke, J. P. (1986), *Bureaucratic Responsibility* (Baltimore: Johns Hopkins University Press).

BVerfG (1960), *BVerfGE*, 8 June.

Cain, M., and Kulcsar, K. (1982), 'Thinking Disputes: An Essay on the Origins of the Dispute Industry', *Law and Society Review* 16: 375–402.

Calavita, K. (1983), 'The Demise of the Occupational Health and Safety Administration: A Case Study in Symbolic Action', *Social Problems* 30: 437–48.

Campbell, C. M. (1976), *The Legal Routine* (Belfast: Queen's University).

Cane, P. (1986), *An Introduction to Administrative Law* (Oxford: Clarendon Press).

Cardozo, B. N. (1924), *The Growth of the Law* (New Haven, Conn.: Yale University Press).

Carter, L. H. (1974), *The Limits of Order* (Lexington, Mass.: Lexington Books).

Casper, J. D. (1976), 'The Supreme Court and National Policy Making', *American Political Science Review* 70: 50–63.

Chambliss, W. J. (1964), 'A Sociological Analysis of the Law of Vagrancy', *Social Problems* 12: 67–77.

—— and Seidman, R. B. (1971), *Law, Order and Power* (Reading, Mass.: Addison-Wesley).

—— —— (1982), *Law, Order and Power* (2nd edn.) (Reading, Mass.: Addison-Wesley).

Chayes, A. (1976), 'The Role of the Judge in Public Law Litigation', *Harvard Law Review* 89(7): 1281–316.

Cherniack, M. (1986), *The Hawks' Nest Incident* (New Haven, Conn.: Yale University Press).

Cicourel, A. (1968), *The Social Organization of Juvenile Justice* (New York: John Wiley and Sons).

Clarke, L. (1988), 'Explaining Choices among Technological Risks', *Social Problems* 35: 22–35.

—— (1989), *Acceptable Risk?* (Berkeley, Calif.: University of California Press).

Cohen, M. D. (1985), 'Stability and Change in Systems of Standard Operating Procedures', unpublished paper presented at the Stanford Workshop on Political–Military Decision-Making, March 1985.

—— (1987), 'Adaptation of Organizational Routines', unpublished paper presented at the Workshop on Organizational Science at Massachusetts Institute of Technology, 10–12 June 1987.

—— and March, J. G. (1974), *Leadership and Ambiguity: The American College President* (New York: McGraw Hill).

Collins, H. (1987), 'Against Abstentionism in Labour Law', in J. Eekelaar and J. Bell (eds.), *Oxford Essays in Jurisprudence—Third Series* (Oxford: Clarendon Press), 79–101.

Comaroff, J. L., and Roberts, S. (1981), *Rules and Processes: The Cultural Logic of Dispute in an African Context* (Chicago: University of Chicago Press).

Conley, J. M., and O'Barr, W. M. (1990), *Rules versus Relationships: The Ethnography of Legal Discourse* (Chicago: University of Chicago Press).

Cook, B. B. (1973), 'Sentencing Behavior of Federal Judges: Draft Cases— 1972', *University of Cincinnati Law Review* 42: 597–633.

Cooney, M. (1988), 'The Social Control of Homicide: A Cross-Cultural Study', unpublished doctoral dissertation, Harvard Law School, Cambridge, Mass.

Cooper, E. H. (1984), 'Timing as Jurisdiction: Federal Civil Appeals in Context', *Law and Contemporary Problems* 47(3): 157–64.

—— (1988), 'Civil Rule 52(a): Rationing and Rationalizing the Resources of Appellate Review', *Notre Dame Law Review* 63(5): 645–70.

Cooter, R., and Ulen, T. (1988), *Law and Economics* (Glenview, Ill.: Scott, Foresman).

Cornell, D. (1985), 'Toward a Modern/Postmodern Reconstruction of Ethics', *University of Pennsylvania Law Review* 133: 291–380.

Coval, S. C., and Smith, J. C. (1977), 'The Completeness of Rules', *Cambridge Law Journal* 36: 364–8.

Craig, P. P. (1983), *Administrative Law* (London: Sweet and Maxwell).

Cyert, R. M., and March, J. G. (1963), *A Behavioral Theory of the Firm* (Englewood Cliffs, NJ: Prentice Hall).

Dahl, R. (1986), 'Power as the Control of Behavior', in S. Lukes (ed.), *Power* (New York: New York University Press), 37–58.

Damaska, M. R. (1975), 'Structures of Authority and Comparative Criminal Procedure', *Yale Law Journal*, 480–544.

Damaska, M. R. (1986), *The Faces of Justice and State Authority* (New Haven, Conn.: Yale University Press).

Danelski, D. J. (1966), 'Values as Variables in Judicial Decision-Making: Notes Toward a Theory', *Vanderbilt Law Review* 19: 721–40.

Davis, K. C. (1969), *Discretionary Justice: A Preliminary Inquiry* (Baton Rouge, La.: Louisiana State University Press).

—— (1976), *Discretionary Justice in Europe and America* (Chicago: University of Illinois Press).

Dean, J. W. (1976), *Blind Ambition* (New York: Simon and Schuster).

Delgado, R., Dunn, C., Brown, P., Lee, H., and Hubbert, D. (1985), 'Fairness and Formality: Minimizing the Risk of Prejudice in Alternative Dispute Resolution', *Wisconsin Law Review*, 1359–404.

Demos, J. P. (1982), *Entertaining Satan: Witchcraft and the Culture of Early New England* (New York: Oxford University Press).

Department of Health and Social Security (1986), *Industrial Injuries Handbook for Adjudicating Medical Authorities* (London: HMSO).

Dicey, A. V. (1915), 'The Development of Administrative Law in England', *Law Quarterly Review* 31: 148–53.

—— (1959), *An Introduction to the Study of The Law of the Constitution* (10th edn.) (London: Macmillan).

Donnison, D. (1977), 'Against Discretion', *New Society*, 15 September.

—— (1982), *The Politics of Poverty* (Oxford: Martin Robertson).

Donovan, J. M. (1981), 'Justice Unblind: The Juries and the Criminal Classes in France, 1825–1914', *Journal of Social History* 15: 89–107.

Douglas, M. (1985), *Risk Assessment According to the Social Sciences* (New York: Russell Sage).

Downs, A. (1957), *An Economic Theory of Democracy* (New York: Harper and Row).

Dworkin, R. M. (1977a), 'No Right Answer?', in P. M. Hacker and J. Raz (eds.), *Law, Morality and Society* (Oxford: Clarendon Press), ch. 3.

—— (1977b), *Taking Rights Seriously* (Cambridge, Mass.: Harvard University Press).

—— (1986), *Law's Empire* (London: Fontana).

Eco, U. (1976), *A Theory of Semiotics* (Bloomington, Ind.: Indiana University Press).

Edelman, M. (1964), *The Symbolic Uses of Politics* (Urbana, Ill.: University of Illinois Press).

—— (1971), *Politics as Symbolic Action: Mass Arousal and Quiescence* (Chicago: Markham Publishing Co.).

Emerson, R. M. (1969), *Judging Delinquents: Context and Process in the Juvenile Court* (Chicago: Aldine Press).

—— (1981), 'On Last Resorts', *American Journal of Sociology* 87: 1–22.

—— (1983), 'Holistic Effects in Social Control Decision-Making', *Law and Society Review* 17: 425–55.

—— (1986), *Contemporary Field Research* (Boston: Little, Brown and Co.).

—— (1991), 'Case Processing and Interorganizational Knowledge: Detecting the "Real Reasons" for Referrals', *Social Problems* 38: 1101–15.

Ericson, R. V. (1982), *Reproducing Order: A Study of Police Patrol Work* (Toronto: University of Toronto Press).

Feeley, M. M. (1979), *The Process is the Punishment: Handling Cases in a Lower Criminal Court* (New York: Russell Sage Foundation).

—— (1983), 'Foreword', in Vera Institute of Justice, *Felony Arrests: Their Prosecution and Disposition in New York City's Courts* (New York: Longman Press), pp. xi–xx.

Feldman, M. S. (1988*a*), 'Studying Change in Organizational Routines', unpublished paper, IPPS, University of Michigan, Ann Arbor.

—— (1988*b*), 'Understanding Organizational Routines: Stability and Change', Working Paper #88/35, Norwegian Research Center in Organization and Management, University of Bergen, Norway.

—— (1989), *Order Without Design* (Stanford, Calif.: Stanford University Press).

—— (1990), 'Organizational Goals and the Use of Analysis', paper presented to Conference on *The Practice of Policy Analysis: Mutual Implications of Context and Methodology*, Austin, Texas.

—— and March, J. G. (1981), 'Information in Organizations as Signal and Symbol', *Administrative Science Quarterly* 26: 171–86.

Felstiner, W., Abel, R., and Sarat, A. (1980–1), 'The Emergence and Transformation of Disputes: Naming, Blaming, Claiming . . .', *Law and Society Review* 15: 631–54.

Finnis, J. M. (1980), *Natural Law and Natural Rights* (Oxford: Clarendon Press).

—— (1987), 'Comment', in R. Gavison (ed.), *Issues in Contemporary Legal Philosophy* (Oxford: Clarendon Press), 62–75.

Fletcher, G. P. (1984), 'Some Unwise Reflections about Discretion', *Law and Contemporary Problems* 47: 269–86.

Florida Civil Liberties Union (1964), *Rape: Selective Electrocution Based on Race* (Miami: Florida Civil Liberties Union).

Foucault, M. (1970), *The Order of Things* (New York: Vintage).

—— (1986), 'Disciplinary Power and Subjection', in S. Lukes (ed.), *Power* (New York: New York University Press), 229–42.

Frank, J. (1949), *Courts on Trial* (Princeton, NJ: Princeton University Press).

Franks, Lord (1957), *Report of the Committee on Administrative Tribunals and Enquiries*, Cmnd. 218 (London: HMSO).

Friedman, L. (1975), *The Legal System* (New York: Russell Sage).

—— (1985), *Total Justice* (New York: Russell Sage).

Friedrich, C. J. (1973), 'Authority, Reason and Discretion', in R. E. Flathman (ed.), *Concepts in Social and Political Philosophy* (New York: Macmillan Publishing Co., Inc.)167–81.

Freire, P. (1985), *Pedagogy of the Oppressed* (New York: Continuum).

Fromm, E. (1965), *Escape from Freedom* (New York: Avon Books).

Frug, G. E. (1984), 'The Ideology of Bureaucracy in American Law', *Harvard Law Review* 97: 1276–388.

Fuller, L. (1964), *Legal Fictions* (Stanford, Calif.: Stanford University Press).

—— (1969), *The Morality of Law* (rev. edn.) (New Haven, Conn.: Yale University Press).

—— (1976), 'The Forms and Limits of Adjudication', *Harvard Law Review* 92: 353.

Galbraith, J. (1973), *Designing Complex Organizations* (Reading, Mass.: Addison-Wesley).

Galanter, M. (1974), 'Why the "Haves" Come Out Ahead: Speculations on the Limits of Legal Change', *Law and Society Review* 9: 95–160.

—— (1980), 'Legality and its Discontents: A Preliminary Assessment of Current Theories of Legalization and Delegalization', *Jahrbuch für Rechtssoziologie und Rechtstheorie* 6: 11–26.

—— (1986), 'Adjudication, Litigation and Related Phenomena', in L. Lipset and S. Wheeler (eds.), *Law and the Social Sciences* (New York: Russell Sage), 151–257.

Galligan, D. J. (1976), 'The Nature and Function of Policies within Discretionary Powers', *Public Law*, 332–57.

—— (1981), 'Guidelines and Just Deserts: A Critique of Recent Trends in Sentencing Reform', *Criminal Law Review*, 297–311.

—— (1986*a*), *Discretionary Powers: A Legal Study of Official Discretion* (Oxford: Clarendon Press).

—— (1986*b*) 'Rights, Discretion and Procedures', in C. J. G. Sampford, and D. J. Galligan (eds.), *Law, Rights and the Welfare State* (London: Croom Helm), 128–49.

Gamillscheg, F., de Givry, J., Hepple, B., and Verdier, J. M. (1980) (eds.), *In Memoriam Sir Otto Kahn-Freund* (Munich: C H Beck'she Verlagsbuchhandlung).

Gamson, W. (1968), *Power and Discontent* (Homewood, Ill.: Dorsey Press).

Ganz, G. (1974), *Administrative Procedures* (London: Sweet and Maxwell).

Gardiner, J. A. (1969), *Traffic and the Police: Variations in Law-Enforcement Policy* (Cambridge, Mass.: Harvard University Press).

Garfinkel, H. (1949), 'Research Note on Inter- and Intra-Racial Homicides', *Social Forces* 27: 369–81.

—— (1967), *Studies in Ethnomethodology* (Englewood Cliffs, NJ: Prentice-Hall).

Garnsey, P. (1968), 'Legal Privilege in the Roman Empire', *Past and Present* 41: 3–24.

Garrison, M. (1987), 'Child Welfare Decisionmaking: In Search of the Least Drastic Alternative', *Georgetown Law Journal* 75(6): 1745–828.

Garson, B. (1979), 'Luddites in Lordstown', in R. M. Kanter and B. A. Stein (eds.), *Life in Organizations* (New York: Basic Books).

Gaventa, J. (1980), *Power and Powerlessness: Quiescence and Rebellion in an Appalachian Valley* (Urbana, Ill.: University of Illinois Press).

Genn, H. (1987), *Hard Bargaining: Out of Court Settlement in Personal Injury Actions* (Oxford: Clarendon Press).

Goffman, E. (1974), *Frame Analysis* (Cambridge, Mass.: Harvard University Press).

Goldman, S. (1975), 'Voting Behavior on the United States Courts of Appeals Revisited', *American Political Science Review* 69: 491–506.

Goldstein, J. (1960), 'Police Discretion Not to Invoke the Criminal Process: Low-Visibility Decisions in the Administration of Justice', *Yale Law Journal* 69: 543–94.

Goodin, R. E. (1986), 'Welfare, Rights and Discretion', *Oxford Journal of Legal Studies* 6(3): 232–61.

Goodrich, P. (1987), *Legal Discourse* (Oxford: Blackwell).

Gottfredson, D., and Gottfredson, M. (1980) (eds.), *Decision Making in Criminal Justice* (New York: Plenum).

Gottfredson, D. M., Wilkins, L., and Hoffman, P. B. (1978), *Guidelines for Parole and Sentencing: A Policy Control Method* (Lexington, Mass.: D. C. Heath).

Gramlich, E. (1981), *Cost-Benefit Anaysis of Government Programs* (Englewood Cliffs, NJ: Prentice Hall).

Gramsci, A. (1971), *Selection from the Prison Notebooks*, trans. Q. Hoare, and G. Smith (New York: International Publishers).

Green, E. (1964), 'Inter- and Intra-Racial Crime Relative to Sentencing', *Journal of Criminal Law, Criminology and Police Science* 55: 348–58.

Greenawalt, K. (1975), 'Discretion and Judicial Decision: The Elusive Quest for the Fetters That Bind Judges', *Columbia Law Review* 75: 359–99.

Greenberg, D. (1974), *Crime and Law Enforcement in the Colony of New York, 1691–1776* (Ithaca, NY: Cornell University Press).

Griffiths, J. A. C. (1990), *British Governmental Conventions* (Oxford: Clarendon Press).

Guiraud, P. (1972), *Semiology* (London: Routledge and Kegan Paul).

Gulliver, P. (1969), 'Introduction: Case Studies of Law in Non-Western Societies', in L. Nader (ed.), *Law in Culture and Society* (Chicago: Aldine), 11–23.

Gurwitsch, A. (1965), 'The Phenomenology of Perception: Perceptual Implications', in J. M. Edie (ed.), *An Invitation to Phenomenology* (Chicago: Quadrangle), 17–29.

Habermas, J. (1986*a*), 'Hannah Arendt's Communications Concept of Power', in S. Lukes (ed.), *Power* (New York: New York University Press), 75–93.

—— (1986*b*), 'Law as Medium and Law as Institution', in G. Teubner (ed.), *Dilemmas of Law in the Welfare State* (Berlin: Walter de Gruyter), 203–20.

Hagan, J., Nagel, I., and Albonetti, C. (1980), 'The Differential Sentencing of White-Collar Offenders in Ten Federal District Courts', *American Sociological Review* 45: 802–20.

Hall, D. (1975), 'Role of the Victim in the Prosecution and Disposition of a Criminal Case', *Vanderbilt Law Review* 28: 931.

Halperin, M. H. (1974), *Bureaucratic Politics and Foreign Policy* (Washington, DC: Brookings Institution).

Ham, C., and Hill, M. (1984), *The Policy Process in the Modern Capitalist State* (London: Wheatsheaf).

Handler, J. F. (1966), 'Controlling Official Behavior in Welfare Administration', in *California Law Review* 54: 479–510.

—— (1969), 'Justice for the Welfare Recipient: Fair Hearings in AFDC, The Wisconsin Experience', *Social Service Review* 43: 12–34.

—— (1979), *Protecting the Social Service Client: Legal and Structural Controls on Official Discretion* (New York: Academic Press).

—— (1986), *The Conditions of Discretion: Autonomy, Community, Bureaucracy* (New York: Russell Sage Foundation).

—— (1987–88), 'The Transformation of Aid to Families with Dependent Children: The Family Support Act in Historical Context', *New York University Review of Law and Social Change* 16: 457–533.

—— (1988), 'Dependent People, the State, and the Modern/Postmodern Search for the Dialogic Community', *University of California, Los Angeles Law Review* 35: 99–113.

—— (forthcoming), 'The Feminization of Poverty and the Malenization of AFDC', *New York University Journal of Law and Social Change*.

—— and Zatz, J. (1982) (eds.), *Neither Angels nor Thieves: Studies in De-institutionalization of Status Offenders* (Washington, DC: National Academy Press).

Harden, I., and Lewis, N. (1986), *The Noble Lie: The British Constitution and the Rule of Law* (London: Hutchinson).

Harlow, C., and Rawlings, R. (1984), *Law and Administration* (London: Weidenfeld and Nicolson).

Harris, J. W. (1979), *Law and Legal Science* (Oxford: Clarendon Press).

Hart, H., and Sacks, A. (1958), 'The Legal Process: Basic Problems in the Making and Application of Law', unpublished manuscript.

Hart, H. L. A. (1961), *The Concept of Law* (Oxford: Clarendon Press).

Hartmann, H. (1987), 'Changes in Women's Economic and Family Roles', in L. Beneria and C. Stimpson (eds.), *Women, Households, and the Economy* (New Brunswick, NJ: Rutgers University Press), 33–58.

Hasenfeld, Y. (1983), *Human Service Organizations* (Englewood Cliffs, NJ: Prentice-Hall).

—— (1987), 'Power in Social Work Practice', *Social Service Review* (September): 469–83.

Hastie, R., Penrod, S. D., and Pennington, N. (1983), *Inside the Jury* (Cambridge, Mass.: Harvard University Press).

Hawkins, K. (1971), 'Parole Selection: The American Experience', unpublished Ph.D. dissertation, Cambridge University.

—— (1980), 'On Fixing Time: Reflections on Recent American Attempts to Control Discretion in Sentencing and Parole', unpublished paper presented to Howard League Seminar Series 'The Future of Parole', London School of Economics, October 1980.

—— (1983), 'Assessing Evil: Decision Behaviour and Parole Board Justice', *British Journal of Criminology* 23: 101–27.

—— (1984), *Environment and Enforcement: Regulation and the Social Definition of Pollution* (Oxford: Clarendon Press).

—— (1986), 'On Legal Decision–Making', *Washington and Lee Law Review* 42(4): 1161–242.

—— (1989), '"FATCATS" and Prosecution in a Regulatory Agency: A Footnote on the Social Construction of Risk', *Law and Policy* 11(3): 370–91.

—— and Manning, P. K. (forthcoming), *Legal Decision-Making*.

—— and Thomas, J. M. (1984) (eds.), *Enforcing Regulation* (Boston: Kluwer-Nijhoff).

Hay, D. (1975), 'Property, Authority and the Criminal Law', in D. Hay, P. Linebaugh, J. G. Rule, E. P. Thompson, and C. Winslow, *Albion's Fatal Tree: Crime and Society in Eighteenth-Century England* (New York: Pantheon Books) 17–63.

Heimer, C. (1985a), *Reactive Risk and Rational Action* (Berkeley, Calif.: University of California Press).

—— (1985b), 'Allocating Information Costs in a Negotiated Information Order: Interorganizational Constraints on Decision-Making in Norwegian Oil Insurance', *Administrative Science Quarterly* 30: 395–417.

—— (1988), 'Social Structure, Psychology, and the Estimation of Risk', *Annual Reviews* 14: 491–519 (Palo Alto, Calif.: Annual Reviews Press).

Heller, K., Holtzman, W., and Messick, S. (1982) (eds.), *Placing Children in Special Education: A Strategy for Equity* (Washington, DC: National Academy Press).

Heritage, J. (1984), *Garfinkel and Ethnomethodology* (Cambridge: Polity Press).

Heumann, M. (1978), *Plea Bargaining: The Experiences of Prosecutors, Judges and Defense Attorneys* (Chicago: University of Chicago Press).

Hill, M. (1969), 'The Exercise of Discretion in the National Assistance Board', *Public Administration* 47: 75–90.

Hindus, M. S. (1980), *Prison and Plantation: Crime, Justice and Authority in*

Massachusetts and South Carolina, 1767–1878 (Chapel Hill, NC: University of North Carolina Press).

Hirschman, A. (1970), *Exit, Voice and Loyalty* (Cambridge, Mass.: Harvard University Press).

Hoebel, E. A. (1940), 'The Political Organization and Law-Ways of the Comanche Indians', excerpted in P. Bohannan (ed.), *Law and Warfare: Studies in the Anthropology of Conflict* (Garden City, NY: Natural History Press, 1967), 183–203.

Hogarth, J. (1971), *Sentencing as a Human Process* (Toronto: University of Toronto Press).

Hollinger, R. C. (1984), 'Race, Occupational Status and Proactive Police Arrest for Drinking and Driving', *Journal of Criminal Justice* 12: 173–83.

Holmes, O. W. (1897), 'The Path of Law', *Harvard Law Review* 10: 457–78.

Holmstrom, L. L., and Burgess, A. W. (1983), *The Victim of Rape: Institutional Reactions* (2nd edn.) (New Brunswick: Transaction Books).

Honoré, A. M. (1977), 'Real Laws', in P. M. Hacker and J. Raz (eds.), *Law, Morality and Society* (Oxford: Clarendon Press), ch. 5.

Horwitz, A. V. (1982), *The Social Control of Mental Illness* (Orlando, Fla.: Academic Press).

—— (1990), *The Logic of Social Control* (New York: Plenum Press).

Hughes, E. C. (1971), *The Sociological Eye* (Chicago: Aldine).

Hummel, R. P. (1987), *The Bureaucratic Experience* (New York: St Martin's Press).

Hutchinson, A. C., and Wakefield, J. N. (1982), 'A Hard Look at "Hard Cases": The Nightmare of a Noble Dreamer', *Oxford Journal of Legal Studies* 2: 86–110.

Industrial Injuries Advisory Council (1973), *Report on Occupational Deafness*, Cmnd. 5461 (London: HMSO).

Jackson, B. (1986), *Semiotics and Legal Theory* (London: Routledge and Kegan Paul).

Jackall, R. (1988), *Moral Mazes* (New York: Oxford University Press).

Janis, I. (1985), 'Problems of International Crisis Management in the Nuclear Age', Kurt Lewin Memorial Lecture, American Psychological Association.

—— and Mann, L. (1977), *Decision Making* (New York: Free Press).

Jasanoff, S. (1986), *Risk Management and Political Culture* (New York: Russell Sage).

Jesch, D. (1957), 'Unbestimmter Rechtsbegriff und Ermessen in rechtstheoretischer und verfassungsrechtlicher Sicht', *Archiv des öffentlichen Rechts*, 163–249.

Jowell, J. (1973), 'The Legal Control of Administrative Discretion', *Public Law*, 178.

—— (1975), *Law and Bureaucracy: Administrative Discretion and the Limits of Legalisation* (Port Washington, NY: Dunellen Publishing).

Kadish, M., and Kadish, S. (1973), *Discretion to Disobey: A Study of Lawful Departures from Legal Rules* (Stanford, Calif.: Stanford University Press).

Kagan, R. A. (1978), *Regulatory Justice: Implementing a Wage-Price Freeze* (New York: Russell Sage Foundation).

—— (1984a), 'Inside Administrative Law', *Columbia Law Review* 84: 816–32.

—— (1984b) 'On Regulatory Inspectorates and Police', in K. Hawkins and J. M. Thomas (eds.), *Enforcing Regulation* (Boston: Kluwer Nijhoff).

Kagan, R. L. (1981), *Lawsuits and Litigants in Castile, 1500–1700* (Chapel Hill, NC: University of North Carolina Press).

Kahneman, D., Slovic, P., and Tversky, A. (1982), *Judgment Under Uncertainty: Heuristics and Biases* (Cambridge: Cambridge University Press).

—— and Treisman, A. (1983), 'Changing Views of Attention and Automaticity', in R. Parasuraman and R. Davies (eds.), *Varieties of Attention* (New York: Academic Press) 29–61.

Kalven, H., and Zeisel, H. (1966), *The American Jury* (Boston: Little Brown).

Kamenka, E. (1978), 'The Anatomy of an Idea', in E. Kamenka and A. Tay, *Human Rights* (London: Edward Arnold) 1–12.

—— and Tay A. (1978), *Human Rights* (London: Edward Arnold).

Kanter, R. M. (1977), *Men and Women of the Corporation* (New York: Basic Books).

Katz, J. (1977), 'Coverup and Collective Integrity: On the Natural Antagonism of Authority External and Internal to Organizations', *Social Problems* 25: 3–17.

—— (1984), *The Silent World of Doctor and Patient* (New York: The Free Press).

Kaufman, H. (1960), *The Forest Ranger* (Baltimore, Md.: Johns Hopkins University Press).

—— (1977), *Red Tape: Its Origins, Uses, and Abuses* (Washington, DC: The Brookings Institution).

Kelman, M. (1987), *A Guide to Critical Legal Studies* (Cambridge, Mass.: Harvard University Press).

Kelsen, H. (1967), *The Pure Theory of Law*, trans. M. Knight (Berkeley, Calif.: University of California Press).

Kevelson, R. (1989), *The Law as a System of Signs* (New York: Plenum Press).

Keynes, J. M. (1956), 'My Early Beliefs', in *Essays and Sketches in Biography* (New York: Meridian Books), 239–56.

Klemmack, S. H. and Klemmack, D. L. (1976), 'The Social Definition of Rape', in M. J. Walker and S. L. Brodsky (eds.), *Sexual Assault: The Victim and the Rapist* (Lexington, Mass.: D. C. Heath) 135–47.

Koch, K. (1974), *War and Peace in Jalemo: The Management of Conflict in Highland New Guinea* (Cambridge, Mass.: Harvard University Press).

Kreps, G. (1989) (ed.), *Social Structure and Disaster* (Newark, Del.: University of Delaware Press).

Kroll-Smith, J. S., and Couch, S. (1989), *The Real Disaster is Above Ground* (Lexington, Ky.: University of Kentucky Press).

Kronman, A. T. (1983), *Max Weber* (Stanford, Calif.: Stanford University Press).

Krueger, A. E. (1978), 'The Organization of Information in Criminal Legal Settings: A Case Study of Prosecutorial Decision-Making in Los Angeles', Ph.D. dissertation, Department of Sociology, UCLA.

LaFave, W. R. (1965), *Arrest: The Decision to Take a Suspect into Custody* (Boston: Little Brown).

LaFree, G. D. (1980), 'The Effect of Sexual Stratification by Race on Official Reactions to Rape', *American Sociological Review* 45: 842–54.

—— (1989), *Rape and Criminal Justice: The Social Construction of Sexual Assault* (Belmont, Calif.: Wadsworth).

Lamiell, J. T. (1979), 'Discretion in Juvenile Justice: A Framework for Systematic Study', *Criminal Justice and Behavior* 6: 76–101.

Landy, D. and Aronson, E. (1969), 'The Influence of the Character of the Criminal and his Victim on the Decisions of Simulated Jurors', *Journal of Experimental Social Psychology* 5: 141–52.

Larson, M. S. (1977), *The Rise of Professionalism: A Sociological Analysis* (Berkeley, Calif.: University of California Press).

Layfield, Sir F. (1987), 'Sizewell B Public Inquiry: Summary of Conclusions and Recommendations', Department of Energy, (London: HMSO).

Lazerson, M. H. (1982), 'In the Halls of Justice, the Only Justice is in the Halls', in R. Abel (ed.), *The Politics of Informal Justice*, i (New York: Academic Press), 119–63.

Lempert, R. (1972), 'Evictions From Public Housing: A Sociological Inquiry', unpublished Ph.D. dissertation, University of Michigan.

—— (1989), 'The Dynamics of Informal Procedure: The Case of a Public Housing Eviction Board', *Law and Society Review* 23: 347–98.

—— (1990) 'Docket Data and "Local Knowledge": Studying the Court and Society Link over Time', *Law and Society Review* 24: 321–32.

—— and Monsma, K. (1988), 'Lawyers and Informal Justice: The Case of a Public Housing Eviction Board', *Law and Contemporary Problems* 51: 135–80.

—— and Sanders, J. (1986), *An Invitation to Law and Social Science* (Philadelphia: University of Pennsylvania Press).

Levi, E. H. (1949), *An Introduction to Legal Reasoning* (Chicago: The University of Chicago Press).

Levin, M. A. (1974), 'Urban Politics and Judicial Behavior', *Journal of Legal Studies* 3: 339–75.

Levine, A. G. (1983), *Love Canal: Science, Politics and People* (Lexington, Mass.: Lexington Books).

Lewis, R. (1987), *Compensation for Industrial Injury* (Abingdon: Professional Books).

Lidz, C., and Meisel, A. (1983), 'Informed Consent and the Structure of Medical Care', in President's Commission for the Study of Ethical Problems in Medicine and Biomedical and Behavioral Research, *Making Health Care Decisions*, ii. 349–53.

Lindblom, C. E. (1959), 'The Science of Muddling Through', *Public Administration Review* 19: 79–88.

Lipsky, M. (1980), *Street-Level Bureaucracy: Dilemmas of the Individual in Public Services* (New York: Russell Sage Foundation).

Lister, R. (1974), *Justice for the Claimant* (London: CPAG Poverty Research Series, No. 4).

Lloyd-Bostock, S. (1991), 'The Psychology of Routine Discretion', unpublished paper, Centre for Socio-Legal Studies, Oxford.

Loftin, C., Heumann, M., and McDowall, M. (1983), 'Mandatory Sentencing and Firearms Violence: Evaluating an Alternative to Gun Control', *Law and Society Review* 17: 287–318.

Long, S. (1981), 'Social Control in the Civil Law: The Case of Income Tax Enforcement', in H. L. Ross (ed.), *Law and Deviance* (Beverly Hills, Calif.: Sage), 185–214.

Lovegrove, A. (1984), 'The History of Criminal Cases in the Crown Court as an Administrative Discretion', *Criminal Law Review* December: 738–44.

Luhmann, N. (1967) 'Positives Recht und Ideologie', *Archiv für Rechts- und Sozialphilosophie* 53: 531–71.

—— (1980), *Trust and Power* (New York: John Wiley).

—— (1985), *The Sociology of Law*, (trans. E. King-Utz and M. Albrow (London: Routledge and Kegan Paul).

—— (1986), 'The Self-Reproduction of Law and Its Limits', in G. Teubner (ed.), *Dilemmas of Law in the Welfare State* (Berlin: Walter de Gruyter), 111–27.

Lukes, S. (1974), *Power: A Radical View* (London: Macmillan).

—— (1986) (ed.) *Power* (New York: New York University Press).

Lundsgaarde, H. P. (1977), *Murder in Space City: A Cultural Analysis of Houston Homicide Patterns* (New York: Oxford University Press).

McAuslan, P., and McEldowney, J. (1985), *Law, Legitimacy and the Constitution* (London: Sweet and Maxwell).

McBarnet, D. (1981), *Conviction: Law, the State and the Construction of Justice* (London: Macmillan).

MacCormick, D. N. (1974), 'Law as Institutional Fact', *Law Quarterly Review* 90: 102–29.

—— (1978), *Legal Reasoning and Legal Theory* (Oxford: Clarendon Press).

MacIntyre, A. (1984), 'The Virtues, the Unity of a Human Life and the Concept of a Tradition', in M. Sandel (ed.), *Liberalism and its Critics* (Oxford: Blackwell), 125, 142–3.

Maihofer, R. W. (1970), *Ideologie und Recht* (Frankfurt: Klostermann Verlag).

Manning, P. K. (1977), *Police Work: The Social Organization of Policing* (Cambridge, Mass.: MIT Press)

—— (1980), *The Narcs' Game: Organizational and Informational Limits on Drug Law Enforcement* (Cambridge, Mass.: MIT Press).

—— (1986), 'The Social Reality and Social Organization of Natural Decision Making', *Washington and Lee Law Review* 43(4): 1291–311.

—— (1987), 'Ironies of Compliance', in C. Shearing and P. Stenning (eds.), *Private Policing* (Beverly Hills, Calif.: Sage), 293–316.

—— (1988a), 'Nuclear Incidents: Accidents, Violations of the Status Quo, or Crimes?', paper presented to the Society for the Study of Social Problems.

—— (1988b), 'Organizational Beliefs and Uncertainty', in N. Fielding (ed.), *Actions and Beliefs* (Farnborough: Gower), 80–98.

—— (1988c), 'Socio-Legal Components of the Definition of Accident', unpublished paper presented to the American Sociological Association.

—— (1988d), *Symbolic Communication: Signifying Calls and the Police Response* (Cambridge, Mass.: M.I.T. Press).

—— and Hawkins, K. O. (1989), 'Police Decision-Making', in M. Weatheritt (ed.), *Police Research: Where Now?* (Farnborough: Gower), 139–56.

—— —— (1990), 'Legal Decisions: A Frame Analytic Perspective', in S. Riggins (ed.), *Beyond Goffman* (Berlin: Aldine DeGruyter), 203–33.

Mansnerus, L. (1989), 'The Rape Laws Change Faster than Perceptions', *New York Times* 138 (19 February): Section 4, p. 20.

Maranville, D. (1984), 'Book Review' (of Mashaw 1983), *Minnesota Law Review* 69: 325–47.

March, J. G. (1978), 'Bounded Rationality, Ambiguity, and the Engineering of Choice', *Bell Journal of Economics* 9: 587–608.

—— (1981), 'Decisions in Organizations and Theories of Choice', in A. Van de Ven and W. Joyce (eds.), *Assessing Organizational Design and Performance* (New York: Wiley Interscience), 205–44.

—— (1988), 'Introduction: a Chronicle of Speculations about Decision-Making in Organizations', in *Decisions and Organizations* (Oxford: Blackwell), 1–21.

—— and Olsen, J. P. (1976), *Ambiguity and Choice in Organizations* (Bergen: Universitetsforlaget).

—— and Sevon, G. (1984), 'Gossip, Information and Decision Making', in L. S. Sproull and P. D. Larkey (eds.), *Advances in Information Processing in Organizations*, i (Greenwich, Conn.: JAI Press) 95–107.

—— and Simon, H. (1958), *Organizations* (New York: Wiley).

Mashaw, J. L. (1974), 'The Management Side of Due Process: Some Theoretical and Litigation Notes on the Assurance of Accuracy, Fairness and Timeliness in the Adjudication of Social Welfare Claims', *Cornell Law Review* 59: 772–824.

—— (1983), *Bureaucratic Justice* (New Haven, Conn.: Yale University Press).

Mather, L. M. (1979), *Plea Bargaining or Trial? The Process of Criminal Case Disposition* (Lexington, Mass.: D. C. Heath).

May, E. R., and Neustadt, R. E., (1986), *Thinking in Time* (New York: Free Press).

Mayer, F., and Kopp, F. (1985), *Algemeines Verwaltungsrecht* (5th edn.) (Stuttgart: Richard Boorberg Verlag).

Maynard, D. W. (1982), 'Defendant Attributes in Plea Bargaining: Notes on the Modeling of Sentencing Decisions', *Social Problems* 29: 347–60.

—— (1984*a*), *Inside Plea Bargaining: The Language of Negotiation* (New York: Plenum).

—— (1984*b*), 'The Structure of Discourse in Misdemeanor Plea Bargaining', *Law and Society Review* 18: 75–104.

Mead, L. (1986), *Beyond Entitlement: The Social Obligations of Citizenship* (New York: Free Press).

Meidinger, E. (1987), 'Regulatory Culture: A Theoretical Outline', *Law and Policy* 9 (October): 355–86.

Melli, M. S., Erlanger, H. S., and Chambliss, E. J. (1988), 'The Process of Negotiation: An Exploratory Investigation in the Context of No-Fault Divorce', *Rutgers Law Review* 40(4): 1133–72.

Meltsner, A. J. (1976), *Policy Analysts in the Bureaucracy* (Berkeley, Calif.: University of California Press).

Menkel-Meadow, C. (1984), 'Toward Another View of Legal Negotiation: The Structure of Problem Solving', *University of California, Los Angeles Law Review* 31: 754–842.

Merry, S. E. (1982), 'The Social Organization of Mediation in Non-Industrial Societies: Implications for Informal Community Justice in America', in R. L. Abel (ed.), *The Politics of Informal Justice*, ii. *Comparative Studies* (New York: Academic Press).

—— (1986), 'Everyday Understandings of the Law in Working Class America', *American Ethnologist* 13: 253–70.

Mileski, M. (1971), 'Courtroom Encounters: An Observation Study of a Lower Criminal Court', *Law and Society Review* 5: 473–538.

Miller, C. R. (1990), 'The Rhetoric of Decision Science, or Herbert A. Simon says', in H. W. Simons (ed.), *The Rhetorical Turn: Invention and Persuasion in the Conduct of Inquiry* (Chicago: University of Chicago Press).

Miller, F. (1970), *Prosecution: The Decision to Charge a Suspect with a Crime* (Boston: Little Brown).

Mills, C .W. (1940), 'Situated Action and Vocabularies of Motive', *American Sociological Review* 5 (December): 904–13.

Milton, C. (1972), *Women in Policing* (Washington: Police Foundation).

Mnookin, R. H. (1975), 'Child-Custody Adjudication: Judicial Functions in the Face of Indeterminacy', *Law and Contemporary Problems* 39(3): 226–93.

Mnookin, R. H. (1985), *In the Interest of Children: Advocacy Law Reform, and Public Policy* (New York: W. H. Freeman and Co.).

Molotch, H., and Boden, D. (1985), 'Talking Social Structures: Discourse, Domination and the Watergate Hearings', *American Sociological Review* 50: 273–88.

Moore, S. F. (1958), *Power and Property in Inca Peru* (New York: Columbia University Press).

Morrill, C. (1989), 'The Management of Managers: Disputing in an Executive Hierarchy', *Sociological Forum* 4: 387–407.

Myers, M. A., and Hagan, J. (1979), 'Private and Public Trouble: Prosecutors and the Allocation of Court Resources', *Social Problems* 26: 439–51.

—— and Talarico, S. M. (1986), 'The Social Contexts of Racial Discrimination in Sentencing', *Social Problems* 33: 236–51.

Nadel, M. V., and Rourke, F. (1975), 'Bureaucracies', in F. I. Greenstein and N. W. Polsby (eds.), *Handbook of Political Science*, v (Reading, Mass.: Addison-Wesley).

Nagel, S. S. (1962), 'Judicial Backgrounds and Criminal Cases', *Journal of Criminal Law, Criminology and Police Science* 53: 333–39.

Needham, C. (1981), 'Discrepant Assumptions in Empirical Research: The Case of Juvenile Court Screening', *Social Problems* 28 (February): 247–62.

Neubauer, D. (1974), *Criminal Justice in Middle America* (Morristown, NJ: General Learning Press).

Nisbett, R., and Ross, L. (1980), *Human Inference: Strategies and Shortcomings of Social Judgment* (Englewood Cliffs, NJ: Prentice Hall).

Noble, D. (1981), 'From Rules to Discretion: The Housing Corporation', in M. Adler and S. Asquith (eds.), *Discretion and Welfare* (London: Heinemann), 171–84.

Nonet, P. (1969), *Administrative Justice* (New York: Russell Sage Foundation).

—— and Selznick, P. (1978), *Law and Society in Transition: Toward Responsive Law* (New York: Harper and Row).

O'Barr, W. M. (1982), *Linguistic Evidence: Language, Power and Strategy in the Courtroom* (New York: Academic Press).

Offner, J. A. (1983), *Law and Politics in Aztec Texcoco* (Cambridge: Cambridge University Press).

Ogus, A., and Barendt, E. (1988), *The Law of Social Security* (3rd edn.) (London: Butterworths).

Olsen, F. (1984), 'Statutory Rape: A Feminist Critique of Rights Analysis', *Texas Law Review* 63: 387–432.

Packer, H. (1968), *The Limits of the Criminal Sanction* (Stanford, Calif.: Stanford University Press).

Parsons, T. (1986), 'Power and the Social System', in S. Lukes (ed.), *Power* (New York: New York University Press), 94–143.

Partington, M. (1980), 'Rules and Discretion in British Social Security Law', in F. Gamillscheg, J. De Givry, B. Hepple, and J. M. Verdier (eds.), *In Memoriam Sir Otto Kahn-Freund* (Munich: C H Beck'she Verlagsbuchhandlung), 619–29.

—— (1989), 'Secretary of State's Powers of Adjudication in Social Security Law: A Research Report'.

—— (1991), *Secretary of State's Powers of Adjudication in Social Security Law*, SAUS Working Paper 96 (Bristol: SAUS Publications).

Partridge, A., and Eldridge, W. B. (1974), 'A Report to the Judges of the Second Circuit', published by the Federal Judicial Center, August.

Pattenden, R. (1982), *The Judge, Discretion and the Criminal Trial* (Oxford: Clarendon Press).

Patterson, W. (1983), *Nuclear Power* (2nd edn.) (Harmondsworth, Middlesex: Penguin Books).

Peirce, C. S. (1931–), *Collected Papers* (Cambridge, Mass.: Harvard University Press).

Peller, G. (1987), 'On Deconstruction', *Tikkun* 2 (July–August): 28.

Pepinsky, H. E. (1984), 'Better Living Through Police Discretion', *Law and Contemporary Problems* 47: 249–67.

Perrow, C. (1984), *Normal Accidents* (New York: Basic Books).

Petersilia, J. (1985), 'Racial Disparities in the Criminal Justice System: A Summary', *Crime and Delinquency* 31: 15–34.

Pfeffer, J. (1981a), 'Management as Symbolic Action', in G. Salancik (ed.), *Research in Organizational Behavior* (Greenwich: JAI Press), 1–52.

—— (1981b), *Power in Organizations* (Cambridge, Mass.: Ballinger).

Phillips, J., and Hawkins, K. (1976), 'Some Economic Aspects of the Settlement Process: A Study of Personal Injury Claims', *Modern Law Review* 39(5): 497–515.

Piliavin, I., and Briar, S. (1964), 'Police Encounters with Juveniles', *American Journal of Sociology* 70: 206–14.

Polsby, N. (1963), *Community Power and Political Theory* (New Haven, Conn.: Yale University Press).

—— (1970), *Power and Poverty: Theory and Practice* (New York: Oxford University Press).

Ponting, C. (1986), *Whitehall: Tragedy and Farce* (London: Sphere).

Pope, C. (1978), 'Sentence Dispositions Accorded Assault and Burglary Offenders: An Exploratory Study in Twelve California Counties', *Journal of Criminal Justice* 6: 151–65.

Post, R. C. (1984), 'The Management of Speech: Discretion and Rights', *Supreme Court Review*, 169–236.

Pound, R. (1908), 'Mechanical Jurisprudence', *Columbia Law Review* 8: 605–23.

President's Commission for the Study of Ethical Problems in Medicine and

Biomedical and Behavioral Research (1983), *Making Health Care Decisions*, i, ii, iii (Washington, DC: Government Printing Office).

Prosser, T. (1977), 'Poverty, Ideology and Legality: Supplementary Benefit Appeal Tribunals and their Predecessors', *British Journal of Law and Society* 4: 39–60.

—— (1981), 'The Politics of Discretion', in M. Adler and S. Asquith (eds.), *Discretion and Welfare* (London: Heinemann), 148–70.

Radelet, L. A. (1986), *The Police and the Community* (4th edn.) (New York: Macmillan) [1st edn., 1973].

Raz, J. (1975), *Practical Reason and Norms* (London: Hutchinson).

—— (1979), *The Authority of Law* (Oxford: Clarendon Press).

—— (1980), *The Concept of a Legal System* (2nd edn.) (Oxford: Clarendon Press).

Reed, J. (1965), 'Jury Deliberation, Voting and Verdict Trends', *Southwest Social Science Quarterly* 45: 361–70.

Reich, C. (1963), 'Midnight Welfare Searches and the Social Security Act', *Yale Law Journal* 74: 1347–60.

—— (1964), 'The New Property', *Yale Law Journal* 73: 733–87.

—— (1965), 'Individual Rights and Social Welfare: the Emerging Issues', *Yale Law Journal* 74: 1245–57.

—— (1966), 'The Law of the Planned Society', *Yale Law Journal* 75: 1227–70.

Reiss, A. J. jun. (1971), *The Police and the Public* (New Haven, Conn.: Yale University Press).

—— (1974a), 'Discretionary Justice', in D. Glaser (ed.), *Handbook of Criminology* (Chicago: Scott, Foresman), 679–99.

—— (1974b), 'Discretionary Justice in the United States', *International Journal of Criminology and Penology* 2(2): 181–205.

Reskin, B. F., and Visher, C. A. (1986), 'The Impacts of Evidence and Extralegal Factors in Jurors' Decisions', *Law and Society Review* 20: 423–38.

Richardson, G., Ogus, A., and Burrows, P. (1983), *Policing Pollution: A Study of Regulation and Enforcement* (Oxford: Clarendon Press).

Roberts, S. (1979), *Order and Dispute* (London: Pelican).

Robson, W. A. (1928), *Justice and Administrative Law* (London: Macmillan).

Rock, P. (1973), *Making People Pay* (London: Routledge and Kegan Paul).

Rosen, L. (1980–1), 'Equity and Discretion in a Modern Islamic Legal System', *Law and Society Review* 15(2): 217–45.

Rosenberg, M. (1970–1), 'Judicial Discretion of the Trial Court, Viewed From Above', *Syracuse Law Review* 22: 635–67.

Ross, H. L. (1970), *Settled Out of Court: The Social Process of Insurance Claims Adjustment* (Chicago: Aldine).

—— and Thomas, J. M. (1981), 'Blue-Collar Bureaucrats and the Law in Action: Housing Code Regulation in Three Cities', unpublished paper presented at the annual meeting of the Association for Public Policy Analysis and Management, Washington, DC; 23 October.

Roy, D. F. (1979), '"Banana Time": Job Satisfaction and Informal Interaction', in R. M. Kanter and B. A. Stein (eds.), *Life in Organizations: Workplaces as People Experience Them* (New York: Basic Books) 192–205.

Roy, D. L. (1955), 'Efficiency and "the Fix": Informal Intergroup Relations in a Piece-Work Machine Shop', *American Journal of Sociology* 60: 255–66.

Rubinstein, J. (1973), *City Police* (New York: Ballantine Books).

Sainsbury, R. D. (1988), 'Deciding Social Security Claims: A Study in the Theory and Practice of Administrative Justice', unpublished Ph.D. thesis, University of Edinburgh.

—— (1989), 'The Social Security Chief Adjudication Officer: The First Four Years', *Public Law* (summer): 323–41.

Salem, S. R. (1983), 'Discretion in Criminal Justice: A Theoretical Analysis of the Concept and a Proposed Framework for Examining its Exercise in the Criminal Justice Process', unpublished Ph.D. dissertation, Cambridge University.

Sanders, A. (1987), 'Constructing the Case for the Prosecution', *Journal of Law and Society* 14: 229–43.

Sanders, W. B. (1977), *Detective Work: A Study of Criminal Investigations* (New York: The Free Press).

Schauer, F. (1985), 'Easy Cases', *University of Southern California Law Review* 58: 399–410.

—— (1986–7), 'Precedent', *Stanford Law Review* 39: 571–605.

—— (1987), 'The Jurisprudence of Reasons' (review of Ronald Dworkin, *Law's Empire*), *Michigan Law Review* 85(5 and 6): 847–70.

—— (1991), '*Playing by the Rules: A Philosophical Examination of Rule-Based Decision-Making in Law and in Life*' (Oxford: Clarendon Press).

Schegloff, E. A. (1987), 'Between Micro and Macro: Contexts and Other Connections', in J. Alexander, B. Giesen, R. Munch, and N. Smelser (eds.), *The Macro-Micro Link* (Berkeley, Calif.: University of California Press), 207–34.

Scheppele, K. L. (1988a), 'Law Without Accidents', presented to the Conference on 'Social Theory and Emerging Issues in a Changing Society', University of Chicago, April.

—— (1988b) *Legal Secrets* (Chicago: University of Chicago Press).

—— (1989), 'Facing Facts in Legal Interpretation', unpublished paper, University of Michigan, originally delivered at the meeting of the American Political Science Association, 1988.

Schneider, C. E. (1985), 'The Next Step: Definition, Generalization, and Theory in American Family Law', *Journal of Law Reform* 18(3): 1039–59.

Schneider, C. E. (1991), 'Rethinking Alimony: Marital Decisions and Moral Discourse', *Brigham Young University Law Review*, 197–257.

Scholz, J. (1984), 'Cooperation, Deterrence, and the Ecology of Regulatory Enforcement', *Law and Society Review* 18: 179–224.

Scott, E. S., Reppucci, N. D., and Aber, M. (1988), 'Children's Preference in Adjudicated Custody Decisions', *Georgia Law Review* 22(4): 1035–78.

Scott, M., and Lyman, S. (1968), 'Accounts', *American Sociological Review* 33(2): 309–18.

Schubert, G. A. (1963), *Judicial Decision-Making* (Glencoe, Ill.: Free Press).

Selznick, P. (1969), *Law, Society, and Industrial Justice* (New York: Russell Sage Foundation).

Shapiro, S. (1987), 'The Social Control of Impersonal Trust', *American Journal of Sociology* 93: 623–58.

Sherman, L. J. (1975), 'Evaluation of Policewomen on Patrol in a Suburban Police Department', *Journal of Police Science and Administration* 3: 434–8.

Sherman, L. W., and Berk, R. A. (1984), 'The Specific Deterrent Effects of Arrest for Domestic Assault', *American Sociological Review* 49: 261–72.

Short, J. F. (1984), 'The Social Fabric at Risk: Toward the Social Transformation of Risk Analysis', *American Sociological Review* 49: 711–55.

Shrivastava, P. (1987), *Bhopal: Anatomy of a Crisis* (Boston: Ballinger).

Simon, H. A. (1947), *Administrative Behavior* (New York: Macmillan).

—— (1956), 'Rational Choices and the Structure of the Environment', *Psychological Review* 63: 129–38.

—— (1964), 'On the Concept of Organizational Goal', *Administrative Science Quarterly* 9: 1–22.

—— (1969), *The Sciences of the Artificial* (Cambridge, Mass.: MIT Press).

—— (1976), *Administrative Behavior* (3rd edn.) (New York: Free Press).

—— (1979), 'Rational Decision-Making in Business Organizations', *American Economic Review* 69: 293–513.

Simon, R. J. (1967), *The Jury and the Defense of Insanity* (Boston: Little Brown).

Simon, W. (1986), 'Rights and Redistribution in the Welfare System', *Stanford Law Review* 38: 1431.

Skolnick, J. K. (1966), *Justice Without Trial: Law Enforcement in Democratic Society* (New York: John Wiley).

—— (1967), 'Social Control and the Adversary System', *Journal of Conflict Resolution* 11: 52–70.

Smith, D. and Gray, J. (1983), *Police and People in London* (London: Policy Studies Institute).

Smith, D. A., and Klein, J. R. (1984), 'Police Control of Interpersonal Disputes', *Social Problems* 31: 468–81.

—— and Visher, C. A. (1981), 'Street-Level Justice: Situational Determinants of Police Arrest Decisions', *Social Problems* 29: 167–77.

—— —— Davidson, L. A. (1984), 'Equity and Discretionary Justice: The

Influence of Race on Police Arrest Decisions', *Journal of Criminal Law and Criminology* 75: 234–49.

Smith, G. (1981), 'Discretionary Decision-Making in Social Work', in M. Adler and S. Asquith (eds.), *Discretion and Welfare* (London: Heinemann), 47–68.

Smith, M. (1966), 'Percy Foreman: Top Trial Lawyer', *Life* 60: 92–101.

Spradley, J. P. (1970), *You Owe Yourself a Drunk: An Ethnography of Urban Nomads* (Boston: Little Brown).

Sproull, L. S. (1981), 'Beliefs in Organizations', in P. Nystrom and W. Starbuck (eds.), *Handbook of Organizational Design* (Oxford: Oxford University Press), ii. 203–24.

Stanko, E. A. (1981), 'The Arrest versus the Case', *Urban Life* 9: 395–414.

—— (1981–2), 'The Impact of Victim Assessment on Prosecutors' Screening Decisions: The Case of the New York County District Attorney's Office', *Law and Society Review* 16: 225–39.

Steinbruner, J. D. (1974), *The Cybernetic Theory of Decision: New Dimensions of Political Analysis* (Princeton, NJ: Princeton University Press).

Suchman, L. (1983), 'Office Procedure as Practical Action: Models of Work and System Design', *ACM Transactions on Office Information Systems* 1(4): 320–8.

Sudnow, D. (1965), 'Normal Crimes: Sociological Features of the Penal Code in a Public Defender Office', *Social Problems* 12: 255–76.

Sugden, R., and Williams, A. (1978), *The Principles of Practical Cost-Benefit Analysis* (Oxford: Clarendon Press).

Sunstein, C. (1988), 'Book Review, Feminism and Legal Theory', *Harvard Law Review* 101: 826–48.

Swigert, V. L., and Farrell, R. A. (1976), *Murder, Inequality and the Law* (Lexington, Mass.: D. C. Heath).

Tammelo, I. (1959), 'On the Logical Openness of Legal Orders', *American Journal of Comparative Law* 8: 187–203.

Tannenhaus, J., Schick, M., Muraskin M., and Rosen, D. (1963), 'The Supreme Court's Certiorari Jurisdiction: Cue Theory', in G. Schubert (ed.), *Judicial Decision Making* (Glencoe, Ill.: Free Press), 111–32.

Teitelbaum, L. E. (forthcoming), 'Individualization, Discretion, and Criminalization', *Brigham Young University Law Review*.

—— and DuPaix, L. (1988), 'Alternative Dispute Resolution and Divorce: Natural Experimentation in Family Law', *Rutgers Law Review* 40(4): 1093–132.

Teubner, G. (1986), 'After Legal Instrumentalism? Strategic Models of Post-Regulatory Law', in G. Teubner (ed.), *Dilemmas of Law in the Welfare State* (Berlin: Walter de Gruyter), 299–325.

—— (1988) (ed.), *Autopoietic Law* (Berlin: Walter de Gruyter).

Thomas, J. C. (1986), 'The Personal Side of Street Level Bureaucrats—

Discrimination or Neutral Competence?', *Urban Affairs Quarterly* (September): 84–100.

Tiffany, L., Avichai, Y., and Peters, G. (1975), 'A Statistical Analysis of Sentencing in Federal Courts: Defendants Convicted after Trial, 1967–1968', *Journal of Legal Studies* 4: 369–90.

Timmer, D. A. (1981), 'Organizational and Phenomenological Determinants of Local Crime Control: The Historical Selectivity of Municipal Policing', unpublished doctoral dissertation, Colorado State University.

Titmuss, R. M. (1971), 'Welfare "Rights", Law and Discretion', *Political Quarterly*, 42(2): 113–32.

Tonry, M. (1987), 'Sentencing Guidelines and their Effects', in A. Von Hirsch, K. Knapp, and M. Tonry, *The Sentencing Commission and its Guidelines* (Boston: Northeastern University Press), 16–43.

Trotman, D. V. (1986), *Crime in Trinidad: Conflict and Control in a Plantation Society, 1838–1900* (Knoxville, Tenn.: University of Tennessee Press).

Türk, K. (1980), 'Handlungsräume und Handlungsspielräume rechtsvollziehender Organisationen', *Jahrbuch für Rechtssoziologie und Rechtstheorie* 7: 153–68.

Tushnet, M. (1986), 'Critical Legal Studies: An Introduction to its Origins and Underpinnings', *Journal of Legal Education* 36: 505–17.

Tversky, A., and Kahneman, D. (1974), 'Judgment Under Uncertainty: Heuristics and Biases', *Science* 185: 1124–31.

Tweedie, J. (1989), 'Discretion to Use Rules: Individual Interests and Collective Welfare in School Admissions', *Law and Policy* 11: 189–213.

Twining, W., and Miers, D. (1982), *How to do Things with Rules* (2nd edn.) (London: Weidenfeld and Nicolson).

Tyack, D., and Hansot, E (1982), *Managers of Virtue* (New York: Basic Books).

Uhlman, T. M. (1979), *Racial Justice: Black Judges and Defendants in an Urban Trial Court* (Lexington, Mass.: D. C. Heath).

—— and Walker, D. (1980), ' "He Takes Some of My Time; I Take Some of His": An Analysis of Judicial Sentencing Patterns in Jury Cases', *Law and Society Review* 14: 323–41.

Ule, C. H. (1985), 'Rechtsstaat und Verwaltung', *Verwaltungs-Archiv* 76: 1–23.

Ulen, T. (1990), 'Cognitive Imperfection and Public Policy Decision Making', unpublished paper for the Conference on Understanding and Improving Public Policy Making, The Institute of Government and Public Affairs, University of Illinois, 19–20 April 1990.

Ulmer, S. S. (1973), 'Social Background as an Indicator to the Votes of Supreme Court Justices in Criminal Cases: 1947–1956 Terms', *American Journal of Political Science* 17: 622–30.

Unger, R. M. (1975), *Knowledge and Politics* (New York: Free Press).

—— (1976), *Law in Modern Society* (New York: Free Press).

Uviller, H. R. (1984), 'The Unworthy Victim: Police Discretion in the Credibility Call', *Law and Contemporary Problems* 47(1): 15–33.

van der Sprenkel, S. (1962), *Legal Institutions in Manchu China: A Sociological Analysis* (New York: Humanities Press).

Van Maanen, J. (1973), 'Observations on the Making of Policemen', *Human Organization* 32(4): 407–18.

—— and Schein, E. H. (1979), 'Toward a Theory of Organizational Socialization', *Research in Organizational Behavior*, 1: 209–64.

Vaughan, D. (1983), *Controlling Unlawful Organizational Behavior* (Chicago: University of Chicago Press).

—— (1990), 'Autonomy, Interdependence, and Social Control: NASA and the Space Shuttle Challenger', *Administrative Science Quarterly* 35: 225–57.

Vera Institute of Justice (1981), *Felony Arrests: Their Prosecution and Disposition in New York City's Courts* (2nd edn.) (New York: Longman Press) [1st edn., 1977].

Venezia, J. C. (1959), *Le Pouvoir discrétionnaire* (Paris: Librairie Général de Droit et de Jurisprudence).

Von Hirsch, A. (1976), *Doing Justice* (New York: Hill and Wang).

—— (1985), *Past or Future Crimes* (Manchester: Manchester University Press).

—— Knapp, K., and Tonry, M. (1987), *The Sentencing Commission and its Guidelines* (Boston: Northeastern University Press).

Waegel, W. (1981), 'Case Routinization in Investigative Police Work', *Social Problems* 28: 263–75.

Wald, M. S. (1980), 'Thinking About Public Policy Toward Abuse and Neglect of Children: A Review of *Before the Best Interests of the Child*', *Michigan Law Review* 78(5): 645–93.

Walker, C. (1983), *Changing Social Policy* (London: Bedford Square Press).

Weatherly, R., and Lipsky, M. (1977), 'Street-Level Bureaucrats and Institutional Innovation: Implementing Special Education Reform', *Harvard Education Review*, 47(2): 171–97.

Weber, M. (1946), 'Bureaucracy', in H. H. Gerth and C. Wright Mills (eds.), *From Max Weber: Essays in Sociology* (New York: Oxford University Press) 196–244.

—— (1947), *The Theory of Social and Economic Organization* (New York: Free Press).

—— (1958), *From Max Weber*, trans. and ed. H. H. Gerth and C. W. Mills (New York: Oxford University Press).

—— (1968), *Economy and Society*, ed. G. Roth and C. Wittich (Berkeley, Calif.: University of California Press).

Weick, K. (1979), *The Social Psychology of Organizing* (2nd edn.) (Reading, Mass.: Addison Wesley).

—— (1989), 'The Vulnerable System: An Analysis of the Tenerife Air Disaster', unpublished paper, University of Michigan.

Weitzman, L. J. (1985), *The Divorce Revolution: The Unexpected Social and Economic Consequences for Women and Children in America* (New York: Free Press).

Werthman, C., and Piliavin, I. (1967), 'Gang Members and the Police', in D. J. Bordua (ed.), *The Police: Six Sociological Essays* (New York: John Wiley), 56–98.

West, R. (1988), 'Justice and Gender', *University of Chicago Law Review* 53: 1–72.

Whitehead, A. N. (1948), *An Introduction to Mathematics* (12th impression) (London: Oxford University Press).

Widick B. J. (1979), 'The Men Won't Tow the Vega Line', in R. M. Kanter and B. A. Stein (eds.), *Life in Organizations: Workplaces as People Experience Them* (New York: Basic Books).

Wikeley, N. (1988), 'Social Security Adjudication and Occupational Lung Diseases', *Industrial Law Journal* 17(2): 92.

Wilkins, L. (1975), 'Perspectives on Court Decision-Making' in D. Gottfredson (ed.), *Decision-Making in the Criminal Justice System: Reviews and Essays* (Washington DC: Government Printing Office), 59–81.

Williams, K. M. (1976), 'The Effects of Victim Characteristics on the Disposition of Violent Crimes', in W. F. MacDonald (ed.), *Criminal Justice and the Victim* (Beverly Hills, Calif.: Sage), 177–213.

Wilson, J. Q. (1968), *Varieties of Police Behavior* (Cambridge, Mass.: Harvard University Press).

—— (1980), *The Politics of Regulation* (New York: Basic Books).

Winkler, J. T. (1981), 'The Political Economy of Administrative Discretion', in M. Adler and S. Asquith (eds.), *Discretion and Welfare* (London: Heinemann), 82–134.

Winter, G. (1985), 'Bartering Rationality in Regulation', *Law and Society Review* 19: 219–50.

Witty, C. J. (1980), *Mediation and Society: Conflict Management in Lebanon* (New York: Academic Press).

Wolfe, T. (1970), *Radical Chic and Mau-Mauing the Flak Catchers* (New York: Bantam Books).

Woolf, H. (1986), 'Public Law—Private Law: Why the Divide?', *Public Law*, 220–38.

Wunderli, R. M. (1981), *London Church Courts and Society on the Eve of the Reformation* (Cambridge, Mass.: The Medieval Academy of America).

Yngvesson, B. (1988), 'Making Law at the Doorway: The Clerk, the Court, and the Construction of Community in a New England Town', *Law and Society Review* 22: 409–48.

Young, K. (1981), 'Discretion as an Implementation Problem', in M. Adler and S. Asquith (eds.), *Discretion and Welfare* (London: Heinemann), 33–46.

Zimmer, L. (1987), 'How Women Reshape the Prison Guard Role', *Gender and Society* 1: 415–31.

Zucker, L. G. (1985), 'Review of *Bureaucratic Justice* (Mashaw (1983))', *Administrative Science Quarterly* 30: 613–15.

Index of Authors

Index of Subjects